PREDICTION AND OPTIMAL DECISION

PHILOSOPHICAL ISSUES OF A SCIENCE OF VALUES

C. West Churchman
University of California
Berkeley

PHILOSOPHICAL ISSUES

PREDICTION
AND OPTIMAL
DECISION

OF A SCIENCE OF VALUES

GREENWOOD PRESS, PUBLISHERS
WESTPORT CONNECTICUT

Library of Congress Cataloging in Publication Data

Churchman, C. West (Charles West), 1913–
    Prediction and optimal decision.

    Reprint. Originally published: Englewood Cliffs,
N.J. : Prentice-Hall, 1961. (Prentice-Hall international
series in management)
    Includes bibliographies and index.
    1. Decision-making. 2. Value. I. Title. II. Series:
Prentice-Hall international series in management.
[HD20.23.C485 1982]   658.4'03   82-6264
ISBN 0-313-23418-3 (lib. bdg.)   AACR2

© 1961 by Prentice-Hall, Inc., Englewood Cliffs, N.J.

Reprinted with the permission of Prentice-Hall, Inc.

Reprinted in 1982 by Greenwood Press
A division of Congressional Information Service, Inc.
88 Post Road West, Westport, Connecticut 06881

Printed in the United States of America

P

In order to keep this title in print and available to the academic community, this edition
was produced using digital reprint technology in a relatively short print run. This would
not have been attainable using traditional methods. Although the cover has been changed
from its original appearance, the text remains the same and all materials and methods
used still conform to the highest book-making standards.

To
Gloria and Danny
who know a lot about values without thinking about them at all

PREFACE

Man, the great discoverer, has shown little aptitude in discovering the solutions to the problems of right and wrong conduct. Every intelligent person today would like to find a clear criterion that would enable him to tell which national and international policies are morally correct, and which are not. But no such guide is to be found in the writings of novelists, politicians, or scientists.

Part of our trouble is ignorance. Even the experts cannot predict the outcome of a proposed policy. The unexpected is too often calamitous.

But part of our trouble is that we do not yet know what we want. Too often we assume that the nature of man's needs and desires is obvious, even though a little self-conscious scrutiny on the part of each individual will tell him that, in his own case, at least, this is not so.

As we approach the egalitarian age when each man will count in the formation of national and international policies, we have a great need for empirical evidence concerning each man's real values. Only then will we be able to solve the problem of morally right and wrong policy-making.

The empirical investigation of what men really want is possible only if men are educated as well as possible concerning the outcomes of policies, and only if men are free to choose. Evidence of man's true values is to be found in his spoken words, or his consumer practices, or his voting behavior only if he is free of ignorance and other constraints. Hence the extreme difficulty in the empirical determination of values, and hence the inevitable conclusion that today we do not know even in a very rough form what the human animal wants.

I have tried in this book to give a personal estimate of the methodological problems of determining human values. If my estimate is correct, there can be little doubt that our greatest unsolved problem of exploration lies in the study of real wants. But I think that one of the rewards of an adequate method of discovering human values will be the resolution of some fundamental ethical problems. Ethics has been a backward science only because it has lacked the kind of empirical evidence it requires for its advancement. The distinction between the so-called "world of fact" and "world of value" has been based on a naïve understanding of the facts about human values. The distinction is, in fact, untenable. A science of ethics is feasible but only possible if there is a science that can measure values. But neither the science of ethics nor the measurement of values is possible unless we become more self-conscious about science itself. I think we shall have our science of ethics if we ever attain a science of science.

A science of science is the study of the critical decision problems of the scientist. It is therefore concerned with the following kinds of questions. What is the decision process by means of which observations become facts? What are the decision rules underlying the establishment of measurements, hypotheses and theories? What are the decision rules for the rejection of established facts, measurements, hypotheses, and theories? The underlying decision-making structure of science is often taken to be logical. That is, many believe that the answers to these questions are to be found in the discipline of formal logic. I do not see how this can be the case, because formal logic, in our day at least, has not been concerned with decision criteria relative to goals. The decisions about observations and theories are good or bad depending on whether they serve science's goals. Hence the basis of judging scientific decisions must be found in an evaluation of the goals of science. Now, science has many goals, short term and long term, practical and basic, specialized and generalized. Science seeks to find knowledge and also seeks to survive. Its goals often conflict. Hence a science of science requires an empirical method of ascertaining the relative importance of goals. Science also, fundamentally, seeks ethical goals. Hence a science of science requires an empirical method of ascertaining the ethical importance of goals. What such a requirement can possibly mean is the problem of this book.

The first draft of this book, called *Costs, Utilities and Values*, was written under a research grant from Case Institute of Technology. The second draft was prepared while I was a member of the Management Science Nucleus of the Institute of Industrial Relations at the University of California.

I have tried to express my intellectual debts within the framework of each chapter. I have tried to write to a broad intellectual audience, and have often repeated what some readers will know very well. The book as a whole is an outcome of many years of work with Russell L. Ackoff, and many conversations with Thomas A. Cowan, Sebastian B. Littauer, Richard S. Rudner, J. S. Minas, Philburn Ratoosh, and my colleagues in the Management Science Nucleus. Alice Tabet, Sue Berger, and Phyllis Dexter put in many tedious and fruitful hours on the manuscript.

TABLE
OF CONTENTS

PREDICTION AND OPTIMAL DECISION

PHILOSOPHICAL ISSUES OF A SCIENCE OF VALUES

SCIENCE AND OPTIMAL DECISIONS

1

Summary

and

Intent.

Probably the most startling feature of twentieth-century culture is the fact that we have developed such elaborate ways of doing things and at the same time have developed no way of justifying any of the things we do. We are great distinction-makers; among the many distinctions we make is the one between science and ethics. We feel comfortable in pointing out that science tells us what is and what will be and that ethics tells us what ought to be. Having made the distinction, we think we are justified in maintaining it. Hence we are not surprised to learn that we know how to do so many things and yet don't know why we do them. Our science is developed; our ethics is not. This is very sad, but not very odd.

It seems to me that philosophy, which is the critic of common sense, must examine this common-sense distinction between science and ethics. Is it possible to have an activity which *merely* generates knowledge of fact, without any ethical commitments? Is it really true that science in its search for knowledge is indifferent about what is good and what is bad or what is wrong and what is right? Furthermore, how do we know that science cannot tell us what ought to be as well as what is?

This book attempts to examine critically the distinction between science and ethics. It conducts this examination by outlining an approach to a scientific verification of ethical judgments. It makes no attempt to show that this method of verification is feasible. Whatever value there may be in this work lies in a reformulation of the problem which common sense so glibly answers. It may be that science cannot verify ethical judgments, but before we can be sure this is so, we must propose at least one way in which science could make such verifications, unless we feel that the distinction between science and ethics is a matter of definition alone.

The development of a scientific method for verifying ethical judgments is a long and tedious process. The present work is only a hesitating step in this direction. There is no intention here to construct a precise, conceptual model for such a methodology, since I am more concerned with pointing out the problems we face than with providing final answers. Ethics is still largely a mystery to the rational, observing mind, and such a mind can only begin to unravel the tangle after a great deal of analysis. For those to whom ethics is no mystery, this work of analysis will inevitably seem intolerably tedious. And to the rational mind, in the end, it may appear fruitless.

2 · Some Presuppositions.

At the outset, it is important to characterize briefly and in general terms some of the assumptions that underlie this inquiry. First of all, I assume that the problem of whether there is a scientific method for verifying ethical judgments cannot be answered by arbitrary definitions of the terms involved, no matter how clear and precise the definitions may be. Some justification of this assumption will be made in this chapter, based on the observation that the problem before us gains its significance from the fact that the concepts of "science" and "ethics" are important in contemporary social policy-making, and that one is justified in asserting that the meanings of the concepts must reflect this importance. Next, I assume that the verification of ethical judgments depends on the values of individual persons, without committing myself as to the exact nature of this dependence. This assumption requires an analysis of the methodology of ascertaining personal values, an analysis that occupies a majority of the present book. It seems to me that the developments that have occurred in this century require a reformulation of the meaning of human values, and I have tried here to estimate what this reformulation entails. Finally, I assume that the use of personal values to verify ethical judgments involves the construction of a theory of values over the domain of social groups and time, in a sense to be explained later in the text. In effect, the present effort is in line with the traditional attempt to construct a scientific methodology for ethics: namely, to construe the evidence for and against an ethical assertion to be facts about the collective wishes of mankind.

In the end, the attempt to find at least one possible methodology for verifying ethical judgments is equivalent to the attempt to outline a scientific discipline of human values. Hence, this work can also be taken as an exposition of the fundamental problems of a science of values.

In general, I am enough of a Hegelian to feel that the problem of ethical judgments must be looked at from many different points of view. For this reason, from time to time I will try to restate the objectives of this book in different terms as I have just now stated one of them in terms of developing a science of values. *The* objective is the resultant of these differing and perhaps contradictory formulations.

3 · *The Social Importance of the Meaning of Science and Ethics.*

Now, suppose that we try to justify the position that "science" and "ethics" are concepts, the meanings of which are important for policy-making in contempory society. Of course, any congenial group of scientists could arbitrarily agree among themselves what "science" means and what "ethics" means and then, by rational analysis, decide whether a scientific verification of ethical judgments is possible. Such an exercise in analysis might be of interest to the group that performed it but would correspond only accidentally to the results of the analysis of some other group. The justification of the position we adopt here is based on the assertion that there is a more significant problem than the analysis of the opinions of specific groups of scientists about the meaning of science. "Science" is a name for a social activity that has a tremendous impact on all that we do and especially on the policies that we adopt as a nation. As a nation, we have to decide what constitutes reliable information in order to decide what we are going to do. Hence, what "science" means depends, in part at least, on what a whole society or culture takes to be reliable information. It may be that the meaning of "science" also depends on judgments and values that transcend cultural boundaries, and later on in the book we shall defend this position. But in any case, the important problem is this. Suppose the meaning of "science" depends in part on the criteria our culture uses to determine whether information is reliable or objective; does this meaning of "science" preclude the possibility of there being any reliable evidence for or against specific ethical assertions? An alternative formulation of the problem is this. Suppose there is a defensible sense in which the whole of a society or culture decides what "science" means; does this decision imply the decision that value judgments cannot be verified or refuted by "science"?

We shall see that these two ways of posing the problem are not the only ones. Indeed, this entire essay is an attempt to state the problem of science and ethics in a number of different ways. For the present, we can postpone these reformulations and turn instead to an illustration to see if this helps to clarify the issues before us.

4 · *An Illustration.*

As a nation we are faced with many critical policy issues. For example, in the early 1950's, the United States was concerned with these questions: Should we bomb the Chinese mainland? Should we attempt to stop the growth of communism in countries where the majority apparently favor it? Should we abolish by force communist politics in this country? Should we fire before trial a government employee who is under suspicion? Does a worker have the right to strike if striking threatens our defense program?

We suspect that the method we use to resolve these issues will have a great deal to do with the future history of humanity. We also suspect that these issues cannot be settled adequately by each man's looking into his inmost soul and voting pro or con on the basis of the dictates of his conscience. Nor do we see how the moral "intuitions" of benevolence and altruism, or moral principles such as the Golden Rule and the Ten Commandments are of much service. Even if a man wants to "do unto others as he would have them do unto him," he is hopelessly confused as to whether stopping communism by force is or is not an application of this moral rule.

Obviously, then, issues like those just mentioned can only be settled adequately if we know a great deal about the situation. We need to know, for example, who are concerned and what will happen to them if a given policy is adopted. Consider now two equally obvious implications of this assertion—implications that often escape us.

First, let it be admitted that most citizens of our country cannot have access to all the information relevant to the issues cited above. This is certainly a modest admission. Even if the information were not restricted by the bonds of security, few would have the time or the inclination to absorb it all. But this modest admission, together with the principle that correct decisions on these issues require a great deal of information, implies that only a very few persons are in a position to decide correctly on bombing China or on restricting strikes by force. And presumably these "few" must rely on those who know how to gather and analyze information in the most objective fashion.

Second, if it is admitted that these issues are the most important ones we face, then one of our most pressing needs today is the further development of relevant, objective information. There is good reason to believe that research into the social consequences of our national policies far outweighs in importance most other research activities.

These implications may seem distasteful to many—so distasteful, indeed, that they may lead to a denial of the premises on which they are based. Perhaps certain issues can be decided without knowing very much about the consequences of the actions. Perhaps in many cases, the relevant information is readily available, and it is the government's responsibility to educate the people properly. Perhaps the information is not obtainable at all. Perhaps the issues are not really as important as some would make them.

For the time being, let us assume that the relevant information on social issues is available only to a few because of cost, time, or risk. Let us state the dilemma which seems to follow from this assumption to see if it is possible to escape between the horns.

The dilemma is this. *Either* we say that national issues can be adequately decided even though the decision-maker has very little relevant information, *or* we say that the issues can be decided only by a very few informed people who must rely on those who gather objective information.

The first horn of the dilemma is not one on which we will be impaled in this study. It was possible at one time in human history to argue that a man's conscience should be his guide—that he should act in accordance with his moral insights. But the issues mentioned above are social issues that are the concern of many people in a social group. It is absurd to say that an executive "should" act independently of a knowledge of the consequences of his actions, or that a legislator need not know what will happen if a proposed law is adopted. If available, information about the consequences of actions is always relevant. However, it may be so costly to obtain that it would be a wise policy not to obtain it. But in this case there must be evidence to substantiate this wisdom.

What of the second horn of the dilemma—that relevant information about social issues is available at the present time to only a few people because, in addition to "security" problems, time and cost are involved in absorbing it?

This horn of the dilemma may not seem very difficult to accept. In our country we have come to delegate authority for certain actions to persons who are informed. Naïvely, we may expect that our Secretary of State and his staff do know whatever is to be known about the possible consequences of bombing the Chinese mainland. Normally, we do not regard this issue of bombing or not bombing as a matter for democratic vote. So the second horn is not so painful at that, since our democratic way of life—if properly defined—does not require all to decide on all issues.

However, is it easy enough to sharpen the horn again. In the next election, voters decide whether the Secretary did a good job or not.

They decide whether their congressman voted correctly on legislation or not. But they must make these decisions in ignorance of many of the consequences of executive and legislative action.

The important point is: Did either Mr. Secretary or Mr. Congressman "use" all the relevant information? What is "relevant" information, and how should it be "used"? These questions cannot be answered in an arbitrary manner. In cases where a great deal of effort has been made to answer the questions, we know that the answers are not easy ones to give. For example, the operations research groups of our Army, Navy, and Air Force are composed of scientists who study the manner in which relevant information should be used in setting military policies. I do not believe that any other government agency has adopted anything resembling this use of scientific manpower for such a purpose. Thus, those who make social decisions fail to gather the relevant information even though it is available. How should this defect in social policy-making be controlled? Presumably, in a democratic society, by a vote of the interested parties. But how can everyone have the available information in order to judge the inadequacy of the policy-makers?

Hence, we seem driven to accept these apparently inconsistent consequences of democratic decision-making:

(a) Ultimately all interested persons should be partners in social decisions,

(b) Good decision-making depends on the selection of relevant information and its proper utilization,

(c) Only a few people have the time and means to obtain relevant information and to ascertain its proper use.

We can avoid the apparent contradition of these assertions if we attempt to define the terms properly. Specifically, we could argue that certain persons in our culture are qualified by training and by mental aptitude to perform the job required for (b), the selection of relevant information. We could also argue that all members of the culture should judge whether or not a specific training and aptitude qualifies a man to do this job. They could make this judgment by delegating the decision to certain people, for example, to university professors. Qualified personnel are called "scientists." Everyone in our culture would have an interest in and help to decide who are scientists. Thus (a) is satisfied. The scientists do what (b) requires. And, as (c) indicates, they are only a small group.

If this argument solves the problem, it clearly suggests another one. For now we must recognize that what "science" means is not an arbitrary matter to be decided upon by a few experts, or by so-called "scientists." Instead, what "science" means is a matter of national policy, just as what "science" means to a business firm is a part of the firm's policy. This conclusion shows that the problem we have posed can be restated as follows: does the meaning of science that our national policy requires in order to maintain its democratic ideals, preclude a science of ethics?

5 · *Science and Decision-Making.*

Before answering this question, we need to understand in more detail how "science" can assist decision-makers. Over the last decades, there has been a growing recognition that science can be useful in decision-making. For example, in the latter part of the nineteenth century there occurred the "scientific management" movement that was intended to improve performance of industrial workers. Many engineers and scientists attempted to study management problems in the early decades of the twentieth century, notably in the communications problems of the telephone companies. Since World War II there has been a tremendous increase of interest in the use of scientific method in solving management problems, under such labels as "operations research," "management science," "linear programming," etc.

In what way do these scientists aid decision-makers? One answer to this question can be obtained by recognizing the traditional attitudes of engineers and physicians. The disciplines of both have arrived at one plausible answer to the problem of how applied science works: The scientist discovers the relevant facts; the decision-maker acts. The "relevant facts" consist of estimating what will happen if a certain course of action is followed or of finding an action which will accomplish a prescribed result.

One point of view, therefore, is that the decision-maker decides what he wants, and the applied scientist tries to tell him what to do in order to gain his objectives. The engineer and doctor do not try to tell their client what he ought to do; they tell him what will happen if he does do so-and-so.

But this point of view will not do because a significant part of modern management science consists, not only of attempts to find out how to accomplish results, but also of attempts to find out what results are really wanted.

The reason why management science has had to consider what is wanted is not too hard to understand. Most policy problems do not involve one objective but several. Threatening to bomb the Chinese mainland might stop the spread of Asiatic communism; it might also result in killing some Chinese; it might also make other Asiatics so furious that our oriental trade would be further impaired. What is the relative importance of these three possible outcomes, Communist check, Asiatic murder, or trade decline? No decision-maker could feel satisfied with an immediate response to this question without any factual support. One might argue that Communist check is the most important because, if it were not checked, eventually there would be no freedom, not even freedom to avoid being murdered, or to trade. But whether one argues in this fashion or not, he has attached relative weights of importance to outcomes. If he can estimate these weights, albeit intuitively at times, this suggests to the scientific mind the possibility of making an estimate in terms of controlled observation. Indeed, the reasons offered for assigning a high value of importance to checking communism seem to depend on "reliable" observations of the behavior of Communists.

If it is true that the scientist can study and determine the relative importance of objectives, he has made an inroad on the activities of the decision-maker. The scientist discovers what will occur and whether it is desirable that it should occur. What is left for decision-making as such?

A number of answers are possible. First of all, one can point out a certain amount of naïvete that has crept into the discussion. It's all very well to picture the objective, fact-finding, cool-headed scientist who calmly puts the facts about consequences and the facts about wants into his machine and as calmly awaits whatever answer comes out. Such a brave new world is as far away in reality as it is present in the pulps.

We said that scientists are sitting at the right hand of policy-makers. But we should also say something more about what they accomplish there. They have discovered that even fairly small business organizations are tremendously complicated phenomena to study. At the present time, there is no model within which the total activity of such organizations can be described. There is no known way of generating even the most important information to test such a model if it did exist, and there is no known machine that could absorb and analyze the information if it could be obtained.

The decision-maker is, therefore, still essential, because someone has to make the leap in the dark and take the risk, even with a scientist at his elbow. The problem of the inability to see the whole organizational picture scientifically is matched by the inability to find satisfactory methods of evaluating the information. Information about an organization comes from many sources, some much more reliable than others. It is not a matter of "plugging information into a machine."

But the present inabilities of science do not remove the problem of the relation between science and policy-making, or science and ethics. Furthermore, these inabilities will be lessened in time if science is permitted to survive by policy-makers and moralists. Does this mean that as science becomes more adept at studying whole organizations, it will gradually replace the decision-maker? Will the decision-maker sit at the right hand of the scientist?

Now the issue becomes speculative and therefore really interesting. If the scientist makes recommendations, he says, in effect, "This is what you ought to do." How are such recommendations possible in view of what the scientist does?

For purposes of speculating on this point, we remove the barriers caused by the current ineptitude of academic science. Suppose that the scientist can successfully estimate what actions are available, what outcomes will result if an action is pursued (or at least the probability of the outcome), and the relative importance of each outcome. How does he put all these "facts" together to come up with a recommendation? What is the significance of the recommendation? That is, why is the recommendation compelling?

Several answers will be examined here: (1) the scientist as such can do no more than gather together the relevant facts without ever verifying any recommendations; (2) the scientist can examine the decision-maker's past behavior and recommend on the basis of rational rules of consistency; (3) the scientist can recommend on the basis of the rules of rational decision-making used in science itself (that is, on the basis of an extension of scientific method); (4) recommendations—what "ought to be done"—are valid because they follow from the notion of measuring the values of the decision-maker's objectives. We want to argue that the final answer is the only sound conclusion. Once the meaning of value measurements is given, the meaning of a recommendation becomes clear. In other words, if the scientist has a method for determining what the decision-maker wants, this method can be made the basis for verifying a recommendation.

6 · Is What "Ought To Be" Nonfactual?

Consider the first answer to the question about the meaning of recommendations; this is merely an extension of an earlier answer. The scientist, so the reasoning runs, is restricted to facts and to prediction by scientific laws. This restriction does enable him to say what is, what will be if such and such is done, and possibly what the relative values of these outcomes are for the people involved in the decision. But the restriction to facts alone prevents his doing any more than this. He may *feel* that as a result of the facts certain actions should be chosen, but he cannot *prove* anything on this score.

This point of view argues that the essence of decision-making is the initiation of action, and this essence lies beyond the scientist's realm. It is, in Kantian terms, *noumenal* compared to the *phenomenal* world of the scientist. What distinguishes the executive from his scientific staff is the fact that the executive must act; the scientist merely advises. So goes the theme. And one might add that since action entails much more risk—of property, life, career, and all—than does advice, the rewards of our culture go to the risk-taker, not to the scientist.

The line of argument is clearly faulty—or else not yet defined clearly enough. What are the "facts" to which science is restricted? Surely, without a comprehensive notion of the resources of science, it is arbitrary and naïve dogmatically to assert that science can do *this* but can't do *that*.

The notion of the limits of science introduces a dualism which never seems to hold up under the pressure of time. The dualism consists of setting boundaries on the scope of human knowledge. It argues that *this* sort of question can be studied scientifically, but *that* sort cannot. God, immortality, freedom, the Human Spirit, the action of the decision-maker, all have been candidates for the "cannots."

The dualism fails on so many counts that it is not necessary to dwell long on its inadequacies. It claims to know enough to know that a certain problem does not lie within the scope of science. Whence comes this knowledge? For a sophisticated knowledge it is indeed. It is a knowledge of what science is and forever will be, as well as a knowledge of what the problem is and forever will be. Such a knowledge is truly astounding.

The real motivation that drives men to deny a science of God or freedom or action need not drive them into the awkwardness of this untenable dualism. The motivation comes about because people are afraid that if certain problems are studied by the methods of *current* science, the results will be disastrous. And this may well be the case, for current science by its own modest admission is replete with inadequacies, lacunae, inconsistencies. Still this is no reason to deny that science is a potential servant of all men for all problems, just as art, production, and politics are. It seems far more prudent to say, "This is something that ought not to be settled by present-day scientists," than to say, "This is something that science can never study."

To deny the dualism is to say that the entire world can be viewed in a great many ways, of which science is one. In terms of our national and cultural objectives, there seems to be a compelling reason for keeping open forever the potential use of science for every human need. This is desirable, even though we're not sure how one decides when that potentiality should be actualized. Indeed, such a decision is itself an ideal of science.

We therefore want a conception of science that enables the scientist to look at all the world. Recommendations are a part of the world, and hence we are driven to inquire how science can verify recommendations. Of course I am aware that the argument just posed is not rationally compelling. But its compulsion for the moment rests on the emotion of intellectual curiosity. If there is a sense in which one decision is better than another—a sense that is clear to the good executive as he views the world—then how can the scientist go about verifying (or refuting) such a judgment?

The natural answer to this question is that there must be some way of putting all the facts together so that the judgment about the value of a decision can be scientifically proven. This leads us to a consideration of the second answer to the problem of the meaning of a recommendation: consistency of behavior.

7 · *Does "Ought" Mean "Consistent"?*

Let us define a "decision rule" as any method which from time to time provides an explicit way for selecting one action from a set of alternative actions available to the decision-maker. A number of different decision rules are available for every decision-maker. He could select actions by repeatedly tossing a coin; or by doing what first comes to mind; or by doing what Uncle Joe says to do. Now, some thinkers would like to assert that the scientist qua scientist makes no choice among the many possible decision rules. But the scientist may find through past history that a company, or government agency, has acted *as though* it accepted one specific decision rule. Their argument concludes: "If your present behavior is consistent with your past decisions, this is what you ought to do." With the one simple premise that one ought to act consistently, the recommendations are "provable" within science. And this simple premise is one which science itself must adopt in its own procedures.

The difficulty with this suggestion is to find suitable rules of consistent behavior. This is a matter which will have to be explored in greater detail later on in the book. But an example may suffice to illustrate such a rule. Suppose in the past that the decision-maker has regularly shown a preference for A over B, and for B over C. Then consistency seems to require that when he is given the choice between A and C, he "ought" to choose A. This is somewhat analogous to the situation where one has observed X to be longer than Y, and Y longer than Z. We agree in such cases that a comparison of X and Z ought to reveal that X is longer that Z. But of course the analogy does not establish the result we want. How do we know that preference comparisons ought to obey the same rule as length comparisons? We can fall back on intuition, or on definition; that is, we can argue that the A ought to be preferred to C because this is intuitively clear given the premises, or because this follows from the meaning of preference. Whether either of these suggestions is feasible will require some scrutiny. For the present we may express some doubts on this score because (1) intuition rarely if ever provides sufficient evidence for a scientific conclusion, and (2) truths based on definitions require a justification of the definition.

Nevertheless, we shall see that this suggestion for verifying "ought" judgments is a fruitful one, and, properly interpreted, may be the best we have attained so far. Before considering how this suggestion can be generalized and made more satisfactory, it is worthwhile to ask whether the rules of consistent behavior are not already revealed in the procedures of science itself. In other words, perhaps the rule: "If *A* is preferred to *B* and *B* to *C,* then *A* ought to be preferred to *C*" is a rule which governs decision-making in science, and its justification lies in the fact that if it were not valid, then there would be no science.

8 · *When Using Scientific Information, Do as the Scientists Do.*

In order to understand this suggestion, it must be pointed out that the scientist himself is a decision-maker. This way of looking at science may seem unusual, but it is a realistic viewpoint. The scientist decides what to study; he decides what model is adequate within which to pose his problem; he decides how, when, and where to make observations; he decides when to accept or reject a conclusion. As a decision-maker he is as much concerned with actions as is the executive. The scientist's creation of "objective" facts and predictions is based on the decisions he has made.

It seems safe enough to assume that the manner in which scientists make decisions is based on rules of consistency. That is, the scientist has rules which tell him what choices ought to be made given previously prescribed choices and his present circumstances and aims. Therefore, when the scientist says to the executive, "This is what you ought to do," perhaps he means, "This is the action that would be selected, given the facts, if you used the same criteria of consistency that science uses." This point of view argues that the scientist's advice is merely an extension of his own decision scheme to the executive's problems. He is *deducing* a decision from the facts plus science's own decision scheme. The compulsion of his recommendation—for this point of view—is a compulsion based on consistency: if the decision-maker accepts the scientist's facts, he "ought" also to accept the decision scheme by means of which the facts were arrived at.

But how does science decide to accept a "fact"? We shall return to this awkward question frequently. For the present, let us assume a somewhat simple and naïve answer: The scientific decision rule for accepting facts is that all "competent" observers agree on the occurrence or non-occurrence of the event. That is, "*A* is a fact" should be accepted if *A* describes an event and all competent observers agree that the event occurred. In general, we have: "Whenever all competent persons agree—and will continue to agree—that something is so, then any assertion that this something is so *ought* to be accepted." We therefore argue that, given the facts about agreements, the "ought" follows from these facts and this rule, a rule that science itself accepts.

Stated otherwise, scientific facts are in the indicative mood: "*X* is *A*." But the decision used by science to accept the facts is in the optative mood: "*A* ought to be done." If this decision rule is generalized, then there is a meaningful sense in which science "verifies" a recommendation; it does so by deducing an assertion in an optative mood from factual assertions in the indicative mood *plus* the generalized consistency rule in the optative mood. We might note in passing that to hold that what "ought to be" cannot be derived from what "is" is to ignore the fact that what "is" is itself a decision—a decision about what "ought" to be done.

This whole argument is rather "neat," and does away with a lot of nonsense about "is" and "ought." —but it won't do—at least in the social environment of contemporary science. For one of the most striking things about science is that it never has tried to conduct a comprehensive study of its own decision rules. Indeed, many practicing scientists have objected strongly to philosophical attempts to analyze their decision procedures. Scientists are often proud of the vagueness that surrounds their activities: the fact that they "believe" in two conflicting hypotheses simultaneously, that they often do not try to resolve apparent inconsistencies, and that they do not need to justify their interest in one type of research as opposed to another. Creative scientists talk about themselves in much the same manner as successful executives. Statisticians are aware of this attitude of scientists; even in such matters as experimental design and sample size, where the scientist's creative genius is not at all threatened and where adequate decision rules have presumably been worked out by statisticians, it is often quite difficult to persuade the scientist to accept assistance. Statisticians often play the same role with respect to scientists as the latter sometimes play with respect to the executive;

the difficulty the statisticians encounter in making recommendations to scientists shows the absurdity of attempting to make the scientist's decision rules a standard for policy-making at the present time.

Even the rule of agreement cited above is often ignored in research because of other considerations. Many scientists will find some scene such as the following familiar enough:

> Scientist A (coming into Scientist B's office with a sheet of data): Well, our little idea didn't work out at all. We've run off the experiment and the results obviously don't check.
>
> Scientist B (ruffling through the pile): Hmm. Let's see. (Frowns) Who made these readings anyway?
>
> A: Well, Smith did most of it. Brown checked over the equipment, though, and said it was O.K., and ran some of the tests himself.
>
> B: Damn it all. Smith's always getting things balled up. Why didn't Jones do it?
>
> A: He was busy on the secret project and Harrison wouldn't let him off.
>
> B: Well, we'll have to run the stuff over again. Smith's competent enough, but I'm positive our idea must be right. Get Jones to recheck the data.

The observers all may agree, but the scientist may not feel he should accept the results. Scientist B may have used good judgment; because perhaps his "idea" is so important that abandoning it on "insufficient" grounds would be disastrous.

In sum, except on a few occasions, such as Bridgman's operationism, scientists have shown a strong disinclination to examine their own decision rules. Logical reconstructionism—an effort primarily initiated by philosophers—has attempted to perform an analysis and a logical purification of scientific activities, but few Reconstructionists would argue that the results of their efforts can be used to set up explicit decision schemes for science.

The reader may be puzzled by the two statements: (a) science is supposed to provide objective information, and (b) science itself has never examined its own decision process. For the moment let us let the paradox remain. No wise man believes that the value of an activity depends solely on a self-consciousness about the reasons for the decisions that are made. We are supposing that science does well, and for the time being we hold in abeyance an analysis of the decision rules by means of which it accomplishes its task.

9 · *The "Ought" and Value Measurements.*

So far, then, we have not given a satisfactory account of the way in which science verifies recommendations. But we might make some progress in this direction by generalizing on a suggestion we made earlier and temporarily abandoned. We said that the scientist might verify a recommendation by inferring what the decision-maker would do if he followed established rules of consistency. New rules of consistency can be thought of as patterns (theories) of behavior. Instead of insisting on *one* so-called "consistent" pattern of behavior, why don't we say that the scientific verification of a recommendation is based on whatever pattern of behavior actually obtains?

At first sight, this viewpoint seems to abandon the entire spirit of a recommendation. All it seems to say is that "X ought to do A" is the same as "X will do A." Such is not the intention—or rather the intention is more subtle. The prediction implied in the "ought" is a prediction of behavior *under certain conditions*. The "ought to do A" is a "dispositional" predicate, and like all such predicates can be specified only by specifying the conditions under which it applies. For example, in the physical sciences, "has length of 3 cm." is a dispositional predicate which predicts how a certain object would compare with a standard under standard conditions.

This example suggests that in trying to arrive at a satisfactory interpretation of the "ought" of a recommendation, we could profit by examining some ideas about measurement in the physical sciences. In particular, I want to turn attention to the use of standards. All along we have been interested in what is meant by the value of an outcome for a person. I take this to be a legitimate factual question that science can attempt to answer. However, it is also legitimate to interpret this question as one of measurement in quantitative terms: How much does a person value an outcome? Since this is so, it is important that we construct the standard conditions and operations that define the measurement process. All measurements of the form "X is k units" presuppose such standard conditions. The statement "X is k units" means "X would exhibit such-and-such properties and behavior in the standard environment." This very brief account will be explained in much greater detail in Chapter 5.

Suppose we could agree on the standard conditions for measuring the values of outcomes. Then we would say "X values an outcome to degree k" means "X would exhibit such-and-such behavior in the standard environment for value measurements." The present suggestion is to assert that the "ought" in a recommendation can be stated as follows: "X ought to do A in *this* environment" means "X would do A in the standard environment that defines value measurements." This suggestion at present is tentative—it will take the rest of the book to defend and make its meaning approximately intelligible.

For the moment, however, the general idea can be understood. If a scientist states that an executive should follow a certain course of action, he says in effect, "I have measured the values of the executive —or his organization—for the various outcomes that may result from his decisions. These measurements predict what he would do if he were making his decision under the standard conditions of value measurements. When I say he ought to exhibit such-and-such behavior, I mean that this is the behavior he would exhibit if these standard conditions held. Of course, he may not do what he ought to do; that is, the standard conditions may not hold in this environment."

What are the standard conditions that define measurements of value? Common sense holds that all standards are "arbitrary," but, as we shall see in Chapter 5, the choice of standards is really based on considerations of economy and fruitfulness. The considerations lead us to conclude that if we want to find out what a person really wants, we have to be sure he understands his choices and is not confused by extraneous considerations. In other words, if a person is not disturbed, can "think properly," and is not confused by irrelevant interruptions, his choices may be taken to express his values. The conditions are vaguely described, and may be very difficult to attain even under laboratory conditions. However, they help to define one possible "standard" for value measurements. Hence, tentatively, when we say "X ought to do A in this environment" we mean "X would do A if he were undisturbed, could think properly, and were not subject to external forces."

Suppose we try to develop this notion more precisely. If we want to find out what a person wants, we could, of course, ask him. However, he may not understand our question, or may not feel that the question is realistic, or he may give the answer he thinks is expected of him. Hence we may try to put him in a situation where he has to make a real choice. But even here a behavioral response may not reveal a true preference, because he may not know all the choices he has, or he may be ignorant of the consequences of his choice.

These remarks lead us to a second attempt to define standards for value measurements, which will be developed further on in the book, and especially in Chapter 7. "*X* ought to do *A*" means "*X* would do *A* if he were aware of all alternative actions and knew the probabilities of the possible outcomes." This standard condition for measuring values is defined in terms of complete knowledge. When we say that a person wants something very much we mean that he would try to get it if he knew how; we predict his behavior under conditions of perfect knowledge.

Thus one meaning of the scientific verification of what a man "ought" to do depends on the scientist's way of measuring what he wants to do. If we know what a man wants, that is, if we can measure his values—then we can say what he ought to do. This is clearly not the answer we set out to find at the beginning of the chapter, because such an "ought" is not necessarily a moral "ought." However, we shall want to see whether we can find a meaning of the moral "ought" once we have satisfied ourselves about the meaning of a prudential "ought."

Admittedly, the phrase "perfect knowledge" is vague and requires further analysis. At this step in the over-all analysis, it is important to point out that a person knows the outcomes perfectly if he can predict the one outcome which would occur after a certain action was taken. But we shall also want to say that he knows the outcomes perfectly if he knows the probabilities of each of the outcomes perfectly, because in many cases the decision-making environment is so structured that exact prediction is impossible.

We have now come to a tentative meaning of a scientific verification of a (prudential) recommendation. According to this meaning, a recommendation is a prediction of behavior when the decision-maker acts in a state of complete knowledge, either knowledge that predicts with certainty, or knowledge of the true probabilities of the outcomes. As an aid to the decision-maker, the scientist must do two things: he must try to improve the decision-maker's state of knowledge, and he must try to find out how the decision-maker would act if his ignorance were removed. We have already discussed the scientist's efforts to tell the executive what is going on around him. Indeed, the traditional conception of applied science restricts the scientist to this activity because it was implicitly assumed that the decision-maker actually knows what he wants. Once this implicit assumption is removed, that is, once it is admitted that the scientist must also measure wants and needs, then the concept of the recommendation includes both considerations: improvement of the decision-maker's knowledge and a prediction of his behavior if such improvement occurs.

This entire analysis of what is meant by a degree of want and the correlative concept of "ought" is not necessarily made in conformity with common usage. It has been arrived at through a chain of reflections initiated by the question of what a recommendation could possibly mean to a scientist (assuming that it has some meaning for him). Some defense of this concept can be made in terms of existing attempts to measure human values in education, attitude studies, consumer behavior, accounting, management science, and so on. But that defense, necessary as it ultimately is, is beyond the scope of this chapter.

Suppose for the moment that we accept the proposal that "X ought to do A" is a prediction of X's behavior under conditions of complete freedom and knowledge, admitting that this proposal requires a great deal of refinement before it becomes very useful. Before we can make the supposition, however, one rather obvious objection can be raised: Can such predictions be made? In one sense, no scientific prediction can be made since all predictions are subject to error. At the present time, even in rather simple laboratory situations, and even there only by dint of a great deal of intellectual effort, the "ought" predictions can only be made crudely. This imprecision is responsible in part for the feeling that "ought" cannot be reduced to "is"; a sophisticated version of this philosophical cliché consists of asserting that "ought" cannot be reduced to "is" because no one will ever be able to predict what people would do if they were not ignorant.

What, then, is the point of all this effort? Several comments come to mind, perhaps the most significant of which is that to be unattainable is one of the properties of the ideals of the scientific enterprise. But—on a more practical level—the point of the analysis is to suggest a framework within which one can reflect on the many diverse efforts to study human wants and to make recommendations. Perhaps thereby one can find a basis for criticism in this area. For the growth of interest in the application of science to decision-making shows that those predictions that can be made do have a great deal of value even if they are subject to error.

10 · *Science and Morality.*

We set out to find a method for verifying ethical judgments. However, defining a method of verifying prudential judgments is so difficult that only at the end of the book will an attempt be made to see how one can go from the prudent to the ethical. The following is a sketch of the more detailed discussion to be pursued there.

It seems natural to consider social morality first, that is, the morality of a given society or culture. It does not seem too difficult to go from the prudential to the social "ought": "X ought to do A" means "A is what the society as a whole wants X to do." But it is amazing how difficult it is to explain social approval in terms that can be useful to a scientist trying to verify a recommendation for a social group. According to the tentative ideas developed so far, "Y wants X to do A" means "given that Y has complete knowledge of the probabilities of the consequences of each action that X can choose, and given that Y knows what X wants, that is, knows what X would do if he were not restrained and had complete knowledge, and given $Y's$ ability to control $X's$ behavior, A is what Y would make X do." If Y represents a social group, then this is an explanation of what X ought to do on the grounds of social morality. If the society believes in a certain amount of individual freedom, A may merely be that action which best serves $X's$ purposes; i.e., for the case of free decisions, society wants X to do what he would do if he had perfect knowledge. For other decisions, society imposes sanctions. But this explanation is in need of further analysis because of the difficulties entailed in defining what a social group knows (Chapter 11) and in defining what it wants (Chapter 12). At the present time, we have few guides to help us choose a suitable definition of social knowledge and social values. But we can at least examine the possibilities.

Reserving these technical details for later discussion, we pass on to the question of ethical "oughts." A society of head-hunters presumably approves of severing heads on occasion, though many less bloodthirsty humans have believed it sensible to say that they ought not to have done so. In the same manner, some wiser generation will surely express the ethical opinion that the rigid and unimaginative life of today's white-collar commuter constitutes an immoral waste of the gifts of reason and creative imagination. Hence, approval of a man's actions by one society is not by itself a good basis for the verification of an ethical judgment. Can we find any basis?

The aim is to interpret the statement "X ought to do A on ethical grounds" or "A is the right policy for X to adopt" so that the scientist can verify the assertion (within certain error limits, of course).

According to the meaning of "science" adopted here, we have to rule out verifications based on assertions that a certain action is a dictate of a superior or supreme being. That is, the "ground rules" of the present discussion preclude our saying that "A is the right policy" can be scientifically translated into "A is the policy approved by a being superior to all men." This translation is not ruled out because the existence of such a superior being cannot be established by the "facts," but because normally we have no satisfactory method of proving that statements are revealed to us by a superior intelligence. I take it to be a tradition of academic science that investigation into any issue is always possible and eventually desirable.

All this amounts to saying that the search for the scientific meaning of the ethical "ought" must lie within the boundaries of humanity. The aim here is not to find out what people normally mean when they advise and criticize on ethical grounds. The aim is to discover one or more plausible ways in which science might verify a moral precept. My own reflections on this matter tend to converge on the idea that ethical judgments are really judgments made for the sake of future generations.

This idea suggests one solution to the problem. One might say that "X ought to do A on ethical grounds" means "A is what X would do if he knew the consequences of his acts, and if he knew what future men will want." This idea has a certain appeal; men sin only because of ignorance. Murder, rape, the aggression of nations, the exploitation of the worker—all would disappear if men knew the future and knew what future men will want. This is a nice idea, but not really tenable with our present knowledge of what men are like. Besides, unethical men do like to influence what people will want, and this conduct would not be judged unethical under the definition just proposed.

We try again. This time we take a hint from those who have searched for intercultural agreements about ethical norms. What relevance does it have to ethics that all men, now and in the past, have agreed on the right way to behave, or on other aspects of ethical problems? No relevance, I think, if the intercultural agreement is all that is offered because the next generation might suddenly realize that all past generations have been ethically sterile. For example, Nietzsche's great message was not so much an attack on Christian morality, but an attack on all moralists who find their criteria of ethical validity in universal conformity with the past. Something more than "all agree that" is needed to understand the import of an ethical judgment. The "something more" is not hard to find: perhaps one needs only add, "and all men will forever agree when they are given the maximum opportunity to disagree." As we shall see later, true agreement (judgment) is based on a pattern of disagreement between free decision-makers.

The significance of the interculturalist's studies can now be seen: Perhaps "X ought to do A on ethical grounds," means "A is what all men will want X to have done." But the hope of finding evidence for so universal an assertion about human wants seems dim indeed. It seems naïve in the extreme to assert that because all men in the past have agreed they will agree in the future. But what other evidence is there for an ethical assertion?

The obvious reply is that we are not really restricted to "static" agreements. In science itself one does not expect to find universal agreement on any issue. There is no proposition that all men will always believe. But perhaps there is some class of propositions that all men will "tend" to agree upon more and more. Similarly, perhaps there is some class of actions open to X at the present time which men will eventually "tend" to want X to choose.

What this idea means is obviously difficult to explain, although an attempt will be made in this direction in Chapter 15. First of all, it is important to become clearer on the motivation for introducing an hypothesis about "converging" human interests. We want a scientific interpretation of the ethical "ought." We accept the position that the ethical "ought" from the scientific viewpoint refers to future man, and specifically to what future man will want. The vague scientific interpretation of "X ought to do A on ethical grounds" is "A is what future man will want X to have done." Some of the vagueness of this translation has been removed by giving a tentative interpretation of "*Y* wants *X* to do *A*," where *Y* is a social group. If *Y* is the social group which includes future man, as the argument seems to demand, then the difficulties of explaining the idea of social approval become very great. However, there seems to be no other way of interpreting ethical judgments adequately.

In a sense, the attempt to view morality through the eyes of science is more fantastic than factual, more visionary than precise. Science still knows so little about what present-day man wants that it is fantastic to talk about what future man will want, and to suggest the possibility of forecasting such wants by scientific method. Nevertheless, it is hard not to talk in this vein even though in so doing one drastically violates the ideals of rigor and clarity. It is difficult not to because science has a stake in morality, that is, in the future wants of humanity. Philosophers of science must ask themselves whether the problems of future men—admittedly relevant to current science—are forever beyond the understanding of current science.

It therefore seems clear that we must consider the feasibility of a scientific discipline which predicts the future interests of men by means of a theory of the development of interests. Such a theory is much like discussions of the origin and ultimate fate of our universe —terribly important but not rigorously defensible at the present time.

A simple theory of men's interests would be one that predicts that interests remain the same throughout all time, for example, that all men will always be interested primarily in maximizing pleasure. The next chapter considers this theory in some detail and concludes that it is untenable. A modified version of the theory that men's interests remain the same at all times, is one that predicts changes in men's interests, but a convergence of these interests towards a common set of ideals. If this theory could be defended, we could adopt the position that the expression "what future man wants" is to be interpreted as "what is required to optimally approximate the ideals." Each age of science would then try to estimate what the ideals really are, as well as estimate those policies which are optimal with respect to the ideals. These estimates would form the basis of a scientific verification of the ethical value of a policy. The last chapter of the book will amplify on this brief account.

At one time I accepted this simple convergence theory much more strongly than I am inclined to do today. Along with Russell L. Ackoff I even attempted to work out a notion of how the convergence might be identified by means of historical data. Further reflection has tempered the enthusiasm and added qualifications.

At this time I cannot help thinking that the hypothesis of ultimately converging interests was unduly simple, at least as I had thought of it earlier. I did think that men might diverge in interest for long periods because, with infinite time as the basis for estimating "trends," one can be quite complacent about erratic departures from trend lines which last many millenia. But the simple notion of converging interests was naïve because it ignored the reasonable thesis that men do not want to agree. That is, an ideal held dear by many men is that men should differ among themselves concerning what is most worth living for. This reflection makes me think that the theory of human interests can be viewed in two distinct but compatible ways. The rationalist will argue that men disagree in order—in the long run—to find ways of agreeing. The individualist will argue that men agree in order—in the long run—to find ways of disagreeing. The rationalist looks at human history as a trend toward less conflict, more consolidation, but realizes that such a theory of history can only be sustained if men disagree both with others and themselves. The individualist believes that men must agree on methods of survival and more profitable living in order the better to express their disagreements.

The viewpoints are not contradictory because both theories see no end to the story. Within this view of eternity, there is no distinction between means and ends. Science can interpret human history as a trend toward peace in which conflict is a necessary sustaining force or a trend toward conflict in which peace is a sine qua non of survival.

In any case, the theory of converging interests is not the only possible framework within which one can find a scientific interpretation of a morally right decision. Furthermore, a more adequate language than that of convergence may be available. For example, a number of thinkers have suggested the language of cybernetics as a more appropriate medium for expressing the complicated structure of human conflict and happiness. Certainly neither a convergence theory nor a cybernetic theory should treat the future goals or states as a priori givens; the study of the development of the human species must permit a redefinition of concepts as well as a reformulation of theory.

Furthermore, lest we forget the pessimist, the effort to find an ethical theory may fail. Ethics, as seen through the eyes of science, is a gigantic, complex anthropological theory. And perhaps no proposed theory will meet the requirements of scientific method. Science must always reserve for itself the right to unearth a tragic truth about man: mankind has no morality. The manner in which science might eventually come to accept such a doctrine is hopelessly obscure to me, as is the meaning which "science" could possibly have after such a conclusion to its history. I cannot help but feel that a science that "discovered" the amorality of men would also discover the total ignorance of men. But this too is possible.

In sum, the possibilities of a scientific interpretation of the ethical "ought" are real enough. It is far too premature to be dogmatic about any one interpretation, since each is based on a theory of human wants so comprehensive as to defy our present scientific powers of testing. And it is certainly premature to argue that no reasonable interpretation will ever be found. None of this detracts from the value of attempted interpretations, however. Such attempts —however tenuous—are guides to future scientific research.

11 · *Freedom and Science.*

It may be fruitful to restate the purpose of this enterprise in looser terms.

In this age of mass communication, it is natural enough that people repeat the obvious. One repetition that has occupied its share of the national print and radio waves is that the decisions of men should be free. Any threat to this freedom is a sin against Americanism, and must be punished by depriving the sinner of his freedom.

Another repetition is the one that pictures the scientist as a cold-hearted machine, which picks up facts like some gigantic crane, digests them like a rock-crusher, and reconstructs them like an automatic mason.

Put these two repetitions together and form a third one—many writers have. This third one pictures the awful day when "science" will decide what ought to be. No more will you, or I, or the man who runs a grocery store on the corner, freely decide what to do. All of us will have our decisions made for us by the perfectly correct machinery of science.

Do modern executives worry about that day when out of their research laboratories will charge a sedate and highly organized body of badly bodied and well minded scientists—who will smoothly eliminate the executive function and replace it by the scientific?

What an awful prospect! Therefore, what "ought to be" will not be defined in terms of what "is." For humanity's sake let us keep the scientist out of the decisions and relegate him to his "facts"!

But just the same repetitions appear on the other side. The scientist, above all, wants to remain free. His great fear in the last decade has been that executives and legislators will not allow him this freedom. He is afraid that what "is" will be decided by someone's notion of what "ought to be."

The scientist's fears are the more realistic ones. It is not hard to find legislators who would like to tell scientists what they ought to do, although most scientists still show little interest in recommending actions for executives. The problem is to get them to show more interest, not to get them to show less.

The world can be seen in many ways. The artist can—and does—construct criteria of aesthetic quality in actions, and for him much of what is decided today by business executives and government officials must look ugly indeed. This does not mean that artists will decide the fate of nations or rob us of our freedom. So too, the scientist may decide what ought to be done—or at least so it has been argued in this chapter. But having decided this, he does not thereby control men's actions.

There is, of course, that pure essence, the "act," the decision in itself, which belongs to every man as his own. Science cannot take that away. Or can it? The one privilege science demands is to understand the world, including the world of decisions. This demand is based on the assumption that decision-making is scientifically interesting to study. Each one of us may hope that his decision-making is so private that no one else will ever see it or understand it. If the decisions to be made are unimportant enough to everyone else, there is no reason this should not be so. But, will granting the scientist the privilege to study decision-making deprive men of their freedom? "Of their freedom," no. "Of their privacy," yes. The important and complicated decisions of men in society are no longer, and I hope never again will be, complete secrets from their fellow men.

12 · *Indebtedness.*

The idea that some decisions, especially moral ones, can be made correctly without information was most fully expounded by Butler (4) and the Intuitionist school of ethics.

Informational schemes for decision-making—in terms of (1) alternative actions ("means"), (2) possible outcomes ("ends"), (3) probability that actions are followed by outcomes, (4) value of the outcomes—have been discussed by many philosophers; one example is Dewey (6). Examples of other writers on decision theory are Savage (13), the authors of *Decision Processes* (17), and Luce-Raiffa (11). See also discussions of maximizing the expected monetary return or expected utility in economics (16). The very important question of the specific time period that includes the outcomes is discussed in some of the references cited in Chapter 3.

Some illustrations of scientific recommendations for decision-making can be found in the journals, *Operations Research,* and *Management Science,* as well as numerous other publications referred to in these journals.

For an example of a scientist's annoyance at an analysis of scientific decision-making, see Wilson's review (19) of a recent book by Braithwaite (3).

Some of the difficulties in constructing standards for utility measurements are discussed in the work of Davidson *et al.* (5).

Discussions of the role of science and ethics are many. Among the recent ones are Dewey (6), Edel (7), Kadish (9), Northrop (12), Kluckhohn (10), Golightly (8), and Ackoff (1).

For a classification of ethical schools that is relevant to the present work, see Singer (15).

For a discussion of the difficulties in defining the preferences of a social group, see, for example, Arrow (2).

Finally, I think it is clear that the concept of value adopted here has some resemblance to well-known classical concepts of value. Thus, "economic man" is an ideal, rational choice-maker who knows all the consequences of his choices. But the difference is that here we drop the "rational" requirement, and the ideal becomes a standard for measurement. The fact that the standard conditions for measuring values are rarely encountered in practice is no more strange than the fact that the standard conditions for measuring length are rarely encountered either.

Furthermore, the dogma of the Catholic Church holds that a mortal sin is committed only if a person acts with full consent of the will and full knowledge of the consequences. I take the intent of the stipulations to be a formulation of the evidence of a person's values: he *wants* evil if his choices are evil under these conditions. But, of course, in this book the stipulations are those an observer requires in order to derive evidence of a person's values, and not to derive evidence of the evil in them.

REFERENCES

1. Ackoff, R. L., "On a Science of Ethics," *Philosophy and Phenomenological Research,* Vol. IX (1949), pp. 663-672.
2. Arrow, K. J., *Social Choice and Individual Values.* New York: John Wiley & Sons, Inc., 1951.
3. Braithwaite, R. B., *Scientific Explanation.* Cambridge: Cambridge University Press, 1953.
4. Butler, J., *Fifteen Sermons.* London: George Bell & Sons, Ltd., 1949.
5. Davidson, D., S. Siegel and P. Suppes, "Some Experiments and Related Theory on the Measurement of Utility and Subjective Probability," *Stanford Value Theory Project, Report No. 4,* Stanford, Calif.: Stanford University Press, 1955.
6. Dewey, J., *Logical Conditions of a Scientific Theory of Value.* Chicago: The University of Chicago Press, 1903.
7. Edel, A., *Ethical Judgment: The Use of Science in Ethics.* Chicago: Free Press, 1955.
8. Golightly, C. L., "Value as a Scientific Concept," *The Journal of Philosophy,* Vol. LIII (1956), pp. 233-245.
9. Kadish, M. R., "Evidence and Decision," *The Journal of Philosophy,* Vol. XLVIII (1951), pp. 229-242.
10. Kluckholn, C., "Ethical Relativity: Sic et Non," *The Journal of Philosophy,* Vol. LII (1955), pp. 663-677.
11. Luce, D. L., and H. Raiffa, *Games and Decisions.* New York: John Wiley & Sons, Inc., 1957.
12. Northrop, F. S. C., "Ethical Relativism in the Light of Recent Legal Science," *The Journal of Philosophy,* Vol. LII (1955), pp. 649-662.

13. Savage, L. J., *The Foundations of Statistics*. New York: John Wiley & Sons, Inc., 1954.

14. Simon, H., *Models of Man*. New York: John Wiley & Sons, Inc., 1957.

15. Singer, E. A., *In Search of a Way of Life*. New York: Columbia University Press, 1948.

16. Stigler, G. J., "The Development of Utility Theory," *The Journal of Political Economy*, Vol. LVIII (1950), pp. 307-327 and 373-396.

17. Thrall, R. M., C. H. Coombs and R. L. Davis (editors), *Decision Processes*. New York: John Wiley & Sons, Inc., 1954.

18. Waddington, C. H., *Science and Ethics*. London: George Allen & Unwin, Ltd., 1942.

19. Wilson, E. B., "Review of *Scientific Explanation*," *Journal of the American Statistical Association*, Vol. 50 (1955), pp. 1354-1357.

PLEASURE AND PREFERENCE

2

Summary

and

Intent.

The last chapter argued that the meaning of a recommendation for action from the scientific viewpoint depends on the measurement of human values and specifically on the construction of standards and the prediction of behavior in standard conditions. But it is possible that ascertaining human values is a very simple and direct process that does not require any elaborate methodology of measurement. The present chapter is an examination of such a theory of values, specifically, the attempt to relate value to an immediate sense of pleasure. It begins by considering Kant's "imperatives," that is, Kant's ideas about different kinds of recommendations. The first, the imperatives of skill, are not really concerned with values at all;

they merely predict outcomes of actions. The second, the assetorial imperatives, do involve considerations of human happiness, and these can be interpreted in terms of a calculus of pleasure-pain units. We are thus led to consider the difficulties entailed in trying to construct a science of values in these terms. In order to overcome the difficulties, one may try to resort to another kind of direct observation: observation of the choices a person makes. Instead of asking the person to decide how much pleasure he feels, one decides from an observation of his behavior what choices he prefers. The simplest form of behaviorism merely transforms the direct observation from the subject to the observer. A number of arguments are given to show that a simple choice between alternative actions is not a sufficient basis for inferring preference. In effect, this discussion is the basis for arguing the need for a much more elaborate analysis of the meaning of value measurements.

2 · Kant's Imperatives of Skill.

Writing in the *Fundamental Principles of the Metaphysic of Morals* Kant distinguishes three kinds of imperatives which are of importance to men. The first he calls the general imperatives of skill. These, he says, belong to the "practical part" of all sciences. How do you make a glass tumbler that won't break too readily and that will hold water? There exists a practical side of chemistry and mechanics which answers this question. The answer is in the imperative mood. To make such a glass, first perform step one, then step two, and so on.

What is the compulsion of these imperatives? Kant felt that they were compelling because it was possible for empirical science to demonstrate that actions which complied with the imperatives would produce the prescribed ends. For him the imperatives of skill are not concerned with the question of whether the end sought is rational or good. The imperatives are compelling simply because the action produces the result.

Kant's first type of imperative is certainly familiar enough today. With the advantage of over a century of development in machine design, we can reflect that this imperative is not really concerned with men as such. The action which the imperative commands could be—and often is—an action of a machine.

In effect, then, an imperative of the form "Do X_1. X_2, X_3, and so on," is another way of saying "Actions X_1, X_2, X_3, and so on, in a certain environment, will produce result Y." The *compulsion* of the imperative in this case is equivalent to the *verification* of the latter expression. Put otherwise, "X_1, X_2, X_3, and so on, *ought* to be done" is verified if and only if Y results when X_1, X_2, X_3, and so on, are done.

We know now that the problem of the imperatives of skill is not as simple as Kant felt it to be. He, of course, recognized that in many cases science did not know what action would produce a given result. But he did not seem to be concerned with that wide class of problems where science can only predict on outcome with a specified degree of probability.

At this point there is a useful distinction to be made. When we say that science cannot predict with certainty, we may mean one of two things. We may mean that the present state of science is such that no one knows enough to predict the exact outcome of an action, but future science might approach the exact prediction much more closely that we can. Or we may mean that the situation itself is so defined that the outcome occurs only a certain percentage of the time. For example, if the action is not defined precisely, then usually any given outcome occurs only with a relative frequency lying between o and 1. In many cases, for example, one does not want to specify the operation of a production machine with exact precision, and one is satisfied with the prediction that the production of an item with certain qualities will occur with a frequency of 0.95, say. Thus there are two types of uncertainty: uncertainty due to ignorance, and uncertainty due to the specification of the problem. In this context, we are interested in the second type of uncertainty.

When the findings of science state that the outcome has a 95 per cent chance of success, does this modify the compulsion of the imperative? At first sight it does not. Common sense tells us that in the face of uncertainty we should choose the action with the highest probability of success. This means that the imperative of the form "Do X_1, X_2, X_3, and so on," is another way of saying "The set of actions X_1, X_2, X_3, and so on, has the highest probability of any set of actions, in a certain environment, of producing Y." The compulsion of the imperative is a verification that a specific set of actions yields this "maximum probability." Or, more generally (since exact verification of the probability never takes place), the imperative becomes more compelling to the degree to which the latter statement is confirmed by tests.

The history of design specifications, however, indicates that the solution is not so simple. For example, a number of outcomes are specified for the production of glass: the strength of the glass in terms of its resistance to an impact blow, and the clarity of the glass, among others. Very often these properties are scalable. There is such a thing as more or less strength, and more or less clarity. Now an action may be excellent in producing strength, and poor in producing clarity. A second action may not be so good with respect to the strength characteristic, and yet a great deal better with respect to the clarity property. Which action should be adopted? In this situation, the common interpretation of the skill imperative "Do X_1, X_2, X_3, and so on," is "The set of actions X_1, X_2, X_3, and so on, have the highest probability of any set of actions of producing the set or results Y_1, Y_2, Y_3, and so on." But very often there is no action set that maximizes the probabilities for every member of the set of results. What does the compulsion of the skill imperative imply in this context?

The answers to this question have constituted the art of the applied sciences: medicine, engineering, agriculture, and architecture, among others. Each practitioner knows that certain actions will produce certain results. Furthermore, he does not know any set of actions that will produce all the specified results with the highest degree of probability for each. He uses his art and experience to find one set of actions, among all of the alternatives, which will "best" approximate the specifications.

Why are the recommendations of such practitioners compelling? One answer is that the recommendations of a practitioner have more and more weight as we begin to see that what he recommends works out satisfactorily. In other words, we shift the basis of our argument from the probability that the specific acts produce results to the probability that the practitioner produces the results. This is certainly the conscious basis which people use in selecting a doctor, lawyer, or executive, for example.

But, in adopting this solution, one sees immediately that the compulsion of the imperative has taken on an entirely different character. The imperatives of skill were compelling because the recommended acts produced the specified results. The imperatives of the practitioner are compelling because the recommended acts "work out satisfactorily." The test of the first could be carried out without using human subjects; the test of the second cannot. The compromise which the practitioner adopts is based on some notion of human happiness—or human utility—or human benefit—or humanly desired monetary gain. There seems to be no other sensible way of accomplishing the compromise than to refer to some standard of human values. This means that the imperative, "Do X_1, X_2, X_3, and so on," is another way of saying "The set of actions X_1, X_2, X_3, and so on, will produce the most satisfactory set of results Y_1, Y_2, Y_3, and so on." We could now explain the compulsion of the imperative if we could explain how the declarative sentence could be tested.

3 · *Kant's Assertorial Imperatives.*

All this amounts to saying that since Kant's time science has become more and more impressed with the fact that it cannot recommend acts which will accomplish with certainty all the specifications that people impose. The art of applied science has therefore had to include principles of compromise which are somehow based on human desires and values. And the consequence is that the imperatives of skill are far less significant than Kant's second type of imperative, which he calls "assertorial." These imperatives are based on two considerations: the probability that the act will produce a certain result, and the desirability of the result. For example, the kind of career one should follow depends in part on what one wants to get out of life. Or, try asking an automotive expert what sort of car you should buy. He'll tell you that it depends on whether you want a fast car, safe car, family car, or roomy car and so on. And again, science can make glasses that are almost perfectly clear and unbreakable but they cost too much; few people want to spend the money for them. Science cannot yet make glasses that are absolutely satisfactory in every way.

These comments sound like common sense, but it would make life much easier for the thinker if all imperatives could somehow be reduced to the imperative of skill. The theory of assetorial imperatives has to face the enormously difficult problem of finding a way to establish desirability. Not much help in this connection is to be found in Kant. He follows a long philosophical tradition which asserts that all men desire happiness. This assertion in Kant's time was on the verge of becoming a tautology; only a few decades later it was turned around by J. S. Mill into the assertion that happiness is empirically identified in terms of what men actually desire. Kant apparently thought science could handle the assetorial imperative; that is, judgments of the type "X produces happiness" could be proved or disproved by empirical observation. One way in which this proof might be accomplished is by direct observation of one's own state of mind. Thus one often hears such expressions as, "I may not know much about music, but I do know what I like to hear." Does one really know what he likes?

4 · *The Immediacy of Sensation.*

The consideration of this question is an important part of the history of philosophy and psychology. The way in which the question is answered determines the way in which science studies the problems of imperatives. In more general terms, the question is whether people sometimes respond to the world about them in such a way that there is no doubt about the nature of their response. If one answers this general question affirmatively, he believes that a person alone can know whether or not the response has occurred, and his knowledge is perfect in this respect. In this book we shall often return to the notion that one can sometimes know directly how he feels or what he observes. It is a position that is rejected here, and its rejection is quite important. The last chapter argued that value judgments derive their meaning for scientific inquiry from the methods of making value measurements. But, if one can directly ascertain what one wants, then all the complicated concepts and operations of measurement are unnecessary.

Advocates of the position that direct knowledge exists have often illustrated their thesis by the so-called "simple sensations," for example, the sensation of a blue patch. Their position is not an easy one to define, and some care must be taken in explaining what is meant. Chapter 4 attempts to analyze the idea in more detail so that here a brief characterization will suffice. When a dentist hits a sensitive spot, the patient "knows" he has a pain. This is apparently common sense. But the refinement of this common-sense idea is extremely difficult. The person has some kind of a sensory reaction.

What is it that he knows? He knows that he is having a sensation of pain. But now a name has been attached to the sensation. The patient not only knows that he has a sensation, he also knows the name of it. How does he know he has named the sensation properly? At this point we could assert that such a question is meaningless and insist that the naming is not the important point. If we did this, the common sense assertion loses much of its significance: The person knows he is having a "something," but *what* the "something" is, is not relevant.

From the point of view of science, such an interpretation of immediate knowledge is senseless. For science, communication between minds is essential. Consequently, from science's point of view it is pointless to talk of the knowledge of a "sensation" where the meaning of the sensation cannot be communicated.

Therefore, let us suppose that a person names his sensations and knows that the names are correct. What can "correct" mean in this context? Of all the possible answers that could be made to this question, only one seems to be feasible and at the same time meaningful to science. What is meant is that if the person is confronted with the same stimulus in the same environment, he will always name the sensation in the same manner if asked to do so. This suggestion itself poses some new problems. To determine whether a person has named correctly, we require an ability to test repeatedly his responses to the same stimulus in the same situation. We also need to know how to ask him to name his response. We need to know that his attitude in this context is sincere, that is, that he is not trying to lie to us, or to be facetious.

If all this is true, then the assertion that a specific person knows his own simple sensations at a given moment of time requires quite an elaborate series of steps to test its validity. In fact, the test requires other minds and their reactions. And it can scarcely be argued that these other minds will have a simple task to perform. There will be no simple tests they can use to guarantee, for example, a "sincere" attitude on the part of the person who has the sensation.

Hence, it may be true that a person knows his sensations at a given moment of time, but there is no simple and direct method of verifying this assertion.

This digression into the theory of sensation can be summarized in the following way: The assertion "X knows he has sensation Y" may be interpreted *either* as "The occurrence of *X's* knowledge of *Y* is indefinable, and hence not communicable," *or* "The occurrence of *X's* knowledge of *Y* means that X responds consistently in a certain manner under certain circumstances." The first choice we have rejected, and the second choice we recognize as having a number of methodological difficulties that will have to be studied.

5 · *The Pleasure-Pain Accounting System.*

The relevance of sensation to our discussion of imperatives can now be made clear. If we could have adopted the alternative we just rejected, then we could believe that people know their sensations of pleasure and pain directly. We would also have a good basis for explaining the compulsion of Kant's assertorial imperative.

In the simplest cases, we could argue that "Do X_1, X_2, X_3, and so on," is another way of saying "X_1, X_2, X_3, and so on, will produce sensations of pleasure, and any other set of actions will not produce sensations of pleasure." If sensations of pleasure are known directly and the knowledge is perfect, then the assertion about the set of actions can be tested, and the compulsion of the imperatives is explained.

In general, if we could adopt the thesis of direct knowledge of pleasure and pain, we might hope that the verification of a prudent judgment ("X ought to be done") could be accomplished by counting up the plusses and minuses of any policy in terms of the directly ascertained pleasures and pains of the persons involved. If this idea could be worked out, then there would be a fundamental and invariant basis for ascertaining the values of outcomes. Perhaps if we were successful, we could reduce such "intangibles" as "good will," and "employee responsibility" to pleasure and pain units. Government as well as business might be run on the same basic data—the coinage of pleasure and pain. But today's government and industrial accounting systems are still largely based on monetary, not pleasure-pain units, and this policy cannot be the outcome of perversity or stupidity. It must be that the determination of pleasures and pains is not as simple and easy a task as a first, naïve outlook might suggest. On the basis of the general rejection of all direct knowledge, this assertion is obvious. Nonetheless it will be worth our while to assume that direct knowledge of pleasure and pain are possible in order to show what difficulties arise from the assumption. We begin by assuming something far stronger: namely, that the quantity of pleasure and pain can be ascertained directly.

6 · Is Pleasure a Sufficient Basis for Value?

The first question that comes to mind is whether the quantity of pleasure and pain can ever be a sufficient basis for measuring human values. "Nature," says Bentham in his *Principles of Morals and Legislation,* "has placed mankind under the governance of two sovereign masters, *pain and pleasure.* It is for them alone to point out what we ought to do, as well as to determine what we shall do." But common sense becomes indignant at this supposed piece of arrogance against morality. It gives me great pleasure, sir, to steal your wife and slit your throat. This is therefore what I ought to do!

Much of Bentham's effort was designed to show that when one counted up the score for the adulterer and murderer, the balance was in the red, despite the immediate pleasures to be derived from adultery or murder. Society and nature cooperate to impose sanctions on actions in such a way that in the long run what common sense calls immorality, the pleasure-pain calculus would prove to be painful.

Bentham was aware that by thus subjecting his method to empirical test, it might come up with results that common morality did not condone. Indeed, his successors, and notably Sidgwick, thought that the system should be bolstered by certain intuitive moral axioms, which in effect impose ethical restraints on the completely free use of the pleasure-pain calculus as a basis of policy-making.

But it should be noted that hedonism of the sort proposed by Bentham is a very flexible doctrine which is only committed to determining values in terms of certain inherently valuable responses to outcomes. Hence, any objection to hedonism on the grounds that it leads us to verify ethical judgments that are obviously faulty must be considered carefully because the objection may be based on the wrong conception of the inherently valuable response. Instead of pursuing the objection, it seems more fruitful to turn attention to more specific problems of method.

7 · *The Uncertainty of Pleasure: Expected Value.*

The central methodological problem of the proposal we are considering is to determine the function which translates pleasure and pain responses into judgments of value. Bentham mentions that in "calculating pleasures," one has to pay heed to their intensity, duration, certainty, propinquity, fecundity, purity, and extent. One must be aware of different sensibilities to pleasure and pain on the part of different people. And so on. The question is how all these elementary considerations are to be combined in order to evaluate policies.

Suppose we look at one of the items on Bentham's list because of its importance in later developments. This is the consideration of the "certainty" of the pleasure or pain. In some cases there is a chance that an act will produce a great deal of pleasure, but the chance is small. It may therefore be sensible to choose an act that produces only moderate pleasures with higher chances of success. This is presumably one reason why most people don't gamble large amounts of money.

A traditional way of handling uncertainty is to argue that a person should select those acts which maximize his "expected value." If p is the probability that an event will occur, and v is the total of the pleasure minus the pain units of the event if it occurs, then pv is the expected value of the event. An action may have several possible, mutually exclusive consequences. If the probabilities of each possible consequence are known, then we add the expected values of all possible consequences and derive the total expected value of the set of actions. Thus gambling one's fortune may produce a consequence (winning) of 100 pleasure-pain units, but it has, say, only 1 chance in 100 of doing so. The expectation of this consequence is (100) $(1/100) = 1$. Gambling may also produce a consequence of -100 pleasure-pain units, and this has a probability of $99/100$ with an expectation of -99. The total expected value of the act is therefore $1 - 99 = -98$.

According to this viewpoint, the imperative "Do X_1, X_2, X_3, and so on," is another way of saying "The set of actions X_1, X_2, X_3, and so on, will yield the highest expected value."

What is the compulsion here? Several objections could be made to this procedure of calculation and therefore to the method of translating the imperative. If probability connotes the long-run frequency with which an event occurs, then the expected value may be irrelevant. Shall I marry the girl or shall I not? You tell me that in the long run, marriages such as this have a 0.75 chance of producing + 25 pleasure-pain units, and a 0.25 chance of producing — 10 pleasure-pain units. But I do not foresee a long sequence of marriages like this for me. Even for inhabitants of Hollywood, the run of possible marriages is not large enough to make long-run frequencies relevant. Furthermore, who could ever calculate the probabilities, since the events (for each person) are so rare?

Leaving the problems of probability calculation for consideration later, in Chapter 6, one could reply as follows. One marriage, yes. But many, many decisions in a lifetime. When the life is over, the faithful selection by the expected value criterion will be seen to have yielded the greatest total pleasure. This is sensible enough unless some action might yield a consequence I could not bear, or take me so deeply into the mire of pain that no action thereafter would ever be pleasurable again. In other words, the defense of expected value for each action seems to assume that the actions are independent of each other as far as the pleasure-pain calculations are concerned. If they are not independent, then we should view all interdependent actions as one large plan or strategy and calculate accordingly. If all actions of a person are interdependent, or a large majority are, as seems likely, then we must calculate a man's life plan as a whole. Apart from the absurdity of this project, the criterion of expected value is again a dubious one because for any man there is only one lifetime. His main comfort in adopting the expected-value criterion is that the whole set of lifetimes lived thereby yield the largest total value—an odd basis for the compulsion of the imperative, to say the least.

This problem of handling uncertainty will reoccur throughout the rest of this book. But one advantage that our subsequent questions will have is that probability of outcome will be a necessary condition for ascertaining a person's values. In this chapter we are considering a theory of values in which it is assumed that the value of an outcome is solely a function of the responses of a person to the outcome independent of the probability that the outcome occurs. This is certainly the simplest assumption to adopt, but it does make it very difficult to defend any method of discounting for uncertainty. In the suggestions to be made in Chapter 7 and after, probability measurement of some kind is essential to value measurement, and an "expected value" assumption is justified if certain predictions about behavior can be successfully made.

8 · *The Determination of Pleasure.*

Thus, even if we assume that quantities of pleasure can be ascertained, we encounter apparently insurmountable difficulties in connection with probabilistic situations. But we should also ask ourselves whether there is any reasonable method for quantifying pleasures if we admit for the moment that pleasures and pains can be known directly. Thus we could ask people what pleasure or pain they feel when they respond to a given situation. If we restricted their answers to such qualitative responses as "There is some pleasure (or pain) in the response" we might elicit a fairly reliable set of answers from most people. But even so, this information would be so meager that it would be useless for the purpose of making recommendations, that is, for verifying prudential judgments. But if we try questions designed to reveal the amount of pleasure, then we find that the responses will not be consistent and often depend on the wording of the question, even for simple tastes (as the fascinating literature on food preferences shows). The unreliability increases in responses to more complicated questions about vocations, family living, and the like.

What has been done in the past to develop an empirical method of quantifying human pleasures and pains? Actually, very little, because those philosophers who defended pleasure as a basis of value for the most part gave up or ignored the problems of ascertaining amounts of pleasure, although they preached a principle of the "greatest" pleasure for the greatest number. Presumably, for them, this principle had value as a guide for action but it was not felt important to construct a quantification of pleasures and pains.

Some economists, in contrast, seem to have been much concerned with the measurability of pleasure or what they called "utility." They adopted the same idea that experimental psychology did when it began measuring aspects of sensation. The idea is simple enough. If a subject reacts to changes in a physical stimulus, and we know the pattern of his reactions, then we can set up a functional relationship between the stimulus and the response. Since the physical stimulus can be measured, we can derive measures of the response from this functional relationship.

To see how this might work out for utility measurements, suppose we want to compare a person's preference for various commodities (apples, beer, pigs, TV sets, and so on). Suppose we could find a physically measurable commodity of this nature: when we present a subject with x units of this "standard" commodity and y units of apples, he feels that he is indifferent as to which he receives. That is, he feels he prefers equally x units of the standard commodity and y units of apples. Then why not say that his degree of "pleasure" associated with y apples is measured by the x standard units? If this could be done for all quantities of every commodity, then we would apparently have a general "pleasure" scale (sometimes called a preference scale and sometimes a utility scale).

One difficulty that economists found with the simple proposal for equating preferences for quantities of a commodity with a standard lay in the fact that indifference points depend on how much the person already has. If I already have a dozen apples my interest in y additional apples may be very slight, and certainly far less than my interest would be if I had none. What is needed, therefore, is a measuring device that will reflect this piece of common sense. But this is not a serious difficulty, for now one looks for a more general function that would determine the indifference points for any given amounts of various commodities held by the person.

Such a concept of human values might be expected to have led economists into lengthy experimental programs. This is what happened in psychology when Fechner and others suggested how the intensity of sensation might be measured in terms of physical stimuli. Their work touched off an enormously expanding series of experiments. But experimental economics has been slow in arriving, although specific efforts are to be found in some preference studies we shall examine later in the book.

9 · *Behaviorism.*

Whatever experimental economics may turn out to be, it certainly seems that its methods must go far beyond the suggestions we have been studying in this chapter. But must they? We have been considering the feasibilty of ascertaining values in terms of certain direct responses of a person to a given situation. Possibly experimental economics can accept the proposal that values can be directly ascertained, by pointing out that it is not interested in the internal, "pleasure-feeling" aspect of the response but rather in the external *choice* made by the subject. Hence, the experimenter does not have to pose questions about internal feelings; he can directly observe what the subject really does. In this view, experimental economics adopts behaviorism and discards introspectionism.

The term "behaviorism" has many different meanings, and connotes many different concepts to the modern student of humanity. One of its philosophical origins represents a common denominator of most behaviorist theories: it is Hegel's notion that there is no "mind" unless there is also a reflecting mind, "another" mind that observes it. E. A. Singer had a succinct way of translating the obscurity of Hegel's thinking into a more comprehensible thesis for modern science: "Mind is an observable object." That is, whatever reflective controls science exerts in its attempts to observe the physical world, it also should exert in its attempts to observe mind.

At first sight, this idea seems to clear up an obscure question. Introspectionism regarded simple sensations as primitive ideas, not definable in any other terms. According to its viewpoint, to know what it means for a mind to have a sensation of yellow, each person must go through the process himself. His own reaction immediately tells him what this idea of yellow actually means. We have already seen that for a scientist the subjective meaning of the sensation, even if it exists, has no relevance and from the point of view of scientific method is meaningless. The scientist's interest is in observing that people react similarly (for example, in terms of verbal behavior) in similar situations. The scientist observes the behavior, and for him the "mind" of the person is the behavior that is observed.

But if we left the matter in this simple form, we would hardly have improved the situation. We would have passed the introspective method from the subject to the observer. We would ask the observer to look and see what the subject does, and we would expect him to be able to make immediate judgments based on his direct observation. We would expect him to be far better in introspecting his own observations than the subject is at introspecting his own feelings.

Science is controlled observation. Therefore, what shall control the observations of human behavior? As a minimum, we need a set of instructions that tell the observer what to observe. We need a basis that will justify these instructions, and enable us to say that if such-and-such behavior is observed, then the subject may be taken to have such-and-such a property. We need procedures that enable us to check whether the instructions have been carried out.

In the case of men's values, these needs may seem fairly easy to satisfy. To test whether a person values pork more than beef, present the choice to him and observe what happens. The instructions are simple. The basis of justification seems obvious, for who would choose what he does not prefer? And only the minimum amount of checking seems necessary, since the behavior of choosing one rather than the other is so gross that the chance of error seems small.

Yet even in this homely example, the problems are not so simple as they sound. The problem of justification is in fact rather difficult. Does the fact that the subject chooses pork mean that the subject prefers pork over beef? Or does it mean that he prefers a certain taste, and what produces the taste is irrelevant?

There is another aspect of the simple choice situation which indicates that the instructions to the observer may be difficult to give and to justify. Perhaps the subject "prefers" the beef, but chooses pork because he thinks the experimenter likes it and he does not want to offend him, or else he wants to be an individualist and chooses what he thinks only a few would choose. In all these cases, the subject is not exhibiting a preference for meats; instead he is choosing between politeness and rudeness, or between conformity and nonconformity.

How is the experimenter to know what the subject thinks about the situation? What things should he do to preclude the existence of all else except the preferred choices in the subject's mind? What should he observe to make sure the subject has understood what the choices mean? These questions recall the theme of the last chapter: that the determination of preference presupposes knowledge on the part of the subject. But how can we observe that knowledge occurs?

Furthermore, to add to our difficulties, we should require that observations be repeated since repetition is the basis of observational control in science. But the subject of a preference test has a memory;

he may know he has been given the same choice before, and this knowledge may change his perception of the choice from pork versus beef to consistency versus inconsistency.

All these remarks lead us to conclude that there is no simple way in which a person's direct responses to a situation can be used to ascertain his values. Throughout this discussion we have restricted ourselves to methodological issues.

We have not at present proved that hedonism is "wrong." In fact, later when we come to talk about theories of human behavior, we may want to take seriously a theory that behavior under conditions of complete knowledge can be predicted solely in terms of a person's responses to the outcomes of his actions. But *traditional* hedonism seems to have agreed that values can be determined from the conscious responses that the person himself knows and can report. This viewpoint we have criticized in order to convince ourselves that there is no easy way to our goal.

Much of the discussion of this chapter undoubtedly seems impractical since the practical mind no longer thinks in terms of "pleasure units," but in terms of maximizing dollar income. The next chapter examines this monetary scale of value, to see whether it provides any clearer basis for deciding what ought to be done.

But at this point it will be worth while to recapitulate the steps we have taken by describing the kinds of imperatives we have considered in this and the first chapter. Specifically, we have argued that the expression "X ought to do A" may be verified in one of the following ways:

(0) *Imperatives of Skill* Verification by proving that if A is done, then B will follow, or if A is done, the probability that B will follow is maximum (Not part of the theory of value).

(1) *Prudential Imperatives* Verification by proving that if A is done, then X's values will be maximized. These Kant calls assertorial imperatives.

(2) *Social Imperatives* Verification by proving that a social group (Y) wants X to do A.

(3) *Ethical Imperatives* Verification by proving that future mankind wants X to do A.

The theory of value is concerned with the meaning of (1), (2), and (3).

Finally in addition to the comments already made in this chapter two additional comments will help to state the purpose of the chapter in different ways.

10 · *A Precautionary Comment.*

There is a difference between an immediate response to an event and a judgment about the event. The distinction is important in what follows since later we shall argue that judgment is an essential step in scientific method. In this chapter the idea of immediate or direct knowledge of human values has been rejected. Judgment is also a personal reaction to a situation or to a question, but it differs from direct knowledge in that no judgment occurs unless there is a system for checking the judgment. In other words, although we have discarded direct intuitive knowledge, we have not discarded the use of intuition in science. When we consider the meaning of measurement, we shall want to argue that judgment is a legitimate aspect of measurement processes as long as personal reactions to events can be put within the framework of standards and controls which all measurement requires.

The point is important, I think, because of the common cliché that some values cannot be measured, for example, friendship and loyalty. These values seem to be "intangibles" because they are "matters of personal judgment." If this assertion meant that the value of a friendship could be ascertained *only* by a direct feeling on the part of a person, then I should agree that the value is not measurable. But if the assertion means merely that personal judgment is one type of evidence that is necessary to establish the value of friendship, then the inability to measure does not follow.

These reflections may give us some hope that the so-called "intangible values" are not so intangible after all. The hope is tempered by reflections on the difficulties in obtaining an adequate system of judgment controls.

11 · *A Comment on Happiness.*

This is a book about human happiness. Because the subject is treated from the viewpoint of science, it undoubtedly tends to become dry and tedious. But the purpose is the same as that of the preacher, politician, or artist, who also try to understand what men want and how they can get what they want.

We have examined hedonism—the pleasure-pain concept of happiness—in a somewhat calm and detached fashion. If we can relax intellectual precaution for the moment, we can afford to express some feelings about *traditional* hedonism, how devoid of any real sense of the depth of human wants this theory is. To think that the slight bubblings of pleasurable titilations on the surface of human consciousness could in any way be thought of as the basis of human happiness! Everyone likes ice cream cones, roller coaster rides and the embracing touch of another's body. But how could serious thinkers still come to believe that these immediately pleasurable feelings were the things that humans wanted most deeply—that the only tragedy is a lack of them?

Human happiness is still the greatest unsolved problem of science. Our ignorance about what people really want is only matched by the jargon intended to hide our naïvete. People want to be "adjusted," though to what standard of adjustment is never made clear. People want "freedom," but freedom from what is still a secret. People want to enjoy the pleasures of life, but let's not ask what these are! People want to maximize their profits, though no one knows what this means.

No doubt we could afford to have a bit more pleasure and a bit less pain in this world. Starvation, sickness and ignorance are all evils, and no one has to set forth a "calculus of pleasures and pains" to prove it. But it is absurd to infer that because people like to enjoy themselves and don't like painful experiences, pleasure and pain completely define human happiness!

But then this book won't tell anyone what happiness is either. It may tell some people how difficult a problem it is to get even some insights on the subject.

12 · *Indebtedness.*

Stigler (8) has written a valuable discussion of the nineteenth- and early twentieth-century economic theory of utility. Edwards (3) presents a summary and extensive bibliography of more recent utility theory.

Some accounts of behaviorism, not necessarily of the simple type discussed in this chapter, are to be found in Singer (6), Skinner (7), and Watson (9); see also Boring (2).

REFERENCES

1. Bentham, J., *An Introduction to the Principles of Morals and Legislation.* Oxford: The Clarendon Press, 1907.
2. Boring, E. G., *A History of Experimental Psychology.* New York: The Century Company, 1929.
3. Edwards, W., "The Theory of Decision Making," *Psychological Bulletin,* Vol. 51 (1954), pp. 380-417.
4. Kant, I., *Fundamental Principles of the Metaphysics of Morals,* translated by T. K. Abbott. London: Longmans Green & Co., Inc., 1898.
5. Schlick, M., *Problems of Ethics,* translated by D. Rynin. Englewood Cliffs, N. J.: Prentice-Hall, Inc., 1939.
6. Singer, E. A., *Mind as Behavior.* Columbus: R. G. Adams & Co., 1924.
7. Skinner, B. K., *Science and Human Behavior.* New York: Macmillan Co., 1953.
8. Stigler, G. J., "The Development of Utility Theory," *The Journal of Political Economy,* Vol. LVIII (1950), pp. 307-327, and 373-396.
9. Watson, J. B., *Behaviorism.* New York: W. W. Norton & Co., Inc., 1930.

PROFITS
AND VALUES

3

Summary

and

Intent.

In this chapter we examine the measure of values in terms of dollars. If the aim of the decision-maker is to maximize cash on hand at the end of a specific period, then a simple meaning can be given to the "best" action for him to adopt. This meaning is the same as that described for Kant's imperatives of skill in the last chapter. No value considerations are involved in the problem of selecting that action which gives the greatest net cash, although the methods of finding an optimal decision may be difficult.

However, no business firm tries solely to maximize cash at a specific moment of time. Instead, firms are often said to maximize "profits" or "return on investment"; but there is no clear way of defining these concepts that will satisfy the requirements of value measurements. To substantiate this viewpoint, we shall argue that in most cases (1) the time over which profits are to be calculated is not adequately defined; (2) opportunity costs, such as alternative uses of capital and lost sales, are not usually included; (3) since a proper allocation of overhead presupposes a knowledge of the correct organization for the firm, the proper allocation is rarely made; (4) since costs act as motivators of human actions, cost accounting designed to measure values should depend on psychological considerations, but it rarely does. This does not mean that accounting figures are useless as far as managers are concerned. It does mean that accounting figures are not measures of the values or the goals of the industrial enterprise, and hence cannot be used directly as a means of verifying recommendation, that is, telling a manager what he ought to do. We turn now to details of the argument, many of which, of course, are already familiar to the student of accounting and economics.

2 · *Is Profit a Value Measurement?*

We are now considering activities the prime objective of which, it seems safe to assume, can be defined in terms of the accumulation of dollars. This consideration merits our attention, because it is easy enough to fall into the misapprehension that business and industrial organizations in a capitalist society have worked out a scheme of measurement which more or less adequately defines correct policy decisions. It looks as though industrial management had evolved a method for deciding which policies are best, and for judging past decisions in terms of an objective standard. Even if management has been successful in this regard, its success, of course, does not constitute a general theory of policy-making because management itself would deny that all national policies should be guided by the dollar considerations.

The conviction that industry has attained a fairly clear set of decision criteria is evidenced by the many clichés that businessmen use to describe their decisions. I like the following illustration:

> Professor Baker: I wonder how much Mr. Kestnbaum thinks a company should vary its policy away from the maximum-profit motive in the interests of general social responsibility.

Mr. Kestnbaum: If it is ever going to be a question of a company adjusting its prices according to what people may want to pay, we will all go out of business. Any firm that starts to lose money because it has altruistically lowered its prices so more people can afford to buy its products will disappear very quickly. The best rule for businessmen to follow, if they want to meet their social responsibilities, is: "Run a good business. . . ." (2)

One may state the thesis implied in Mr. Kestnbaum's reply to the professor in its strongest terms as follows: Companies are equipped with objective measures of profit; the primary objective is to maximize the measure of profit; it is possible to judge whether one policy does or does not increase the total profits; a "good" business is one that adopts a profit maximization policy.

Even if one abhors the existence of men who are motivated primarily by monetary profit, and believes their activities to be socially undesirable, this would not alter the thesis as it stands; for we have not argued, any more than Kant did, that "value" must be defined solely in terms of what is socially right and wrong. Our primary concern has been to make some sense out of Kant's assertorial imperative: the imperative that tells us the "best" way to accomplish a person's purposes. We have seen that the traditional hedonist runs into the inescapable vagueness attached to the term "pleasure." But this vagueness seems to disappear when we examine the operations of a business where the standards of measurement are set by a well-organized accounting system.

It is almost needless to say that what seems to be the case is not the case at all. Step by step, it is not difficult to show that a deeper analysis reveals the vagueness of the theory of decisions based on the "profit" motive.

3 · *What Time Period Is the Basis for Measuring Profits?*

Consider, then, the proposal that "X ought to do A" is to be verified or refuted depending on whether A, among all the alternative actions, does or does not result in the largest net profit for X.

We may begin with a more-or-less obvious objection to the proposal. Suppose we can satisfactorily develop a measure of net profit. Over what time period is this measure to be applied? Few businesses know that they are going to be out of business in *x* years. With an indefinite life span ahead, what is the proper time segment to use? The number of plausible answers to this question show that the issue has no clear answer at this time, and that, in this respect at least, the decision theory of modern business is not even defined, far from being verified.

One suggestion for a suitable time span for planning is a cautious version of the "eat, drink, and be merry" theme. Make the time period a brief one, say a year, where the forecasts seem fairly definite and the uncertainties are not so great as to obscure the picture. Maximize profits for this period under the condition that the financial status of the company will be no worse at the end of the period than it was at the beginning.

This kind of narrow planning has not received favorable attention from large companies, primarily because it throws away a lot of useful information. Even where the forecasts have elements of uncertainty, they do supply data, and to ignore this information is to plan poorly. One should, on this account, plan for the foreseeable future, and build the uncertainties into the planning. It is foolish merely to plan to have the company in sound financial condition at the end of a coming year. Perhaps now is the time when the company can begin to organize for some new product. This might result in a smaller annual profit for the year but in much larger profits in subsequent years.

This idea is sometimes referred to as "planning to the horizon." It has an analogy with the planning of the pioneer, and the poetically minded can easily picture an alert business enterprise in terms of its pioneer spirit with respect to the future. The wise pioneer, you see, sends his scouts as far ahead as is feasible to plan the route. The foolish pioneer will plan as far ahead as he can see, and follow the easiest route of today which leads him to the rugged mountains of tomorrow. The wise pioneer knows of these mountains, or at least has some information about them. He makes today's detour (and thus sacrifices some ground) in order to make far greater progress tomorrow.

Enthusiasts of horizon-planning even find therein the answer to the alleged "selfishness" of the business enterprise. The ethical wrongs of business activities are the result of narrow planning; as Mr. Kestnbaum suggests, social responsibilities will automatically be considered by a business that is "run correctly." Some people today may be derived of good clothes because they cannot afford the prices;

but in the long run—out to the horizon—the maximum social benefit will accrue if the company maintains its price level and seeks long-range profit maximization. Otherwise, I suppose the argument runs, all *good* clothes companies would "disappear" and nobody would have any good clothes.

There are really two issues here which we should keep apart for the purposes of the present discussion. One is whether profit maximization out to the horizon is a sound policy for companies whose primary motive is taken to be profit-maximization, that is, whether this is a reliable way of acting prudently. The other is whether such planning resolves all matters of ethical right and wrong in the planning operations of such companies. In the spirit of this chapter, let us examine the first of these: Is planning to the horizon a satisfactory method for verifying prudential judgments about what a company should do?

A reply to this question is that the question itself is too vague: What does "horizon" mean? Furthermore, even if we could maintain some analogy between the scouts of the pioneers and the forecasters of modern business and speak sensibly of the limits of human knowledge with respect to the future, we would still have to face the two critical questions of discounting for time and discounting for uncertainty. There are, then, at least three questions concerning horizon-planning, none of which has yet received a definitive answer: how to define the horizon, how to discount for time, and how to discount for uncertainty. Since this chapter is primarily designed to show the difficulties entailed in policy-making for profit, rather than to provide answers, let us examine each of these questions in order to understand why they are complicated and why no satisfactory answer is forthcoming at the present time.

Suppose we say the horizon is the point in time beyond which one has virtually no information. Quite apart from the enormous difficulty of ascertaining this point, there is a more subtle question to be pondered. The definition seems to presuppose that there is just so much information "there" and once we have "taken" it all, that is the end of the matter. But in truth, information is always created, not taken. Specifically, one of the policies which a company can adopt is to lengthen its horizon, that is, to invest heavily or lightly or not at all in research which creates information about the future. The analogy of the scouts will not do simply because the pioneer had to get along with the scouts he had, but business can create new ones or fire the lot of them. The matter is simple enough to express: If a present-day executive could make requests of an executive of twenty years ago, what information would he ask him to gather which would best serve his present needs? None other than what the earlier executive did gather? Or a whole new class of data on sales or production costs? The answer has a lot to do with the horizon of today's executive. This all amounts to saying that the horizon is in part what the company plans it to be; it is not separate from its planning function.

4 · *Discounting for Time and Uncertainty.*

Consider now the question of discounting for time and for uncertainty. Discounting for time is essentially an opportunity cost. If I receive the dollar today rather than tomorrow, then I can invest it today, and tomorrow I will not only have the dollar but also the return on the investment. For this reason, discounting for time looks like a comparison of annuities. The suggestion is that the company should adopt that policy which has payoffs that provide the highest annuity rate. Even if the payoffs are known with certainty, this notion of time-discounting is what the economists euphemistically call a "first approximation." Why is a policy based on the highest annuity rate compelling? Indeed, it is not hard to find examples where it would not be. Perhaps by adopting a policy of a loss for ten years the company can eventually make so much money that the corresponding annuity is maximum. But few companies would follow such a course of action. Discounting for time involves a consideration of certain psychological properties, such as patience, which may quite outweigh favorable annuity rates. In sum, there is no obvious and simple way of generating an adequate discounting function.

A possible solution to the problem of uncertainty would be to use the idea of expected value discussed in Chapter 2: Multiply the probability of the return by the amount of the return. The difficulties discussed in Chapter 2 apply here as well because this proposal separates the value of the outcome from the uncertainty of the means of attaining it. The expected return might be the logical thing to try to maximize, provided one visualizes himself as a gambler. In this case, the probabilities are the frequencies of events; and to adopt the policy of maximizing the expected return is virtually equivalent to maximizing the total return over a long period of time. However, in the case of business-planning, the probabilities are usually judgments about the likelihood of future occurrences. There is the legitimate question whether these judgments can safely be taken as estimates of long-run frequencies. One technical point on the use of probabilities has attracted a good deal of attention in recent years. The probabilities which a business faces are not fixed; the probable success of an action which the company takes may depend on the actions of its competitors. If a competitor knows what action a company is going to adopt, or can make a pretty close guess, then he may act to reduce the probability of its getting a high return. This leads the researcher into the rather complicated task of formulating optimal policies by means of "game theory."

In summary, one begins to suspect that the criterion of profit maximization is as vaguely defined as the criterion of maximizing pleasure. "Planning to the horizon" is a phrase that virtually begs the question because the meaning of the horizon cannot be defined without a plan; and the definition of profit maximization requires methods for discounting for time and uncertainty, neither of which is simple to determine.

There is, however, one way in which the profit-maximization criterion seems to constitute an improvement over the hedonist calculus. The dollar figure is there, and does represent a common unit of value that was lacking in the hedonist theories. As long as we can assume that the entrepreneur wants to maximize the profit measured in dollar units, and we do not ask why he has such a motive, we seem to succeed in developing a scale of value, even though there are serious difficulties in using this scale to define a profit maximum. We shall devote the rest of this chapter to showing that in fact no such scale does exist, or more moderately, there is no known accounting system which supplies the kind of data needed to permit us to use maximization of profits as a basis for evaluating decisions.

5 · *Opportunity Costs.*

Suppose we start by considering the Profit-and-Loss statement, since this supposedly does supply managers with a scale in terms of which they can judge past performance just as a budget supposedly supplies them with a scale with which they can make plans for future actions.

It is important to bear in mind what this discussion is trying to do. There is no denying that P-and-L's and budgets are useful to managers, and this study provides no evidence that this use has been an illusion. But the intention here is to look at the accounting process from the eyes of a scientist. The scientist wants to determine whether there is a value scale which would provide a basis for predicting managerial action when the manager is completely informed and free to choose. However, one cannot help feeling that if a convincing case can be made for the thesis that no such scale exists, the results may be of service to managers who scrutinize carefully what it is they are trying to do.

The reason why the profit score on the P-and-L is not a measure that management should try to maximize is easily enough stated. Every business and industry faces the problem of the acquisition or nonacquisition of assets, and of their use or nonuse, once they have been acquired. In the case of this type of decision, only the acquisition and use are matters that are recorded in the usual P-and-L statement. If the manager fails to acquire an asset, no "cost" is directly recorded. Similarly, if he "holds" the asset without using it (for example, inventory, cash, and so on) there is no direct cost reported on the statement. These hidden costs are the well-known and well-neglected "opportunity" costs. As long as it is admitted that they are costs at all, it is clear that the "profit" line of the P-and-L is not necessarily a measure which the manager should try to optimize.

Of course, one may point out that opportunity costs do appear in P-and-L statements in an indirect way because inefficient holding of an asset, or failure to acquire an asset, generates lower profits in the long run. Indeed, this is exactly why these inefficiencies are taken to be "costs." But the question is: How do we know when a profit line is lower than it ought to be? The answer to this question is difficult to give simply because no business or industry keeps its records in such a manner that an answer to the question can be determined. It is clear that a "wise" management does invest in assets which it does not continuously use. For example, the policy of maintaining a certain level of working capital is a recognition that there are serious "costs" entailed in letting the working capital drop too low; it is also implicitly admitted that there are costs involved in letting the working capital become too high. What constitutes the correct level, and how should the costs of "too low" or "too high" be recorded when poor planning incurs such costs? No one knows the answer to this question yet, despite the fact that working capital plays an important role in financial planning.

Indeed, there is not even an adequate definition of working capital itself. The concept on which it is based is the notion of "current" availability of funds. The distinction between "current" and "long run" is a vague one dependent on "judgment." But in view of the fact that current assets may include cash and accounts receivable, as well as certain types of inventory, it is apparent that management thinking has thrown a number of assets into one category based on availability of from one day to a month or more. This certainly raises a question about the concept of "current" from the point of view of the decision-maker, especially if the enterprise demands emergency uses of assets. The costs of holding excess working capital, or the costs of shortages of working capital, are surely a function of time, and to make an arbitrary split of the time dimension may be an unnecessarily crude method on which to base important policy decisions.

To sum up, once it is admitted that the holding of assets and the proper timing of the acquisition of assets are critical problems for policy decisions in industry, then we have no adequate way of showing that the profit line of the P-and-L constitutes the basis for policymaking.

This will come as no news to students of industrial management. It has long been argued that other indices must be used to supplement the information contained in the P-and-L statement, or in the balance sheet. A large profit does not imply necessarily that the managers have done their job well: perhaps the investment with which they worked, or the nature of the market, was such that even an inadequately managed enterprise was bound to show up with a favorable result, and a better managed enterprise would have made twice the profit.

There has undoubtedly been a disinclination to put all the additional factors together into one coherent set of figures that would form the basis of policy-making and the criterion for judging past performance. Apparently industrial managers like the vagueness of accounting figures, like to point out that no figure by itself means very much, and like to point out that the significance of this or that piece of accounting information "depends on the circumstances." Thus, there exists no coordinated and understandable scheme for setting up measures which will unequivocally determine optimal policies, or unequivocally measure the value of past performance.

It is sometimes argued that the costs which we have been discussing —the "opportunity" costs of holding, or not holding, or not acquiring assets—are "intangibles" which, like Good Will and Social Responsibility cannot be accurately measured, at least in dollar terms. This viewpoint seems to assume that the figures in the P-and-L are accurate, or can be made accurate. If "intangible" means "partly a matter of judgment" then all figures of the P-and-L, and indeed all scientific results, are intangibles. All measurement involves judgment. If "intangible" means "cannot be measured accurately," then again large portions of the P-and-L are intangible; besides, inaccurate measures that are highly important are less "intangible" than accurate measures that are trivial.

It is hard to understand why industrial management has not attempted to set up accounting schemes that include all the costs relevant to management decisions. There are undoubtedly serious problems to be faced in such a program. But there are problems in any data-gathering and data-processing system. One cannot help but be impressed by the potentialities of an accounting system where the figures, however crudely estimated, are directly relevant to policy-planning and the judgment of past decisions.

6 · *Return on Investment.*

In addition to profit, a number of indices of managerial performance have been suggested. Suppose we examine one of these: return on investment. This index seems to incorporate some of the ideas contained in the holding or nonacquisition of assets. It tries to measure how well a manager has done with the assets at his disposal, or, in terms of the future, it tries to provide a basis for decision concerning capital expansion based on the available funds of the company.

In considering "return on investment" it is important to recognize the motivation for the use of this measure. If an individual has a fixed sum to invest, and *after investment he no longer makes decisions about the manner in which the investment is to be used,* then the return on investment is clearly the measure he should maximize,.

provided what he wants to do is to maximize his dollar return, and provided the problems of discounting for time and uncertainty could be solved adequately. Indeed, these provisos make the assertion a tautology.

Return on investment also seems to be the basis on which many business managers try to gauge the advisability of setting up a new plant, or going into a new line of endeavor. But such a basis for decision-making involves a subtle fallacy. There is an analogy between the stock market investor and the company contemplating a new development requiring an investment of funds. But, like all analogies, there are aspects in the two situations that are not similar, and in this case one of these aspects is critical. The investor does not, but the company does, make decisions subsequent to the investment. The investor chooses that investment which will yield the highest return, and no action on his part (except possibly the original act of investing) will alter the size of the return. But the entrepreneur not only decides how to invest, but also how to use the investment. There are many ways in which the investment can be used once it has been made, and these ways depend on decisions of managers. How can the entrepreneur decide what the return will be on his investment if he must make decisions about the manner in which the investment is to be managed? Presumably he measures the rate of return in terms of the best known method of management.

Now, if industrial organizations were such that the return on any increment of investment could be ascertained, then such a measure would supply a basis for decision-making, provided a "return" figure can be determined. In such a case, return on investment is no different from the return on stock investor's money. But industrial organizations are not so constructed that it is feasible to measure the marginal return of each additional dollar invested. Instead, the manager may be "scored" in terms of the over-all return on investment for a given period of time. But this score may actually prevent the manager from making the best decision, and hence this score is not a measure of the value of managerial decisions.

A specific example will serve our purposes here. Let us suppose that a company manufactures products for sale, and suppose, as quite frequently happens, that by increasing the in-process and raw-material inventories fifty per cent, the costs of production can be reduced by ten per cent. Is, or is it not, wise management to increase the inventory?

A straightforward analysis of this problem might proceed as follows. If it is reasonable to assume that the fifty per cent increase in inventory will represent an average increase over a long period of time, then in effect the company has tied up funds in an asset, which are no longer usable for other purposes. The simplest manner of conceptualizing this situation is to think of these funds, if they were *not* used for inventory, as investable funds at some maximum rate of return on the stock market (for example). In other words, the use of the funds for increasing inventory is competing with some specific alternative use. If there are obsolescence risks, or deterioration risks in carrying the inventory, these would have to be estimated, just as the risk of the loss of the investment in the stock market would have to be estimated on the other side. The decision over whether or not to increase inventories would then be a straightforward comparison of the specific return on the (optimal) "outside" investment (which can be called the "cost" of carrying the inventory) and the reduced production costs accruing from increasing the inventory (which can be called the cost of *not* carrying the additional inventory). Assuming that the basic motive of the company is dollar maximization relative to all possible alternatives, these two costs—the cost of increasing the inventory and the cost of not doing so—should be value measures of the management decision.

But suppose now that the manager is scored, not in terms of a return on the inventory investment, but by the over-all return on investment for some period of time. To simplify the discussion, let us define the return on investment as the gross return, minus the costs, divided by the specific investments, of which inventory is one:

$$RI = \frac{GR - C}{I + A}$$

where:

RI = return on investment

GR = gross return

C = costs

I = inventory

A = other types of investment

Now if inventories are increased 50 per cent, and costs reduced 10 per cent, then the new return on investment appears as follows:

$$RI' = \frac{GR - C + (0.1)C}{I + (0.5)I + A}$$

The manager guided ultimately by an over-all return-on-investment criterion, will decide to increase inventories if RI' is greater than RI, that is, if and only if

$$\frac{GR - C + (0.1)C}{I + (0.5)I + A} = \frac{GR - (0.9)C}{(1.5)I + A} > \frac{GR - C}{I + A}$$

or, alternatively, if and only if

$$\frac{(0.1)C}{(0.5)I} < RI$$

That is, do not increase inventories if the additional investment does not yield a relative cost reduction at least as great as the return on the total original investment. Such a decision rule argues that it is always possible to invest funds "outside" the enterprise with a return at least as great as the return on investment within the enterprise. This concept of the real world of the manager pictures him as at best making one more penny than could be made if investments were placed elsewhere. This illustration is not a "theoretical" one; examples do exist where managers have not increased inventories— even though it was economically advisable to do so—because such increases would have shown up poorly in the return-on-investment score.

The only sensible method for deciding on the increase in inventory is first to assign an inventory carrying cost (measured in terms of the real potential for alternative investment of each additional dollar of inventory assets), and compare this with the cost saving resulting from increasing inventories. This implies that the cost of carrying inventory depends on the firm's optimal policy of investment of funds released from inventory. We begin to sense, what will indeed turn out to be true, that the meaning of "cost" for decision-making purposes depends on the determination of optimal policies for certain functions of the business.

7 · *Overhead Costs.*

To illustrate the point that the measurement of costs presupposes the determination of optimal policies, consider "overhead" costs. The problem of overhead costs turns out to be a rather complicated one from the point of view of management decisions. In assigning costs to a given policy, to what extent should overhead be counted in? The obvious answer—only to the extent that the adoption of the policy affects overhead costs—is merely a statement of the problem, not a solution. Consider this example already reported in the literature (3). Mechanics in a machine shop come to a counter to get tools and other equipment. How many service people should be assigned to this counter? If there are too few, the mechanics will have to wait, and there will be a rising cost because of their idle time. If there are too many servers, they will accumulate idle-time costs, because for periods of the day there will be no one to wait on.

How are these costs to be measured? In computing the cost of the idle time of the mechanics, should one include supervisory overhead? If so, to what level of supervision? Should machinery idle time be included? If so, how is it computed? The "answer" to this question is: "Include the cost if it varies depending on how many servers there are at the counter." For example, if the optimal policy of running the shop will require the same supervisory staff whether the mechanics wait or do not wait, then supervisory overhead should not be included because it is irrelevant. It is asserted to be irrelevant because every "policy" (number of servers) will be penalized equally in this respect. But we could only know it to be irrelevant if we knew the optimal way to run the shop in terms of supervisory personnel.

Hence in order to determine the costs of waiting time and idle time, one requires another model which depicts the organizational structure of the shop. If the machinery has alternative uses when the mechanics are waiting, or if the servers can be alternatively employed, then the costs of idle equipment or idle servers will be measured in terms of this model of the operations of the department. In other words, we are not seeking to find out how supervisory costs *actually* vary with the numbers of servers, but how *they ought* to vary as determined by an organizational model.

8 · *Managerial Accounting as a Branch of Industrial Organization.*

This amounts to saying that the assignment of costs to policies in an industry depends on the organization of the operations of the industry; organization theory and accounting for management decisions are inseparably tied together.

The point we have just made can be illustrated by other "costs." For example, how much does it cost a shop to "set up" for a run of items? The obvious reply is that one should compute the direct labor and materials involved in the setup, plus the idle time caused by the setup. But the "setup man" may be used for other jobs, and the timing of the setup might be so designed that setups occur only during meals or coffeebreaks. This means that the cost of setup is *not* computed in terms of the outlays the company *actually* makes, but in terms of the outlays it would make if the shop were organized optimally. As before, the true cost depends on an optimal policy. This is a point to which we will return in Chapter 13.

The role of organization planning in the determination of costs can be illustrated in other ways. It is possible to formulate the "best" policy for a group of persons to adopt, and yet to provide no way in which the group could implement the policy because of their limitations as human beings. If production, marketing, finance, and administration were all in one person's head, then certain actions could be adopted much faster than they are in industry; for example, there would be no time lost in transmitting and interpreting information, and few errors made in interpretation. But industry is organized on the basis of a division of labor, because this "one mind" concept is not feasible, and a division of labor is.

The idea of the division of labor implies that each person will attempt to maximize a certain measurement (for example, gross sales), or else minimize a certain measurement (for example, costs). The objective of an organization based on a division of labor is that each division can feasibly come near to maximizing (or minimizing) its "score" and that such efforts will be the best way in which the group as a whole will attain its over-all objective. Consequently, the assignment of costs (and returns) to a division is—from the point of view of the division's policy-making—a problem of organization.

Something approaching this idea is recognized by those who design standard cost systems. Here the "variances" really act as the type of cost which we have been discussing. The purchasing department (say) is interested in minimizing the unfavorable variances on purchases of raw material. The "standard cost" is often set as a goal. The production department is also given a set of labor and material standards, and it tries to minimize its unfavorable variances. Much of the argument about standard cost systems is concerned with the question of whether or not a given manager can do anything about the variances he is supposed to minimize, that is, whether or not the realities of the organization are reflected in the standard cost system.

In most instances with which I am familiar, there is a serious doubt that the persons who set up the standard costs were fully aware of the proper way to relate organizational structure to cost standards. Since we have as yet only very tentative ways of proving what organizational structure is optimal, the cost accountant cannot be blamed. But until we do know more about this problem, it would be ridiculous to assert that industrial management has satisfactory measures of management performance and planning.

9 · *Managerial Accounting, Errors and Psychology.*

Mention should be made of two other aspects of costs that are definitely relevant to policy formation and are definitely lacking in accounting systems. Few (I'd be inclined to say "No") costs are known with certainty. The errors in cost figures (or return figures) are clearly important in decisions of management. They are important in deciding how much effort to put into the task of gathering cost information and transmitting it. The errors are also important in understanding the risks entailed in decisions. Yet company data-processing systems do not generate information about the errors of estimated costs, and in this respect, again, we lack a sound basis for verifying managerial decisions based on costs.

The second aspect may be less important, or at least its importance has not yet been ascertained. This concerns the "constant" costs (sometimes called "sunk" costs) which are irrelevant in the sense that they equally penalize all alternatives. There is a real question whether such costs should or should not be included. Formally, the question is trivial, since a policy that minimizes a certain measure will also minimize this measure plus some constant. But psychologically, the problem may be quite serious. Suppose the standard cost for an activity is $100,000 per month. A variance of $1,000 does not look very serious, although it may very well occur as a result of bad management. A much larger variance, but less controllable, may attract an unwarranted amount of attention. Thus, it is certainly important to know to what extent the numerical size of the measurement scale influences, favorably or unfavorably, the attitude of the decision-maker. As we shall see in Chapter 8, in recent years there has been some stress put on the fact that the measurements which the business-man tries to maximze (or minimize) are not "unique" numbers, and can be transformed into a number of other scales (for example, from dollars to pounds to francs). Such arguments may make the somewhat naïve assumption that the legitimacy of a transformation is independent of the personality of the decision-maker.

10 · *Currently Calculated Profits Are Not Values.*

This concludes our discussion of the theme that business and industry at the present time have no satisfactory scale of value—even if value is measured solely in terms of dollars. It isn't that accounting systems are "slightly" defective here and there, and that the wise manager will ignore some figures and add or subtract from others. In view of the fact that asset utilization and nonutilization, and organizational policy are both highly critical in management decisions, and because the values of these policies are not measured by accounting information, it is safe to say that cost and profit information is seriously defective relative to a scientific understanding of policy information.

In sum, we don't know what value measures characterize the activities of business firms, that is, we do not know what it is that business is attempting to maximize.

11 · *A Practical Reflection.*

The practical import of this chapter can be brought out most forcibly by emphasizing one of the points made in it that managerial accounting is a branch of organization theory. No company of any size can act as one mind, and it is absurd to characterize the firm as though it were a single player of a game, or the man who runs the

corner drug store. The rational entrepreneur of classical economics
is a many-headed monster. The attempt to develop a single-minded
organization is much too costly. Instead, the business organization
divides the labor and assigns functions. Large corporations tend to
decentralize and permit division managers to pursue their assigned
objectives without a large amount of home office interference. The
question is how to score the performance of the divisions and subdivisions of a company. This is the same as asking what functions
ought to be assigned to the divisions and subdivisions. No clear idea
of the "profit" which the company is trying to maximize can be given
unless these scoring methods have been worked out for the divisions.
Return on investment has become a popular scoring method because
it is assumed to be a first approximation of a score that validly depicts
what the division manager's function actually is. In Chapter 13 we
shall consider what might be entailed in a second approximation.
This consists in trying to set up objective value (or cost) measures
that are relevant to the decisions of the manager or superintendents
of his subdivisions. The production superintendent, say, is given an
explicit cost of holding idle inventories and equipment, cost of
shortage, cost of setup, and labor cost. If the organization is so constructed that these are the only relevant costs, then we have both
defined the manager's function and can measure his performance: to
minimize the total of *these* costs for any specific assignment of output. In the same manner, the division manager is assigned, among
other things, a specific cost for capital received from the home company. Once this and other costs have been assigned, his function is
also assigned, and so is the scoring method for his performance. Managers have more or less "freedom of decision" depending on the types
of cost that are assigned to them. This "second approximation" to
value measurements for organizations is undoubtedly very difficult
to work out. So is any value measurement for any decision-maker.

12 · *Managerial Accounting.*

In a very general sense we are talking about managerial accounting
in this book, if I understand the true intent of this term. The "profit-
maker" doesn't have to be the manager of a business organization.
Business organizations were discussed because one can talk about
them more concretely than other organizations. But the moral is

general. What are the United Auto Workers trying to accomplish? Increased take-home pay, fringe benefits, old-age security, guaranteed wage, and so on, for their members. Did they make a profit last year? The question is legitimate because profit is not a word reserved only for the activities of the entrepreneur. The UAW certainly had costs. Count in its outlays for staff, and buildings, among others, as well as the time spent by its members at meetings. Count in lost work opportunity of its members. Count in, too, its "opportunity" costs— the failures to act when it could have, the delays in processing grievances. The UAW had a "return" in terms of the objectives outlined above. Is it sensible to ask for a managerial accounting system for labor organizations?

13 · *Indebtedness.*

The discussions of the problems entailed in defining profits are so numerous that detailed references would be far too extensive. Similarly the problem of the proper horizon for planning, besides being a topic that the Soviets worried about and "solved" in terms of five years, is also discussed widely in this country. Dean (6, pp. 556-558) has some wise things to say on both topics. Modigliani-Hohn (7), and Charnes *et al.* (4) have made contributions to the problem of the "horizon" of planning in certain contexts.

Return on investment is talked about extensively; see, for example (1).

Remarks on accounting similar to those given in this chapter can be found in Churchman-Ackoff (5).

REFERENCES

1. *Improved Tools of Financial Management, Financial Series No. 111.* New York: American Management Association, 1956.
2. Bursk, E. C., and D. H. Fenn (editors), *Planning the Future Strategy of your Business.* New York: McGraw-Hill Book Co., Inc., 1956.
3. Brigham, G., "On a Congestion Problem in an Aircraft Factory," *Journal of the Operations Research Society of America,* Vol. 3 (1955), pp. 412-428.
4. Charnes, A., W. W. Cooper, and R. Mellon, "A Model for Optimizing Production by Reference to Cost Surrogates," *Econometrica,* Vol. 23 (1955), pp. 307-323.

5. Churchman, C. W. and R. L. Ackoff, "Operational Accounting and Operations Research," *The Journal of Accountancy,* Vol. 99 (1955), pp. 33-39.
6. Dean, J., *Managerial Economics.* Englewood Cliffs, N. J.: Prentice-Hall, Inc., 1951.
7. Modigliani, F., and F. E. Hohn, "Production Planning over Time and the Nature of the Expectation and Planning Horizon," *Econometrica,* Vol. 23 (1955), pp. 46-66.

THE THEORETICAL CONTENT OF FACTS

4

Summary

and

Intent.

Chapter 1 proposed a thesis about the scientific verification of recommendations. In the earlier discussion, the term "scientific" was taken to characterize a set of activities of academic scientists. But the program needs to be made more explicit by attempting to say what these activities are. This is the aim of the next two chapters. Obviously, it will be impossible to develop a thorough analysis of scientific method here. Instead, the emphasis will be placed on those aspects of scientific method that are apt to be ignored in popular treatments of "what is science?" Indeed, these aspects may be ignored as well in more sophisticated treatises by writers with a different philosophical bias from my own, so that there is some point in bringing out the salient properties of scientific method which this treatise presupposes. This can best be done by beginning with one popular account of the method of science, and then discussing why this somewhat obvious description of what science does is rather obviously false. The ultimate aim is to argue that in one important sense, to be explained, *facts, measurements* and *theories* are methodologically the same. Once this aim has been accomplished, the stage is set for the more detailed discussion of measurement in the next chapter.

2 · *An Unsatisfactory Concept of Scientific Method.*

A popular account of scientific method asserts that it consists of proceeding from the simple to the complex. This philosophy of science can be depicted by the accompanying diagram.

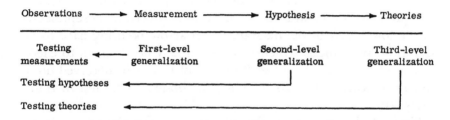

The upper line of the diagram indicates that science begins with "elementary" observations. The observations are then transformed into measurements of various types. To do this, one requires, in addition to the observations, an abstraction—a "model" which establishes relationships between the empirical entities. The combination of observation and the measurement model produces descriptions, orderings, numbers, and the like. These "constructs" often may be regarded as elementary data by practicing scientists; for example, a metallurgist might think of a Rockwell reading as an "elementary" observation. But further reflection shows that such readings are partially made up of "direct" observation and partially made up of some sort of an abstract construct that defines relationships between observations.

Next, the scientist constructs hypotheses, which are simple generalizations about the measurements. Finally, he constructs theories, which are more elaborate generalizations. Measurement, hypothesis, and theory represent levels of generalization. Each of these higher levels can be "tested" by the lower levels. To see how this works out, suppose we examine the way in which measurements are "tested" by direct observations. For example, suppose "preference" were to have a clear empirical meaning. That is, "X prefers A to B" is to be considered as an "elementary" observation: we assume the statement is true if and only if X is observed to choose A instead of B. In order to rank preferences, one introduces a first-level generalization based on the notion of transitivity: If A is preferred to B and B is preferred to C, then A is preferred to C. This rule, together with other ideas, permits one to construct "rank-orders" among choices. The scientist has passed from the elementary language of observations (in this case, "X prefers A to B") to another level of language ("A is higher in the rank order than B").

The legitimacy of this passage from lower order to higher order can be "tested" by observing whether A is preferred to C whenever A is preferred to B and B to C. This testing procedure is represented in the lower part of the diagram by an arrow pointing back to observations from measurements. A person may be observed to choose A instead of B, and to choose B instead of C, but be observed not to choose A instead of C. In this case, the observational test of transitivity fails.

Similarly, hypotheses—under this conception of scientific method—can be tested by means of measurements—or possibly by means of the observations themselves. For example, one might test the hypothesis that persons of one race are more intelligent than persons of another race. Intelligence measurements (based, say, on observable choices in a paper-and-pencil test) would first be made on a sample of each race, and a test of significance would be run. Perhaps a "significant difference" appears in the analysis. One may therefore accept the hypothesis of a true difference in intelligence. But as the diagram suggests, one could just as reasonably argue that the measurements themselves were not legitimate. That is, one can always pass back to the test of the measurements in testing an hypothesis. This is less apt to occur if the measurements have had a long tradition, as in the case of measurements of length. But where agreement on the meaning of terms and methods of measurement has not been attained, one will expect to find—not that the hypothesis in question is accepted or rejected—but that the measurements are rejected. Such "dual testing" is represented by a continued line running back from hypothesis through measurement to observations. Thus—and this point may be glossed over in elementary textbook expositions of the logic of hypothesis-testing—the experimenter has a choice between rejecting the hypothesis or rejecting the measurements.

Theories can be regarded as sets of hypotheses (usually infinite in number). According to the viewpoint we are expounding here, the distinction between hypotheses and theories is really a matter of degree. At the extreme "lower" end of the hypothesis concept are statements which can be tested by one experiment, that is, by computing from the measurements one "statistic-vector" which acts as a decision-criterion for acceptance or rejection. In this context, a statistic-vector is a set of numbers derived from measurements. For example, an average and a standard derivation would form such a vector. Thus the student t test for differences in means of two static populations provides a method of using two statistics (t and degrees of freedom) to decide whether to accept or reject the hypothesis.

We would come closer to a "theory" if we considered the dual problem of equivalence of means and of variances in two static populations, for in this case the hypothesis would consist of the conjunction of two propositions ("The means are equal" and "the variances are equal"). This suggests that "theories" are conjunctions of many logically independent propositions, that is, propositions that do not logically imply each other. For example, the assertion that some specific linear relationship exists between two continuous variables in a certain range is really a conjunction of an infinite number of propositions; for each value of one variable, there is a hypothesis about the value of the other variable, and each hypothesis is testable by a method similar to the one mentioned above.

As the diagram indicates, theories are tested by testing a suitable sample of the hypotheses included in the theory.

This is a general account of a popular conception of scientific method. It is true that we have discussed some subtle points that a popular treatment would have to avoid—for example, the testing of measurements—but the account we have given represents the common viewpoint that the scientist is a generalizer anchored to reality by his objective observations.

What's wrong with this viewpoint? First of all, because it is a popularization of the meaning of scientific method, there are a number of both obvious and subtle errors of omission. Then there is a more fundamental error of commission, concerning the role that observations play.

Turning first to the omissions, we may note that the problem of language structure has been glossed over in the account we have given. As recent literature in the philosophy of science has shown, the linguistic distinction between observation, measurement, hypothesis, and theory is not simple to give. But my main concern here is not with the decisions as to whether a sentence is observational or theoretical, but rather with the decision as to whether it should be accepted or rejected or considered to be meaningless. In this sense, there are a great many omissions in the diagram we have been considering because there ought to be a great many more "arrows," which of course, would destroy the usefulness of the diagram itself. For example, there are other tests of the measurement construct besides the one we mentioned. It is sensible to ask whether the measurement language is unambiguously clear and also whether it is intuitively satisfactory. Thus, in preference rankings one might introduce the notion of "closure" as follows: "If *A* and *B* are distinct, then either *A* is preferred to *B* or *B* is preferred to *A*." But this concept is not clear for it does not tell us whether the "or" includes the possibility that both preferences occur (*A* preferred over *B and B* preferred over *A*), or excludes this possibility. Hence the "arrow" in the diagram which signifies the test of the measurement construct is not complete; there should be an arrow pointing to a column called "sense of rigor."

Furthermore, it is perfectly legitimate for scientists to criticize and reject a measurement construct because it does not meet the demands of intuitive adequacy. Indeed, in the example of testing the intelligence of two races, mentioned above, the "rejection" of the intelligence measures would probably be based on such a criterion. Another example is discussed in Chapter 8 which considers some constructs used in measuring utility. These may "test out" as far as observations are concerned and also meet the requirements of rigor, and yet a person might meaningfully assert that whatever these constructs measure, they do *not* measure utility. He might demonstrate his assertion by showing some examples of behavior that meet the requirements of the measurement construct but "obviously" do not constitute evidence of the utility of outcomes for the person. For example, one might feel inclined to say that given two choices, *A* and *B*, the utilities of the two are equal if a person chooses each one with about the same frequency as he chooses the other. But a critic might argue that such behavior does *not* imply equality of utilities, because *A* and *B* may be incomparable as far as the subject is concerned (for example, *A* is a Picasso painting and *B* is the Emperor Concerto). The equal frequency of choice in this case might be evidence of confusion, not indifference. Hence the diagram ought to include another arrow pointing to "sense of intuitive adequacy."

Furthermore, the measurement construct may be empirically valid, rigorous, and intuitively adequate, but absurd and therefore useless. The number of hairs on a person's head is a useless measure (it does not even measure degree of baldness), as is the ratio of the square of a person's height to the cube root of his intelligence. Hence, we need another "test" arrow pointing to a "sense of significance and usefulness."

If we pass on to hypotheses and theories, the difficulties of the diagrammatic representation of science become even more apparent.

Decisions about hypotheses may be made on grounds other than the directly relevant observations or measurements. Hypotheses may be considered meaningless because they are not rigorously stated. For example, "The majority of the people approve of the present administration" may be considered meaningless because "people" and "approval" have not been rigorously defined. Hypotheses also may be "rejected" without observational test because they are obviously false. A beginning student of statistics often states a "null" hypothesis in the form: "The true means of the two populations are the same," although to a more reflective mind such an hypothesis is obviously false because in the nature of things it is incredible that the true means would be exactly the same. What is meant is that the true means do not differ "very much"—which is a vague hypothesis but perhaps no longer trivially false. Again, hypotheses may also have no significance—for example, testing whether the majority of people approve of "white lies," or disapprove of stealing pennies. In other words, in the diagram we need "test lines" to columns representing a sense of rigor, and of usefulness of hypotheses.

But the diagram is defective in other ways as well. These ways were also inherent in measurement constructs, but not so obvious there. To test an hypothesis one needs to make observations and measurements. Consequently, there is the problem of selecting a sample of information which will give maximum information at minimum cost or, rather, a sample that minimizes the total cost of sampling plus sampling errors. This is a problem that falls under the head of experimental design and/or sampling plans. It is sometimes ignored as a critical part of the description of scientific method because it may be argued that overtesting, though inelegant, is not a fundamental defect in scientific method. Such an argument is based on the naïve idea that science faces no economy of scarcity. Furthermore, even if one does adopt this viewpoint, *under*-testing is a significant problem in scientific method. When is an experimenter justified in asserting that sufficient evidence has been gathered to decide whether or not to accept or reject an hypothesis? The answer depends on criteria for accepting and rejecting hypotheses. Every student of the foundations of statistics knows how difficult it is to find such criteria. Hence, our diagram needs some superstructure built along the "testing" line. This might be said to designate the economic criteria that act as guides for the design of the test and the ultimate acceptance or rejection of the hypotheses. Such a superstructure is also required for measurement constructs, as we shall argue in more detail in the next chapter.

We might go on to point out that test criteria also should include decisions concerning the economics of computations, ease of communication of results, and so on. But enough has been said to establish the idea that hypotheses are not "simply" tested by so-called "direct observation" or measurements based on them.

Consider now the question of theories. If it is true that theories are sets of hypotheses, then the test of a theory raises other questions in addition to those of observation, measurement, rigor, usefulness, and economy, which we have already discussed. Not only must we select a sample of measurements, but we must also select a sample of hypotheses to test. Anyone who has spent time worrying about sampling procedures for inspection of a continuous process will recognize this problem; *when* and *where* to test are as important as *how much* to test. The "theory" that is being tested is (say) that the mean and standard deviation of some population each remain within some interval over a period of time. There are an infinite number of hypotheses contained in this theory. Which ones should be tested?

One might appeal to common sense and assert that the tests should be "spread out equally" over the interval. Thus, if the theory predicts what will happen in the time interval from January 1 to July 1, then one should test hourly, or daily, or weekly. "All other things being equal," this is probably so—perhaps trivially so if we suitably define this vague expression. But in inspection practice "all other things" are not equal, and a great deal of research is required in order to determine how to test a theory. Thus, we require a theory of theory-testing. In this respect, inspection procedures have vastly outstripped other branches of science for no other discipline has developed a theory of theory-testing. That production inspection has made strides in this direction may of course be due to the fact that inspection theories are apt to be simpler than (say) solar-system theories. But this fact, if true, does not imply that the problem is unimportant in the other disciplines of science. Most scientists recognize that the mere accumulation of measurements that "confirm" a theory do not add to one's confidence in the theory for they may merely overtest one or more hypotheses, and undertest the rest. Thus, on a vague level, one feels that a theory ought to be tested under "widely different" circumstances, but this prescription is difficult to define.

Suppose we try to formulate some guiding principles relative to the problem of theory-testing. These may help to illustrate its complexity:

(1) The more dubious the hypothesis, the more testing effort is required.

(2) If equal doubt exists concerning all hypotheses, then the testing should be "equally spaced" over the variables.

(3) Every "variable" of the theory should be tested at least once if there is any doubt as to its effect.

Each of these "principles" raises serious problems. Principles 1 and 2 require a specification of prior confidence in the hypotheses, and the role this confidence should play in testing. Furthermore, principle 1 may be impossible to fulfill if the set of hypotheses is infinite because inevitably there will be an infinite set of untested hypotheses, many of them "maximally" dubious. Principle 3 may seem trivial, provided the variables of the theory have been isolated. But it also may be false, if the effect of a variable is estimated beforehand to be slight. This principle is a first approximation to the notion that theories should be tested as broadly as possible. But "breadth of testing" evidently requires more analysis if this principle is to mean anything.

I hope these remarks make it evident that the degree of confirmation of a theory—if such a measure exists—does not depend solely on the number of instances in which the theory has been "confirmed" by observation. Criteria other than consistency with observation play at least as important a role.

It must be clear, therefore, that "testing" in empirical science is not a straightforward and routine process. The contrast that is sometimes made between the routine of testing hypotheses and the creativity of discovering hypotheses is surely faulty. The process of testing hypotheses and theories puts severe demands on the creative abilities of the scientist.

The discussion has shown that there are multiple choices that must be made in testing, and none of these can be "routinely" prescribed. The inconsistency of an hypotheses with observation does *not* necessarily mean that the hypothesis is to be rejected: the measurements themselves may sensibly be rejected on any of the grounds we have cited. Hypothesis- and theory-testing are delicate operations, and as yet in the history of science we have no very clear ideas how they should be performed. This is so, despite the many texts and manuals on testing hypotheses and the voluminous discussions in professional philosophy on "inductive" methods.

These remarks recall the discussion in Chapter 1, where it was argued that at present we do not know the decision rules that govern scientific activity. The present discussion leads us to conclude that we do not know what these decision rules ought to be. For example, we do not know how science ought to decide when to accept or when to reject a theory. This reflection on the decision processes of science will be a recurrent theme in this book because it seems quite impossible to discuss the scientific verification of recommendations without at the same time discussing the problem of how science itself should make decisions.

3 · *Are There Levels of Generalization in Science?*

We now turn to a basic error in the diagram we have been considering. This concerns the "levels" of generalization which, according to the diagram, exist in the process of science. Seemingly, the problems at each "level" become more severe: observation is the "simplest and most direct" operation, "measurement" next, and when we come to theories we are obviously faced with the tremendously difficult problems of multiple-hypothesis-testing. Observations are therefore thought to be an anchor—or system of anchors—which supply rigidity to the structure of science. The superstructure must be so framed that it does not "float away" from this anchor system. For this reason, so the argument runs, the criteria of rigor and significance are important, but they are secondary compared to the "ultimate" test of "objective" fact.

But by what process does science accept the "facts" of observation? This is the crucial question for any philosophy of science based on "levels" of generalization. The most obvious answer is one that we have already discussed in Chapter 2: direct, immediate sense experience.

As Chapter 2 indicated, much has been argued about the issue of immediate sense knowledge in the philosophical literature. But, interestingly enough, much has also been said about it in the "practical" world of industry and business. It is "common sense" in the business world that some assertions are clearly established facts, and others are theories. For example, "cash on hand" is often taken to be an objective fact; allowance for depreciation is taken as a "guesstimate"; Good Will is thought to be a mythical figure. Businessmen too distinguish between the ideas (like cash) which they can more or less directly grasp, and the ideas they have to think about (depreciation or cost of carrying inventory). The naïve student of business administration is often led to believe that the more directly an idea can be grasped, the more valid it is. This is one reason that "smart operators" often represent their vague hunches in terms of numbers—because the numbers can be grasped directly.

Now we can raise a rather obvious objection to the thesis that science accepts objective facts in a simple or direct way—or that business accepts a cash-on-hand figure by a simple, one-step process. All we need do is observe that scientists recheck their observations before finally accepting them just as firms use elaborate internal controls to confirm their cash-deposit figures.

But it is easy to make a common-sense reply to this observation. It is true that "direct" confirmation does not mean a one-step process.

Everyone knows that nothing is ever known with certainty, and that no idea is ever completely clear. But "clearly" some experiences are known to occur with much greater certainty than others, just as some ideas are known to be much clearer than others. When I look at the clear-blue sky, or at a report of cash on hand, I know that my belief in the occurrence of a sensation of blue or the actual existence of the cash in the banks is much more likely to be correct than my belief (say) in the ultimate origin of the universe or a depreciation figure.

This is common sense, and therefore it is only natural for a scientist to ask whether it is true and, if so, why it is true. Why are certain beliefs and estimates much more reliable than others? The only conceivable answer is because experience has shown them to be. But then the answer, if sensible, implies that the reliability of a certain kind of information is based on a *theory*, namely that the information has had and will have a certain degree of reliability over time and over a class of "normal" observers.

In other words, everyone admits that cash on hand may be in error —company cashiers and bank clerks are not infallible. But accountants will argue that they know that cash is a "more accurate" figure than depreciation or Good Will. They may feel that this is intuitively obvious. But when pressed to explain the meaning of "accuracy," they must develop a theory of accounting information in terms of which their intuition can be confirmed.

We can now pose the issue in a more formal manner. Throughout this chapter—as well as the rest of this book—we consider propositions in terms of the decision process by which they are accepted or rejected. This may be what some philosophers call the pragmatic interpretation of the proposition, but I prefer to use the phrase "methodological meaning." We began by considering a classification of propositions in terms of their methodological meanings, a classification suggested by the diagram which was so unmercifully criticized. This classification was based on the following idea: some propositions are accepted or rejected depending on whether an observation of a certain kind occurs in a specific circumstance. These are the directly confirmable propositions. Next, some propositions are accepted or rejected depending on whether a "sufficient" number of directly confirmable propositions of a certain type are accepted. These propositions are either measurements or hypotheses. Finally, some propositions are accepted or rejected depending on whether a "sufficient" number of directly confirmable propositions of "sufficiently" different kinds are accepted. These propositions are—methodologically speaking—theories. If all this could be adequately formalized, we could then go on to classify scientific propositions into one of these types. But the argument has shown that, except for the last type, all the other classes are empty. In particular, the practice of science shows that such a proposition as "An observed object X weighs k pounds" or "An observed object X is blue" are, methodologically interpreted, elliptical for "If X is observed under any of the conditions C_i belonging to the class of conditions C, by any observer O_j belonging to the class of observers O, the recorded observations will all belong to a class of propositions P." The confirmation of this proposition belongs to the last type—the theories. By a similar argument, all other propositions of science are—methodologically interpreted—theories.

What are the implications of this conclusion relative to the meaning of scientific method? It should be emphasized that the conclusion does not lead one to infer that "facts" are "theories" in a syntactical or semantic sense. Recent studies in the structure of factual and theoretical propositions seem to be irrelevant to the present discussion—or, rather, the relevance is a subtle matter that would take us too far afield. Parenthetically, however, the problem of confirming counterfactual propositions ("If this had happened, then that would have happened") is relevant; obviously in a philosophy that takes all propositions to be methodologically theoretical, the analysis of the problem differs considerably from the analysis of a philosophy that recognizes methodological distinctions between observation and theory.

4 · *Science and Communication.*

There is one more reflection to be made on the basis of the preceding discussion of fact and theory. If one purpose of science is to communicate information, then there is no such thing as immediate and personal knowledge for science. Facts are theories about the acquisition and transmission of information.

Consider, for example, the following conundrum: "If a physicist were wrecked on a desert island with some equipment, and spent the rest of his lonely life conducting experiments, only to end by perishing with all his results in a typhoon, would you say he had behaved as a scientist and that his results were scientific?"

The answer—methodologically speaking—must be "no." More precisely, the answer is that since the communication was restricted to that of one man to himself at various times of his life, the "science" of such a biography was small indeed.

It may be true that deep within each rational individual there is a true sense of validity and a true sense of clarity each of which can act as a control on his behavior and his thought, and thus supply him with some sound basis for deciding what is true and what is clear. But the inner thoughts and experiences of such a mind do not constitute science because in the practice of science, personal conviction is never the sole basis for the acceptance of scientific results. There may be cases where no scientist feels the need or the desirability of checking one man's conclusions; for example, a mathematician has recently calculated the value of 1000! Probably no one else will do so ever again. But in this case the scientific community uses a multitude of other experiences to satisfy itself that personally acquired results of this kind would turn out to be confirmed by other observers if they were to take the time to do the work.

Consider the point about science and social communication in another way. I've sometimes heard it said, in defense of the use of this or that term in scientific discourse, that it doesn't matter what terms are used "as long as one is clear as to the meaning." This is just another cliché gone wrong because "clarity" is not something that each person can create in himself. Clarity is a social concept, not a personal one. The use of a certain term may preclude communication because of the social interpretation of the term. I cannot say "Democracy is a social form of government in which one person dictates all the decisions of the group and is not himself controlled by any decisions other than his own." Even if what follows "Democracy is" consists of very clear ideas, the whole definition is not clear at all. It is not clear because the term "democracy" already has a social meaning.

We are thus led to make one conclusion—which is certainly not new —about the meaning of science: science seeks to communicate experience as widely as possible. Even if there are experiences which, when they occur, are fully understood by each person, this fact plays only a minor role in the communication process. What is of major importance is first the method by which experience can be transmitted from person to person and generation to generation, and second the translation of the information into specific purposeful responses on the part of the individual.

Enough has been said to indicate how the verification of observations involves the same methodological problems as those that underlie the verification of theories. We turn now to a similar discussion of measurement.

5 · *Measurements and Theories.*

We want to examine now the sense in which—methodologically speaking—measurements are theories. For this purpose, suppose we select one well-known example of measurement: length.

Philosophers and scientists have long marveled at man's ingenuity in creating measurements of length. Some marvel because of the simplicity of certain length measurements; even a child or housewife can perform them (if *that* is evidence for simplicity!). But what is really marvelous is that A can speak of the length of a table, B can speak of the height of a mountain, C can speak of the distance of the planet Mars from the Sun, D can speak of the width of a tiny indent in a piece of steel, and all mean essentially the same thing by their experiences! The experiences are indeed "incomparable," yet they can all be described by the same measurement concept.

This is a question that cannot help but fascinate the student of science: How can so many diverse experiences mean essentially the same kind of thing? But before we examine this question in detail, we can observe that since the concept of length has such a widely divergent application in the study of nature, it has well satisfied the requirement of communication. It is possible to transmit information about many diverse experiences by means of one concept. We have become so accustomed to this scientific result that the wonder of it has worn thin. Yet to a mind unfamiliar with western science it might very well seem strange to throw into one category the experiences relating to the distance between stars and to the distance between electrons, especially since neither of these two distances is experienced in the same manner, nor is either similar to the experience of a distance between two points on a table top.

The "secret" of the success of length measurements consists in translating all measurements into a comparison with a standard, that is, in predicting what would have occurred if the length measurement had been made against a standard in such-and-such a manner in such-and-such a circumstance. In broad outline, the steps of this process consist of observations ("readings"), rules for adjusting observations, the adjustment of the observations to standard conditions, and a theory of errors which acts as a control on the previous steps. Measurement of length is a prediction of the observations that would have occurred if a comparison were made under standard conditions:

> The International Prototype Metre is a bar of platinumiridium alloy (90 per cent platinum, 10 per cent iridium) of a special winged X-form section devised by G. Tresca to give maximum rigidity in relation to the weight of metal used; the neutral plane of the section is exposed throughout the length of the bar, and the metre is defined as the distance between two transverse graduations on the neutral plane, near the ends of the bar, when the latter is at the temperature of 0° C. (2; p. 152)

The implications of this definition are somewhat astonishing at first sight. If the concept of length has the same meaning throughout science, then any assertion of the form, "The distance between *A* and *B* at moment *t* is *x*," must be translated into an assertion of the form, "If the straight line joining *A* and *B* were compared with the standard meter rod, the straight line would be seen to be so many meters—that is, so many of the distances between the transverse graduations mentioned in the description of the standard."

What is remarkable from the point of view of the economies of scientific activity is that the scientist will seldom actually attempt a comparison with the standard. What is even more remarkable is that in many cases such a comparison is impossible. For example, neither the distances between stars nor the distances between electrons can be compared with a standard in this "direct" fashion.

The reason that science can measure length even when the standards cannot be applied directly has already been suggested: the scientist is equipped with predictive laws that enable him to estimate what would have been experienced under the standard conditions. Thus it is not ridiculous to say that an astronomer of 1956 can measure the distance between two planets in 1976—or the depth of the ocean in mid-Pacific—or the distance between two nerve fibers in a live brain—even though in none of these cases can direct comparisons with a standard be accomplished. This means that if we ask what the length of an object *really* is at a given time and in a given environment, the answer depends on an ability to predict what would happen in another environment. The distance in question is compared with some measuring rod with marked gradations. The reading obtained is not, of course, the true length of the object. Even a series of readings would not necessarily constitute a basis for estimating the true length. They would do so if we knew that the distances between the gradations would compare exactly with the gradations on the standard meter rod under standard conditions. Usually, we expect that the distance between the marks on the measuring device will remain invariant—or almost so—but this is not necessary, of course. There are still some subtle issues to be settled concerning this account, but we'll postpone these until the next chapter.

We are led to conclude that what property a thing really has depends on what would occur under other circumstances. In a sense, the "factual" depends on the "counterfactual." We shall argue in the next chapter that qualitative and quantitative properties are ascertained by essentially the same method, and both may be measurements. Thus we decide that an object has a color blue only because certain comparisons would be observed under some standard set of conditions. All description methodologically entails prediction. In general, all measurement takes place within the context of a theory.

According to the present account of measurement, it also follows that there are no "primitive concepts," methodologically speaking. In order to understand the standard, that is, to specify the standard conditions and operations, certain other concepts must be understood and certain other measurements must be made. For example, in the case of measurements of length, the following considerations apply:

> It is necessary, of course, to maintain a close control and make accurate measurements of the temperature of the bars during comparison. For this reason the comparator is arranged so that the bars can be immersed, during measurement, in the inner compartment of a double water-bath, provided with stirring devices to maintain a uniform temperature. In the case of metric standards it is permissible to immerse the bars in distilled water, together with suitable thermometers, during measurement. . . . Measurements cannot readily be made at 62° F. the British specification, and still less can they conveniently be made at 0° C. Since different bars will have different coefficients of thermal expansion, it is necessary to determine these

and make allowances for them in computing the results of comparisons actually made at other temperatures. (2; p. 154)

Which "comes first"—the measurement of length or the measurement of temperature? Which is a simpler or clearer idea—length or thermal expansion? The answer is that these questions are not meaningful, since in the procedures of science it is not possible in general to rank the steps in terms of a preferential order to be followed, nor is it possible to rank concepts in terms of over-all simplicity or clarity.

Of course, for specific purposes—or in specific circumstances—it is sensible to say that one step ought to come before the other or one idea should be made basic relative to others. We are describing here the strategy of science, not the specific tactics. In a given battle, it may happen that the infantry ought to precede the tanks. But this is not a valid strategic principle of military activities. In the same way, in a given piece of research on values, "preference for actions" may be easier to understand than "value of outcomes" in the sense that work can begin with one concept as a base and cannot begin with the other as a base. But this does not imply that in the over-all strategy of research into values, either preference for acts or value of outcomes is "simpler" or "clearer."

We could now examine in detail how hypothesis-testing is also a type of theory-testing. Some of the points here are quite subtle, and their detailed discussion would not be profitable in this context. We may merely note that in the earlier discussion hypotheses were taken to be tested by one or more "statistics." Essentially, this account was incorrect. To test an hypothesis in this manner, it is essential that we be able to make estimates about the probability of erroneous rejection or acceptance, and that we know how low the probabilities of such errors should be. The required probabilities of error turn out to be theories in the sense defined above: they are multiple hypotheses concerning the samples that will occur under various possible "states of Nature." These "background theories," which play so definitive a role in hypothesis testing, have recently become quite important in discussions of the foundations of statistics.

Thus the hierarchical levels of scientific activity—observation, measurement, hypothesis, theory—which may have seemed so sensible in a first glance at science, are untenable. Indeed, this "first glance" was not even a good approximation. The idea of direct observation cannot be simpler and more direct than the idea of measurement because its explication requires a concept of measurement (for example, measurement of agreement). The notion of measurement cannot be simpler and more direct than that of a hypothesis or a theory because its explication requires the notion of a theory (to adjust readings). Consequently, the purported hierarchy is not based on criteria of simplicity or clarity of ideas. Nor is it based on "operational" criteria, since the operations that validate an observation or a measurement are no simpler and no more likely to be correct *per se,* than the operations that validate a theory.

6 · *Where are the Anchors and Controls of Science?*

Although it is not difficult to attack the notion of a methodological hierarchy in science, nor to show that "observations" and "measurements" are theoretical constructs, nevertheless once the attack on immediacy and simplicity has been successful, an embarrassment sets in. For in terms of a hierarchy in science, it is possible to provide a clear notion of the checks, controls, and ultimate authority of science; the simpler operations are used to define and control the more complicated. But if the ultimate authority of observation or fact is removed, what has become of the objectivity of science?

Of course, to say that observation and measurement are theoretical constructs is not to say that they are fantasies of the mind or rational constructions without any ties to reality. But one must now think of reality and objectivity in different terms. Once the notion of "ultimate" authority is given up, one can no longer assert that the *real* is what is *directly observed.* Wherein lies the objectivity of science?

The answer that most naturally comes to mind is that the objectivity of science lies—not in what it takes to be the ultimate authority—but in what it seeks to accomplish.

No doubt the science of the Renaissance had to declare a platform in which all dogma and metaphysical superstructure were denied as authority for scientific decisions. The ultimate decisions that the philosophers of the Renaissance science took to be acceptable were highly individual and personal: clarity of idea and immediacy of sensation. Perhaps the historian of science will recognize why such a platform was essential. As do all platforms and philosophies, it spelled its own doom. For the authority of sensation and clarity which seemingly formed the foundation of the new science, eventually showed—via the development of the psychological and social sciences—that neither clarity nor observation are personal and individual.

Modern science cannot adequately be described in terms of a philosophy of Renaissance science. The "modern" of the twentieth century is self-conscious about his decisions, that is, about the purposes of his decision-making. Even a casual glance at the shifts in American culture from 1900 to the present provides an enormous amount of evidence to support this viewpoint. Nineteenth-century industrial management seems to have done very little thinking and research into its goals. Modern management spends a significant part of its time on this problem. City-planning boards, social-service agencies, psychiatrists, management consultants—all are evidence that modern man has turned seriously to the problem of what he is trying to accomplish.

Hence, there is at least some plausible basis for asserting that science is "objective" because of what it seeks to do, and not because of some ultimate authority it selects to check its results.

What does science seek to do? This aim has been variously described, and subsequently we shall want to pursue the question in greater detail. Some have argued that the ultimate aim of science is to provide an unambiguous way of communicating human experiences. Some think that science strives to predict with certainty. Others have thought in terms of reducing the error of measurement to zero. Still others think that science seeks to control Nature, that is, to provide perfect ways of accomplishing tasks. All of these—and similarly described objectives—are notably vague but surprisingly similar in the sense that the approximation to any one of them would seem to entail an approximation to the others.

Assume for the purpose of this discussion that science's aims can be given meaning, although the meaning is admittedly not precise. It is not enough to say that science is objective because it is interested in these aims. Everyone is more-or-less interested in communicating unambiguously, or predicting with certainty, and so on. One also must assert that science seeks actively to find the best means to approximate these ideals.

Thus the seventeenth- and eighteenth-century philosophers were not "wrong," although they were quite naturally restricted by the knowledge of their day—just as we are in our own. One can think of Leibnitz and Locke—not as people trying to find ultimate authorities for the truth or falsity of assertions—but as people interested in the resources that science has at its disposal in the pursuit of its aims. From this viewpoint, the attack on dogmatism was an attack on the notion that dogma provides one such resource. The problem is not too different from the problem that human production faces: What are the resources that enable productive effort to pursue its aims?

In this sense, observation is a resource of science, just as thinking is. We do obtain from observation more than the abstract framework of theory. But this amounts to saying that the *act* of observing is a fruitful way of approaching the ideals of science. The act in and of itself means nothing; combined with other acts the effect constitutes the best estimate we can make at the present time of the optimal strategy of science.

How do we know this? That is, what method does science use to evaluate its strategies? In the past, the two primary criteria of evaluation have been consistency and error. The concept of consistency was used as an evaluation of the formal framework of theories; the concept of error was used to determine whether measurements and theories were in a satisfactory alliance. "Too much" of a deviation in the measurements from the predictions of theory meant that the system had to be revised by readjusting measurements or rejecting theories.

Today, we have come to realize that these two criteria are not sufficient to act as the basis of evaluating scientific effort. In fact, today we do not feel confident in any specific set of evaluative criteria. In this respect, science and industry share a common confusion —a confusion that will be examined in more detail in Chapters 13 and 14.

7 · *Recapitulation and a Moral.*

These remarks have led us to the conclusion that science is identified by its aims; that science does not have any clearly identifiable actions which are "best" with respect to its aims; that all scientific actions must be examined in the light of their effectiveness as strategies or tactics.

The moral for the future discussion of value measurements is this: we must be on guard against any claims that one approach to a science of human values is more fundamental or "clearly better" than another from a scientific point of view. We shall see that some researchers into value have stressed the need for setting down "simple" and "precise" foundations, and for constructing operationally feasible test methods for generating value measurements. Others (for example, in accounting and management research) have approached the problem from a broad point of view that will provide useful and meaningful methods of studying values in "real" situations. Neither approach can lay any a priori claims to being a better way to study values.

8 · *Communication and Values.*

We can state the theme of this chapter in another way, namely, that science is man's way of communicating with man in the cooperative attempt to control his environment. A science of values is therefore a way in which men can communicate their wants and needs. If values are the inmost secrets of each man's soul, then no one can appreciate fully another's wants and needs, and no one could legitimately recommend to another what he ought to do. Such individualism would permit persuasion, or force, but not understanding. Similarly, if man's moral sense lies too deep in his inner conscience, then no man can tell another what ought to be done on moral grounds.

The possibility of a science of values is the same as the possibility of a science of communication about values. Insofar as one man cannot understand the values of another, just so far is there no science of values or science of ethics.

Communication is not the same as consciousness; that is, a science of values does not depend on every man's being *aware* of his neighbor's needs. Communication occurs between two people when each has all the relevant information about the other in order to make a correct decision.

The contrasting viewpoints about science and values described in Chapter 1 can now be stated in another way. Those who think that science is restricted to the "facts" about the outside world and cannot therefore make recommendations, believe in effect that man can communicate with Nature but not with himself. Others think that man can communicate with man about values if each regards the other as a natural object. In such communication, the experimenter prods the subject by means of a carefully controlled stimulus in a carefully controlled situation, and carefully observes the verbal or overt response. In other words, the "facts" about a man's values are the results of laboratory tests of much the same sort as one would administer to a rat. If the subject is allowed to talk too much, or reflect, or come in contaminating contact with others, the experimenter becomes confused and can't codify his data.

At all costs, keep the experimenter from being confused! So the "facts" about human values are exhibitions of written or overt behavior in situations which the experimenter fully understands. Such "facts" are also of very little use in communicating man's values. Since all realistic decision-making occurs in situations that are confusing and partially unintelligible to the experimenter, the "science" of values is retricted to the laboratory. Is it?

No. Because the laboratory is also a very confusing place, too, and if one were honest about it and insisted that all aspects of the situation be as clear as possible, then men don't even communicate about values in a laboratory setup.

The cost of clarity can be too high. Men are not like rats, at least in two respects: they can talk more and are usually somewhat more expressive in their behavior.

This is tantamount to saying that a science of value is not going to come out of some laboratory. Laboratory work is good, of course, because thereby a scientist can learn to look at human behavior. The laboratory is a training ground for observation of behavior. But I question whether laboratory tests will ever provide much evidence for statements about human values.

Where can one learn about human values? In organizations. Organizations are based on schemes of communication. The organized group tries to squeeze the maximum of information out of its members—as many a zealous security officer has learned to his chagrin.

As scientists we may find it fruitful to study organizations in laboratories. But beyond this, what we need most of all in the science of values today is an ability to observe "live" organizational behavior in such a manner that we can develop evidence for and against certain theories of human behavior.

Won't this distort the "true" values of each man, if we study him as a member of an organization? No. Because the natural habitat of modern man is in the deep waters, tangled bushes, and spring storms of organizational activity.

9 · *Indebtedness.*

For philosophical discussions on the need for comparability of values in order to measure values, see, for example, Lewis (5), Perry (8). These discussions seem to ignore the role of standards and predictions in measurement methodology.

Some recent descriptions of scientific method are to be found in Margenau (6), Mosteller and Bush (7), and Coombs (3).

A fuller treatment of the argument that there are no methodological "primitives" is to be found in (2). An earlier attempt is in (1).

REFERENCES

1. Churchman, C. W., "Statistics, Pragmatics and Induction," *Philosophy of Science,* Vol. 15 (1948), pp. 249-268.
2. ———, "Concepts Without Primitives," *Philosophy of Science,* Vol. 20 (1953), pp. 257-265.
3. Coombs, C. H., H. Raiffa, and R. M. Thrall, "Some Views on Mathematical Models and Measurement Theory," in R. M. Thrall, *et al.* (editors), *Decision Processes.* New York: John Wiley & Sons, Inc., 1954.
4. Darwin, C., J. E. Sears, *et al.,* "A Discussion on Units and Standards," *Proceedings of the Royal Society of London,* Vol. 186A (1946), pp. 149-217.
5. Lewis, C. I., *An Analysis of Knowledge and Valuation.* LaSalle, Ill.: The Open Court Publishing Co., 1947.
6. Margenau, H., "The Competence and Limitations of Scientific Method," *Operations Research,* Vol. 3 (1955), pp. 135-146.
7. Mosteller, F., and R. R. Bush, *Stochastic Models for Learning.* New York: John Wiley & Sons, Inc., 1955.
8. Perry, R. B., *General Theory of Value.* New York: Longmans, Green & Co., Inc., 1926.

THE
TELEOLOGY OF
MEASUREMENT

5

Summary

and

Intent.

What is the meaning of measurement? In this chapter we shall argue that measurements are a specific type of information which co-determines decisions in a wide variety of contexts. In other words, measurements are pieces of information that have application in many different places and times. The chapter will outline the problems entailed in obtaining information of this type. We begin with the common-sense notion that one should specify *what* is being measured; that is, the measurer ought to specify the objects (or actions) he intends to measure as well as the properties of these objects. He ought to do this in such a manner that a decision-maker can interpret the measurements and know how to use them. This

93

could be done satisfactorily if there were some common language of things and their properties that all (reasonable) persons understand. But in this book we have adopted a sceptical attitude with respect to the existence of any such language. Instead, it is argued that the identification of objects and their properties must be made within a large framework which interrelates a number of different concepts. The framework is constructed to permit the greatest possibility of correct interpretation by its users. No one knows exactly how such a framework is to be constructed, but a theory is offered here, namely, a framework with a number of different "bases"—so that two interpreters with different sets of primitive ideas can both communicate within the framework and make use of information expressed in terms of the framework.

Once the items and their properties are defined, the measurer further clarifies the nature of the information he supplies. He does this by relating the information to other kinds of information. Some decisions can be made if the decision-maker knows that an item has a certain property or belongs to a certain class of items (for example, that the traffic light is red or green). Some decisions can be made if the decision-maker knows that an item is at the top (or bottom) of a list of items (for example, priority assignments). Some decisions require information about how much an item has of a certain property (for example, how heavy a package is). A classification of measurement languages provides the decision-maker with choices for relating the information to the kind of decision which he is to make.

The measurer must also consider the use of his information in a wide variety of contexts and times. He does this by providing the decision-maker with rules that enable him to adjust information collected in one time and place so that it is usable in another time and place. Thus, although a concept may be defined independently of any specific environment, the measurement activity pertinent to the concept must take place in specific environments. Hence, the measurer must be able to adjust the results obtained in one environment to the results that would be obtained in any other environment. In this manner, the environmentally free definition, which originally is no more than a research program, becomes meaningful in specific contexts.

The measurer accomplishes the adjustment of information by constructing "standards" or reference points for the comparisons of information in different contexts. The standards are expressed in the language of the broad conceptual framework and add to this language rules for the adjustment of information expressed in the language.

It is possible to have good or bad information, and it is also possible to have good or bad measurements. The measurer must therefore provide the decision-maker with information about the accuracy (value) of the measurements. In other words, measurement entails the construction of measures of accuracy, and the examination of the consistency of all adjusted information. A set of measurements made at one time and place may agree very closely, but when adjusted to information to be used at another time and place, may exhibit poor agreement. Consistency of all adjusted information is the basis for asserting that the measurements are real instead of fictitious. When consistency occurs, we say that the measurement process is "in control." Accuracy and control are both essential aspects of measurement; a series of measurements may be in control and yet have low value for the decision-maker since they don't measure what he needs to know in order to make decisions properly (that is to say, the series of measurements is inaccurate).

This chapter does not emphasize the operational problems of the measurer, that is, the specification of the operations of measurement and the training of observers, except insofar as these problems relate to the communication patterns and ultimate objectives of the process. This book is concerned primarily with the general design of measurements and specifically with the conceptual framework and standards for value measurements.

2 · *Functional Definitions.*

Since we plan to define measurement in a certain way, it is important to explain the kind of definition that is being proposed.

This book has tried to rephrase each methodological question in terms of a decision and to answer it in terms of certain decision criteria based on objectives. The earlier chapters have argued that the meaning we assign to concepts is a decision designed to serve certain interests; for present purposes, this argument needs to be generalized and made more precise. By a "functional definition" of a concept, we mean a definition which makes explicit the usefulness of the concept for certain purposes. One way of accomplishing this explication is to make clear what activities or things are denoted by the concept, and what purposes these activities (or things) serve.

An example may help to make the process more explicit. It is an amusing parlor game for idle intellectuals to ask each other to define their respective fields. The answers usually reflect the personal experiences—and ambitions—of the definer. This does not imply, of course, that the meaning of an idea depends only on a person and his problems. But it does suggest that the meanings that are offered depend on what the definer thinks are the purposes of his field of study.

To be more specific, suppose we consider an area of applied science which has recently come to the attention of management in business and industry: "operations research." During the last war the activities of certain scientists were labelled "operations research" because these men studied and analyzed military operations. How shall those who "believe in" the values of these studies make the meaning of their endeavor more explicit? Suppose we compare the problem of the man who tries to define operations research with the problem of defining so simple a concept as "table."

An ostensive, but nonfunctional definition of these two concepts could be accomplished if all reasonable men recognized that there are only a finite number of operations-research activities, or tables. We could then "point" to all such activities and objects, and associate with our pointing some such utterance as "*this* is to be called operations research," or "*this* is to be called a table." If the pointing really did individuate the activities and the objects, then such a process of ostensive defining would succeed in separating operations research, or tables, from other activities or things. But it is difficult to think of instances where such definitions satisfy either intellectual or material needs, and few people would feel inclined to try to reduce all defining to such a "simple" method.

A more fruitful extension of this idea of defining would be to find a set of properties that all reasonable persons would recognize to exist if they were pointed out, and to define operations research, or tables, in terms of a subset of these "ostensive" properties.

Thus, operations research might be defined as the activity of scientifically studying the management problems of complex organizations. Or, a table is an object with a flat top, rigidly supported by legs. Each of these properties: "activity," "scientifically studied," "rigidly supported," and so on, could (presumably) be explained by the simple act of pointing to activities and objects in the world about us which have these properties. Thus, if we give a few examples, everyone may know what a flat top is—shelves and buildings have them, people other than comic-strip characters do not.

But it is reasonable to ask how we decide that a property is to be associated with a concept. Why must all tables be flat? That is, by what decision criterion do we decide that flatness is a necessary condition for tableness? One is inclined to answer, by tradition, until a little reflection shows that man is quite willing to throw over traditional uses of terms when the traditional uses become awkward. The top of a table need not be perfectly flat; it is awkward and ridiculous to insist on such a rigid use of terms.

These rather obvious reflections lead us to conclude that decisions about the meanings of concepts depend on at least two partially conflicting aims. We want to keep open the lines of intelligible communication, and at the same time we want the meanings to reflect our real interests—to be fruitful relative to our most important activities. The "right" definition cannot be ascertained arbitrarily. It cannot be ascertained solely by examining common usage because this decision criterion would only emphasize the aim of mutual understanding. It cannot be ascertained solely by convenience because this decision criterion would only emphasize the aim of reflecting one's interest of the moment. The "correct" decision criterion for the meaning of a concept may be as difficult to provide as decision criteria for other activities of men. These, at least, were the reflections that in Chapter 1 drove us to declare that the meaning of "science" is a problem of national or world-wide policy.

For the time being, we can at least observe that the attempt to find a finite set of properties which all agree are essential and sufficient to define a class or a concept may be quite futile. In the case of tables and operations research, the aim of communication and the aim of fruitfulness both seem to be better served by saying that the definition of a table depends, not on specific structural properties, but on the use to which tables are put. In other words, *what* a table is depends on what tables are for. For example, when is a table not a table? When we cut its legs in half? In quarter? How could one decide when to stop pointing? How does one decide that some monstrocity or creative masterpiece of the modern interior decorator is *not* a table? Just by deciding that the object with legs so short or a top so recessed no longer does what tables are taken to do.

Similarly, when does a scientific study of management become unscientific? When no observation occurs—and the research is just a mathematical exercise? How does one decide that some ingenious intellectualism of a scientist is *not* operations research? Just by deciding that the research with mathematics so long and observation so brief no longer does what operations research is taken to do.

With this much defense of functional definitions, we can conclude the discussion by a more formal characterization of this method of defining. We may begin by noting that objects with totally different properties may produce the same type of result. For example, living things that vary widely in their properties may produce their own type, that is, reproduce. The class of reproducers is defined in terms of the products of its members and not in terms of some inherent structure the elements may have. Now objects that produce never are sufficient conditions for their products: they all require an "environment" or "natural assistance." Thus operations research produces optimal managerial decisions by means of the most economic use of available information—but it only does so if executives cooperate. Or, tables "produce" various activities like writing and eating—but only do so if certain environmental activities also occur.

Hence, there are two conditions which constitute a functional definition: (1) differently structured objects have products with common properties, and (2) the objects alone are never sufficient for this productive activity. Functional definitions consist of a specification of the common products. More exactly, functional definitions classify things or actions in terms of their common *potential* or *probable* products (since not all tables need ever produce that which characterizes tables). More generally, functional definitions may be combined with structural definitions. Thus, a table might be defined as an object with a flat top which potentially produces (along with certain actions) certain types of activity such as eating or writing.

There still remain certain technical problems in clarifying the concept of functional definitions. For example, we have contrasted the "structural properties" of an object with the "potential products" of the object. Vaguely, "structural properties" are components which the researcher uses to construct a state of nature at a specific moment of time, provided his construct includes a principle of individuation and a set of relations between individuated elements. "Products" are the individuated elements of a later state of nature which bear a certain relationship to the components of the earlier state. A more detailed account of "properties" and "products" can be postponed until the Appendix of Chapter 7 because we do not now intend to develop a precise functional definition of measurement but rather to suggest the technical problems that a functional definition implies.

3 · A Functional Definition of Measurement.

Our discussion has led us to ask the very obvious question: Why measure? A functional definition of the process of measurement is a statement of the relevant products of this process in terms of which one might answer this question.

We begin by making a suggestion in order to see where it leads us: the potential product of a measurement process is a certain type of information. What seems to characterize this information is its precision and its generality. Measurements are used when we feel the need for making "fine" distinctions. Measurements are also used when we want to employ results obtained in one circumstance (for example, a laboratory or an inspection station), in totally different circumstances (for example, in building a plane). Can we capture these two desiderata of the measurement process in one general functional definition? Suppose we say that the potential product of the measurement process is information which will have a "wide use" in decision-making. "Width" of usage will be taken to include both the satisfaction of the need to distinguish and the need to generalize. In other words, in the same environment one piece of information has "wider" usage if it can be used for more (potential) decisions, and in a set of environments one piece of information has "wider" usage if it can be used (potentially) in more environments in the set.

If it is true that we measure because we want to create widely useful information, then we must also recognize that we sacrifice a great deal of time and effort in the process of obtaining the information and defining the circumstances and procedures of its use. In contrast, another type of information which is *not* measurement is one in which we sacrifice very little time or effort in obtaining the information, but the information has very restricted use. This contrast will be important when we turn to the economics of measurement: it will be clear that there is no virtue in measuring *per se*. Measurements are expensive products.

It should be noted that by "information" we mean recorded experience which is useful for decision-making. In other words, in the sequel we will be considering information from the point of view of its effect on decisions that people make. Information in this sense differs from information as the term is used in some aspects of current information theory. See Ackoff's discussion in (2).

In the sense in which we use the term, the statement that a pill contains 5 gr. of aspirin is information if it partially determines the actions of a patient or a doctor. But the statement that Lincoln died in 1865 may not be information—unless it is useful on a quiz show, or "satisfies curiosity."

This meaning of information is not restricted to the everyday activities of everyday man. A scientist or artist may use information to decide on the correct experimental design, or the correct color. The action choices relative to which statements become information may be political or criminal, esoteric or communal.

There are, of course, a number of questions to be raised about this characterization of information. For example, it makes the existence of information dependent on the person and the context. For the astronomer, the speed of light *in vacuo* may be information; for most of the rest of us it is not. For an executive reading a report (for example, a monthly Profit-and-Loss Statement) the variances reported by the production department may mean very little. For him, the variances are not information—yet. But gross sales, or trends in sales by product lines, may determine specific actions on his part, and these are information.

If we think of the potential future of a certain empirical report, we may begin to conceptualize a meaning of the "amount" of information contained in the report which is independent of particular decision-makers. We could define the "amount" of information contained in a statement in terms of the utility of the statement for various potential decision-making purposes in various contexts. Of course, we have no such scale, and for present purposes we will have to rest content with an intuitive notion. Presumably information has high or low utility depending on the scope of its usefulness to various decision-makers, in various contexts. The technology of developing a scale of "amount of information" in this sense would involve the difficult considerations of defining "potential decision-makers," their "potential" problems, and the usefulness of the information for problem-solving. But we may note that if such a scale could be developed, we would then be in a position better to define the measurement process: its potential product is information high on this scale.

This characterization of measurement seems reasonable because it does encompass the notion of precision and usefulness. It gives point to the costly efforts men must make to generate satisfactory measurements. It highlights the fact that numbers "by themselves" are not measurements, no matter how carefully assigned. It does imply that many of the statistics about populations which load our reference books are not measurements. Finally, it contrasts the costs of information with the amount of information. This contrast will be the theme of the remainder of this chapter.

Before proceeding to this theme, we should recognize one aspect of measurement which may be implicit in the characterization just offered, but which needs to be made explicit. One of the most significant aspects of modern science is the realization that one does not measure unless one also measures the error of the measurement. In plainer language, measurement includes the process of control. In lessplain language, measurement is an organization of experience in which information is "fed back" concerning the accuracy of the measurements. "Accuracy" entails information about the possible deviations of the measurements from reality. According to the philosophical viewpoint adopted here, this means that accuracy is information about the value of the measurements from the point of view of the outcomes of the actions which have been partially determined by them. One of the most significant results of modern scientific method has been the ability to estimate accuracy without knowing exactly what reality is, that is, what the best action is.

We can therefore restate the proposal of this chapter in the following way: measurement, defined functionally, is the organization of experiences in such a way that they codetermine purposive decisions in a wide variety of contexts—where the organization is subject to control.

4 · *Decision Problems of Measurement.*

This proposal is, of course, very tentative. It needs defending in terms of the historical usage of the term measurement and the practice of measurement. And, as we mentioned earlier, we have no scales that precisely define "wide variety," that is, amount of information. But in a book that is frankly programmatic, we can go ahead and act as though we knew what the proposal means to a sufficient extent to enable us to develop the problems entailed in such a functional definition.

We can begin by noting one striking consequence of the proposal. The objective of measurement can be accomplished in a number of ways. The qualitative assignment of objects to classes, or the assignment of numbers to objects are two means at the disposal of the measurer for generating a high degree of useful information. But which means is better? The striking consequence of the proposal is that measurement is a decision-making activity, and as such is to be evaluated by decision-making criteria.

In this sense, of measurement taken as a decision-making activity designed to accomplish an objective, we have as yet no theory of measurement. We do not know why we do what we do. We do not even know why we measure at all. It is costly to obtain measurements. Is the effort worth the cost?

I have no intention of developing a complete functional theory of measurement here. Instead, I want to reconsider some of the well-known aspects of measurement in the light of the tentative proposal given above. In each case, I want to ask what alternative decisions the measurer has, and to what extent he has guides that enable him to select the best alternative. The topics selected for discussion do not necessarily represent the best way of organizing measurement activities; I have selected them because they have each received considerable attention in the literature on measurement. In each case it will be found that the measurer is caught between at least two desirable aims, and the more he attempts to succeed in one aim, the more he must sacrifice another—which is the typical problem setting of the decision-maker.

The topics to be considered are: (1) the selection of a *language,* (2) *specification* of the items and their properties, (3) *standardization* of the information to permit adjustment to various times and places, and (4) *accuracy* and *control* of the measurement process.

There is a distortion which I will have to introduce in order to discuss these topics: the method of deciding how to handle any one of the problems does eventually involve consideration of all the rest. But the main point here is to show that a true decision problem does occur in the case of each of the four topics, rather than to suggest how the decision problem is to be solved.

5 · *Language.*

The measurer must develop a language which adequately communicates to another person what the user must do to utilize the information contained in the measurement. The emphasis here is on the language of communication.

One aim of the language of measurement is to communicate to as many potential users as possible since this will increase the scope of utilization. But another aim is to enable the user to employ the information when there is need for fine distinctions since this also will increase the scope of utilization. These two aims are apparently in conflict—the more common the language the more difficult it is to use the language for portraying fine distinctions.

In order to understand the nature of this conflict, we need to consider certain aspects of the philosophy of language. Indeed, one such philosophy suggests how one can escape through the horns of the dilemma we have introduced. Suppose there are some "fundamental" operations which can be described in unequivocal language, so that virtually every intelligent person will understand what is meant, or can be trained to understand. Suppose, too, we can find a process by which other operations can be understood in terms of these more elementary ones, and that these operations permit greater and greater refinement. If this were so, then we could accomplish *both* a wide scope of communication and a great depth of utilization of measurement. One example of a simple operation might be the comparison of straight rods; by successive steps we go from the "simple" language of comparison to the more complicated language of measuring the distances between the planets. Another example of a "simple" operation is the preference comparison of commodities; we may try to go from the "simple" language of preferences to the more complicated language of utilities.

It should be noted that "simplicity" in this account has a two-fold meaning. A concept is semantically simple (1) if we can simply verify or refute certain statements containing the concept, and (2) if we can simply transmit the information to others. As we mentioned earlier, it is not sufficient in science for an idea to be clear to one person since science is a communicating activity. Hence, if there are simple ideas, they must be simple to communicate as well as simple to identify empirically.

But throughout this book there runs the theme that the search for ultimately simple and clear ideas is bound to fail because the test for clarity itself involves ideas that are not clear according to any acceptable definition of clarity (for example, "agreement of usage," or "similarity of response to the same stimulus"). Hence, though there may be clear ideas, there is no clear way of defending their clarity, and from the point of view of science, which insists on the permission to test everything testable, there is no basis for asserting that some ideas are ultimately clear.

The second approach to a language of measurement consists of giving up the notion of a hierarchy of meaning altogether. Instead, one tries to construct a conceptual framework in which there are a number of "ultimate" bases—or sets of semantically primitive ideas. This approach, which is the one adopted here, is similar to that used by most dictionaries, though the exact methodology of dictionary construction is often difficult to discern. Dictionaries usually do not list a set of ultimately clear ideas and then attempt to define all other notions in terms of them. Instead, the dictionary assumes that each reader has some set of ideas that are clear for him, and with such a set he can intelligibly read the dictionary and understand other ideas. Two readers do not have to agree with respect to the ideas that they understand; each will "look up" different words, and each will use different aspects of the definition the dictionary gives.

No dictionary attempts to provide the rules for the intelligibility of the dictionary—if such were feasible. But the language of science is circumscribed, and it is at least conceivable that a conceptual framework could be constructed for scientific measurement in such a way that there are alternative sets of ideas which can form the basis of intelligibility of the whole language. One such attempt which has been made in this direction will be discussed in Chapter 7, where we shall recognize that "X prefers A at least as much as B" may be taken as clear in a provisional sense, by asserting that this sentence is to be accepted as valid if and only if X chooses A instead of B. But this meaning of preference depends on the meaning of "choice." We then try to explain the conditions which define a true choice. This explanation will introduce other terms; specifically, "X chooses A" is true if and only if X is actually a producer of his own act. This explanation requires an explanation of "producer." And so on.

Now we do not know enough—yet—about the process of communication to be able to specify how concepts should be interrelated. The extension of the scheme discussed in Chapter 7 is essentially a circular one. A set of concepts of logic, mathematics, and physics are used to define certain biological, psychological, social, and ethical ideas which can then be used to define the ideas of logic, mathematics, and physics. The construction of the scheme is such that at various points in the circle one can determine sets of ideas sufficiently rich to define all the rest. But a circular scheme is itself somewhat restricted and probably not realistic as a representation of a communication system. For one thing, it is unnecessary in many cases to develop all the intermediary ideas on the rim of the circle in order to connect two given ideas intelligibly. For example, some sociological concepts can be defined in terms of biological concepts only, without the intermediary concepts of psychology. A "lattice" framework probably represents the most general model of a conceptual scheme for science.[1] Hence the communication scheme

---

[1] The following comments seem important in clarifying this discussion of a "lattice theory" of meaning:

(1) The argument for eliminating semantical primitives in scientific language has no relevance to the role of primitives in purely formal languages. The formal logician does not assume that these primitives are ultimately clear—indeed he often constructs alternative sets of primitives for a given axiom set. The formal logician does seem to assume that certain ultimately clear ideas exist in what is called the metalanguage, that is, the language which talks about the formal system and tells one what can and what cannot be done in it. However, the purpose of the metalanguage is much like the purpose

developed in Chapter 7 is only tentative and suggestive of the further research needed to characterize adequately an optimal communication system for science.

We assume, then, that one ultimate aim of the language of measurements is to relate the meanings of the measured items and their properties to all other meanings of science. A more restricted aim consists of relating these meanings to a set of meanings assumed to be understood by a given class of decision-makers. Thus, although physicists may be able to explain the ideas of physics to other physicists (that is, decision-makers of their own class), it may not be possible or desirable to explain them to psychologists or business executives.

If the aim of the language of science can be described in terms of the interrelationship of concepts, then the decision problems to be discussed in the subsequent sections of this chapter are real ones. These problems do center around a conflict of objectives—often between the objective of a wide range of communication and the objective of precision. The objectives conflict, because the more we succeed in attaining the one, the more costly it is to attain the other. The methodology of the language of measurement is a decision process by means of which we try to establish at any given stage an optimal balance between the two basic objectives of measurement: breadth and depth of information.

The conflicts entailed in reaching an optimal solution can best be illustrated by considering one aspect of the language of measurement which is concerned with the logical relationships between entities. In some measurements, one attempts to assign objects to classes, in others one tries to establish specific relationships, in still others one

---

of the rules of a game or the programming of a computing machine, so that a good deal of informal testing of the adequacy of the metalanguage's "primitive ideas" actually takes place.

(2) The notion of reductionism and primitive ideas in the empirical sciences is relevant to the present argument. Operationism, for example, seems to have been taken by many writers as a successful insistence on reduction of ideas to a set of "primitive operations." If operationism means that the system of scientific concepts must include operational notions, there could be no objection. If it means that all concepts are definable in terms of a set of operational ideas, then it is no more than a hypothesis—albeit a rather plausible one. If it means that unless all concepts are explicitly defined in terms of operational ideas, they fail to be clear, then it is also an hypothesis—and a very dubious one. Sociologists might reasonably be expected to insist that the "ultimate" tests of clarity and meaningfulness of scientific ideas is their institutional reference— *not* their relation to "simply performable" operations.

attempts to assign numbers. These attempts constitute an important part of the definition of the informational reports. The decision making conflict between simplicity of operations and precision requirements occurs for each type of logical relationship, but generally the assignment of numbers serves precision more adequately than does assignment to classes. It is for this reason that some writers have defined measurement in terms of the generation of informational reports in which numbers are assigned to objects. However, a functional definition of measurement makes any such restrictive definition untenable; assignment to classes may provide very precise information which can be widely used, while certain types of number assignments may be useless.

6 · *Class Assignments.*

Certain informational reports presuppose a language within which one can speak of classes, each defined by a specific set of properties, and that it is clear to the person making the report as well as to the persons receiving the report, what it means to say that an item belongs to one of the classes. Furthermore, it is operationally clear to the observer, in terms of his observations, when an item does belong to a class and when it does not.

This means that the information is in the form "x is in classes a, b, c, and so on, but not in classes d, e, f, and so on." A rather obvious example of this type of information is the stop light. If the light is red, then one adopts no action; if it is green, one moves. The use of litmus paper provides essentially the same kind of information. The assignment of living bodies to species is yet another example. Again, a housewife wants to buy untainted pork, and needs to know which items do and which do not fall into this category. In industrial decision-making, class assignment occurs when production items are reported "good" or "bad," or accounts receivable "collectable" or "uncollectable," and so forth.

At first sight, the language of classes seems to be the most adequate for communication purposes, that is, it is apparently least costly in time and effort to transmit information in this way. But, although class assignment is sometimes simple to understand, it does not follow that it is easy to accomplish: it may not be simple to ascertain whether an item belongs to a class, and it may not be simple to communicate the information. Deciding that a piece of meat is untainted does require the construction of refined standards, and in all likelihood the decision will presuppose measurements involving numbers. Hence, one should not assume in general that class assignments are the cheapest way of transmitting information.

Suppose we examine the costs entailed in the proper utilization of a class-assignment language. The language itself, as are all communication languages, is governed by certain rules. These rules are, in effect, the means by which a decision-maker uses the information expressed in the language. What are the rules of the language of class assignment? This is a question familiar to the student of logic, but a review of some of the textbook answers will help us to understand better the assumptions that underlly this type of informational report.

Suppose, then, that a set of classes has been constructed, which we may designate as *a, b, c,* and so on. In order to make a report about every item, we must be able to show that each item belongs to at least one of the classes. Is this requirement so obvious that its mention serves only to prolong the discussion? The answer depends on human experience: Is it often the case that information is requested as to whether an item is in *a* or *b* when it turns out to be in neither? For example, do executives ever ask whether a new plant should be located in *X, Y,* or *Z* when it shouldn't be located in any of these places? Or whether inventories should be continued at the present level or decreased, when they should be increased? I assume that this type of experience occurs often enough to warrant some consideration of the "obvious" principle stated above, which requires that the classes exhaust the possibilities. A lover of sea shells is said to have constructed the most beautiful and perfect classification of all conceivable shells, so perfect indeed that when he chanced on one that belonged to none of his classes—he stepped on it.

The point is that a perfectly "adequate" language of class assignments must meet all potential informational requirements, that is, must provide an exhaustive classification. There is one rather easy way to develop a language that meets this requirement: let *a, b, c* be any three classes given initially. Then the universe of items can be divided neatly into eight compartments—and every item must belong to one, and only one, of these compartments. We accomplish this by letting Part I be the class of items belonging to *a* and *b* and *c;* let us call it *abc*. Part II is the class of items belonging to *a* and *b* but not to *c;* call it *abc'*. It's easy to see that the remaining parts are *ab'c, a'bc, ab'c', a'bc', a'b'c, a'b'c'*. We need not worry if some of these compartments are empty; our only concern is whether they exhaust the possibilities.

Now our executive can't go wrong. For if *X, Y, Z* stand for the locations of the new plant, *X'Y'Z'* will stand for none of these locations, and this possibility is automatically included.

Has this simple device solved the problem? It has met the formal conditions that every item must belong to at least one of the classes. But measurements are useful information. In the case of the executive worried about plant location, the information should enable him to make a decision. But the report might be useless if, for example, no new plant should be constructed. Then the partition is faulty, because *X'Y'Z'* may mean "no plant" or "plant at some place other than *X, Y, Z.*" One criterion for a suitable partition, therefore, is that information about the membership in each part is useful in arriving at a decision. Thus, although it is not too difficult to partition a universe in the manner just described, it may be quite difficult to show that the partitioning is optimal relative to the users of the information. The "basis" of the language is an assumption that the partitions do convey an adequate amount of information.

Thus a language structure which provides a very simple set of classes can be widely understood, and the cost of transmitting the information may be small. On the other hand, such a language will be inadequate for the purpose of detailed decision making. The objectives of wide usage and precision conflict.

There are other examples of the way in which formal rules of a language become the basis of defining a not-so-obvious measurement decision problem. It is often desirable from the point of view of the decision-maker that, if an item is assigned to one partition, it can be assumed not to belong to any other. But guaranteeing this rule may be very costly because it can easily happen that on one occasion an item is assigned to one class and on another it is assigned to some other. This is not at all improbable; anyone familiar with inspection procedures knows that even the most carefully controlled inspection process may accept an item today, and, on reinspection by the same process tomorrow, reject it. Personnel managers are undoubtedly aware that the screening of prospective employees does not necessarily select people for employment in a consistent fashion. The point here is that the stated rule for assigning items to classes may not in practice lead to a consistent assignment, where "consistency" means that an item is assigned to one class only. In other words, in order to be informative, it is better that the report be so designed that if an item is assigned to a class, it will not be assigned to any other class. If this structure is known by the recipient of the report, he knows in part how to use the report. But the only way to guarantee the structure is to test the rule of assignment, and this may be very costly. The decision problem is again a problem of balancing two conflicting objectives.

We may mention, in concluding the discussion of this type of measurement language, some other desirable rules of class assignments: (1) if x is assigned to a and a is so defined as to be included in b, then x must be assigned to b as well; and, (2) if x is assigned to a, and to either b or c (or possibly both), then x must be assigned to a and b or to a and c (or possibly both).

These "laws of logic" constitute some of the criteria of consistency of class assignment. Logic, which often seems the most trivial of the sciences to the beginning student, actually forms the basis of some of the most difficult problems of science—so difficult that on occasion a philosopher will feel inclined to modify the logical principle in despair of finding a method of class assignment that meets its requirements. Too often logic courses emphasize the rules of deduction, which are the least-useful aspect of logic for the college student. One cannot help feeling that elementary logic courses should attempt to teach the student how to organize a system of assignments of objects to classes which will meet certain consistency requirements and, at the same time, be informative.

Before leaving this subject, we should point out that the "consistency" rules are not absolute or fixed. Rule (1), above, could fail, for example; in this case, "is included in" would have a special (and unusual) meaning. But if this meaning were understood by the recipients of the report, there would be nothing essentially wrong with the procedure.

7 · *Relations.*

Another type of informational report consists, not in assigning items to classes, but in assigning a relationship between items. Essentially the same comments that were given above apply here as well. The formal aspects of the relation must be set down by deciding how the report about a relation between two or more items is to be used. The reports that are generated by the measurement process must then be tested to see if they meet the formal demands.

For example, one might be interested in deciding whether two living beings have the same ancestral line. There are a number of ways of doing this, but the "sibling" relationship will serve as an example. The items to be studied are organisms that have two parents, and "is the sibling of" means "has both parents in common with." We may agree on certain properties of this relationship (R) over a given set of individuals, $x, y, z, \ldots$:

(a) Either $x R y$ holds or $x R y$ is false, and not both. (This is similar to the exhaustiveness and exclusiveness criteria mentioned in connection with class assignment).

(b) If $x R y$ and $y R z$, then $x R z$ (x and z being distinct). This asserts that the sibling relation is "transitive." It may be noted again that a certain process of establishing a sibling relationship may fail to satisfy this "obvious" formal property; for example, if comparisons of certain features were made the basis of establishing siblings, x and y might satisfy the comparisons, as might y and z, but x and z might not.

(c) If $x R y$, then $y R x$. This asserts that the sibling relation is "symmetrical"—again an obvious result of the meaning of the concept. But (naïvely, to be sure) one might test for the absence of a sibling relationship by determining whether, for opposite sexes, x tries to mate y. Thus x and y might satisfy all other sibling tests, and x fail on this test and y not. The measurement process would thus fail relative to its purposes since symmetry would not hold.

The last example brings out the decision problems of relational languages. One way of assigning a relation such as "is the sibling of" may be cheap in terms of time and effort, yet fail to convey a certain type of precise information, for example, for legal decisions. In order to improve on the amount of information, for example, by guaranteeing symmetry, one incurs operational costs. The measurement problem is the proper balance of these conflicting objectives.

8 · *Orderings.*

The class of relations most commonly used in scientific measurements are the relations that place items in an order. Such relations are clearly important as codeterminers of action since many human decisions are based on whether one object lies "below" or "above" another with respect to some property: industry wants to minimize costs or maximize returns; students are judged on the basis of the highest, or lowest, point average; and so on. In each case, the kind of ordering depends on the uses to which the measurements are to be put. If the action is based on the "highest" or "most" or "best," then a simple ordering relationship may suffice.

Any ordering relationship, R, satisfies at least these three conditions:

(a) If $x \, R \, y$ and $y \, R \, z$, then $x \, R \, z$ (R is transitive over the set of items).

(b) Either $x \, R \, y$ or $y \, R \, x$ (R has closure over the set).

(c) If both $x \, R \, y$ and $y \, R \, x$, then x and y have the same position in the ordering (R is "antisymmetric" over the set).

If a finite set of items satisfies these conditions, and R means "at least as good as," then there will be at least one item that is at the "top," that is, a most-preferred item.

As in the other types of measurement, there may be an insufficient guarantee that the rules of ordering a set of objects actually hold. A very common example of this failure occurs when the "items" do not remain stable in time. It is well known that "x beats or ties y" does not, in general, enable one to order the teams of a baseball or football league. That is, if one tried to establish "x is at least as good as y" by the condition "x beats or ties y," the transitivity axiom quite commonly will be found to fail. Yet in many instances there is no other feasible way of ascertaining whether one team is better than another except by trying to adapt the easily discernible condition of being a victor to fit the rules of ordering.

In general, it is extremely difficult to find measuring methods that order items "consistently" *and* significantly. It is not so difficult to find methods for ordering objects—any arbitrary assignment of numbers does this. What is difficult is to find an ordering method that does what it is supposed to do. In many cases, condition (c) is quite important in this respect. This condition assigns equal rank if both $x \, R \, y$ and $y \, R \, x$. The class of items with the same rank is sometimes rather aptly called an indifference class. In preference orderings, if x and y have the same rank, then the action, say, of selecting x has about the same effectiveness as selecting y. Thus one might tell a visitor that "all other things being equal" Department Store A is as good as B for quality and variety, meaning that it is a matter of indifference which one he selects to shop in.

One could "order" a set of objects by constructing a relationship that puts them all in the same indifference class, which would clearly be a nonsignificant measurement process. In practice, therefore, there is an additional requirement imposed on the size of the indifference classes—or at least on the size of the "top" or "bottom" class—often to the effect that it have but one member. This means that there is one and only one item that stands in the relation R to all other items, provided $x \, R \, y$ means that x is at least as high as y in the ordering. It is this restriction on the size of indifference classes that poses one of the most difficult problems or ordering, as any executive has come to realize who is faced with the problem of choosing his successor without recourse to flipping a coin.

9 · Number Assignment.

So far, we have said nothing about numbers, which may appear odd to a mind accustomed to thinking of measurement as quantification. Of course, the ordering of a finite set of objects does assign a rank number, and we usually assign "*1*" to the lowest (or to the highest) and consecutive digits for each of the other items in order. But for communication purposes other numbering schemes may be better. In the selection of an applicant, the decision-maker may want to avoid any argument; he gives the highest candidate a "score" well above the next in line. Most college administrative offices prefer that professors omit the minus or plus after a grade, and many professors have found this to be a wise policy in order to avoid discussion.

Thus a given way of assigning numbers to rank orders may be

preferable to another way because it communicates clearer information. It is certainly unrealistic to say that the number assignment to rank orders is purely arbitrary—as though the measurer could safely ignore the attitudes of the recipients of the measurement report. Quite often, a method of number assignment to rank orders introduces confusion. For example, the assignment of intelligence scores has undoubtedly led some of the "lay" public to think that the difference of ten points is like the difference of ten inches in measurements of length.

There are ways of assigning numbers to objects and people that do more than express a rank order. There is, for example, a legitimate sense in which we can say that one object is twice as long as another. Evidently, this says a great deal more than the assertion that one object is longer than another.

One way to organize experience to go beyond an ordering of objects, is to set up a process that permits comparisons of *differences* in the rank orders assigned to items. Thus one is able to assert that the difference between item *a* and item *b* is greater than the differences between *c* and *d*. This kind of assertion cannot be made about some intelligence or attitude scores, or many of the other methods of assigning numbers used by psychologists and sociologists. Yet at some time it may become important to know that the difference in intelligence between *A* and *B* is greater than that between *C* and *D*: for example, in the optimal design of cooperative teams which may depend on differences in intelligence of the team members.

Similar remarks apply to costs in industrial organizations. Very often, there is no way of establishing the relative seriousness of cost differences. A "variance" in a standard cost-accounting system is supposedly a measure of the deviation of a given cost from a "standard" cost. That is, a variance is a measure of a cost difference. But to date there is no generally accepted method of comparing different variances. We do know, of course, that one variance is much greater than another in dollar magnitude. But variances only become measurements if they are useful for decision-making purposes. In this respect, a large dollar variance for one type of operation may be insignificant compared to a small dollar variance for another operation, especially if no one is to blame for the first, and someone is clearly to blame for the second. In such a case, it is quite sensible to say that the smaller *dollar* variance is actually a greater "cost" difference than the larger dollar variance. Indeed, the larger dollar variance may be a zero "cost" relative to managerial decision-making. As Chapter 3 indicated, we often have no general way of making such managerial cost comparisons.

There is another formalization of experience which yields a different meaning to number assignments. In the case of rank orders, we argued that the assignment of numbers to ranks may not be arbitrary. There may be one assignment, or a class of assignments, which represents the optimal way of transmitting information. In many cases, we do not know what assignment is best because we cannot state all the desirable uses of the information. But there are measurement processes which can be shown empirically to conform to certain formal requirements from which it can be deduced that only a certain class of number assignments is permissible. That is, the class of number assignments is restricted by the nature of the measurement process, and not by the ultimate uses of the measurements. Such is the case of measurements of length or mass. We can measure length in inches, meters, rods, fathoms, and so on. But once we have agreed on the unit for any item, we are committed to that unit for all other items. A somewhat stronger and more precise statement is the following: if the measuring process assigns numbers $x_1, x_2, \ldots x_n$ to each of n items, then there is an alternative and legitimate process that assigns numbers $ax_1 + b, ax_2 + b, \ldots ax_n + b$, where a and b are arbitrary constants. But also *only* those processes that assign numbers of the form $ax_1 + b, ax_2 + b, \ldots$ are legitimate. In this case we say that the number assignment is "unique up to a linear transformation."

But to construct a method of assigning numbers which satisfies this requirement is usually very costly. The contrast of objectives which has been the theme of this discussion is all the more apparent here. A large amount of information may be conveyed by a number assignment that is unique up to a linear transformation in the sense that rather refined predictions are possible for decision-making purposes, but the effort entailed in guaranteeing the requirement may be very great. Furthermore, as Chapter 8 will suggest, the generality of the information may be very low.

Enough has been said to illustrate how measurement reports can be classified and the kinds of decision problems that occur. Reference (10) and works cited in the articles appearing there give a fuller

treatment of this subject and more precise descriptions of the classifications.

10 · *Economics of Measurement Language.*

The point that has been made here is that the measurer has to decide
which form of informational report is optimal for his purposes, and
for any choice he makes he must optimize between the economy of
reporting and the need for detail. The informational reports are said
to be measurements if they have wide use for many decisions, regardless of their form. One could argue instead that measurement consists
of finding the methods of complying with "ideal" languages, that is,
ones in which at least certain minimal rules are met. The most extreme viewpoint would be that measurement is the process of assigning numbers unique up to a linear transformation, and that processes failing to do this are not measurements. But such a viewpoint
would be inadequate for the problem proposed by this chapter because it fails to consider measurement in functional terms. The position would be defensible only if it could be shown that a certain type
of language always provides the maximum amount of information, and
even in this case we would feel justified in asking whether alternative methods exist which provide as much information at less cost.

So far, there exists no acceptable theory for deciding on the proper
measurement language for any given situation. We have become
sophisticated enough to know that "scaling" and "scoring" are not
necessarily valuable; we have yet to provide a basis for determining
which measurement method is most valuable in a given context.

The implication of this conclusion is that we have no adequate
basis for deciding what kind of measurement is most appropriate for
measuring values. The next chapters present various kinds of value
measurements without commitment concerning the relative merits of
each kind.

The discussion so far has shown that our ignorance of the economics of value measurements is not peculiar to the study of values.
Measurement theory, in the sense of a theory that establishes an
optimal measurement process, does not exist—even if the utilization
of the measurements is restricted to "pure" science. It is true that in
this book the illustrations of decision-making are usually drawn from
the world outside the ivory tower, but this is only because so little is

known of the structure of decision-making inside the tower. In Chapter 14 we shall try to develop some hypotheses about this structure.

We turn now to some of the other aspects of measurement, in which similar economic problems will appear.

11 · *Specification.*

The problem of the specification of measurement is one of deciding what objects are being described and under what circumstances. This is simply the problem of deciding on the scope of application of the measurements in terms of time, place, and individuated items. This is not a decision about how the application is to be made, which will be considered under another head.

The economic problem is easy to discern in this instance. It would be very valuable if we could develop information that could be used in connection with all our problems. But the more general information becomes, the more expensive it becomes to acquire, or else the more useless it becomes in any specific context.

Perhaps one illustration will suffice. In the theory of detonation, we would like to measure the sensitivity of various compounds. It would be very satisfactory if we could measure how sensitive a piece of mercury fulminate is wherever the piece may be, no matter what its size, and no matter what is happening to it. But we do not do this at all. The term "sensitive" applies only to compounds which have a specific kind of shape and which exist in a specific class of environments (for example, in a laboratory). We restrict the term to these items and environments because we feel it would be entirely too costly to try to extend the scope beyond them, relative to the gains made from the more extensive information. Generalizing, each measurer is involved in the economic problems of balancing the "costs" of extending the application of measurement, and the "returns." We shall call the environments in which a given set of measurements can be used for decision-making purposes the class of "relevant" environments of the set. The (unsolved) economic problem is to determine the optimal class of relevant environments. The solution of this problem clearly depends on our ability to adjust information so that it can be used in various contexts. This ability depends on the process of standardization, to which we now turn.

12 · *Standardization.*

Measurements enable one to use information obtained in one circumstance in any other circumstance belonging to the class of relevant environments. In searching for a suitable title under which this problem could be discussed, I could find no better one than "standards." Standards of measurement are designed to provide a basis for adjusting experience in widely different contexts. And though the term is usually meant in a narrower sense than the one adopted here, the purpose of standards so exactly corresponds to the concept of "extent of applicability" that the use of the term seems legitimate.

Briefly, the standardization of measurement has two parts: (1) a specification of the circumstances under which observation should take place, plus properties that constitute qualified observers, plus the operations to be performed by the observers in order to arrive at a measurement report, and (2) a specification of the steps required to utilize the report under conditions different from the "standard" conditions where the observations were made. Both of these parts entail many problems. The first has occupied a great deal of attention in recent years, especially because there has been some attempt to make it central to the whole meaning of measurement, that is, the operations are supposed to define what the measurement means. It is not clear why this aspect of the total scheme of measurement should be singled out for such an important role. Certainly any comprehensive theory of measurement must also include a theory of the standardization of measurement: that is, the utilization of measurements in many different contexts. Perhaps this aspect of measurement is often neglected because it is assumed that the problem is trivial, or not nearly as important as setting up an adequate language or satisfactory operational meanings. And yet even a casual inspection of the process of measurement shows how very intricate and delicate is the operation of standardizing measurement readings.

The problem we are considering is based in part on an almost obvious observation that not all human experience takes place at the same time or in the same circumstance. Even if there were but one mind in all the world, such a castaway would need to compare the experience of one moment and place with that of another moment and place. He would have to communicate with his own past. The devices that men have used to make these comparisons are many indeed. One of the most direct methods consists of reconstructing each experience into an experience of a given moment and a given time; that is, the present experience is "adjusted" into the experience that would have taken place under some standard set of conditions. This is not the only way in which experiences of various moments can be communicated, but it is a very powerful device. Robinson Crusoe cannot bring along his hut as he searches for a flagstone for his hearth. But he does need to compare an experience on the beach with a past experience in his hut. He does this (say) by the use of a piece of string. He argues that if the string length fits the flagstone, the flagstone will fit the hearth. What he is really saying is that each experience—of the hearth and the flagstone—can be adjusted to a comparison with the string under "standard" conditions.

The general purpose of standards can now be made clear. One wants to be able to assert that x has property y under conditions z at time t in such a manner that the information contained in the assertion can be used in a wide number of other conditions and times to enable many different kinds of people to make decisions. The assertion that company x had a net income of y dollars in the United States during 1919 means nothing at all unless there is some way in which this property can be compared with a net income in 1956, say —or in England. Hence, the need for a "standard" dollar. Even the standard dollar doesn't accomplish the desired result of transmitting meaningful information, if the circumstances in which the company operated (for example, in the postwar economy) are different from the circumstances of today (cold-war economy).

The decision problem of standards arises because of two rather obvious needs. First of all, one wants to find a method of measurement such that a minimum amount of adjustment is required when times, places, and people change. This desire for simplification is based on an economic motive. For example, it is well known that the length of a metal rod may change radically under different conditions. Therefore, rather elaborate and often expensive procedures have to be followed in order to know how to utilize information about length in a given context. But now consider a report that an item is blue, or that a bar is "long." Even though circumstances change, the report will still be valid. Thus, very little effort may be needed to adjust such reports.

Opposed to this cost of adjusting data is the cost of imprecision. There is a need to differentiate aspects of the world we live in. The planning of a large meeting only demands a rough notion of the size of the crowd—say, between 2000 and 3000—in order to select a meeting hall economically. But the planning of a dinner meeting requires much greater precision. And decisions about the qualities of drugs, bridges, and planes, all demand extreme precision. This is the same point that was made in connection with the form of informational reports; class assignments frequently, but by no means always, require less effort to adjust than do certain number-assignment reports.

It requires little reflection to see that the aim of minimizing the effort to adjust data usually conflicts with the aim of precision. In effect, the "cost" of adjusting data rises as more precision is attained, just as the cost of the absence of precision goes up as we attempt to find "simpler" data. For example, suppose a witness reports on an accident. Is the report useful? Perhaps he reports that one car was going faster than the speed limit, or that it hit the other car. Naïvely, we might think that this report needs no adjustment. It is good as it stands. But there are countless instances in which such reports have been shown to be faulty, and these instances have pointed to the need for adjusting the reports. For example, what is meant by saying that one car was seen to be speeding more rapidly than another? As a first approximation, the witness who saw this was "reliable." What does "reliable" mean? As a second approximation, had any other normal person been at the scene, he would have made the same report. What does "normal person" mean? As a third approximation, a normal person has an intelligence quotient in a certain range, with emotional factors below a certain level of intensity, with vision in a certain range, and so on. The adjustment procedure consists of infering what would have been observed had a normal observer made the report.

It may be noted that defense attorneys often argue that the witness's report is *not* adjustable to this standard because the witness is too excitable, or prejudiced, or known to exaggerate, and so on. Usually, when the witness is shown to have a property significantly different from the standard, his report is rejected. In this case, we can say that the "adjustment" has been a rejection. This terminology will enable us to emphasize the economic gains that occur when "unreliable" reports can be adjusted to reliable ones, rather than rejected. If we knew, for example, that a witness was normal on all counts except that he had an emotional instability of a certain type, then we might be able to adjust his report to the report that would have occurred if a completely normal person had been at the scene of the accident. Thus, we might say, "Even granting that the witness was excited, still his report that the car was going faster than the speed limit is valid." We could make statements like this if we could establish a law relating visual reports in various circumstances to the degree of a specific emotional disturbance. Thus in laboratory work it is not necessary to discard the readings of a "slow" observer if we can find a method of adjusting his readings, perhaps by adding a constant to each one.

Hence there are three "levels" of standardization of data. The first tries to restrict itself to data reports that are virtually certain to remain invariant with time and place so that zero adjustment is required. This level minimizes the cost of adjustment, but the data themselves have little precision and consequently little value where refined distinctions are needed. The second level consists of rejecting data not collected under standard conditions. The method of adjustment is simple—but the waste of information may be considerable. The third level consists of adjusting all or almost all data to standards by means of "laws" that enable one to say: if report R_1 was made at time t_1 in circumstance z_1 by a person having properties w_{11}, w_{12}, and so on, then report R_0 would have been made at time t_0 in circumstance z_0 by a person having properties w_{01}, w_{02}, and so on. The last level most closely approximates the function of measurement, because it permits the broadest use of the information.

It seems natural enough to ask why reports should be adjusted to a standard report. If laws exist that enable one to adjust in the manner stated above, why not adjust directly from one circumstance to the problem context, without going through the medium of a standard? The reason for standardized data is easy enough to give. Without standards, one would have to report all the relevant information about the time, place, persons, and so on, in addition to the data report itself. Otherwise, no one would know what values to assign to the variables in the laws that enable one to use the report in other circumstances. But once a standard has been given, then all data reports can be adjusted to the standard, and all that is needed is the data report itself. Thus the standard conditions constitute a data-processing device that simplifies the amount of reporting that is required. The construction of an optimal standard is a very complicated problem—as anyone knows who has followed the literature on the selection of a standard of length. Indeed, the whole problem of standards is one that has received a great deal of attention by various professional societies.

Before leaving the topic of standards, it will be worthwhile restating the results of the discussion in the language used earlier in the book to discuss values. Consider the sentence "x has property A." We now recognize that this can be taken to mean, "Report R would occur if x were examined under standard conditions . . ." or "x would be observed to behave in a certain manner in standard conditions." Thus a metallurgist may report on a Rockwell hardness of a metal. If he says, "x has a reading of 67," he means "if x were indented in a specific way, and then placed under a microscope in a specific position at a specific temperature, and other specific conditions hold, then a specific reading would be observed." His report is a prediction. In other words, when we say that "x *really* has a (standardized) hardness of amount n," we mean that "x ought to exhibit certain properties in some standard environment."

I have stressed this point about standards because, as the first chapter indicated, I want to argue that the real values a person holds are also predictions of his behavior in certain standard conditions.

13 · *Standards and States of Nature.*

There are one or two points of interest to the philosophy of science in the conclusions we have just reached in the discussion of standards. Suppose we were to consider a model of Nature in which Nature is imaged as a series of states. Each state is comprised of entities and their properties. Our conclusion is that if the properties are to be measured, then the assertion "entity e_i has property P_j in state S_k" is meaningful if and only if we can standardize the measurement of P_j, that is, if and only if we can make a series of statements about e_i in some state S'_k. But assertions about entities in S'_k will be meaningful if and only if we can assert statements about entities in S''_k, and so on. If we allow ourselves a certain amount of generalization, we can therefore say that the meaningfulness of any measurable property depends on our ability to predict. This remark is of some relevance to the discussion of the classical problem of induction because we can restate it in this form: the assertion of an ability to predict that an entity will have a (measurable) property in the future is logically equivalent to the assertion of an ability to assign the property in the present or past. If we know the "past" we must also know the "future."

14 · *A Sensitivity Measurement: An Illustration.*

In order to illustrate the description of measurement given thus far, suppose we consider an example of measurement in physical chemistry—the "sensitivity" of a specific detonative compound. We start by defining the item and the properties which concern us. Item identification has been partially worked out already—we can specify the composition and its purity in the language of inorganic chemistry in order to relate the concept to other concepts of physics and chemistry. However, the shape and density of the items is not initially clear. Nor is "sensitivity" easy to define. Vaguely, the sensitivity of a detonative compound describes how likely the material is to "go off." We begin by defining "going off" in physical terms by saying "detonation" is the development of a shock wave within the material of at least a certain velocity v_0. We then have to face the problem of defining "likelihood of detonation." But detonative compounds have a number of uses. They may be subjected to the blow of a firing pin made of various metals and in various shapes. They may be packed as a pellet and laid on a flat anvil, or else inserted in a cup under pressure of a curved anvil. They may be subjected to an electrical impulse, or to a temperature stimulus. Hence, when we say that the sensitivity of a compound is the probability that it will "detonate" when subjected to a stimulus, we have given a program for research.

We attempt to make this program operational by defining some observational steps: pellets are to be manufactured to a given specification, are then to be laid on a flat steel anvil manufactured to given specifications, a firing pin of a specified radius and hardness is to be placed lightly on the pellet and a ball with a known mass falling from a known height is to strike the pin, and the coefficient of elasticity between pin and falling mass is to be 0.95. We then say that the sensi-

tivity of the compound is the relative frequency of detonations in
this environment. But we find that these instructions are not sufficient to obtain consistent results. The temperature of the testing
room must be set at a given level, as must the relative humidity. Perhaps, now, the results are consistent so that when different observers
in different places test the compound in this manner, they all report
essentially the same result within a desired level of agreement. If so,
the property "sensitive" has been partitioned into a number scale
ranging from 0 to 1, and has been defined in terms of a set of other
properties: flatness, hardness, temperature, and so on.

Evidently this definition is very restricted as far as the use of the
information is concerned. We only know the frequency of detonation
for one mass and one height of drop, for example. Our selection of
the operational steps given above has favored precision above generality of use. We can make precise distinctions whenever it is important to make decisions about pellets when they are hit by a certain
kind of blow, but our results are of little use for other decisions, for
example, whether to use the compound in detonators. But first we
need to specify the language of sensitivity more precisely.

For some masses and heights, some pellets detonate, and some do
not. For some masses and heights, virtually all pellets detonate, and
for other values of the mass and height virtually none detonate. We
can plot a curve relating the frequency of detonation to the kinetic
energy of the striking mass. We could now assign pellets to classes
depending on the shape and location of this curve. We can go further
than this in most cases. We can ascertain that many of the curves
have the same shape and can "locate" them on the graph by means
of two numbers: the kinetic energy at which 50 per cent of the pellets
detonate, and the "standard deviation" or measure of dispersion
around this 50 per cent point. We now say that these two numbers
(rather than the simple relative frequency at one height of drop) constitute the measurement of sensitivity in the conditions already stipulated. Both these numbers are in units of kinetic energy. The "standard" for the measurement of sensitivity is the environment and
operations specified above.

We now try to generalize further, by developing a measure that
is useful in other environments. First, we discover that within a wide
range the temperature of the room has only a very small effect—that
is, that zero adjustment is required for temperature within this range.

But relative humidities over 60 per cent do affect the sensitivity numbers. We determine what effect they have and can adjust our readings accordingly. Thus, if we want to use the material in the tropics, and we know its sensitivity at, say, 30 per cent R.H., we can estimate its sensitivity at 90 per cent R.H. Then we discover that if the anvil has a hardness number above a certain level, the kinetic energy of the falling mass is alone important; that is, the sensitivity numbers remain the same regardless of what masses or heights we use for the striker as long as the kinetic energies are the same. We also discover that the velocity of the striker is important if the pellet is placed on softer matter, and again we find a way of adjusting the sensitivity numbers for various types of supports for the pellet. The measurement has become richer in its application. Next, we study the firing pin. We discover that within limits its mass is unimportant but that the radius and shape of the pin are important; we then ascertain laws for adjusting for mass, radius, and shape of the pin.

Thus, if we know the R.H. of the room, the pellet support, the shape of the pin, and so on, we can measure the sensitivity of the detonative material by means of the two numbers that locate the curve relating probability of detonation to kinetic energy.

This means that the measurement of sensitivity has meaning in a wide variety of contexts. In other words, as we increase our ability to adjust our data to a standard, we begin to approach the objective given in the definition of the concept of sensitivity. The new measures of sensitivity are the parameters that enable us to predict fire or misfire under changing conditions of temperature, relative humidity, hardness of support, and so on.

Suppose the material is placed in a cup under slight pressure of a curved anvil. We have, as yet, no way of adjusting the results of firing tests to the standard given above. Because of our inability to make adjustments, we have to construct another standard, that is, define another concept of sensitivity, for cupped pellets. The same procedures can be used to define and generalize on this standard, but the method of adjustment from the first standard to the second is still an unsolved problem. This means that we have to live unhappily with two separate notions of sensitivity, and two separate testing procedures. The situation is really not so unfortunate as might be supposed. We can predict detonation under a wide variety of circumstances, but we have to test the material in two different ways to do so.

This would also have been the case for the first standard if, say, we could not learn how to adjust for relative humidity; in this case, we would have required separate tests for various R.H.'s that might occur in practice. Actually, at the present time, there are several mutually unadjustable standards for sensitivity. For example, we do not know how to adjust results obtained from pellets in cups to results obtained when the cups are pushed into ammunition cases, nor to adjust for electrically delivered impulses.

If our objectives had remained pure and simple, for example, to study the laboratory behavior of the compound, then the first standard would have sufficed. Indeed, many researchers in detonation despair of ever making measurements outside the laboratory. The multiple standards are consistent, however, and valuable for the non-laboratory users of the product. The reason why we would like to unite the standards is an economical one—we could thereby reduce testing and/or increase accuracy.

Thus the "sensitivity" of a compound consists of the sensitivity numbers for a set of standards. But we still think the program of uniting the standards is sensible, and hence we *programmatically* define the sensitivity of the material as the sensitivity numbers for any relevant environment, and for items constructed out of the compound in any manner. This is what we think "sensitivity" ultimately means, even though at present we do not know how to attain this ultimate meaning. Our programmatic objective defines the concept as long as the objective is feasible and important.

But it should be emphasized that the program described above has entailed a number of important decisions. For example, we assumed at first that the "real" sensitivity was the frequency of fires under a specific impact and specific conditions. This choice permitted some degree of consistency and precision, but the measurement reports were of very little use to those using the compound outside the laboratory. We could have decided that the frequency of fires in actual field use should be the measure of sensitivity, in which case the reports would have had low consistency but would have been more generally useful. Or, as we suggested above, we can regard both as measures of sensitivity and suffer the costs of a dual system of reports. Which is the best choice? The "pure scientist" picks the first, the "practical engineer" the second, the "applied scientist" the third. However, these are merely labels for the decisions and not indicative of the value of the choice. Of course, the answer depends on what we are trying to do; but *how* it depends on this is a very difficult problem of decision-making and values.

The message in all this digression on sensitvity has been the same as that given in the last chapter: the program of finding the *measurement* of sensitivity of detonative materials is the same as the program of finding the correct *theory* of the sensitivity of detonative compounds.

The message is important for an understanding of the present undertaking. Chapter 7 will argue that human values are programmatically measured in terms of the probability of behavior when the subject knows the probability of the consequences of his behavior. There may be no way of adjusting all situations involving human choices to one standard. But the program must be stated because it alone gives some point to specific attempts to measure human values —or to find a theory of human values.

14 · *Accuracy and Control.*

There are two other aspects of measurement, each fully as important as those just discussed. Indeed, both of these have already appeared in the account because accuracy and control are the concepts which define the consistency of measurement reports.

In the standard environment the reports generated according to a set of specifications need not all be exactly alike. Also, in the construction of measurements from these reports, the formal assumptions need not hold exactly. The problem of accuracy is the problem of defining the allowable limits in these processes.

These allowable limits must be defined in part in terms of the uses to which the measurement is put. This might seem to have the awkward consequence that accuracy is a highly relative term, the meaning of which depends on the individual decision-maker. But measurements are pieces of information applicable in a wide variety of contexts and problems. This means that it must be possible to find accuracy measurements which are applicable in a wide variety of contexts and problems. The detailed discussion of this enormously difficult problem would take us too far from the central theme of this book. It will suffice here to point out that the concept of accuracy of measurement can be used in at least two senses. First, a measurement process may fail to be accurate in the sense that it is not consistent. For example, repetitive observations differ "too much" or fail to agree sufficiently well with the formal stipulations. Second, a measurement process, though consistent, may have very poor accuracy for a specific purpose. Thus, we can say that a set of data are inaccurate and mean either that the set is inconsistent relative to certain formal rules, or that the set has a very low measure of accuracy. Which statement is made is usually a free decision of the scientist. An inconsistent set can be made consistent by relaxing the formal rules. For example, a set of data describing preferences may be inconsistent under the formal stipulation of strict transitivity because sometimes the subject "prefers" A to B, B to C, and C to A. But if we relax the rules and permit deviations in responses within certain limits, then the set may be consistent, though the measure of preference may have a low degree of accuracy.

Control is the process of deciding when to test for accuracy and what corrective action to take when it is decided that the accuracy requirements are not met.

Although it is not our chief concern here to discuss accuracy and control, except as they enter into the general pattern of measurement, a few remarks seem in order. In statistical literature accuracy is sometimes defined in terms of a "confidence interval." In so far as this computed interval has any meaning, it tells us that a certain range of numbers constructed out of observations has a specific probability of including the "true" measurement. On the basis of a set of observations, a net is constructed to "catch" the truth, and the confidence interval tells us the probability of a successful catch. But this analogy to fishing only has meaning provided the situation remains stable, that is, the nets and the fishing pools come from the same population. One function of control is to ascertain whether this stability exists.

Although confidence intervals have become a rather popular method of expressing results in many of the scientific disciplines, their usefulness as measurements remains somewhat obscure. It is difficult to understand how the assertion that an interval will probably catch the true value is useful to a decision-maker. The decision-maker does want to know what it means to act as though x were the correct measurement when actually $\xi = x + \triangle x$ is the true measurement. He also wants to know how likely he is to arrive at the conclusion that x is the correct measure, that is, how likely he is to make an error of magnitude $\triangle x$. Neither of these questions is answered by a confidence interval. The second would be answered by what are called tolerance limits, that is, numbers that measure the probability of deviating from the true measurement by a specific amount. But tolerance limits are often difficult to measure unless the system is known to be in control over a long period of time.

Control seems to be a frequently neglected problem in science, except for such processes as production where repetition of data occurs because of the nature of the operation. Even in the so-called "exact sciences," control of measurement has not been attained in any of the accepted senses of the term, to judge from the few studies that have been made. Normally, control is said to exist only if the adjusted observations are statistically consistent. Detailed discussions of statistical consistency may be found in the references of this chapter. They can be briefly summarized by Shewhart's concept of "assignable causes." A measurement process is in control provided there are no assignable causes for the fluctuations in the adjusted readings. To date, the only measuring systems that meet these rigorous qualifications seem to occur in production inspection and certain simple data-processing systems of business and government.

But it may be that the concept of control defined in terms of many repetitions of adjusted observations is too narrow for measurements made outside of the laboratory or outside a precisely controlled production line. If scientific method is to be extended to decision-making in general, the ideals of accuracy and control will also have to be redefined.

It may be noted that control is in effect the test of a good standard. If adjustments can satisfactorily be made to a standard in accordance with the criteria of control, then the standards have been sufficiently specified. If not, then either the laws of adjustment must be changed, or else additional specifications must be added to the standard.

15 · *Fact and Theory.*

Enough has been said in this and earlier chapters to the effect that when we delve deeply into the "facts" of a scientific discipline, as expressed by its measurements, we see hidden therein a world of theory. Perhaps Leibniz's monadology might prove a helpful analogy;

to paraphrase him, if one could look deeply enough into any particle of the universe, one might find reflected therein all the universe. It is towards some such viewpoint that the present discussion has taken us: reflected in the process of correctly deciding to accept a fact about the universe is (perhaps) all the truths about all the universe.

It does seem that in some disciplines there has been a strong attempt to avoid any such conclusion. In other words, the workers in the discipline want to feel that what makes valid information does not depend on theory and what makes valid theory does not depend on information. One historical justification of the argument of this chapter would consist in showing that whenever a discipline does reach this position, there are usually signs of instability as evidenced by useless intellectual warfare. Such an historical study is well beyond the scope of this book. But an outsider may be excused, I hope, for attempting to phrase at least one such historical hypothesis about a very important field. Up until about ten years ago, economics seems to have been characterized by such an independent division of activity. On the one hand, statistical economists collected data on the transactions of business and industry; on the other hand, theoretical economists attempted to describe the form of these transactions. The economic models of the theoretical economist contained "parameters" the values of which could supposedly be supplied by economic data; but the theoretical economist was not primarily interested in what values these parameters might actually have on various occasions. His interest lay in the form of the equations, and the form of the equations was derived by making certain "simplifying assumptions" about the activities of business and industry. The statistical economist, in contrast, did not collect data that were directly relevant to the models of the theoretical economist. This independence of activity was reflected both in the large and in the small. In the large, there were economic theories of the capitalistic enterprise (Smith, Marshall, and others), and a growing large-scale collection of the national statistics of income, production, and distribution. In the small, there were theories of the firm, and the data collection of accountants.

The situation was undoubtedly unstable. In order to make simplifying assumptions that were agreeable to all economists, one had to get further and further away from reality. For one thing, some economic theories ignored the fact that businesses are organizations, and as such never act as an individual who is fully aware of what every part is doing. The economic theory of motivation ignored the organizational theory of motivation. In this and other respects the economic theorist was driven to devise more and more abstract models of business activities. The end result seems to have been that the mathematical economist was turned into a mathematician. Such an economist may still cling to the notion that his mathematics has relevance to business operations, but he ought not to claim that his theory is necessarily descriptive or prescriptive of economic realities. For example certain economists, industrial engineers, operations researchers, and management scientists have attempted to develop mathematical systems that seem to have some potential value for the study of business and industrial operations. But these branches of mathematics have received rather confusing names, such as inventory theory, waiting-line theory, replacement theory, and linear and dynamic programming. The names suggest that the researcher believes the theories describe such industrial processes as inventory control, waiting lines, replacements, and programming. But in view of the fact that all so-called "inventory theories" make no reference to any organizational concepts and rarely make reference to any other motive than minimizing costs (or maximizing return), the wise researcher will view his efforts in the construction of an inventory theory as mathematical research having *potential* use in the study of industrial operations. This attitude is wise on other counts as well; the so-called "inventory theory" may be applied to the control of other assets (such as cash or working capital) and is clearly not restricted to inventory studies.

"Inventory theory" is not economics, nor does it tell the businessman what to do. Economic research or research in the operations of the firm, must be something more. What? A first approximation to the answer to this question would be the following. Research into the operations of a firm begins with an examination of the firm's activities and its objectives. Out of this examination arises what John Dewey called a "felt need," a problem that clearly calls for solution, that all recognize to be vital in the firm's operations. The researcher then asks himself "What is now being done in the area of the problem, What are the results of present policy, and What would be the results if other policies were followed? He may see that he can turn to the body of mathematical knowledge and choose a mathematical system within which he can express the operations that are relevant to the problem. The manner in which he "sees" this is largely intuitive, though he is aided by similar experiences, his own and that of others, which are reflected in such names as "inventory theory," "waiting-line theory," and so on.

The mathematical forms, expressed as equations or inequations, now need to be made explicit because they usually contain coefficients and constants, and the exact nature of the results of following any given policy cannot be ascertained unless these coefficients and constants are estimated. The researcher therefore turns to the problem of the data and in terms of his model specifies what kind of information he requires. He does not specify how the information is to be obtained, but in terms of the problem and the model he can specify how accurate the information should be.

This research procedure is a first approximation to economic research of a firm's operations. It is only an approximation relative to the meaning of measurement adopted in this chapter. A more complete theory of research would require that the researcher's model of the operation specify how the relevant information is to be gathered. No measurements have been made in the complete sense unless this is so. For example, at the present time the "costs" of carrying inventory, of shortages of inventory, of setups, are all determined independently of the inventory "model." The thesis of this chapter is that no theory of inventory exists unless the theory dictates the manner in which the measurements of the parameters of the theory are to be made. This amounts to saying that today we have no theory of inventory. We will only have such a theory when we can specify the information necessary to test the theory and can justify this specification. Thus, to be specific, most inventory models contain concepts such as the cost of shortage, or the cost of setup. As Chapter 3 has indicated, the cost of shortage reflects a model of the firm's operations in the sense that the real cost of shortage is the (opportunity) cost incurred when the firm does not have an item that some consumer wants *when the firm is operating optimally under this condition* (and *not* the cost actually incurred); the cost of setup is the cost the firm incurs when the production line is operated optimally and setups occur (and *not* the actual cost of lost time and materials). The empirical costs are meaningful only under a model of the firm's operations.

In other words, theories of science are not tested by a set of data arrived at independently of the theory itself. Data-collectors are not objective arbiters of truth who have never been embroiled in the disputes they arbitrate. Data-collectors have used a theory to collect their data. Unification of specific effort occurs when we can understand the relation between a theory and the theory of data collection used to test the theory.

Thus, as long as information is "open ended" and not tied down to theory or to any other specific purpose, there can be no controls on the amount and kind of information that is collected, other than a budget and the specific interests of those in control. The problem of the amount, kind, and quality of data is certainly well recognized by our national information agencies, such as the Bureau of the Census. The problem is not so well recognized within business firms, where enormous investments are made to sustain accounting systems and other types of data-processing activities without any investigation at all of the amount, kind, and quality of data that is required.

In sum, to the outsider reflecting on economic research, there seems to be an untenable distinction between theoretical and empirical economics. By the same arguments, there seems to be an untenable distinction between normative and descriptive economics, for an ability to describe presupposes in the end a theory which will predict, and a theory which will predict will enable one to prescribe. Furthermore, *what* one describes depends on what one wants; the acceptance of the facts is itself a normative judgment.

16 · *Indebtedness.*

Prior attempts to discuss definition and measurement on my part (along with others) are to be found in (9), (10) and (11); (9) discusses the notions of intensive and extensive measurements—a distinction that seems to be important for Campbell (7) and Nagel (18). Chapter 4 in (10) is an earlier and shorter draft of this chapter.

Other discussions of measurement that I've found useful are to be found in Ackoff and Pritzker (3), Ackoff (4), Bergmann and Spence (5), Dingle (13), Lorge (17), Reese (19), and Scott Blair (20). Dorsey (14) wrote a magnificent work on the problem of the measurement of light, together with valuable reflections on the part of the author.

Ackoff (2) discusses some meanings of "information," including the one adopted in this chapter.

Formalization in measurement is discussed by Stevens (23) and by Coombs *et al.* (12).

The most useful work on control in measurement seems to be contained in Ackoff (1), Singer (22), Shewhart (21), and Wiener (24). An excellent summary of the contributions of some of this work, as well as an extension of its ideas, occurs in Littauer (16). Some studies of control in the physical sciences have been made by Birge (6). The ideas are also discussed in Churchman (11) and Churchman and Ackoff (9).

Some general and specific problems of measurement in the area of values are discussed in (8).

Finally, I'd like to make clear a very great indebtedness to Kant. In a very meaningful sense, the problem of the methods of measurement is not vastly different from Kant's problem of his first *Critique* (15). Kant was trying to discover how human experience is organized. He differed from Locke and Hume, who felt that the organization of human experience consisted in compounding and comparing sense impressions. For Kant, the sense impressions themselves were organized experiences. What was *not* organized, that is, the elements of experience, were simple, unnameable receptions of the mind, which Kant, having mentioned, ignores. Kant's theories have a vital importance for philosophy of science. For philosophy of science is interested in the manner in which scientists organize human experience. In this sense, Kant's "categories" are comparable to the "methods of scientific measurement." Now for Kant, there was but one way to organize experience: the categories of experience are fixed in number, in form, and in the content that they organize. The organization of experience consists in giving experience a shape (in space), and in interrelating experiences by first identifying each experience, and then putting it into a rational system. Despite the difficulty in style, Kant's work is a quite simple application of organization theory to the workings of the human mind. He believed in fixed principles of mental organization, just as organization theorists of human groups have sometimes talked of *the* principles of human organizations. That he believed in fixed principles was no real error in thought because the science of his time had not come to view the mind as an essentially expanding entity; the only things that were thought to grow in the mind were ideas and sensations, the structure remaining the same. Yet, despite the fact that nowadays we don't like to accept fixed and unalterable principles of organization, Kant's message is important. He emphasized that human experience—and the quest for knowledge—is an organized pursuit and that the problem of organization is a much deeper one than his predecessors had thought.

REFERENCES

1. Ackoff, R. L., "The Concept and Exercise of Control in Operations Research," *Proceedings of the First International Conference on Operational Research.* Operations Research Society of America, 1957.

2. ———, "Towards a Behavioral Theory of Communication," *Management Science* (1958), *4*, pp. 218-234.

3. ———, and L. Pritzker, "The Methodology of Survey Research," *International Journal of Opinion and Attitude Research* (1951), *5*, pp. 313-334.

4. ———, *The Design of Social Research.* Chicago: University of Chicago Press, 1953.

5. Bergmann, G., and K. W. Spence, "The Logic of Psychological Measurement," *Psychological Review* (1944), *51*, pp. 1-24.

6. Birge, Raymond T., "The General Physical Constants," *Reports on Progress in Physics,* VIII (1941), pg. 90.

7. Campbell, N. R., *An Account of the Principles of Measurement and Calculation.* New York: Longmans Green & Co., Inc., 1928.

8. Churchman, C. W., R. L. Ackoff, and M. Wax (editors), *Measurement of Consumer Interest.* Philadelphia: University of Pennsylvania Press, 1947.

9. ———, and R. L. Ackoff, *Methods of Inquiry.* St. Louis: Educational Publishers, 1950.

10. ———, and P. Ratoosh (editors), *Measurement: Definitions and Theories.* New York: John Wiley & Sons, Inc., 1959.

11. ———, "A Materialist Theory of Measurement," in R. W. Sellars, *et al.* (editors), *Philosophy for the Future.* New York: Macmillan Co. 1949.

12. Coombs, R. H., H. Raiffa, and R. M. Thrall, "Some Views on Mathematical Models and Measurement Theory," *Psychological Review* (1954), *51*, pp. 132-144;—also in Thrall, R. M., *et al.* (editors), *Decision Processes.* New York: John Wiley & Sons, Inc., 1954, pp. 19-37.

13. Dingle, H., "A Theory of Measurement," *British Journal for the Philosophy of Science* (1950), *1*, pp. 5-26.

14. Dorsey, N. E., *The Velocity of Light*. Philadelphia: The American Philosophical Society, 1944.

15. Kant, I., *Critique of Pure Reason*.

16. Littauer, S. B., and E. R. Bowerman, "Operations Engineering," *Management Science*, 2 (1956), pg. 287.

17. Lorge, I., "The Fundamental Nature of Measurement," in E. F. Lindquist (editor), *Educational Measurement*. American Council of Education, 1951, pp. 533-559.

18. Nagel, E., "Measurement," *Erkenntnis* (1931), II, pg. 320.

19. Reese, T. W., "The Application of the Theory of Physical Measurement to the Measurement of Psychological Magnitudes," *Psychological Monographs* LV, No. 3 (1943).

20. Scott Blair, G. W., *Measurement of Mind and Matter*. London: Denis Dobson, 1950.

21. Shewhart, W. A., *Statistical Methods from the Viewpoint of Quality Control*. Washington: The Graduate School of the Department of Agriculture, 1939.

22. Singer, E. A., *Experience and Reflection*. Philadelphia: University of Pennsylvania Press, 1959.

23. Stevens, S. S., "On the Theory of Scales of Measurement," *Science* (1946), *103*, pp. 677-680.

24. Wiener, N., *Cybernetics*. New York: John Wiley & Sons, Inc., 1948.

OBJECTIVE PROBABILITY

6

Summary

and

Intent.

In the last two chapters we have defined measurement as broadly and deeply useable information. We now want to apply the results of these reflections to the concept of value. In this case, we are interested in the study of human behavior. This means that we want to predict how humans will behave under certain circumstances. The measures of value will be information that assists in this prediction.

For the time being we will adopt a fairly simple scheme of purposive behavior, which will be examined in more detail in the next chapter. According to this scheme, there are three classes of elements entailed in any purposive act. These are (1) the decision-maker, (2) a set of alternative actions, and (3) a set of goals. This triad is to be considered in terms of three binary relations: (1) the relation of the decision-maker to the actions, (2) the relation of the decision-maker to the goals, and (3) the relation of the actions to the goals. We have a number of ways of defining these relations, but the simplest and most common are the following: (1) the relation of the decision-maker to the actions is expressed in terms of the probability that the decision-maker will choose the action; (2) the relation of the decision-maker to the goals is expressed in terms of the value of the goals to the decision-maker, and (3) the relation of the actions to the goals is expressed in terms of the probability that if one of the actions takes place, a given goal will occur. In the next chapter we shall consider relations (1) and (2), and in this chapter we consider relation (3). We are specifically interested, therefore, in the meaning of "probability."

Two plausible definitions of probability are discussed here. One consists of defining the concept in terms of the relative frequencies of a subclass of items in a reference class. The second is a definition of probability in terms of opinions or judgments. Essentially, the first definition "grounds" probability in a logic of classes, the second in psychology or social psychology.

Each definition will be examined in order to gain some general idea of its formal meaning. Then the two concepts will be studied relative to actual procedures of measurement. The relative frequency concept has received most attention with respect to the operations of measurement. If the reference class of items can be ordered, then the theory of random numbers provides an explicit method of adjusting observations to a standard set of conditions for measuring probabilities. If the reference class cannot be ordered (which is typical of most decision-making problems), then it is difficult to understand how to proceed, and a number of different suggestions will be dicussed. It does seem as though people's judgments must be included as a part of the standard, but there is no agreement as to what kind of judgment is best suited for the purpose.

2 · General Remarks on Probability.

The concept of probability is important in all the empirical sciences because for the empirical scientist every situation contains elements that are not known and at best can only be estimated. Sometimes the "uncertainties" are a result of human inability to measure precisely; sometimes they are inherent in the manner in which the scientist conceptualizes the situation. These two types of uncertainty fall in the same category since human inabilities are an aspect of every situation in which a scientist works.

Despite the clear need for a concept of probability, there has been no clearly satisfactory method of defining the concept. The difficulty, in part, has arisen because of a desire to find an "objective" measure of probability, and because of the curious fact that proposed definitions of objectivity do not hold up under analysis. This fact is really not so curious when probability is compared with other concepts of science; many other concepts (for example, "mass" and "force") are also "clear" to the lay mind that has not indulged in attempts to analyze them. Analysis discovers difficulties, and the attempts to overcome the difficulties reveal the complexity of the "simple" idea. Thus, almost everyone knows what it means to say that an event is only probable—except those who have devoted their lives to thinking about the matter.

To illustrate this point, suppose we see how the search for an objective definition of probability seems to result in a vicious circle. In order to explain what it means to measure the probability of an event, one must (apparently) assume a meaning of probability. We have already noted that every measurement process becomes involved in assuming the meaning of other types of measurement, which themselves assume the meaning of the first measurement. The "trick" of scientific method is to make circular defining fruitful—that is, not vicious. But in the case of probability, the circle does seem to become vicious if so-called "objectivity" is required throughout the measuring process.

"Objectivity" seems to imply a meaning of probability that does not depend on a state of mind of a person, but rather reflects some "objective fact" about reality. Thus, we try to give meaning to the assertion, "The event X will occur with probability p" in such a manner that the measure of probability is independent of the beliefs of individual persons.

Now there are certain easily observable events that do seem to follow a random pattern and that can be described by the relative frequencies of occurrences. Most people are familiar with the "random" occurrences of heads and tails when a coin is tossed, and the more intellectually curious may have tried such tosses many times to see whether the relative frequency of heads and tails is "about" equal.

The search for an objective measure of probability can be illustrated in terms of such a sequence of events. We note two characteristics of the heads-tails sequence that are relevant: (1) the occurrence of a head or a tail on any given toss cannot be predicted, and (2) the relative frequency of heads and tails turns out to be "about equal" after a great many tosses.

Each of these characteristics is somewhat vague, but for the moment let us accept the vagueness in order to see where we are. The first characteristic looks like a standard of measurement in the sense of the last chapter. It tells us that the measurement of a probability in this instance occurs where exact prediction is impossible. The second characteristic looks like a specification of the measurement of probability: the measure of probability of an event is the relative frequency of its occurrence in a long sequence of observable tries.

The vicious circle to which we alluded above is readily apparent in the notion of the standard. What does it mean to say that a head cannot be predicted on any given toss of a coin? The first answer that comes to mind is: "Prior to any toss, a head is as likely to occur as a tail," or (more generally), "Prior to any toss, a head has only a probability of occurring." Thus the standard of measurement directly presupposes that which is to be measured. The "simple" idea of measuring the probability of a head leads us to the absurd conclusion that in order to perform such measurements one must set up a standard which presupposes the measurements. More plainly put, one *can* measure the probability of a head if one "knows" something about the probability of a head.

The impasse suggested by this argument may seem to be illusionary. How did we arrive in this cul-de-sac? By insisting that some probabilities can only be measured under a standard condition where one cannot predict which event will occur on any given try. This requirement seems to be imposed by common sense, for if the event could be predicted, then the probability would be either 0 or 1 (certain not to occur or certain to occur). But we do recognize probabilities of events that lie between these two extremes.

However, the argument may seem to lack force because it is not clear why we have to know anything about the events beforehand. Why can't we say that in measuring probabilities we are simply counting the number of occurrences of various kinds that can occur, and that the prediction or lack of prediction of the next event is quite irrelevant? In other words, perhaps we can give up the first criterion above, and assert that the probability of an event *is* the relative frequency with which the event will occur in a stated series of trials; we make no stipulation about our attitude or knowledge before the trials commence.

In order to examine this suggestion, we first develop a concept of probability which depends solely on the concept of counting membership in classes of items. We call this a "relative frequency" meaning of probability. Throughout the discussion we should bear in mind a methodological defect in the relative-frequency theory, namely, that class membership and counting are taken to be primitives. The discussion of the last two chapters has shown the inadequacy of any such supposition. There is no doubt that many adherents to the frequency theory do ignore the methodological suppositions underlying the "data" and we will want to turn our attention to these. But, for the time being, we proceed as though the assignment of objects to classes and the counting of classes were clear concepts.

3 · *Probability as a Relative Frequency.*

We first introduce the notion of classes of items. That is, we suppose we know what is meant by the assertion that an item x belongs to a class X. We also suppose that the classes themselves belong to a larger class, which we call a "reference class." For example:

Items	*Subclasses*	*Reference class*
Results of tosses of a coin	"heads," "tails"	Class of heads and tails of a long sequence of tosses
Persons	"blue-eyed," "brown-eyed," etc.	Class of members of the same family tree
Results of bombing	"hit," "near miss," "miss"	Class of results of a long sequence of bombing attempts

Each item belongs to one and only one subclass. Each subclass is included in the reference class, and the set of all subclasses exhausts the reference class. We also suppose that we know what it means to count the items of any subclass, and of the reference class. For the moment, we assume that all subclasses and the reference class are finite. Finally, we know what it means to compute the ratio of the number of members of any subclass to the total number in the reference class.

Equipped with all these assumed meanings we can propose the following definition: the probability that an item belongs to a subclass is the ratio of the number of members of the subclass to the total number in the reference class. For example, suppose the reference class is the set of actions of every person in a community at twelve o'clock noon of a certain day. One subset might be the set of actions subsumed under "eating lunch." The reference class is finite and (according to the definition we are considering) the proportion of people eating lunch *is* the measure of the probability that a member of the community eats lunch at twelve o'clock on the given day.

We have said nothing so far about the process of determining the proportions of subclasses in a reference class. This could clearly be done if we could make a complete and accurate count of existing items, or, by predictive laws, of future items. It can also be done even if only a partial count is made, as we shall see.

For the time being, suppose we examine some of the formal consequences of defining probability measures in terms of proportions. There is nothing new in this procedure, of course, but it will show on what basis certain well-known "laws of probability" hold. If an alternative meaning of probability is adopted, these "laws" may no longer be valid.

We let p stand for the probability measurement; p is a measure that applies to the subclasses, which we symbolize as X_1, X_2, etc. Thus, for every X_i belonging to the reference class R, there is some number p_i. Some of the more- or less-obvious formal properties of the p_i are the following:

(1) The p_i are real numbers falling in the interval $o < p_i < 1$. The "proportion" of members of a subclass in a reference class cannot be less than o ("negative membership" is nonsense) nor can it be greater than 1 (the subclass cannot exceed the reference class).

(2) X_i "is larger than" X_j if and only if $p_i > p_j$.
That is, the notion of the size of the subclass X_i can be defined in terms of p_i. It follows that the relation "is larger than" defined over subclasses is transitive, closed, and asymmetrical, that is, orders the subclasses in one of the senses of ordering discussed in Chapter 5.

(3) If X_i and X_j have no members in common, then the measure of the subset made up of X_i and X_j (all those and only those events that belong to either X_i or X_j) is $p_i + p_j$.

This statement is the well-known "law" of probability that if E_1 and E_2 are exclusive events, then the probability of E_1 or E_2 is $p_1 + p_2$.

(4) If X_i and X_j have a subset X_i-and-X_j in common, then the measure of the subset made up of X_i and X_j is $p_{ij'} + p_{ij} + p_{i'j}$ where the $p_{ij'}$, p_{ij}, and $p_{i'j}$ are the measures of the subsets shown in the accompanying diagram.

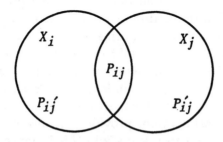

This "law" is merely a generalization of the law of exclusive events.

(5) If $X_1, X_2, \ldots X_m$ are a set of mutually exclusive subclasses that exhaust the reference set, then $p_1 + p_2 + \ldots + p_m = 1$.

This is another way of saying that at least one of the types of event must take place (1 representing "certainty").

4 • *Dependent Events.*

Suppose now we consider some of the ways in which the definition of probability in terms of proportions of finite classes may seem to be inadequate. We said in the beginning that our interest in probability lies in an attempt to relate actions to goals. In any given instance, we want to measure the probability that, if an action is adopted by a decision-maker, a specific goal will occur. But this implies that the decision-maker faces a particular event—not a class of events. That is, the decision-maker wants to know what he should do in a specific instance. However, probability measures defined as proportions are measures of classes—not individual events.

This objection to defining probability in terms of a proportion may or may not carry weight depending on the manner in which we consider the effectiveness of actions for ends. If we think that effectiveness cannot be applied to one decision by itself, but to a collection of decisions that maximizes certain human values over a long period, then the notion of a probability as a proportion may be quite justified. Indeed, in market surveys, the interest is not so much in any one customer but in the proportion of customers that will buy. In census counts, too, the chief aim is to ascertain the proportion of a population that belongs to a certain class.

But the decision-maker often wants to know more than the proportion of times he will be successful. Too long a sequence of bad guesses may be fatal even though the total proportion of good guesses is high. Can the notion of proportion be used to define this sort of information, that is, information about the order in which items appear as they are "drawn" from the reference class?

In order to arrive at a satisfactory answer to this question, suppose we first consider the concept of "independent" events, and the "laws" of probability that govern them. In tossing a coin, the occurrence of a head on one toss does not provide any information about what will occur on the next toss. We say in this instance that the events are independent. Most familiar gambling devices and games of chance are based on this idea: a good bridge hand theoretically gives no indication of what will occur on the next deal. However, in census-taking or market research, one may find that persons who dwell close to each other are apt to exhibit similar properties. Whether the dependence is spatial or temporal, information about one item may tell us something about the probabilities associated with another item, or it may not.

We can extend the language of classes to include classes of events the members of which are identified by location in space and/or time. If we do this, we can give an understandable meaning to the probability measure of a subset X_i *given* that certain "occurrences" have already taken place, or *given* that certain items occur in the neighborhood of the members of X_i.

The idea of dependence or independence of items of the reference class is explained in terms of the patterns which the items exhibit. If the items are spread out over time, then several of the same subclass may occur together—or each member of one subclass may occur as far away from any other as is possible. In other words, when a decision-maker worries about the next decision, he may be considering the whole pattern of successes and failures in the sequence of his decisions. If he knew the pattern exactly, he could predict the next outcome. If he knew the pattern approximately, he could predict the next outcome within a certain limit of accuracy.

Can the notion of pattern be defined within the language of class proportions? There are actually a number of definitions that could be given, among which is the following. Suppose there are just two subclasses A and B. First construct a class of all couples, each member of which is composed of two items that "lie next to" each other according to some precise definition. If the items are individuated by time, then "lies next to" means "comes immediately before" or "comes immediately after." A similar definition can be given if the items are individuated by space coordinates.

Count all the cases where the couples are made up of a member of A and a member of B. Call this $N(A,B)$. Count all the cases of couples. Call this N. The ratio of $N(A,B)$ to N is a measure of the pattern of the occurrences of *A-then-B* over time—or space—or any other individuating property.

Other measures of patterns can also be defined, and are to be found in most statistics texts under the heading of correlations.

Does the extension of the frequency meaning of probability to the counting of "couples" adequately convey the uncertainty which a decision-maker faces when he has to choose an act? We could try to conceive of the situation as follows: associated with each action there is a definite probability that a specified outcome will occur. This probability, if we maintain the frequency meaning of the concept, must be the count of the times the outcome occurs divided by "all" the possible tries. But here we are assuming that the situation remains essentially the same for each try—an unrealistic assumption, certainly. Hence we extend the concept, as we did above, to a series of tries spread out over a period of time. For each "try," which represents a choice of a specific action, the outcome will occur (which we represent by S for "success") or will not occur (which we represent by F for "failure"). We now obtain a sequence *SFFSSFF* . . . over the period of time. We can count the series in couples (or of triplets, or n-tuples if we wish) and thus discern the probability, at any given try, that an S or an F will occur given that a certain pattern of F's and S's has already occurred. This information, collected for each action, is therefore taken to be the basis for the manager's decision.

It is easy to see the chief difficulties of this account. The observer of the decision-maker must know, or have some reliable estimate of, the exact pattern which occurs over the time period. The well-informed observer is therefore watching the choices of an ill-informed decision-maker. Knowing the pattern, he asks himself how the decision-maker "ought" to act, given that the decision-maker does not know the pattern. The observer says to himself: "The decision-maker ought to choose the action which has the highest probability of yielding an S given the past sequence of F's and S's. In particular, if we restrict ourselves to couples of events, he ought to choose the action having the highest probability of success, *given* that either S (or F) has just occurred." The only way to estimate this probability is to take the entire sequence, and count the times an F occurs after an S (or the times an S occurs after an F) and divide by the number of couples in the series. So well informed an observer could just as well say "The decision-maker ought to choose the action which will be successful—if any," because in order to make either judgment the entire series must be known. This leads us to conclude what is surely absurd: that the only way to study choices is to know the outcomes with certainty.

In other words, the frequency concept of probability which defines probability in terms of counting elements in classes, is apparently incapable of conveying the notion of decision-making under uncertainty. If we adhere to the concept, we have no apparent way of describing how a scientist could possibly make recommendations to a decision-maker, unless he (the scientist) were certain about the future himself. Put otherwise, the frequency theory defined solely in terms of class membership does not contain the logic of inferring the properties of a whole class from the data of a sample.

Of course, it is easy to see one way out of the difficulty. We have used class membership and counting as the basic concepts of probability, whereas the meaning of probability very often depends on the *method* of drawing items. Thus, when we consider coin-tossing, we may not want to apply the concept of probability to any method of generating heads and tails. Instead, we may mean that only "random" methods of tossing the coin are susceptible to probability assertions. But introduction of the concept of randomness will not answer one fundamental objection to the frequency theory, even if randomness can be defined. This is the objection that the concept of probability should be applicable to very small reference classes (that is, rare events), and that the frequency notion is quite inadequate to convey any fruitful meaning in such contexts. Before we examine small reference classes, we should pause long enough to ask whether infinite reference classes (such as coin-tossing, for example) pose any difficulties relative to the frequency interpretation.

5 · *Infinite Reference Classes.*

The answer is that there are no technical difficulties in extending the class membership concept to infinite classes, although the consequences sometimes seem odd. For example, if we interpret the classes in the sense of "sets" in set theory, we can introduce "measures" of infinite classes. Thus, the measure of all rational numbers in the interval o to 1 is o. The measure of all reals in the interval is 1. Hence, according to the class-membership meaning of probability, the probability of a rational number is o if the reference class consists of all reals in the interval. It must be remembered that this consequence follows from the definitions; it does not assert that it is impossible to "draw" a rational number from the reference set because the definition is not based on the idea of draws.

We could also apply the definition of probability as a relative frequency to the situation where the items are generated according to a specific rule. In many cases we can speak of the limit of a ratio (for example, of "heads" to total tries), provided we can guarantee a limit according to the rule. For example, suppose the reference class R is composed of two mutually exclusive and exhaustive subclasses A and B. One simple rule would be to the effect that A occurs every third time. In an infinite R the "probability" of A would be simply $1/3$.

But, as before, this extension of the frequency meaning to infinite classes would not permit us to develop a methodology for studying the uncertainty of the decision-maker, unless the scientist knew beforehand the rule of generation of successes and failures. Hence, we can conclude that "probability" can be defined in frequency terms for some infinite reference classes, but the definition is not a fruitful one unless we can somehow define the concept of randomness.

The problem of infinite reference classes becomes more complicated if we consider continuous probability density functions. In effect, the number of subsets becomes infinitely large, and the meaning of the proportions in a subset has to be treated differently. But these problems of definition and theory construction need not concern us here since our purpose is to examine whether the relative-frequency concept is adequate for our purposes and this examination can be carried out without reference to continuous probability-density functions.

6 · *Relative Frequencies and Rare Events.*

We turn now to the opposite extreme: Is it sensible to define probabilities as proportions when the reference class is very small?

The answer, of course, could very well be "yes," since there are in this case no technical difficulties in defining the counting of subclasses and reference classes, and dividing the former count by the latter, as long as we exclude null reference classes. But the more serious point is whether the frequency concept in these instances really conveys anything at all, and if it does not, whether there is any point in studying decision-making when the reference class of events is very small.

It is true that the sense in which people use the adjective "probable" in "rare-event" situations does not seem to depend at all on the relative frequencies of the events. During the 1956 political campaign, people frequently asserted that "Eisenhower will probably win." Yet in this case there were at best only two members of the reference class—the 1952 and the 1956 elections. According to a strict application of the frequency concept, the probability of Eisenhower's winning in 1956 was either 1/2 or 1. This in no sense conveyed the meaning that most people had in mind—assuming they had some meaning in mind at all.

One can attempt to preserve the concept of relative frequencies by asserting that when a person says "Eisenhower will probably win" he means in situations of this kind and with opposing candidates of this type, the frequency of wins of one type over the other is large. In other words, one must suitably enlarge the reference class. This indeed may be the form of argument of some political analysts. But one can reply that in many instances we do not think of "similar" cases when we speak of the probability of an event. We simply mean that in this special instance we do not feel that an event is likely, or else we do feel that it is very likely. The relative-frequency concept does not seem to explicate this feeling.

However, the failure of a definition to convey a common meaning is not necessarily serious, especially if the common meaning is not a very fruitful one for scientific communication. The challenge here must be posed in another manner: Instead of restricting "probability" to situations where reference classes and their subsets can be completely counted, why not introduce a meaning of probability which describes how people feel or believe about the future, especially if this meaning would enable us to overcome some of the objections that have already been posed against the frequency meaning?

7 · *Probability Defined in Terms of Belief.*

Suppose we consider one of the chief advantages of defining probability in terms of beliefs: we no longer are faced with the awkward necessity of insisting on omniscience for the observing scientist. Thus, when we study decisions of importance in politics, business, war, and so on, where we have only the most meager evidence as to the outcome, we can recommend choices based on the collective beliefs of experts. It would be foolish to assert that the scientist of executive decision-making can ever total up the pros and the cons of all "similar" events. Virtually no critical decision-making situation is similar enough to those that have come before to permit a precise relative-frequency measure. Or, again, we have been schooled to believe in the genius of executive "know-how" in this country; this schooling amounts to saying that executives can estimate the probability of an outcome without the explicit use of relative frequencies. Their own beliefs are the best evidence (or perhaps the only evidence) for probability estimates. There has never been any test of this American myth (it may merely be the case that only executives who survive by the laws of chance have been "successful"). But the allegation makes sense, and the "personal" notion of probability needs to be examined.

The other argument against the relative-frequency definition of probability is that it is awkward or impossible to apply in the case where the reference class is small, and there is a very reasonable definition of probability (in terms of personal belief) which can be applied to such cases. The point of the argument seems to be greatly strengthened when it is very difficult to enlarge the reference class by introducing "similar circumstances." An enlargement of the reference class may constitute some loss of meaning, and the scientist has the right to ask whether this loss is worth the gain in precision which the frequency meaning supposedly supplies.

Thus, despite the fact that it may be possible to give a relative-frequency meaning to the probability of so-called "rare events," the real question is whether we should. If the proponents of the relative-frequency position insist that this is the only way in which probabilities can be defined within the conceptual model of science, then they must defend this position. And the definition of probability in terms of belief or opinion seems to provide the scientist with a convenient and powerful method of studying nature—especially the nature of the decision-maker. The real problem is to define the issue, that is, does the researcher have a choice between definitions, and if so what is the nature of each choice, and how should he decide?

8 · *Probability Defined in Terms of Judgment.*

In order to assess the advantages of an alternative definition of probability, we begin by trying to explain what is meant by probability when the concept is defined in terms of personal beliefs. The first suggestion is to say that the probability of an event is defined in terms of the "degree" to which a person believes the event will occur. Hence "degree of belief" needs to be defined, but there is the prior question of whether personal beliefs can provide a "stable" and valid basis for a *scientific* definition of probability. It is true that subjective beliefs may provide a good basis for predicting behavior, but they do not seem suitable for making recommendations to decision-makers. For one thing, we would have to assert that the probability that an outcome follows some adopted action varies from person to person. This means that there would be no generally accepted measure of effectiveness of actions relative to goals. But we might maintain the aim of attaining a stable and nonrelative meaning of probability, and at the same time define probability in terms of belief if we could define what we mean by a "well-substantiated" belief—that is, a "judgment."

There seem to be at least two characteristics of the phrase "well substantiated" which could be used as a basis of the definition we are seeking. A belief is considered to be "well substantiated" if most people have it. It is also "well substantiated" if no believer feels inclined to give it up no matter what arguments are presented. The former we might call the breadth of belief, and the latter the depth (or intensity). In order not to prolong the present discussion, we postpone (until Chapter 11) a more-detailed account of these concepts. At present we can note that each way of characterizing belief suggests a scale, the one in terms of the relative frequency with which the belief is held, the other in terms of the tenacity with which it is held under a barrage of counterarguments. It seems clear that a belief which is widely held but which easily breaks down under counterarguments is a poorly substantiated belief, just as a belief that is held tenaciously by a very few is poorly substantiated. This suggests—but does not prove—that we could construct one measure of "degree of substantiation" in terms (say) of a product of the breadth and depth.

We are now in a position to propose an alternative meaning of probability, namely, that the probability of an event *is* the measure of the degree to which the event is substantiated in the beliefs of a group of people. In the relative-frequency theory, the probability measure is relative to a reference class; so here the probability measure is relative to a social group. But if this group is the group of "interested" scientists, and the arguments which are used to define tenacity of belief are all the arguments accepted as relevant by these scientists, then we could say that the scientific probability of the event is the measure of degree to which the event is substantiated in the beliefs of the scientific group. In Chapter 14 we shall argue that in fact this is the way in which the "probability of a theory" or the "probability of a fact" is often measured, or at least vaguely estimated, in the scientific community. There we suggest, in effect, various interpretations of tenacity of belief under counterarguments and try to see whether there is any basis for accepting one interpretation rather than another.

Of course, it may still seem odd to say that the probability of an event is the degree to which it is well substantiated in the beliefs of "experts." This may appear to be entirely too subjective, for one thing. But a broader understanding of the implications of this question can be obtained if we return to the question we posed earlier: Is there any sound basis for selecting one definition of probability rather than another?

9 · *Judgment and Relative Frequencies.*

First of all, we ought to be sure that the two definitions we have been considering are distinct. Indeed, there is at least one way in which the judgment definition could be subsumed under the relative-frequency definition. We could observe that there is a very high correlation, as measured by the relative frequency of agreements, between the judgment probability and the frequency probability when the latter is applicable (that is, when there is a reference class and observable instances of membership in the subclasses). We could then argue that judgment probabilities have a high probability (in the frequency sense) of being correct, the reference class in this case being the class of all judgments. But this argument will not do because the proposed measurement procedure is faulty. In general, suppose R is a reference class composed of two subclasses S_1 and S_2. Suppose instances of S_2 can never be ascertained, and we lack a theory which will predict instances of S_2 from other available information. Then, whatever may be the properties of items in S_1, we have no basis for inferring anything about items in S_2. Thus judgment probabilities may agree with frequency probabilities in all cases where frequency probabilities apply (S_1), but this is no basis for inferring anything about them where frequency probabilities do not apply (S_2).

Of course this argument is based on a tautology, and a more subtle analysis of the method of ascertaining data about frequencies and judgments might reveal a connection between the two. Thus it may happen that any procedure of counting elements in subclasses and reference classes eventually depends on judgment estimates. So far, we have assumed that the elements of the subclasses and reference class can be ordered and completely counted. The description of the frequency meaning was based on the unanalyzed assumption that we know the meaning of class assignments and of counting the members of a class. But in any description of the methodology of counting one would expect to find a need for a judgment, as the discussions in Chapters 2 and 4 indicate, and as we may now see in detail.

10 · *Standards and Operations for Counting Classes.*

Presumably, any method of counting the membership of any class requires: (a) a rule for individuating each member, (b) a rule for ordering the members, (c) a rule for pairing each ordered member with one and only one integer such that the resulting set of integers are in sequence and start with 1. These rules are, in effect, a partial specification of a set of standard conditions for counting, in the sense of "standard" which Chapter 5 provides. Each of the rules require a whole list of further specifications.

Also, the standard conditions for counting must specify the conditions under which "X is in class A" is to be verified or refuted. This means that the standard conditions define "normal" observers, and define such things as the lighting, the location of X and the observer, and the surrounding conditions.

None of these standard conditions is simple to establish, as previous discussion in this book has argued. The important point is that any report of the form "X is A" is not operationally verified unless it is shown that virtually all normal observers in the standard conditions would verify it. In other words, "X is in A" is true only if it is "highly probable" that all normal observers would agree. But what does "highly probable" mean here? Could it be interpreted as a frequency probability? There is the awkward threat of an infinite regress of meanings: to determine relative frequencies we must be able to verify membership in a class; "X is in A" is verified if "0_1 observes X in A" is very probable; but "0_1 observes X in A" is verified if "0_2 observes that 0_1 observes X in A" is highly probable, and so on. In practice, of course, we often feel that it is obvious that X is in A, for example, when a subject gives a particular response in a psychological experiment. Sound judgment tells us that this, in all likelihood, is the response he really gave, and that the standard conditions really did apply. But then "X is in *A*" is accepted as true on the basis of a judgment probability ("it is quite unlikely that it is false").

Thus we *apparently* arrive at the conclusion that the frequency concept of probability depends on the judgment concept. Whether this dependence is also mutual is not clear. Before making an assessment of this issue, we must ask ourselves again whether there is not a way to overcome the awkwardness of the class-membership concept of probability by introducing in addition to classes and their counts, the concept of a random draw. The point can be made simply enough. For a specified method of drawing items from a reference class, there may be a theory which predicts how, on frequent draws, the items of each subclass will occur. In other words, there may be a theory which describes the reference class of a sequence of draws of length n and the relative frequency of draws that have $0, 1, 2, \ldots,$ members of a given subclass. If such a theory exists, we might be able to overcome objections raised earlier in the text, and even indicate how judgment could be subsumed under a relative-frequency theory. We turn, then, to the consideration of probability applied to methods of drawing items from a reference class.

11 · *Sampling.*

We have before us a set of objects; suppose it is clear how any given object is to be assigned to a subclass. We want to estimate the relative sizes of the subclasses by only examining a sample. Shall we "dip in" and take a handful? Even if the reference class is physically contained in a bowl, it has been shown that "dipping" is a vaguely defined rule, and there is generally no easy way to discover what is being done. In other words, the choice of a standard based on a "careless and carefree" selection of items is not feasible—even for fairly small reference classes. This much is an often-repeated lesson of texts in sampling theory.

What we seem to require is a sample that is "representative" of the whole. If we knew of a method to acquire a sample that would be exactly representative of the reference set, then the same proportions would equal the true proportions. But such a "standard" of measurement is not applicable, that is, no feasible operations could be used either to create the standard or else to adjust data to it.

It is natural to suggest that we make use of the concept of judgment which we have already introduced. Why can't we define the standard for sampling in terms of the "judgment of experts"? In other words, we select items in accordance with what the "best available judgment" decides is a representative sample. This is certainly the procedure that is followed by many decision-making agencies. But experience has shown that there are serious pitfalls involved in using such a standard—even assuming that "best available" can somehow be defined. The count based on a judgment sample apparently is not a reliable basis for estimating the total count of a class. This is because some people (motivated by conformism?) tend to identify "representative" with "average" and therefore try to select a sample that has elements of the more-common types. Other people (motivated by individualism?) tend to exaggerate the unusual in the sample. In either case, the sample fails to reflect the true proportions.

The point can be made more precisely as follows. Suppose that we are given a reference class, a method of assigning members to subclasses, and a method of drawing items that is defined in terms of the judgments of a group of persons. We can now construct a new reference class. This consists of the class of all sequences of draws of a given length, where each draw is determined by the judgment of the group, that is, by a specific method of reaching group agreement. We ask ourselves whether we can develop a theory of these judgments which would enable us to predict the frequency of draws having x members of a given subclass. If we could do this, we could then define the probability that x members of the subclass occur in any draw. Further, if the theory can also show how this probability is related functionally to the relative frequency of the subclass in the reference class, we could use the results of an actual draw to estimate the structure of an unknown reference class. We could, in fact, say which structures are apt to produce the draw that was made, and which are not apt to do so. The word "apt" can be defined by the concept of relative frequencies. That is, we could state in frequency terms the probability that the actual draw would occur if the reference class had a certain structure. For a given level of probability (say 0.05) we could determine all the likely reference classes, that is, all the reference classes for which $p > 0.05$. Thus, we could "estimate" within a range the structure of the unknown reference class.

To date, however, no such theory of judgment is available for any specific group of persons. But this does not preclude the eventual use of judgment standards for selecting samples. The fault may lie with the method of estimating the reference class structure from the sample. Usually a very simple estimating procedure is used, whereas it may be important, as suggested above, to take into account the psychology of the sampler in the estimation formula. Further, it may be possible—indeed in some cases it seems to have been possible— to train people to select "reliable" samples, that is, samples that provide data from which satisfactory estimates of the structure of the reference class can be made. This point is sometimes overlooked in discussions of "judgment" or "purposive" sampling. Writers who claim to prefer more "objective" methods may criticize judgment samples because their unadjusted results are unreliable. But the same writers do not hesitate to employ rather elaborate adjustment techniques for the "objective" samples.

There has been comparatively little research on the development of personal or group judgment in the selection of samples for measuring proportions of subclasses in a finite reference class. Thus, although it is true that a great deal of business and government data is derived from judgment samples, we have as yet no good way of evaluating the methods used by businessmen or government workers to select sample information.

One reason for the lack of research of this type is that there does exist a theory of sampling which apparently avoids the necessity of giving judgment so prominent a role.

12 · *Random Numbers.*

In order to introduce this theory, one pictures the sampler to be engaged in one of a whole sequence of similar experiences. If this were the case, there would be at least two things he would like to see happen. He would like to have his estimates average out to the correct value in the long run, and he would like to have each estimate based on the sample come as close to the truth as possible. These somewhat vague desires provide the basis for the design of a standard. For suppose that on each try every element of the reference class not already drawn has an equal chance of being selected. Then it would seem to follow that, in the long run, the sample proportions should average out to the true proportions, and, in some sense, each sample is as "fair a trial" as could be expected—assuming that there is no prior knowledge about the reference class.

Of course it is obvious that, formulated in this vague way, the proposed sampling standard presupposes the type of measure it tries to estimate. The standard says to select items in such a manner that prior to the selection each item has an equal chance of being selected. The standard is defined in terms of the frequency concept of probability. The reference class of the standard is the set of all possible attempts to sample. Such a reference class is presumably infinite. Furthermore, to establish the equal likelihood of drawing items, many tries at sampling would have to be made. This would defeat the whole idea of sampling a finite reference class.

In other words, to sample a population of items adequately, we need to know how the sample is to be drawn. But, if the specifications for drawing the sample are written in the language of probability, we should set up a new experiment to measure the probability that each item will be selected. This new experiment would itself require another standard, and another set of probability measurements. And so on.

But so costly a regression into an infinity of measurements need not actually occur. Suppose we call a method of selection that has equal probability of selecting any item "random." Furthermore, suppose it were possible to generate a sequence of digits by some method, and to verify, within limits, that the digits are random, that is, obey the theorems of probability that follow from the assumption of equal probability. Then, if a population of items could be "listed" by assigning numbers in sequence, we might use the random digits to select a sample. A universal standard of this kind could be tested for the validity of the assumption that each integer is as likely to occur as any other in a long sequence of the integers. If the tests work out satisfactorily, standard conditions for sampling could be constructed which are applicable in many diverse sampling problems. The legitimacy of the standard could not depend on any property of the reference class other than its being ordered in an "arbitrary" manner. Hence the universal standard of random selection could be used on any finite reference class as long as each item is assigned a distinct integer.

There are some difficulties in this account that need to be considered—especially the problem of assigning a sequence of integers to the items of the reference class. For the moment, though, we want to see whether a set of random digits could be constructed. Can we define a random infinite sequence of integers just as mathematicians have defined other infinite sequences of numbers? The point is that if such random sequences could be constructed, one might apply portions of the sequences to drawing samples from an ordered set of items.

For example, suppose that the sequence

7 3 9 1 3 0 4 3 4 7 8 2 6 0 8 . . .

is a portion of an infinite sequence of digits that comply with the necessary and sufficient conditions for a random sequence.[1] Then, if we had a reference class made up of 100 items, such a sequence could be used to draw samples, provided the items were put in some order and numbered from 00 to 99. We would merely take the digit couples of the random sequence 73, 91, 30, 43, and so on, and these would designate the elements of the sample (duplications would be ignored). The regression in probability measurements would be overcome by our having first defined an objective standard of randomness, and then having applied it to the ordered objects in the reference class. Furthermore, such a standard would operate just as well for one method of ordering as for another, so that the standard for drawing the sample merely specifies a careful ordering of some kind, and a tagging of items in terms of this ordering.

It does not take much ingenuity to sense the extreme difficulties entailed in trying (1) to define infinite random sequences, and (2) to generate specific examples of portions of such sequences. Perhaps this difficulty can be illustrated by pointing out that the sequence given above is the first fifteen digits of the decimal expansion of 17/23. Of course, *any* fifteen digits is the first fifteen digits of the decimal expansion of some fraction (actually an infinite set of fractions), so that this remark alone does not mean much. But it does suggest the complexities entailed in trying to define "patternless" sequences. Furthermore, the example suggests that generation of

1 These conditions are not easy to state, but we can give some hint as to their nature: the relative frequency with which any integer appears in a long sequence should "converge" to $\frac{1}{10}$; the relative frequency of any fixed pattern of n digits (for example, 7257) should "converge" to some definite and calculatable fraction; the frequency of distances of a given length between the occurrences of a given integer, or a pattern of integers, should converge to a definite fraction.

portions of random sequences is not even sensible as stated since *any* finite number sequence is as likely as any other to be a portion of a random sequence—by the definition of randomness. Thus

0 1 0 1 0 1 0 1 0 1

is a portion of some infinite random sequence, though it, like any other such sequence, "very rarely" occurs.

But the natural question is What do we want a random sequence of digits for? The answer is to select a sample from a class so that we can estimate the total from the sample. The critical point is this: if the procedure of generating a "random" sequence of integers is correlated with the procedure for assigning integers to the items of the reference class, then it will not be true that every item has an "equal chance" of being selected. This means, technically, that we would have no general way of estimating the total and computing the accuracy of the estimate; in each case we would have to know how the "random" sequence was correlated with the reference class sequence, and adjust for this correlation. Therefore a more specific answer to the question just posed is that we want a "random" sequence of such a nature that the adjustment for this correlation is unnecessary in a wide variety of circumstances. Indeed, we can now suggest that this be the definition of a random sequence of digits; namely, a sequence of digits is random relative to a set of ordered classes if (1) it can be used to select samples, (2) the rules of estimation of totals do not require an estimate of the correlations between the random digits and the class ordering, and (3) the probability (in the relative-frequency sense) that the estimate falls within a given range of values can be estimated. In other words, a set of digits is random with respect to a given ordering of a reference class if these conditions are satisfied. A set of digits comprises a random-number standard if these conditions are met for a wide variety of ordered reference classes.

Despite severe technical difficulties, standards for sampling have been developed and to date represent the most successful attempt to solve the sampling problem. We first generate finite number sequences by some device which presumably will "scramble" the digits rather severely. The resulting sequences are tested to detect certain patterns that might exist if the scrambling were poorly done. If no such patterns are detected, the finite sequences of digits are called random. One method of scrambling consists of using rather complicated machinery. Another consists of squaring certain numbers and selecting digits in the "cores" of the squared numbers. Further details are given in (19) cited in the References of this chapter.

Not all conceivable tests are run on "random-number" sequences. For one thing, the number of possible tests is obviously enormous if we are dealing with a sequence as large as a million digits (for example, perhaps the multiples of seven appear "too frequently" or perhaps every fifth digit in the columns is too frequently odd). Besides, finite random-number sequences are like people in that every one of them is probably quite unusual in some respect. Indeed, a sequence that "passed" every significance test would be quite improbable: "improbable events are probable" in the sense that most sequences have some improbable characteristic.

The point of the tests is to provide as much initial assurance as can be given that when a set of items have been sampled by the random-number tables, the proportions can be estimated and the errors of the estimates can be computed.

We can now define a measure of probability for a finite reference class in terms of random numbers as follows. Every item of the reference class is to be assigned an integer. Independently, a random number sequence is selected—a sequence purporting to have the desirable property given above. The items are drawn from the reference class in terms of the integers of the random sequence. A method of estimating the proportion of the subclass in the reference class is provided. Hence there is an explicit definition of probability in terms of random-number tables and the estimation formulas.

We argued in the last chapter that any definition of a property presupposes a theory which guarantees a certain type of empirical consistency. This is true of the definition of probability given above.

The use of random-number tables is based on a theory, namely, that the estimated proportions will fall with a certain range of the true proportions with a certain relative frequency of failures. To date, this theory has been "tested" on a large number of reference classes, with considerable success.

We can see that judgment has been assigned a workable role within the theory for judgment is used to list the items of the population and apparently can be relied upon to do this satisfactorily. Furthermore, judgment is used to determine the randomness tests of a given sequence of digits. The ultimate purpose of these tests is to provide assurance that the numbers have wide applicability and not to test statistical properties as such. Indeed, many digit sequences which do not satisfy certain statistical conditions may be random relative to a large number of reference classes. The aim is to find a way of weeding out digit sequences that may fail. The objection that the random-number theory is not "fully tested" is, of course, not an objection at all since no theory is ever fully tested. Further, whether the tests used to establish random numbers are really the best tests that could be used is a problem that falls within the general scope of theory-testing discussed in Chapter 4. Since at this time no adequate theory of theory-testing exists, the theory of random numbers can hardly be singled out as especially deficient in this regard.

However, having admitted that the use of random numbers presupposes a theory, the need for judgment reappears in another form. Whatever may be the test of the theory, the test will have to be expressed in terms of probabilities. For example, a successful test will result in an assertion of the form "the theory is probably correct." Should we interpret "probably" in this assertion to mean "according to well-substantiated judgment"? Such an interpretation makes sense, certainly. Well-substantiated judgments are beliefs that are widely accepted even in the face of strong arguments, and this indeed seems to be the case for the theory underlying random numbers: the "strong arguments" can be construed as the tests of a set of random numbers. But then, the definition of probability in terms of relative frequencies apparently presupposes the definition of probability in terms of judgment.

Of course there is one possible answer to this argument. After all, the numbers in the random-number tables are generated by some definite method, and it is possible that if we knew enough about the method we could predict when the tables would be successful and when they would not.[2] But such a prediction would itself be based on a theory, and presumably such a theory is only "probably" correct. In any case, at the present time, no such analysis of random-

[2] There is always the possibility that the occurrence of the digits is "absolutely" unpredictable, for example, if we accepted an indeterministic theory of electron position and somehow used electron position to generate random numbers. This procedure would ground the concept of randomness in nuclear theory and have the interesting consequence of making the indeterminism of electron position a tautology. However, it would also require an interrelation of the concept of probability in nuclear physics with other scientific concepts—an analysis that has yet to be accomplished.

number tables is available, or perhaps even feasible in terms of costs.

In sum, it has been possible to capture the meaning of uncertainty within the framework of the frequency meaning of probability. We can speak of the probability that a sequence of draws of a given type will occur, without having to know the exact structure of the reference class. We can do this by introducing the concept of a random draw in addition to the concepts of class membership and class counts. The concept of a random draw depends on a theory of random numbers, the validity and application of which depend on judgment. But judgment has been given the same role it plays in any theory-testing; it is not required as evidence for the uncertainty itself, but rather as a guide for the construction of a general theory.

However, we have restricted our consideration to finite classes; or in more general terms, to reference classes which can be ordered.

13 · *Probability Standards for Nonordered Reference Classes.*

What shall we say about reference classes that either cannot be ordered, or, even if ordered, cannot economically be sampled by the procedures prescribed by the random-number standard? An example of the latter occurs when the reference class is spread out over a large area (for example, items in geographically dispersed warehouses, or persons in the United States). This problem has been intensively studied, and various ingenious sampling plans have been developed which enable one to concentrate the sample in certain randomly selected areas and then adjust the sample data to the "pure" random-number standard. That is, on the basis of observations in selected parts of the reference class, one predicts what would have occurred if the random-number standard had been applied.[3]

The real difficulties in using the random-number standard occur when the ordering of the reference class cannot feasibly be accomplished. This may happen because the reference class is infinite, but the more troublesome instance of the problem occurs when the items of the reference class are events spread out in time. This is the typical situation which faces the decision-maker. He wants to know his

[3] In actual practice, this "adjustment" is not made explicitly. Instead, one estimates properties of the reference class and also estimates the variances of these estimates. The variance of the estimates is a measure that can be used to predict how far many similar estimates would deviate from the true measure in a random sequence of experiments.

chances of success if he adopts a certain policy. If "chances" are defined in terms of relative frequencies, he wants to know the proportion of times in which he will succeed or fail. If the various applications of his policy consist of contacting a potential consumer, one might be able to estimate the proportion of successes by a selection of existing potential consumers—and random numbers would be useful. But if the various applications consist of events in the future, then he cannot use random-number tables to sample the reference class since some of the items of the reference class are not available.

In such cases there is a strong temptation to accept whatever comes along as a "random" sample. In psychological experiments, for example, the easiest course is to believe that subjects are "random samples of a college population," or perhaps "random samples of *the* college population," or of "normal" human beings. The a priori probability assumption in this case is clearly quite strong: it asserts that the process by which a subject gets into a sample is essentially the same as the process by which he would have got into the sample if random numbers had been used. Similar problems supposedly arise in the biological and medical sciences. Here there seems to be an inclination to make the mice or guinea pigs as uniform as possible in order to make meaningful comparisons. With a uniform population, one may feel safe in making inferences about the future of the population—but at the cost of making only weak assumptions about other populations of mice or guinea pigs.

When we turn to the areas of main interest to decision-making, the problem becomes even more acute. As we have seen, in order to apply probability measures to the selection of a "rational" decision, we must estimate the probability of some specific outcome of an act. Apparently, therefore, any given act is a randomly selected item from a reference class of acts; the reference class in this case is the set of all such acts in a certain environment.

Here the assumption that the process of generating decision-making situations is like a random-number process seems to be extremely dubious. Indeed, it is absurd to picture the drama of the business executive as made up of "random" scenes, so that today's ventures are merely random draws from a large urn consisting of equivalent ventures of yesterday and tomorrow. No doubt many decision-makers do rationalize their choices on this basis. They like to think that a sequence of successful decisions of a certain type is evidence that a similar decision today has "high probability" of success. If life were a carefully guarded roulette wheel, this notion might have some justification. One would learn which plays have the highest chance of success and would live accordingly. The past frequencies of success, or in general, the past frequencies with which an act has been followed by a consequence, would be adequate measures of probability. The "standard" would be automatically built into every situation by Nature.

In other words, is it safe to say that the manager of an enterprise is analogous to a player of a game of chance? The player needs to know that the game is "fair," and he has at his disposal various physical tests he can run on the gambling device to check his assumption. Indeed, a fair game is constructed by generating events in a manner similar to the generation of random numbers. For example, as much care as possible is taken to assure a zero correlation between the deals of the game and any particular way a player decides to play. But no manager can feel sure that the events that he faces come from a system that generates randomness. Thus, we can define and measure uncertainty if we can find a "well-substantiated" theory of the manner in which draws of various types occur for a given reference class. In the case of the gambler, such a theory may be available; in the case of the executive, there is no such theory. There are so many arguments against any proposal that cannot be answered.

One way out of this difficulty, a way which is considered seriously in current statistical theory, is to add another concept to the theory of probability, in addition to class membership, class count, and random draws from an ordered class. This additional concept could be called the "basic attitude."

14 · *Minimax and Bayesian Attitudes.*

To illustrate this concept before defining it, consider two men engaged in a game, such as that form of Twenty-one in which each player is dealt cards until he decides to stop. Thus Player A has to decide whether to draw another card. He could proceed to estimate the probability that the additional draw would take him over twenty-one. The "simplest" assumption is that any card (other than those he can see) is as likely to be dealt as any other. If the game is a friendly one (or held in a reputable establishment) this assumption may be consistent with the available information. But one could criticize *A's* use of this assumption *in estimating his chances of winning* (not in merely estimating his chances of going over twenty-one). Suppose his opponent still has a choice of drawing or not drawing a card; perhaps past experience has shown him that his opponent more frequently than not will overdraw when the observed cards are on the table. This should surely be taken into account in estimating the probability of winning. Now, Player *A* may adopt an attitude to the effect that the probability of the opponent's overdraw is to be estimated by past experience plus an a priori assumption that aside from the data any probability is as likely as any other.

Alternatively, he could adopt the attitude that the opponent has been trying to create the impression of overdrawing too frequently in order to trap him at the strategic moment. If he adopted this attitude, he would be wise to estimate in such a manner that the chance that the worst outcome occurs is minimized. In this case his attitude is based on a pessimism regarding the unknown.

Depending on the attitude *A* adopts, he usually arrives at a different measure of the probability of winning. Other attitudes also are possible with other resultant measures. It should be emphasized that one cannot remove the need for a basic attitude by urging *A* to study the past behavior of his opponent because the same indeterminacy will arise with respect to this expanded set of data.

The same situation occurs if we consider *A* to be "playing against Nature." For example, in the conduct of an experiment the data might be conceived as "moves" of a player; a basic attitude is required here as well and defines what kind of a player Nature is taken to be. If we assume that Nature plays by means of random-number table, we adopt one form of what is called a "Bayesian"[4] type of attitude; if we assume that Nature is like a clever opponent in a game, we may adopt what is called the minimax attitude.

Neither attitude can be called a judgment because, according to this account, neither can be regarded as a well-substantiated opinion.

[4] After Thomas Bayes, an eighteenth-century contributor to probability theory.

15 · *Probability, Values, and Opinions.*

This is surely a very curious state of affairs, especially when contrasted with the classical theory of probability, where there was
supposedly a clear distinction between the "facts" and the subjective
opinions of the decision-maker. Now we learn that the measures of
the probabilities of outcomes depend *in part* on the decision-
maker's attitudes. The "in part" is an important qualifier because,
in addition to the basic attitudes, there are other factors which form
the basis of probability measures.

Thus two people may agree on what has occurred in the past relative to adopting a certain action, but they will not necessarily agree
on the probability of a future outcome of this action. There is nothing very surprising in this. But, in addition, it seems that no one
else, not even the scientists, can say which one is right when one
adapts a Bayesian attitude and the other decides on the attitudinal
basis of pessimism.

Such a theory of probability leads to an ontological pluralism
which asserts that there are many worlds, not one. If this theory
were adopted, there would be no ultimate basis for determining
correct decisions—a decision that is best for one world based on one
attitude may not be best for the world based on another. Furthermore, there is no basis for argument between the inhabitants of
these worlds. They may agree fully on what has happened, yet the
future worlds of each are different—and what is "best" to do is also
different.

16 · *Untenable Division of the World into Fact and Value.*

Before accepting any such scepticism regarding the science of
decision-making, we need to go back and see where the argument
may have led us astray and in particular to recall the problem of
verifying class membership and counting. And, indeed the fallacy
of the argument is clearly one of omission. The argument has divided the world of the decision-maker into the area of comparative
light where the illumination comes from the evidence of the past—
and the area of darkness—the obscurity of the future.

We recall the old lesson of earlier discussions: we have already assumed the world to have a certain characteristic in deciding what constitutes good evidence as opposed to bad. Therefore, the basis for a decision about the "next event" may very well have been already inherently established in decisions about the relevance and accuracy of the data. The conclusion reached at the end of the last section only arises because we have accepted the data to be "given," and not taken according to some decision criterion.

"To be" is to be decided about. This quite obvious reflection on the facts of man's experience, past, present, or future, may be the insight by means of which the indeterminacy of many worlds is resolved.

Once we glimpse the idea that facts are based on decision criteria, the issues that face the theory of probability become vastly changed. A fact is a system of decisions of a rather complicated sort, as we have already indicated. The basis on which an event is decided to have occurred, may be the basis on which one estimates the probability of future occurrences. This is so as long as we demand some system in the total collection of decisions about past and future events, and man's wants. For example, we have already argued that the decision procedure for accepting facts about the past is based on a predictive theory about the future, for example, repetition of the same observer reports in various circumstances. As for scientific facts—that is, measurements—the theoretical base is quite complicated because it must include a predictive model about the properties of items in various environments. Evidently judgment plays an important role in the acceptance or rejection of these theories. But it is by no means clear that we have alternative choices in selecting criteria of good judgment, no one of which can be proved better than the others. A satisfactory meaning of good judgment is not only a basis for predicting the future: it is a basis for description of the past as well.

The point is that we need to understand the judgment process which generates facts.[4] If we knew this process, we might then be in a position to understand how to measure the probability of future events because the theory that underlies a fact also predicts the future; it predicts continuing acceptance of the evidence, for example. As we shall see in Chapter 14, many scientists adopt a Baye-

---

[4] In connection with this criticism it should be mentioned that I am not discussing methods of estimation of true values from a sample of observations, but rather am talking about the acceptance or rejection of the observations themselves.

sian attitude with respect to the theory of facts: a given datum is taken to be valid because virtually all observers and critics agree, and therefore will "probably" be taken as valid by all future observers. If this attitude provides an adequate theory of factual evidence, then we need to understand why it does not provide an adequate basis for measuring all probabilities. Alternatively, we need to know whether a minimax theory of facts is possible and if so what it is like; we need also to develop other theories of facts.

Our problems of probability measurement are therefore the consequence of our lack of alternative theories of factual evidence, and not the consequence of ignorance of "Nature." Indeed, one cannot help being astonished at the naïve metaphysical presupposition underlying some of the thinking in current statistical theory, namely, that there is a Something-I-know-not-what, who in Her motherly way gives us mortals our data. This metaphysical theory is borrowed without benefit of the scrutiny of critics of the intervening centuries from the empiricism of John Locke. Anyone adopting such a theory must at least try to answer the devastating theses of Berkeley and Kant: data are not moves of Nature; they are in part our own moves, created by our judgment. What neither Berkeley nor Kant provided to our full satisfaction is the theory of this creative process; but the study of such a theory seems far more fruitful than the study of strategies against an indefinable Great Mother.

17 · *A Tentative Conclusion.*

The story of this chapter can now be briefly retold. We began with the hope that an objective measure of probability could be found in the operations of counting membership in classes. We conclude that no matter what major aspect of this definition we choose to analyze, we are always driven to the necessity of introducing judgment: the operation of verifying class membership is based on judgment; the operation of verifying the theory of sampling is based on judgment; the verification of a theory of the generation of events is based on judgment.

Should we conclude that ultimately what probability really means is the measure of the breadth and tenacity of expert opinion? We could certainly say this, and argue that in many, but by no means all, cases this measure depends on relative frequencies because expert judgment is highly influenced by relative frequencies. We could thus be led to consider the definition of probability in terms of frequencies to be a special case of the more-general definition in terms of judgment.

The crucial question is whether we could do the opposite, as we suggested earlier (p. 152), and define good judgment in terms of relative frequencies, that is, could we say that "good" judgment is opinion that frequently predicts correctly? Our earlier discussion decided that we could not, because the form of the frequency definition we were considering precluded our talking about the frequency probabilities of future events. But now we see that the possibility of estimating the future is based on a theory that also permits us to describe the past. The crucial question now becomes: Can the frequency concept of probability be used to express the degree of validity of a theory? It would certainly be naïve to suggest that we "count" the instances where the theory has held and the instances where it has failed—because our data are never of the form that clearly provides positive and negative instances. But we could count instances that are judged to confirm and instances that are not judged to do so. We could also count favorable expert opinions and unfavorable ones. Indeed, the whole idea of well-substantiated judgment seems to rest on such a counting procedure.

Hence we conclude that either definition of probability is feasible. Reflection on the last chapter leads us to see that the issue is not one of logic but of decision-making. In effect, we want to know which is the better standard for probability measures: relative frequency or well-substantiated judgment? Relative-frequency standards have been much more carefully studied and developed; the judgment standard is often much easier to apply. Which is the better standard cannot be decided by an intuitive feeling about what probability "really" means. But whichever standard is chosen it is essential that data collected under the other standard be adjustable; this means, simply, that relative frequencies must agree, by some acceptable method, with judgment probabilities and that judgment probabilities must agree with relative frequencies in those cases where both methods are applicable.

Thus viewed, there may not be many worlds—we may be lucky

indeed if we find one world that even begins to integrate systemati-
cally all the decisions that go into one estimate of a fact—or a probability—or a desire.

18 · *A Reflection on the Chapter.*

These considerations about probability lead me to a rather loosely
formulated reflection about the future of the science of decision-
making. Because probability theory has been primarily of interest
to mathematicians and logicians, those scientists who are concerned
with decision theory under uncertainty find themselves in an awkward position today. Their intellectual resources are rather unsuit-
able for many important problems of decision-making. The intellectual resources demand a "population," and some knowledge or
assumption about how the "events" are "drawn" from the population. This is not too embarrassing a requirement if the sample is
meager, provided one does know that the sample is (say) a random
one. But we often do not know that the so-called "past" of a decision-
maker is in fact his past, and we do not know that it is a sample of any
given population. We have two choices before us, it seems to me. One
is to turn our backs on all decision problems where the past cannot
be known or cannot safely be regarded as some sort of a sample of
the past-present-future. This choice amounts to turning our backs
on virtually all the important problems. *Or* we can admit that our
intellectual resources are inadequate, and attempt to do something
about them. One obvious suggestion along this line is to study judgments of probabilities. Such judgments are made every day; for example, they form the basis of decisions of many planning boards. But
the amount of research on the subject is still very small. When is a
certain action to be construed as a probability judgment? How are
probability judgments to be measured? How are they related to other
evidence about the future? Are there satisfactory criteria of good
judgments? If we began to get some answers to these questions, we
might be able to advance much more rapidly in the study of "real-
life" decisions.

19 · *Indebtedness.*

Works which try to develop a basic language and theory of probability are Carnap (6) and (7), Jeffries (11), and Reichenbach (16). All of these develop the theory from a set of primitives. Carnap wants to distinguish between a relative-frequency concept and a "degree of confirmation," which he apparently thinks is akin to a logical relationship. He believes that probability is used in at least two different senses in science. It seems that he is trying to establish a criterion of "good judgment" in terms of an explicit set of rules connecting evidence statements with hypotheses. If this is so, then his approach differs from the present one in at least three ways: he is not concerned with the role of probability in the process of accepting or rejecting evidence statements; he does not try to define good judgment in terms of the "breadth and depth" of belief in a social group; and he is not concerned with the relation between probabilities and optimal decisions. Laplace, of course, is well known for his statements about probability defined in terms of "insufficient reasons," and perhaps he too was struggling to find a basis for good judgments about probabilities. Nagel (15) discusses different philosophical approaches to probability, and the *Symposium on Probability* (18) represents some typical disputes in the area.

Blackwell and Girschik (4), Savage (17), and Wald (20), (21), are interested in probabilities and decision theory—at least to the extent of trying to formalize the subject. Savage discusses "subjective" probabilities and much of what he says seems to me important for the development of objective probabilities based on judgment. Wald and Blackwell-Girschik treat the problem of the relation of statistical decision theory to game theory (for example, to minimax rules). McKinsey (13) and Williams (22) provide introductory readings for the study of game theory. Luce-Raiffa (12) is the most recent text on the subject. Bross (5) has written a more-or-less popular introduction to the concept of uncertainty relative to decision-making. Tukey (19) discusses random numbers and gives a list of references for further readings on the subject. On Bayesians, see Schlaiffer (17a).

Some of the difficulties in determining a person's real opinions in surveys are discussed by a number of writers, for example, Ackoff (1) and Ackoff and Pritzker (3). I take these difficulties to be directly relevant in the search for probability measures based on judgment. Ackoff (2) gives an example of a method for ascertaining collective judgments of executives.

My own previous attempts to discuss probability are in (8), Chapter 12, which is chiefly concerned with analyzing randomness, and in (9), which is concerned with the nature of statistical inference, and in (10), which suggests that we ought to put into one scheme decisions about how to measure values and decisions about how to measure probabilities.

REFERENCES

1. Ackoff, R. L., *Design of Social Research.* Chicago: University of Chicago Press, 1954.
2. ———, and W. S. Glover, "Five-Year Planning for an Integrated Operation," *Proceedings of the Conference on Case Studies in Operations Research.* Cleveland, O.: Case Institute of Technology, 1956.
3. ———, and L. Pritzker, "The Methodology of Survey Research," *International Journal of Opinion and Attitude Research.* V (1951), pg. 313.
4. Blackwell, D., and M. A. Girschik, *Theory of Games and Statistical Decisions.* New York: John Wiley & Sons, Inc., 1954.
5. Bross, I. D., *Design for Decisions.* New York: Macmillan Company, 1953.
6. Carnap, R., *Logical Foundations of Probability.* Chicago: University of Chicago Press, 1950.
7. ———, *Continuum of Inductive Methods.* Chicago: University of Chicago Press, 1952.
8. Churchman, C. W., *Theory of Experimental Inference.* New York: Macmillan Company, 1948.
9. ———, "Statistics Pragmatics and Induction," *Philosophy of Science,* 15 (1948), pg. 249.
10. ———, "Problems of Value Measurement for a Theory of Induction and Decisions," *Proceedings of the Third Berkeley Symposium on Mathematical Statistics and Probability.* University of California Press, 1956.
11. Jeffries, H., *Theory of Probability,* 2nd ed. New York: Oxford University Press, 1948.
12. Luce, R. D., and H. Raiffa, *Games and Decisions.* New York: John Wiley & Sons, Inc., 1957.

13. McKinsey, J. C. C., *Introduction to the Theory of Games.* New York: McGraw-Hill Book Co., Inc., 1952.

14. Mises, R. Von, *Probability, Statistics and Truth,* trans. by J. Neyman, D. Sholl, and E. Rabinowitsch, New York: Macmillan Company, 1939.

15. Nagel, E., *Principles of the Theory of Probability.* Chicago: University of Chicago Press, 1939.

16. Reichenbach, H., *The Theory of Probability,* trans. by G. H. Hutten and Maria Reichenbach, 2nd ed. Berkeley, Calif.: University of California Press, 1949.

17. Savage, L. J., *The Foundations of Statistics.* New York: John Wiley & Sons, Inc., 1954.

17a. Schlaitfer, R., *Probability and Statistics for Business Decisions,* New York: McGraw-Hill Book Co., Inc., 1959.

18. "Symposium on Probability," *Philosophy and Phenomenological Research,* Vol. V, 1944-45, pg. 449 and Vol. VI, 1945-46, pg. 659.

19. Tukey, J., "Review of the RAND Corporation's *A Million Random Digits,*" *Journal of the Operations Research Society of America,* 3 (1935), pg. 568.

20. Wald, A., *On the Principles of Statistical Inference.* South Bend: University of Notre Dame, Department of Mathematics, 1942.

21. ———, *Statistical Decision Functions.* New York: John Wiley & Sons, Inc., 1950.

22. Williams, J. D., *The Compleat Strategyst.* New York: McGraw-Hill Book Co., Inc., 1954.

A STANDARD
FOR VALUE
MEASUREMENT

7

Summary

and

Intent.

The general aspects of the measurement of values can be stated in the same terms as those used in the measurement discussed in Chapter 5. We have argued that the process of measurement is defined in terms of its function: to provide useful information in a broad number of contexts. The technology of this process involves a specification of the situation where the information is obtained, and a procedure for adjusting the original information so that it has maximum usefulness in other contexts.

In this chapter we do not attempt to show how value measures can be performed. We do try to show what use these measures may have: namely, as predictors of behavior in certain circumstances.

To this end, the discussion of value is primarily concentrated on the concepts which at the present time seem to be most closely related to value measurements. These concepts are the basis in terms of which a suitable "standard" environment for value measurements is defined. In this effort, I want to follow the suggestion made in Chapter 1, and argue that the standard environment must in some sense be "free of disturbing influences," namely, such things as outside control, and ignorance, among others. Of course it may happen that other standards are ultimately more suitable; the primary purpose is to illustrate a method rather than to defend one particular approach.

2 • *Personality.*

When R. L. Ackoff and I wrote *Psychologistics,* we tried to consider what is entailed in studying personality by means of measurements and to define a number of psychological and sociological concepts within a general framework of scientific concepts. The exposition given in this chapter is a brief summary of certain parts of this work revised in a few respects. (Details of the argument are to be found in the earlier work.)

The chief purpose of *Psychologistics* was to define personality. In the initial stages of our thinking, we had held that personality is a measure of the typical ways in which an individual is inefficient. In other words, we thought that a human being—or a machine—performing exactly as it "ought to" has no personality, and the typical behavior deviations from "perfection" constitute the personality of the individual. We tried to set up a useful classification for the study of personality by categorizing the ways a person could typically deviate from an optimal behavior pattern. Thus a "patternizer" tends to follow the same course of action even though it is no longer effective. A "dispatternizer" tends to change before he should. And so on.

As we delved deeper into the problem, we felt that this way of classifying personality concepts was not rich enough for our purposes and that a more general system of concepts was required which would relate personality properties to other properties which science studies.

Psychologistics begins by provisionally accepting certain concepts of logic, mathematics, and mechanics as basic and gradually develops concepts which are ultimately used to define a "psychological individual."

A psychological individual is defined as someone who is faced with at least two alternative actions either of which he could "choose." These actions (we called them "means") lead with varying degrees of success to one or more objectives or ends. The aim of the study of personality, we said, was to predict the probability that a person will choose a certain action, given the probabilities that the actions produce each of the ends, plus other relevant information. The detailed explanation of this account was the aim of the book. Before recapitulating this explanation, it may be useful to make some general critical remarks concerning the purpose of the enterprise.

First, we had evidently adopted a theory as to what psychology is trying to accomplish. Of course, human behavior can be examined from a number of different viewpoints depending on whether the viewer is a chemist, physician, personnel manager, or whatever. Out of the set of such viewpoints we had chosen one which seemed to us to characterize the aim of psychology. It should be noted that we were not asserting that the probabilities that actions produce ends *determine* what actions a person chooses. There is no denying that people's actions are produced by many different things, but they are almost never produced by the real chances of gaining ends. Nevertheless, one can define a personality concept in terms of these probabilities; information about the determinants of behavior, in effect, provides the basis for adjusting observations of behavior so that the information is useful in many contexts. The point is important because one can sensibly ask why we define personality concepts in terms of the true probabilities that actions produce ends, rather than the believed-in probabilities. This is a question to which we shall return later on in the chapter.

Next, we did commit ourselves to accepting one schema for the study of people, namely, a behavioristic means-end model. This commitment images a person as a "free-chooser" who by means of his choices seeks specific goals in the present or future. The commitment is a methodological one. We were not asserting that people "really" behave in this manner because such an assertion is meaningless or else poorly phrased. Instead, we were proposing the methodological hypothesis that this schema for studying human behavior was the most economical: in terms of it, one could provide the "richest" way of studying behavior. The test of such an hypothesis depends on the future development of personality studies, and particularly the study of values, which was our central interest in writing the book. This is not to say that the means-end schema is "simple," or "convenient" to apply. As the subsequent discussion will show, there are many difficulties to be faced. But the schema does enable one to proceed in an economical way from persons to social groups to ethics; it provides a very rich method of generating personality concepts; and it enables one to relate the study of personality to other kinds of research. However, before we finish, we shall want to reexamine the question of the suitability of a means-end scheme in the light of other desirable criteria of research methodology.

Finally, there was one specific aspect of psychological research that we thought could be vastly clarified by an explicit means-end model. Many psychological tests consist of verbal or paper-pencil responses to certain "items" which have been screened by judges and experimenters. All the experimental and computational work leading up to "measures" seemed to us to ignore the criteria for selecting an item in the first place. This remark applies not only to the older attitude measurements of Thurstone and Likert, but also to the more sophisticated methods of "factor analysis" and "latent attributes." In all cases, the original population of items is selected intuitively, which seems to mean that there is an unanalyzed agreement among the experimenters that a given item is relevant. Thus, to study attitudes toward the church, one may make up statements that apparently refer to the church in a favorable, unfavorable, or neutral fashion. But, aside from a vague inspection or a subsequent statistical check, one never knows why the item should be included. Some of the work in scale analysis indicates that the items are all measuring the same thing, but again there is no explicit and testable basis for asserting what this "same thing" is.

In effect, attitude and opinion measurement in the past seemed to us to pay far too much attention to setting up operational procedures and far too little attention to the definition of the measurements. Thus, every effort was made to characterize the nature of the test and the conditions under which the subject is to be tested. But Chapter 5 argues that no measurement exists unless one can adjust information from one environment to a whole set of environments. The measurement definition explicitly defines the set of environments. Of course, one can always restrict the "set" to one member; but it seems absurd to say that a person's attitude with respect to the church *is* the set of his replies to a series of statements presented by an experimenter in a more-or-less controlled situation.

We thought psychological measurement should begin programmatically with an explicit definition which would itself be the basis for justifying the items selected in a questionnaire as well as any other procedures used by the measurer. Instead, we found that attitudes were "defined" as tendencies, inclinations, and so on. The words in the definition were merely attempts to clarify what the writer had in mind. In effect, we felt that personality psychologists had adopted a form of Platonism. They assumed that everyone had a hazy idea of what an attitude is, and it only required some reminding by the use of other terms to make this idea universally clear. Furthermore, they seemed to argue that people's responses to the acceptable items in a questionnaire were indications of this commonly known idea of an attitude.

It is worth noting that the need for a self-conscious selection of items applies to so-called "behavioral" tests as well as paper-and-pencil or verbal responses. In order to observe behavior, one must know under what conditions behavior is to be observed and what properties of the response are to be noticed. For example, consumer-preference studies might be considered more "objective" if they consisted of observing the consumer's actions when he was given a choice between items. But such a behavioristic test might not indicate preference, if by preference one means what the person really wants to use. "Objective" tests must also justify the selection of specific test situations, and the legitimacy of the selection for consumer-preference testing is no easy matter to define.

Or, again, it is not very revealing to say that a person scores a low degree of Negro prejudice on a test, but "behavioristically" he is "really" prejudiced, unless one knows explicitly what real prejudice means and how it can be measured. One does not define a measure of prejudice by merely asserting that it is the degree of unwillingness to associate with a member of a group, because "unwillingness" and "association" are not clear concepts that direct the kinds of operations which one must perform to ascertain real prejudice. The dictionary definition of "unwarranted or unreasonable judgment" similarly provides very little help in pinpointing the concept. Evidently, prejudice is an aspect of a person's values. But determining the nature of this value is no simple matter that can be readily translated into behavioristic tests.

We were not advocates of "operationism" in the sense in which the term is commonly used in psychology. We did not think that "attitude towards the church" is to be identified with the operations necessary to arrive at numbers. But we did believe that a specification of the operations was a *necessary* condition for measurement and that the justification of the operations must follow from the definition. Consider a simple case. Someone says, "The length of this rod is 3 cm." What does "length" mean here? It is hardly helpful to say that "length" is undirectional extension. Instead, we say the length means the comparison of distances and then proceed to make this idea explicit by constructing a standard environment and set of operations, together with methods of calibration. We can then say that the length of an object *is* the ratio of the distance between its extremities to a standard meter rod under these standard conditions. The operations performed to obtain length measurements (using a ruler, or micrometer) are justified because the results are approximately those that would occur in standard conditions. The definition of length justifies and explains what was done to obtain specific measurements.

We were impressed by this contribution to scientific thinking which has grown up with the development of the physical sciences. We did not see how social science could develop measurements without adopting much the same procedure.

These comments on psychological testing are relevant to value measurement, because, except within modern utility theory, they have very often been ignored. For example, vocational guidance tests are often based on a list of items that are accepted on the basis of an unanalyzed agreement among judges. Similar remarks apply to the study of values in the fields of consumer preferences and public opinion polls.

3 • *Measuring Ascendance and Submission.*

These rather general remarks on the fruitfulness of an explicit means-end schema can be illustrated by discussing one measure—

ascendance and submission—to which we gave considerable attention. This discussion will reveal another possibly serious defect in the "scores" assigned to people by the usual test procedures.

What is meant by saying that a person is ascendant, or submissive? We begin by reflecting that if someone interferes with the subject while he is trying to do some important task, and he ignores the "aggressor," he is submissive. If he retaliates by reducing directly the aggressor's effectiveness he is ascendant. The definitional problem is, of course, more subtle than this brief account suggests. The submissive does not really "ignore" the aggressor. A more-complete definition stipulates that the aggressor is pursuing some goal himself, and this pursuit accounts for the aggressive act. The submissive is one who does not try to interfere with the aggressor's pursuit of *this* goal.

Even this account requires further refinement. Each one of the terms of the description can be defined in terms of the means-end schema: "interference" means reducing the probability that the subject's action will produce the desired results; "importance" is defined in terms of certain behavior choices, as we shall see; "ascendant response" means the choice of an action which decreases the probability that the aggressor will gain his desired goal.

We arrived at the tentative conclusion that ascendancy can be defined in terms of the probability that a person will respond aggressively if he is himself aggressed against; "aggressive" behavior is behavior which reduces the effectiveness of another's behavior relative to his intended goal. The highly ascendant person is one who directly retaliates—the submissive is not (though the latter may retaliate in devious ways).

This is a broad characterization of ascendancy. It sets up a program of research into retaliatory behavior under many different circumstances. The broad approach needs to be narrowed by further specifications which more clearly define the notion of a preference for retaliation.

A person may not retaliate because he does not know of any retaliatory action; or because he is restricted physically from such choices; or because any such choice would clearly be detrimental to his own interests (for example, physical harm might result). Any of these circumstances might very well make a difference in the kind of behavior he would exhibit.

In trying to explain the meaning of preferences for acts, it does seem essential that we remove those conditions which would prevent the free choice of an act. An act may not be chosen because it is not "available" (the subject physically cannot exhibit it); or because the subject does not know that he can choose it; and so on. The acts are "free" choices if they are equally available, and the subject knows the probabilities of the outcomes. In other words, acts are "free" if there are no physical, emotional, or intellectual restraints on choice. Discussion of the technical problems associated with a precise definition of a free act can be postponed for the moment.

We now can tentatively define ascendancy as the probability of a retaliatory choice against aggression, given a set of free actions that include varying degrees of retaliation.

What is entailed in constructing a measurement of ascendancy?

In trying to approach this problem, we are, of course, flying blind because the methods of adjusting observations of behavior from one circumstance to another are not yet well developed. But as a beginning, since we are interested in preference for acts rather than outcomes, it seems that we ought to try to purify the environment of all the influences that outcomes might exert on the subject's choices. This would mean that the choices are to be equally effective relative to the subjects' intended goal. In other words, a sensible standard for ascendancy measurement is one in which the person is free to act as he wishes, is fully aware of the consequences of his choices, and the choices have essentially the same value for him *except* for their retaliatory property.

This does not mean that the study of ascendancy is restricted to such a purified environment. Perhaps the most interesting examples of ascendant behavior occur when a person retaliates even at the risk of severe harm to himself. By setting up one standard, we do not give up the general program inherent in the definition of the concept. But there is some advantage in trying to conceptualize such a standard because thereby we can construct some more-or-less simple questionnaire situations which purposely have been structured to meet the standard conditions as closely as possible. For example, we asked the subject what he would do if he were studying for an important examination, and someone started to play a radio rather loudly. The "someone" is the aggressor, whose action has presumably decreased the subject's effectiveness for a desired goal. We then tried to make the situation appear to be one in which the subject could accomplish his aim of studying equally well whether he retaliated or not. That is, we tried to approximate a "purified" environment.

The details of the procedure are not relevant here and can be read in Ackoff's *Design of Social Research* (1). But the general motivation is quite relevant. In the first place, we did not assume that the questionnaire measures ascendancy, which it clearly does not. Rather, the questionnaire seems to be a reasonable and economic method of finding out what needs to be put into a standard. To this end, we designed our tests by varying the "degree" of aggressiveness, which was defined in terms of the amount of interference inflicted and the importance of the goal the subject is pursuing. We did this because it seemed reasonable to suppose that retaliatory behavior would vary with the degree of aggression and the subject's interest. Whether it did or not, this information could be used in the ultimate search for a satisfactory standard. Again, it became obvious that the social relationship of the aggressor (friend, stranger, foe, relative, and so on) was important and would have to be specified in the standard.

One result of this research was that even in the paper-and-pencil tests, a person's choice does depend on the intensity of his interest in his goal, on the intensity of the aggressive act, and on his relationship to the aggressor. What, therefore, is *the* measure of ascendancy or submission? One number by itself does not enable us to predict behavior. Indeed, the "score" on an ascendant-submissive test can at best be a sort of "average" response culled from many different situations; such an average is perhaps analogous to averaging the distance between two planets. We could not find any basis for a single score because we lacked a theory of behavior which enabled us to predict a person's responses in various ascendant-submissive environments on the basis of one number. To pursue the analogy, if we knew the distance between two planets at a certain moment of time, and we had other information about the masses, positions, and so on, of other bodies, we could predict the distance at another time. But if we know how a person responds when he is intensely interested, the aggression is severe, and the aggressor is his friend, we do not know how to predict his response when he is less interested, or the aggression is mild, or the aggressor is a stranger. Hence, an average score is probably meaningless, and, like the average distance between two planets, may never be very helpful in research work.

This seems to be a devastating indictment of test scores in an age when personality-testing has become so popular, and it was meant to be. Our results illustrated how mere number assignment may not measure.

We turn now to a more explicit characterization of the means-end schema. A formal definition of the schema is given in the Appendix.

4 · *Probability of Outcome and Probability of Choice.*

We think of a personality as an individual existing in a series of environments. In each environment, there is a set of actions any one of which the individual can adopt, and these actions lead with assignable probabilities to certain outcomes at a later point in time. The ingredients of a means-end schema are, therefore, the following: (1) an individual who can be identified over time; (2) a series of environments; (3) in each environment a set of actions which the individual can choose; (4) possible states of nature occurring later than the series of environments in which specified "outcomes" may or may not occur; (5) a set of numbers which measure the probabilities that the outcomes occur, given that a certain action has been chosen in a specific environment. It should be emphasized that the "environment" of a set of action choices consists of all the conditions sufficient to arrive at (5), the conditional probabilities of outcomes given a specific action. The model assumes that such an environment exists for a given moment of time.

The reader may be bothered by other assumptions which underly this means-end schema, for example, the assumption that people "really" have choices. But it seems sufficient to point out that a specific type of action is defined in terms of a range of properties, just as a specific type of animal is defined by a range of chemical properties. Also the "environments" are not rigidly defined. Hence, there is no methodological inconsistency in saying that a person can act differently under much the "same" set of circumstances, and in saying this we make no commitment concerning "free will" or "determinism" in some of the classical meanings of these terms.

It should be noted that in the spirit of the pragmatic methodology which pervades *Psychologistics* and this book as well, the decision-maker, alternatives, and goals are not given but are the products of the research design. For example, in a large organization we could define the decision-maker as the entire group in a collective sense and define the alternatives in terms of the group's behavior. Or we could concentrate attention on (say) the chief executive, and suitably modify the set of alternatives. If we make the executive the decision-maker, we recognize that he is limited in his choices by the attitudes and values of other members of his organization, and that these members are as much a part of the description of his environment as the weather or the stock market. If we make the organization the decision-maker, the environment is not the same as the environment of the executive, but possibly the set of alternative actions is the same. Indeed, "top" management might very well be defined as that individual whose alternatives are essentially the same as those of the total organization.

5 · *Measuring Preferences for Acts (Habit and Tastes).*

Our inquiry now turns to the question of the fruitfulness of the means-end schema. How much of human behavior can be adequately understood within this framework? It seems best to let the schema suggest the kinds of properties it more-or-less naturally assigns to the individual decision-maker, and then ask whether these properties reflect any recognizable characteristics of personality. Suppose we concentrate on one environment in which there is a decision-maker with alternative courses of action, and a prospective later environment where certain goals may or may not occur. It seems natural enough to ask:

(1) How does a person behave when the goals are irrelevant and only the actions themselves really matter?

(2) How does a person behave when only the goals matter, and the actions are irrelevant?

Consider for the moment the first of these questions. Suppose a person is interested in just one objective, and that in a given environment the actions open to him have equal probabilities relative to this objective and he knows that this is so. Then what does he do? In this case the goal is irrelevant in the sense that every action is equally effective. Only the actions themselves matter. This seems to be a formalized version of questions that are frequently asked about people—questions about tastes and habits. Does a man prefer wearing dark flannel suits or not? Granted that either type of action equally well accomplishes his desired aims and that there is no question about social disapproval of alternative garb, the matter becomes one of taste. "There is no disputing tastes" seems to mean that tastes describe the selection of actions when the value of the selection is a matter of indifference as far as any desired outcome is concerned. Tastes, habits, and traits are important in the study of personalities, and in *Psychologistics* we believed we had character-ized what is common to all such studies. The experimenter in these cases is not concerned with whether the subject solves a problem or wants a certain possible outcome to occur, but rather is interested in the subject's preference for acts as such.

More precisely, and generally, one program for measuring prefer-ences for acts can be defined as follows. Let $A_1, A_2 \ldots A_n$ be a set of available actions in an environment with known conditional prob-abilities relative to a set of m objectives, $O_1, O_2 \ldots O_m$. Let $P(O_i/A_j)$ be the conditional probability that O_i will occur if A_j is chosen. Then we can construct a matrix which defines the kind of standard we have in mind, where the entries in the body of the matrix are the conditional probabilities $P(O_i/A_j)$:

	Outcomes			
	O_1	O_2	$\ldots$	O_m
A_1	a_1	a_2		a_m
A_2	a_1	a_2		a_m
.		.		.
.		.		.
.		.		.
A_n	a_1	a_2		a_m

Available ("free") actions

That is $P(O_k/A_i) = P(O_k/A_j)$ for all i, j, and k. If there is only one in-tended outcome, the matrix contains only the first column.

We now introduce the concept of "probability of choice," namely, the probability that a given A_i will be chosen by the individual. This concept is essential but by no means easy to define. As we shall see, "choice" itself is conceptually a very subtle term. In the Appendix to this chapter it has been defined in terms of a producer-product relationship, which itself is defined in terms of a causal schema. But even if we knew what choice meant, we still have not adequately defined "probability of choice," because we need to know the refer-ence class (see Chapter 6). Are we asking about choices of the individual in any state, or about his choices when his state is prescribed in some manner? The concept of taste suggests that the individual must himself be aware of what is going on. That is, he must know that the actions are available and that each action is equally effective for the goals. We are therefore asking for the probability of choice of an action when the individual is in this state.

The study of ascendancy belongs in the "act-preference" category of psychological studies. Our previous discussion suggests that ascendancy studies are studies of a subject's preference for retaliatory actions against aggressors.

It should be emphasized that we have not shown how act-preferences can be measured because measurements also would enable us to predict action choices when the environment changes. For example, we have already suggested that in ascendancy tests the social relationship between the aggressor and the subject may be important. Hence, we may estimate the probability that an ascendant choice is made when (say) the aggressor is friendly but not be able to predict the choice when the aggressor is a stranger. Furthermore, we would normally be interested in the probability of choice when the actions were not equally effective. In other words, we might try to predict the choice of action when one "penalizes" the most-preferred act by (say) reducing its chances of attaining a desired outcome. The subject, therefore, is presented with a conflict choice. He wants to choose the act for its own sake, and he wants the outcome to occur. In effect, the measure of the preference for the act will tell us the (marginal) sacrifice he is willing to make of a desired end in order to go on choosing the act.

Furthermore, even if the alternative actions are equally effective and the subject has no preference for one act over the other, he may choose one act consistently because he does not like to change. This prediction could be made, of course, if we knew how to include preference for change or nonchange in the value scheme of the subject and, hence, knew how to adjust for it. There are obviously a number of technical difficulties in doing this.

Finally, a measure of preference for acts should tell us how the subject would behave when he believes (rather than knows) the probabilities of the actions' outcomes. Can we safely say that if a subject chooses an action when he knows the probabilities are P_1, $P_2, \ldots,$ he will also choose the action when he believes the probabilities are P_1, P_2, . . . , even though they do not objectively have these values? Some consideration of this question needs to be given, but we will postpone it until we have discussed other aspects of the means-end model.

6 · *The Presuppositions of Preference Measures.*

A person's preference for acts has been defined in terms of his choices, given that the acts have equal effectiveness for his desired outcomes and that he knows this. But "desirability" and "knowledge" have not yet been defined. Haven't we implicitly assumed the meaning of these concepts?

But this question recalls a familiar theme of this entire book: that knowledge and value are "inseparable" concepts whether we are talking about individual persons or the whole of science. The theme in the present instance appears in the following form. Given the means-end schema, we can define preference for acts in terms of the concepts "knowledge" and "desirability of outcomes." As we shall see, we can also define knowledge, given the schema, in terms of the meaning of act-preference and outcome desirability. Finally we can define desirability of outcome, given the schema, in terms of act-preference and knowledge. Thus act-preference, knowledge, and desirability of outcome are an integrated set of concepts not really separable in the context of the whole problem of studying personality. But saying this much does not help the psychological-researcher to find practical procedures. His problem, however, is no more difficult than that of any measurer. We have already seen how length measurements have become involved in a similar "circularity" of concepts. A very subtle methodological question is the statement of the conditions under which a mutual interdependence of concepts is or is not viciously circular. In any case, it is essential that we examine in more detail the nature of the circle of psychological concepts which is assumed here.

7 · *Knowledge.*

Imagine that we have succeeded in finding a set of actions which satisfy the matrix given on p. 185. Suppose the subject chooses each action of the set with an equal frequency. But suppose that we no longer assume that he knows the probabilities that each action will lead to a given outcome. We still assume that the subject is aware of the availability of the actions, and that he wants the goal or goals to which the actions may or may not lead.

Consider a test in which one tries to ascertain how "sensitive" the subject is to the effectiveness of an action for a desired result. Such sensitivity could be tested if the effectiveness of one of the equally preferred actions is slightly altered in such a manner that it is somewhat more effective than the others.

This simplified concept of knowledge can be represented by the following matrix, where the symbols are the same as those given on p. 185, and ϵ is a suitably small number greater than 0:

		Outcomes			
		O_1	O_2	$\ldots$	O_m
Set of	A_1	$a_1 + \epsilon$	$a_2 + \epsilon$	$\ldots$	$a_m + \epsilon$
available	A_2	a_1	a_2	$\ldots$	a_m
and	.				
equally	.				
preferred	.				
actions	A_n	a_1	a_2	$\ldots$	a_m

Suppose that (as indicated in the matrix) one of the actions is more effective relative to the desired outcomes and that the person selects the action. His selection is only partial evidence of knowledge because knowledge is a comparison of performance when the effectiveness of actions is changed. Thus we would have to know how the subject acted when $\epsilon = 0$, or when $\epsilon < 0$. Hence we can think of a measure of knowledge in terms of a positive correlation between the probability of adopting an action and its effectiveness. Or, if we had a model of a subject's behavior in which, for any set of effectiveness measures of the actions, we could predict the subject's choice (assuming that he wants certain outcomes), then knowledge would be a measure that enables us to predict how a person will change his choice given that changes occur in the effectiveness measures.

Again we have not defined a measure of knowledge. Instead, the discussion indicates how knowledge is related to other concepts and poses the programmatic problem of developing measures of knowledge. It can be seen even in the relatively simple matrix given above that the separation of act-preference from knowledge cannot readily be made. Suppose that in the original matrix on p. 185 the subject chooses all actions with equal frequency, and that in the revised matrix given above on p. 188 he chooses only A_1. One explanation of his behavior would be that he knows the effectiveness of each action in both cases and has no preference for the actions as such. Since he wants the outcomes, he is indifferent with respect to the actions in the first matrix and chooses only A_1 in the second matrix. An equally plausible explanation is that in the first case he did not believe that A_1 was as effective as the other actions, but he sometimes chose it nevertheless because he preferred it to the other actions. Under this interpretation, he is actually indifferent between the value of the outcome that is sacrificed by choosing A_1 and the value of choosing A_1 for its own sake. But if A_1 is given an increment ϵ of effectiveness, he may choose it consistently because now he regards it to be as effective as the alternative actions, and he prefers A_1 more than the other actions.

The example suggests that either explanation may be suitable and that the optimal choice of explanations depends on certain decision criteria. Before considering this point in detail, it will be advisable to introduce other concepts implied in the means-end schema.

8 · *Intelligence.*

Knowledge is a measure of rate of change (relative to efficiency) in behavior choices under specified conditions. This notion of knowledge, as a "velocity" of change relative to the effectiveness of actions naturally leads one to ask about the "acceleration" of change—the rate at which knowledge improves. This acceleration could be defined relative to time, and if this is done, we have in effect a definition of the "intelligence" of an individual relative to a specific problem. Thus we have arrived at three quite distinct areas for the study of choices of action: preference for acts, knowledge (rate of change of choice relative to the effectiveness of acts), and intelligence (rate of change of knowledge relative to time).

We can now turn our attention to the outcomes themselves,

rather than the immediate choices of action which are the basis for studies of preferences for actions and knowledge of actions.

9 · *Values of Outcomes (Intention).*

Suppose for the moment that we have a suitable classification of the outcomes that might occur if a person makes certain choices of behavior. How can we determine which outcome he prefers, and in general measure his preference for each of the outcomes? In other words, how do we ascertain a person's true intentions?

Again, we start off with our chief resource, common sense, and proceed to refinements. Suppose someone says, "I didn't intend to step on your toe, and indeed had I known you had your foot out in the aisle, I would have avoided it." The hint from this remark is that unintended outcomes are outcomes that occur because of ignorance, or because of other factors beyond the person's control. When we talk of intentions we are inferring that the person would act in a particular manner if the restraints were removed.

This is precisely the same conclusion we reached in talking about preference for acts: such preferences mean action choices when the choices are "free." When we talk of intentions, we are estimating which outcomes a person would pursue if a set of actions were freely available and if he knew the conditional probabilities of these actions relative to the outcomes. But if we are interested in the value of the *outcomes* only, then we must stipulate that for the subject no *act* has any greater value than any other act.

In other words, we define the value of outcomes in terms of a selection of an act from among a set of "free" choices: each choice is available, is known to have a specific probability of leading to an outcome, and is preferred equally with respect to other available choices.

As an example, suppose we could set up alternative actions each with a conditional probability of $a > o$ for an outcome, and conditional probabilities of o for all the other outcomes. If the actions are all available to a person, if he knew these conditional probabilities, and if the actions were equally preferred, then his choice would be evidence of what he intends. The scheme for this simplified intention standard is given in the following matrix, where the values shown in the body of the matrix are the conditional probabilities.

| | Outcomes | | | |
	O_1	O_2	$\ldots$	O_n
A_1	a	o	$\ldots$	o
A_2	o	a		o
A_3	o	o		o
.	.	.		.
.	.	.		.
.	.	.		.
A_n	o	o		a

Set of equally preferred and available actions

There is certainly nothing very new or sophisticated about this analysis. In consumer preference tests of a simple sort, we present the subject with alternative brands and ask him to make a choice. Presumably he knows that he can have only one of the brands, and presumably he knows that he will receive the brand he chooses (that is, he knows that $a = 1$). Hence, when we say that a person's choices are an indication of preference, we mean that we can predict the way in which the future outcome influences his choices when he is equally familiar with all the alternatives, knows what outcomes will result from each choice, and knows that each action-choice leads to only one of the outcomes. There is no denying the tremendous technical difficulties involved in inferring behavior under such conditions. But it is true that in practice people use the matrix given above to test a person's interests. An additional example occurs in the study of a person's relaxations. Which objective does he want: painting, seeing a play, or solving a chess problem? The frequency of choices of actions leading to these objectives is often taken to provide a ranking of the person's interests, and assuming that the means were roughly equivalent in effectiveness, one might even call the resulting frequencies a measure of intention (preference). Similarly, a Hooper rating is an estimate of the frequency of choice of one TV program over another by a population of listeners at a certain hour. In this case the conditions of the simple-choice situation are presumably closely approximated. The subject knows each available program by reading the newspapers. He presumably has no preference for turning the dial in one direction or the other, so that the means for getting any of the programs are equally familiar (with the possible exception of lazy listeners who never turn the dial or nervous ones who always do). Thus Hooper ratings for single listeners or for groups of listeners might be taken as measures of preference for objectives. A similar use of the matrix is often the basis for policy decisions on adult-education programs, freeways and toll roads, transportation routes, and types of theatre, to mention a few examples. In each case, the measure of preference is taken to be the relative frequency with which the objective is sought once the means for attaining it are available. The planner attempts to estimate what this frequency would be if the social group knew of the existence of the means and the manner in which it can be used to pursue the goal.

But in all these instances we may have good grounds for doubting whether the "purified" conditions really apply. When a man buys apples, or cars, or houses, it is extremely difficult to determine what he knows or does not know. Further, we rarely can be sure that he does not have preferences for certain actions as well as the outcomes, so that the choice is not clear evidence of his intentions relative to the outcomes. Finally, we often do not know what his choices will be at other times (for example, when the choices are not all equally effective for their respective outcomes) and hence cannot infer behavior in the standard environment.

Admitting the difficulties of empirical application, we can nevertheless define the values of outcomes as predictors of behavior when a person is aware of the alternative actions, can freely choose any one of them (in the sense that he has no preference for any act as such), and knows the conditional probabilities. This is really more a characterization of values than a definition of measurement of values. It relates the concept of value-of-outcome to other concepts in the means-end schema.

One specific point concerning this characterization is worth mentioning since it will recur in the discussion of rational behavior in the next chapter. There does seem to be a distinction between saying that a person acts in a certain way *when* he knows the conditional probabilities of the alternatives and saying that he acts in a certain way *because* he knows the conditional probabilities. And further it seems reasonable to assert that values, preferences, and intentions are concepts that refer to acts that are made because (not just when) the subject has knowledge. Indeed, the concept of "choice" seems to imply that the subject acts because of his knowledge. In other words, "choice" is not directly ascertainable, nor is it a primitive concept of value theory. The Appendix to this chapter defines the concept within the framework of the means-end schema.

We can now reappraise the relationships we have been discussing. Within a means-end schema we can define "free choices" if we are willing to accept the meaning of certain concepts as given. But since we have abandoned the methodological use of primitive concepts, we are faced with a circle. Is the circle vicious? Apparently not, if we consider that we were driven to the concepts of knowledge and value by a distinction prevalent in common language. We are really searching for ways to predict human behavior, and it may be that in the end we will not have any simple way to distinguish between knowledge and value measurements. For the present, the distinctions are worth keeping. Indeed, they suggest ways in which a practical approach to the study of behavior can be made. This practical approach is one that is frequently adopted in empirical studies of behavior: the experimenter, using his intuition or any other available resources, makes certain assumptions about the state of knowledge of the subject, as well as the subject's attitudes towards the available choices. As he conducts his tests, he begins to gain increased reliance on the assumptions he has made, as well as on the measurements that have been made.

Hence, the separation of knowledge and value as concepts enables the researcher to categorize his assumptions. More to the point, in terms of a pragmatic theory of measurement, it enables him to categorize his alternative decisions. If a subject makes a choice—even repeatedly—he may do so because he prefers the associated outcome, or he may do so because he likes the choice itself, or because he thinks the alternatives are riskier for their respective ends, or because there is some other end he thinks this choice also serves. The researcher's decision problem is to select the optimal inference from among such a set of alternatives. Thus in our earlier discussion of knowledge on p. 189, we suggested how certain evidence might be construed as evidence of knowledge or evidence of preference for acts. Similar choices for the researcher occur in studies of the values of outcomes.

Since these choices are typical of all measurement, as Chapter 5 argues, we can proceed on the basis that there is justification in talking about "the area" of value research defined by a means-end schema. This area, like all areas of research, is definable in terms of a program.

10 · *Critical Appraisal of the Program for Value Research.*

In terms of the research scheme we have been studying, the program of value research is characterized by the aim of predicting what the person would do if he has equal preference for all available actions and knew the respective conditional probabilities for each of the outcomes.

This concept certainly requires some defense as well as elaboration. Many students of value theory have offered a more restricted concept of value, namely, an exhibition of preference based on a "rational choice." "Rational behavior" is a prediction of behavior of rational people, and "rationality" is regarded as an ideal not always met by normal men. But, so runs this argument, the true values of a person are defined in terms of what he would do if he were rational. What "rational" means in this context is no easy matter to decide. It may mean that the person chooses on ethical grounds, that is, the only values are those that follow from ethical principles. But it does seem sensible to say that a man can be rationally selfish, even though his selfishness is unethical. "Rational" behavior is more often defined as behavior that meets the demands of consistency. Some examples of definitions of rational behavior will be discussed in the next chapter.

There is no denying the usefulness of the concept of rationality in providing the researcher with a model that, at least on intuitive grounds, seems to be a valid basis for predicting behavior under the ideal conditions of completely free choice. In other words, if we know that the subject is "rational" in some precise sense of the term, we have a model in terms of which we can actually construct value measurements.

But the real issue is whether we are to insist on making a rationality model an integral part of the program of value research. Must we assert that "X ought to do A" means "X would do A if his choices were free and he were rational?" If we do assert this, then we must either (1) exclude from the program of value research the study of all persons whose behavior cannot adequately be interpreted as rational, or (2) construct a model that enables us to predict how these persons would behave if they were rational, or (3) spend time and effort training subjects to be rational. In the last case, persuasion becomes an integral part of the meaning of value: "*X* ought to do *A*" means "*X* would do *A* if his choices were free and he were persuaded to adopt rational decision rules according to some definition of rationality."

There seem to be at least two strong reasons why we ought not to bind ourselves to these choices. First, as the next chapter argues, the meaning of rational behavior which is commonly adopted depends on certain "intuitions" of the researcher, and we have as yet no way of analyzing the origin of these intuitions (for example, are they culturally biased, in terms of our language, or our economic history?). Second, the rational behavior models are often very restricted, and there is the question of whether attempts to enrich them are really the most economical way of proceeding. Both of these points will be discussed in the sequel; that is, we shall want to consider whether a long-run commitment to the concept of rationality is a desirable choice for the researcher, admitting that the concept has obvious short-term advantages. For the present, the program of value research, which defines the concept of value, should be stated in very general terms.

The remainder of this chapter is a series of footnotes on various aspects of this program.

11 · "*Ought.*"

First, we return to the discussion of Chapter 1, and reconsider the meaning of "ought." Assume that the value measures of outcomes have been obtained. They enable the experimenter to predict the person's behavior choices if the person knew the true conditional probabilities. This behavior may, of course, be described in terms of a set of "probabilities of choice," and not in terms of some one specific choice.

We have argued that expressions of the form "*X* ought to do *A*" can be interpreted as "*X* would do *A* if *X* knew the conditional probabilities," or, more precisely, "*X* would do *A* if *X* had perfect knowledge, and had no preference for any of the action choices as such." Hence prescriptive sentences are translatable into predictive sentences.

We may note one technical point which the earlier discussion glossed over. In general, one cannot predict behavior when perfect knowledge and equal act-preference are the only information available. Other aspects of the environment also influence behavior choices. Hence the question "Ought X to do A?" may only be answerable in the form "X ought to do A under conditions C_1," with no implied commitment about his optimal choice under conditions C_2.

But the important point for consideration is the translation itself. We have used a device that is basic in any general process of measurement to interpret an obscure common-sense expression. In this regard, we have done no more than is customary in an attempt to move from a common-sense basis to a scientific one. But the translation should still have some appeal to common sense, even though it is usually impossible to catch all the nuances that common sense entails.

If we were measuring the length of an object, it would not be very reasonable to assert that the object "ought to have" length l at time t, meaning thereby that it would have this length under standard conditions. But we have already noted in Chapter 5 that the assignment of a length to an object enables one to predict how the object would compare with other objects in various environments. *What* number is assigned is determined by the economic conditions entailed in any construction of standards. These economic conditions depend on the actual utilization that is made of information about lengths, namely, certain kinds of comparisons. The analogy can be carried this far, at least. We can say that in measuring the values of goals we are interested in predicting a person's behavior. It seems reasonable to assert that we are trying to find out how these goals "determine" what he does. This last statement is interpreted, in this book, to imply that we are interested in the way goals determine behavior when a person's choices are not restrained by ignorance or compulsion. If he were not aware that he had a choice leading to a certain goal, his actual behavior would not indicate how the goal would influence him. Also, if he were forced by someone else to make a certain choice, the goal would not "freely" determine his behavior; but "equal preference" for the acts is supposed to imply that no compulsion exists for one act rather than another. That is,

the conditions that must be satisfied in order to infer equal preference include implicitly the stipulation that no outside force restrains
the person's choices. Hence, the suggested form of a standard for
measuring goal values is supposed to reflect this common-sense need
for the measurement of values. Note that we have not "purified" the
standard by removing all determinants of a person's values: he may
value a goal very highly because some person or situation forced
him to. The origins of a person's value structure are not made a part
of the standard for measuring his values.

Another way to defend the present thesis is to recall that "X ought
to do *A*" is some sort of a recommendation. Thus, the "force" of a
recommendation is something like the force of an assertion that a
mechanic might make after fixing an automobile: "This ought to
work now" means, "If all the operating conditions have been met,
this will work." The "operating conditions" of human performance
include knowledge and freedom of choice. I do not mean to force
this analogy of course; it merely suggests why a recommendation
entails a sense of compulsion. The force of a recommendation lies
in the fact that an improvement of the subject's *knowledge* (of the
conditional probabilities of his actions) will result in his adopting
the behavior being recommended.

It is clear that the measurement of value and the structure of a
recommendation depend on how the alternative choices and the
objectives are classified. These classifications are the scientist's
choices—just as in any measurement process the scientist has a choice
of the manner in which he will view the world. What choice is correct depends on research into the aims of the scientist—or on some
more ultimate values of science, such as those discussed in Chapter
14.

In general, it is sensible to say that the proposed definition of
value is an hypothesis. We have, for example, excluded preference
for acts from the definition, though these preferences may be the
most important "values" a person has. The dichotomy of the act and
the goal is primarily one of conceptual convenience, and there is no
reason why a scientist might not want to make act-preference measures the inseparable components of goal values. More important,
we have made no mention of one set of "objectives" of men—ideals
that by their nature are unattainable (perfect knowledge, perfect

cooperation, and so on). Here the conditional probabilities are o and usually known to be so. In Chapter 15 we shall return to this question.

But further comments on the hypothesis proposed here need to be made before we can decide on its adequacy.

12 · *The Horizon.*

For example, it is a commonplace that the objectives one seeks to attain at a future moment of time may very well be the means for other objectives lying even farther ahead in the future. A man may seek a promotion as a step in his more ultimate goal of the presidency; or, a firm may try to increase its share of a market in order to attain a larger profit over a five-year period.

But the suggested general standard for value measurements makes no commitment concerning future objectives. Specifically, it does not include in the definition a knowledge about the probability of all possible outcomes over time, but only of the outcomes of a specific time. Quite clearly a person who knew the chances of success for outcomes at t_1, but *not* for outcomes at a later time t_2, might make different choices from a person who knew the chances relative to both times.

This means, as we have already suggested, that the general program for value measurements requires information about other properties of the situation and the person in order that a prediction of choice of behavior be made. Whenever a person's values for more-distant objectives at t_2 do influence his present choices, then the standard for measuring his values for nearer objectives at t_1 must presuppose a knowledge of the conditional probabilities of the alternative choices relative to the objectives at t_2. Otherwise, we would not be able to measure the importance of the later objectives for him, and hence we could not ascertain their influence.

Thus, in order to measure the values of objectives at time t_1 we may have to know a great deal about the values of objectives at some later time t_2, because these long-run objectives influence present choices. In contrast, some outcomes may be terminal in the sense that a knowledge of what comes after them in time has no effect on a person's behavior. These objectives seem to be what certain philosophers call "immanently" valuable—valued in and of themselves.

An objective is immanently valuable if its value measurement remains the "same" (that is, is used to predict behavior in the same way) no matter what the person's state of knowledge about the consequences of attaining objectives at a later time may be. In contrast, more-distant outcomes may determine all the intermediate behavior of some decision-makers in the sense that a knowledge of their chances of attaining these outcomes completely predicts behavior with respect to all intermediary outcomes. In Chapter 3 we suggested that "net profit" over a long period might be such a determining outcome for certain firms, although at the present time we do not know how to estimate behavior relative to such distant goals.

Thus it depends on the personality of the individual being studied, whether values of objectives are terminal, determining, or have some other characteristic. There is, however, a more-subtle question to be raised about this point. Hitherto we have linked the concepts of value measurements and recommendations together by saying that a person ought to do what he would do if his choices were free. But his "free choices" in the sense we have used the phrase may be influenced by his values for certain future goals. They may also be influenced by his erroneous conception of these future goals, or his erroneous estimate of the probabilities of gaining them. We have not insisted that the influences on a person's values must also take on one standard form. In other words, we could say that a recommendation is always relevant to some specific future time t_1, and makes no commitment about some later time t_2; or we could say that a recommendation for objectives at t_1 must be a recommendation for the decision-maker for all future times that are relevant. Nothing seems to force a choice upon us, but as we proceed to social values and ethics we will be classifying various kinds of recommendations. We can therefore note that the present discussion differentiates between temporal and atemporal recommendations for a single decision-maker.

13 · Can Learning Be Valued?

Consider now a further critical problem about the concept of value measurements which has been developed here. We often say that a person "wants" to know more about the conditional probabilities of the actions available to him. Indeed, this is a central issue of the theory of information-gathering and analysis: whether to stop acquiring evidence and make a decision to act, or whether to go on acquiring evidence. In *Psychologistics* we treat this idea under the head of "doubt." We said that the measure of intensity of doubt was the person's desire (intention) to increase his knowledge of the conditional probabilities of an action. Thus very intense doubt is exhibited when the person sacrifices a great deal to learn more about the situation, a common failing of faculty committees.

But does this notion of intention to increase knowledge make sense if we accept the theory of value measurements discussed above? At first sight it does not. "Increased knowledge" is now one of the possible outcomes of the actions. What sense does it make to say that a measure of value for this outcome is a prediction of how the subject would behave if he knew the conditional probabilities of all actions? Or rather, the answer is trivial. If he knew the conditional probabilities, he could not choose an action that led to increasing knowledge.

This question reflects again the manner in which knowledge and intention are so closely interwoven. One solution to the difficulty is to treat the subject as a reflective agent—a person who is trying to decide which of two agents he wants to be. Suppose a person could view himself in two ways: one as the ignorant agent he now is, the other as the agent he would be if his ignorance were removed. Thus the researcher tries to predict the choice of the subject if he did know the conditional probabilities of the outcomes when this (partially ignorant) agent acts, and he did know the conditional probabilities if an agent with improved knowledge were to act. He also knows the conditional probabilities of the outcomes if the agent sacrifices time, effort, or some other value, in order to bring himself into a state of complete knowledge. We want to predict which choice he would make. Does he choose to be the partially ignorant agent or to be the agent that increases his knowledge? The measurements required for such a prediction are measurements of the value of increased knowledge. Thus "increase in knowledge" can be assigned some value measurement if we classify the subject's choices in this manner. In many studies we may find that additional information, although it improves the accuracy of our estimates, is not worth the expense. We estimate what we would gain if we had the additional information and we estimate what we would lose by trying to acquire it, and decide that the "net" is negative.

This discussion indicates that "knowledge of the conditional probabilities" was ambiguously characterized in the earlier discussion. We said earlier that a person knows the probabilities, *not* if he merely makes the correct choices, but if he is "sensitive" to changes in the probabilities, that is, continues to make the correct choices even when the probabilities change. But such a person may still want to acquire more information in the sense defined above. Such a desire would be evidence that he does not know the true chances of increasing his knowledge. Hence, when we say that a person "knows" the conditional probabilities, do we also mean that he "knows he knows" or do we impose no restraints on his knowledge of his own state? The question perhaps has more relevance to the history of philosophy than it does to practical applications of decision theory, but the lesson of this history seems to be that "knowledge" must include self-knowledge. Hence, we are trying to predict behavior when the decision-maker knows the conditional probabilities, and does not (erroneously) wish to increase his knowledge.

The concept of the value of learning is important because, as Simon and March suggest in *Organizations* (9), the most fruitful theory of behavior may be one which predicts choice based on the supremacy of the value of learning rather than direct maximization of clearly perceived values. But the observing scientist cannot verify that the learning objective is optimal unless he estimates the values of other objectives; it may be desirable for the decision-maker to simplify his deliberations, but in order to prove that this is so the observer may require a more complicated model where all alternatives and objectives are included.

14 · *Maximization and Value Measurements.*

It is important to note that the purpose of this chapter is not to develop a theory of behavior, but to provide a standard for measuring values which a theory would enable us to use. Hence, we are not chiefly concerned with whether man is typically a learner or a maximizer. Suppose, though, that we briefly characterize these two theories, reserving for later discussion some of the important details.

A theory of maximization can be characterized in the following way: associated with each action-outcome combination there is an efficiency measure and with each outcome a value measure of such a nature that the maximization of a function of these measures alone is a sufficient condition for predicting the behavior of a person if his choices are "free" in the sense defined above. More generally, there may be more than one measure associated with each goal or each action-goal combination, or alternatively, one measure may apply to a subset of two or more goals (or action-goal combinations).

The chief candidates for suitable measures for maximization theory have been the following: with respect to action-outcome combinations, either the true conditional probabilities, or the best-available estimates of these probabilities, or the subject's estimate (belief); with respect to outcomes, either the amount of pleasure, or the amount of net discounted monetary return, or the utility in the contemporary sense of this term, or approximation measures to unattainable goals. The maximizing function is often taken to be a product of one of the probability measures and one of the outcome measures, but not always. None of the advocates of pleasure or monetary measures has yet been able to exhibit a function which acts as a reliable predictor in any but a very restricted set of contexts, as Chapters 2 and 3 try to show. Contemporary utility theory, as we shall see in the next chapter, has attempted to construct a general axiom set sufficiently strong to establish a product function as a predictor in specifically defined contexts.

A very pertinent question about "maximization theories" is to ask how they could fail. Suppose we try to state the basic assumption of the theory in mathematical terms. Consider a function of two variables, $f(x,y)$. Suppose it is possible to associate with each alternative action A_i a unique number couple (x, y) belonging to the domain of this function; for example, x might be the conditional probability, y the utility of the outcome. Then if this can be done, for each A_i there corresponds a value of the function $f(x,y)$. Suppose further that A_i will be chosen if and only if the value of $f(x,y)$ associated with A_i lies in a certain range, or has some specific property. Maximization (or minimization) theory states that A_i will be chosen if and only if the associated $f(x,y)$ is a maximum (or minimum) over all the values of $f(x,y)$ of the alternatives. Maximization theory would be "wrong" relative to some $f(x,y)$ which could be used to predict behavior if the prediction did not depend on maximization. For example, a man might decide that he does not want to maximize his income, but instead wants an income of exactly $5000 per annum. A student of his behavior could then construct a function $f(x,y)$, where x is a probability vector and y an income vector, and he would decide that A_i will be chosen for which the associated value of $f(x,y)$ is $5000. But then a "maximization advocate" could point out that this theory is too restricted (for example, no such A_i may exist) and that the appropriate function to be used is not $f(x,y)$ but a function that measures the difference between $f(x,y)$ and $5000; the subject is, in this case, minimizing this function. This example suggests that it may be quite difficult to construct a theory of optimal behavior which cannot be translated into a theory of maximization. This is true, but the essence of most maximization theories is not maximization per se, but the thesis that optimal decision-making consists of scanning all alternatives and choosing the one having the maximum return. It may be much more fruitful to assert that optimal decision-making consists of simplifying the situation by examining only a few alternatives relative to a less-comprehensive criterion of effectiveness. One might reply that this is a good description of how choices are made but not of how they ought to be made. Also, the advocate of maximization might point out that the decision-maker has a choice between attempting to scan all alternatives (at some cost to himself) or being satisfied with a less-exhaustive and complicated survey, and his optimal choice may be the latter. No doubt such a theory of behavior could be subsumed under a more general theory of maximization in which learning is one of the goals, but whether this would be the most useful way of reconciling the theoretical viewpoints is difficult to say. In any case, as was pointed out above, the proof of the optimality of simplification must be found in a more-general and complicated theory.

Later on we shall want to examine another, quite different theory of optimal choice in which the decision-maker is taken to be a pursuer of unattainable ideals.

As was suggested earlier, some researchers defend a type of maximization on the grounds that the maximization follows from the axioms of "rational" behavior; they would argue that "X ought to do *A*" means that "*X* would do *A* if his behavior accorded with rational criteria." In this respect, these researchers might agree with the minimal conditions of value research and yet disagree with the interpretation of "ought" that is proposed here. In effect, the minimal conditions proposed here do not include any stipulation about the manner in which the subject uses his knowledge of the conditional probabilities. If "ought" connotes rational choice in some sense, then there may be a strong case for adding further conditions. This is a matter to which we can profitably devote the whole next chapter.

15 · *Subjective Probabilities.*

Before turning our attention to these topics, we shall consider one final problem, which in effect raises the question whether the minimal conditions suggested here are too strong, rather than too weak. Specifically, value research might be defined in terms of predicting choice, given the decision-maker's *beliefs* about the conditional probabilities; or, it might be defined in terms of predicting choice, given the best available evidence concerning the probabilities.

Whether or not the first suggestion really differs from the one proposed here depends on the definition of belief or, more generally, on the definition of subjective probabilities. Suppose we have some method of measuring a person's belief that an outcome will occur if a certain action is chosen. Suppose, too, that the measurement is such that we can test whether a person's beliefs are "correct," that is, whether the subjective probabilities "equal" the true probabilities (or the best estimates of these). Then the goal of a program that tries to predict behavior given any set of subjective probabilities would be the same as the objective of a program that tries to predict behavior given the true probabilities. The suppositions required to bring about an equivalence of the two programs are quite strong, and may not hold in a given research program. In this book we are primarily interested in defining a program of value research that enables us to verify a recommendation. We have argued that a recommendation is valid if it (implicitly) predicts behavior when the decision-maker knows the true probabilities. It seems patently wrong to say that "*X* ought to do *A*" means simply that *X* will do *A* because the subjective probabilities have a certain value.

16 · *Estimated Probabilities.*

We turn now to the second suggestion: Why shouldn't the program of value research be defined in terms of "best estimates of probabilities" instead of "true probabilities," especially since any predictive formula using probabilities will have to use the best estimates of any given time? Clearly the researcher himself never knows the true probabilities.

This question is, above all, important for an understanding of the purposes of this book. Anyone who has studied decision-making cannot help but be impressed by the abysmal ignorance that pervades the subject; even the most-careful analysis probably fails to discern all the alternatives and certainly fails to provide precise estimates of the conditional probabilities. Therefore, what use is it to define optimal choices in terms of "a complete set of alternatives" with known outcomes? The answer is that all measurements are defined in terms of ideal standards, and accuracy is used to estimate how close a given empirical process comes to the ideal. Thus, the inability to construct a standard condition is no evidence pro or con for a given proposal for standardization. Perhaps in some cases we can estimate the optimal very closely by means of a mathematical model and accounting procedures; in other cases, the best available methods may be a set of judgments based on personal opinions. In either event, we are trying to approximate as closely as possible using the resources available. This is all that scientific method can require a scientist to do.

But there is one aspect of this question which is quite relevant to the history of man's values, a history which is central to the development of social morality and ethics. Consider the two assertions:

(A) "Value measurements are estimators of behavior when the subject knows the best estimates of his social group concerning the conditional probabilities and is free to make choices."

(B) "Value measurements are estimators of behavior when the subject knows the true conditional probabilities and is free to make choices."

The only apparent difference between these two assertions—and an important one certainly—is the issue of how one should regard the estimates of past or "culturally deficient" societies and peoples. As has just been argued with respect to our present culture, there can be no methodological difference between the two positions, for the "best estimates of the true probabilities" will be the measures which the experimenter will use in his predictions, that is, he will provisionally take these quantities to be correct in order to make value measurements.

But the question of past or scientifically deficient societies and their beliefs is an important one. Which statement more adequately represents the aim of value research: the measurements of the values of the Romans are estimates of those actions they would have performed had they been able to apply science as they best knew it to their policy problems—or, the measurement of the values of the Romans are estimates of those actions they would have performed had they known the "true" effectiveness of the courses of actions available to them. Another way of stating the second viewpoint is to say that our present-day measures of the values of the Romans are estimates of the actions they would have performed had they known what we know today—that is, our measurements of their values are adjusted to our estimates of the true probabilities.

First let us note that the two statements are quite different because they lead to distinct notions of what the Romans valued. Did the Romans really wish to abolish slavery? The argument that they did not could run as follows: the Romans were willing to make large sacrifices of lives and capital to maintain the institution of slavery. As they understood the social world, slavery was the only manner in which other institutions and conditions, such as education, high standard of living for the wealthy, or games, could be maintained. Their actions showed that these conditions were the ones they wanted to pursue, given their knowledge of society, even though it meant that certain people remained in bondage. But if one adopts the second position, one has to show that even with an improved knowledge of how to manage their society with the means available to them, the Romans would still have chosen courses of action that maintained the institution of slavery.

The first position makes the study of the values of the past become closely dependent on the science of a culture or society, to the extent that primitive peoples must be said to want certain diseases or unsanitary conditions because, relative to their best science, they would choose actions that lead to these outcomes.

Thus if we define values in terms of the state of knowledge of a social group, then we would have to say that some classes of society, or some peoples of the world, do not "value" a better standard of living, meaning that even if we gave them the opportunity to improve they would do nothing about it because the social group to which they belong believes that the means are bad. Such an argument would enable one to serve the needs of a social group by keeping them in ignorance. It is interesting to note, therefore, that the question about the suitable interpretation of the term "value" is in this context an ethical one. I cannot help but feel that the answer on ethical grounds is rather obvious: we ought to define "value" in terms of objective probabilities in the sense of Chapter 6, that is, in terms of the best estimates of the science of all ages.

17 · *Reflections on this Chapter.*

One somewhat startling consequence of the foregoing discussion is that if we say we are the most scientifically advanced culture up to the present time, it is possible for us to know more about the values of the Romans, or even of some contemporary cultures, than these societies could know about themselves. It is possible for us to do this if we have as much relevant information as they did, and in addition we have better estimates of the probabilities that actions available to them lead to specific outcomes. No one can deny that adopting this position places a tremendous burden on our faith in our own science. Do we really know more about the true values of the primitive than he does himself? This smacks of the missionary—and indeed it is intended to. But it implies a social policy relative to science that perhaps the older missionary would have shunned: social scrutiny and criticism of the scientist's efforts and inferences.

If there is to be a science of values, a science that measures value, then such a science is not merely a matter of tacking on one more discipline to the family of sciences. For a science of values makes a strong, important, and dangerous assumption: it is possible to know a man's values better than he does himself. The contribution of the scientist is not merely to show a man how he can better gain his goals. It also estimates for him what his goals really are—something he may not be aware of at all.

Dangerous? Surely. What do the workers of the world really want?

And be "objective" about your answer! If "objective" means "divorce yourself from all your notions of political and social objectives," how can this possibly be done? The scientist makes decisions, and his decisions that have an influence on society are subject to the review of that society. What American scientist today would be willing to accept the hypothesis that today's worker really wants a "proletarian dictatorship"?

The science of values, if it exists or ever will exist, makes the scientist, as a scientist, an important and a potentially dangerous man. This may or may not be a new role for the scientist. It is certainly one that is well recognized relative to the businessman and the worker: both are important and potentially dangerous.

Actually science has no choice as to whether or not to develop a science of values if such a development is possible. For science in its own inference-making presupposes a theory of decision, and hence if value measurements are possible, science must make them at least for its own activities.

Furthermore, the scientist today need not be surprised if he must appear before Congressional committees; if his "aloof foundations" are investigated for subversion; or if scientists are drafted or fired for their know-how and public assertions. For every significant development in science eventually leads to better estimates of the probabilities that actions lead to specific outcomes. And these "better" estimates provide a better basis for determining values of people and groups. That is, *if* they are better. If they are worse, then science as an institution creates a dangerous lie: it leads men to wrong conclusions concerning their wants and needs.

The scientist need not be "surprised" at an increase in scrutiny by his society—it is what his own actions have led to. But, by the same token, he need not accept any form of scrutiny and control, no more than the businessman and worker have. In fact, the present-day scientist is a worker, and has much to learn from workers as to methods of safeguarding his rights.

The conception of value measurements which is offered here has social implications for the science that is coming. The science of the past has been through at least two great epochs. In its deductive period it sought to find "fundamental" principles from which all truths would follow. In the Renaissance, these bases became rooted in man's own reason, and, when ultimately it became clear that pure reason could yield nothing but formal science, the epoch of induction was introduced. In that epoch, no matter how odd the hypothesis—no matter how contrary to one's fixed beliefs—the ultimate test was the evidence of the senses. Science could now assume the cloak of objectivity, and carry a certificate of immunity. Above all, science must observe what is there, not what it wants to be there. It is therefore immune from political and religious attack because its sole object is the truth, and it maintains an indifference as to whether or not the truth hurts.

But suppose we grant the possibility of a science of decision-making, so that "*A* ought to do *B*" can be supported by scientific evidence.

A science that goes this far will have given up both objectivity and immunity. No doubt in the past, the meaning of an "objective fact" depended on certain decisions of the scientist, as Chapter 5 tries to show. But few cared to scrutinize these decisions as long as the results of science could be used profitably and did not interfere with other decision-making activities.

However, everyone will want to scrutinize the decisions that lead a scientist to accept a fact about someone's values and what he ought to do.

Tomorrow's science will not be objective. Rather, the dichotomies, objective-subjective, biased-unbiased, will cease to have their present significance. Future science will not be politically immune.

Actually, this is not a prediction at all. The day of "objectivity" and immunity are over already. It is no longer the privilege of any rational man to "test for himself" whether a factual assertion in the physical sciences is true or false because establishing the privilege may be too costly, or threaten our national security. The true "facts" are the assertions accepted by a few whom our society trusts. As a culture we tend to trust our physical scientists, and tend not to trust our social scientists. We trust no one if we can see the direct relevance of his assertions to changes in our national policy and our personal lives. Hence we can hardly expect that a "science of values" will be represented by assertions accepted by a few in our culture. Somehow, such a scientific discipline, if it is ever to exist, must be very democratic in its rules of membership—possibly to the extent that it incorporates other social institutions; in other words, the difference between the policy-maker, the administrator, and the scientist may very well disappear.

18 · *Indebtedness.*

Much of the debt for the development of the ideas in this chapter is owed to Thomas A. Cowan, whose guidance led both Ackoff and myself into writing *Psychologistics*. Cowan, of course, is not responsible for the final outcome. That is, there is no evidence that he values this outcome in the sense of value adopted in this chapter. The treatment of ascendance and submission is to be found in Ackoff's book (1). Some discussion of *Psychologistics* and its relation to other psychological theories is to be found in Brant (2). Evidently, the whole chapter is the outcome of Ackoff's and my collaboration; he, however, is not responsible for the errors and excessive caution in the present treatment.

Simon (10) and March and Simon (9) discuss theories of "satisficing"behavior and compare them with maximization theories.

Finally, a great deal is owed to E. A. Singer, Jr., and especially to his *Experience and Reflection* (12), as the Appendix shows. Singer was the first, as far as I know, to define the basic concepts of teleology within a physical model of nature: producer-product, function, and means-end.

REFERENCES

1. Ackoff, R. L., *Design of Social Research*, Chicago: University of Chicago Press, 1957.
2. Brant, H., *The Study of Personality*. New York: John Wiley and Sons, Inc., 1954.
3. Churchman, C. W., and R. L. Ackoff, *Psychologistics* (mimeographed). Philadelphia: University of Pennsylvania, 1946.
4. ———, "Purposive Behavior and Cybernetics," *Social Forces*, 24 (1950), pg. 32.
5. ———, "Towards an Experimental Measure of Personality," *Psychological Review*, 54 (1947), pg. 41.
6. ———, "An Experimentalist Definition of Personality," *Philosophy of Science*, 14 (1947), pg. 304.
7. Churchman, C. W., "Concepts without Primitives," *Philosophy of Science*, 20 (1953), pg. 257.

8. ———, "Notes on a Pragmatic Theory of Induction," *Scientific Monthly,* 79 (1954), pp. 149-151.
9. March, J. G., and H. A. Simon, *Organizations.* New York: John Wiley & Sons, Inc., 1958.
10. Simon, H. A., "Theories of Decision Making in Economics and Behavioral Science," *American Economic Review,* Vol. 49 (1959), pp. 253-283.
11. Singer, E. A., *Mind as Behavior.* Columbus, O.: R. G. Adams & Co., 1924.
12. ———, (C. W. Churchman, editor), *Experience and Reflection.* Philadelphia: University of Pennsylvania Press, 1959.

APPENDIX

We recognize the following components of a system:
(a) a finite set of n elements,
(b) a finite set of m properties of these elements,
(c) assertions about the elements.

We now suppose that the world of elements has been ordered in some way so that we can meaningfully speak of the x_1th element, where x_1 takes on the integers from 1 to m. The properties have also been classified so that those that are alike have been grouped into one "morphological" class. The properties belonging to any class have been ordered, as have the classes themselves. We can therefore speak meaningfully the x_2th property in the x_3th class of properties.

By means of this linguistic equipment, we can introduce a notation for the assertions about the elements of the system. We want these assertions to be dependent on time for their validity so that we introduce a set of real numbers, defined along a continuum. We now let the vector $\mathbf{X} = (x_1, x_2, x_3, t)$ stand for the assertion that x_1th element has the x_2th property, of the x_3th class of properties, at time t. Thus the domain of x_1 is the set of integers from 1 to n, where n is the number of elements. The domain of x_2 is the set of integers from 0 to k_{x_3} (where k_{x_3} is the number of properties in the x_3th class), the domain of x_3 the set of integers from 1 to m, and the domain of t the set of real numbers in the interval 0 to ∞.

The vector $\mathbf{X} = (x_1, x_2, x_3, t)$ is a propositional function, and hence the language of the system can be expressed in terms of the language of propositional functions. Our intent here is to sketch the system and not to display it in detail. Hence we will describe the relevant aspects of **X** in ordinary language as far as possible.

(1) Given any element and any class of properties, the element can have only one value within the class at any time; in other words, for a fixed value of x_1, x_3 and t, there is only one value of x_2 that makes the assertion **X** valid.

(2) Every element has some value within each class of properties at any given time; in other words, for every x_1, x_3 at a fixed t, there is some value of x_2 that makes the assertion **X** valid. In order that the system have a real interpretation, we understand that in each class of properties there is a value of x_2 that stands for "irrelevance." Let this be the value for which $x_2 = 0$. Hence the assertion that an element belongs to the first subclass of a morphological class of properties is to be interpreted as meaning that the class of properties does not apply to the element.

(3) There is an individuating class of properties, and we let this be the first class ($x_3 = 1$). This means that only one element can have a particular value in this class at a given moment of time. In other words, given a specific value of $x_2 > 0$ for the first class of properties at a fixed time, there is at most one x_1 that makes the assertion **X** valid. If $x_2 = 0$ for the first class, then this is to be interpreted as meaning that the element has no position (is not individuated). We therefore assert that if, for a given element, $x_2 = 0$ in the first class at a fixed time, $x_2 = 0$ for every other class; in other words, the element in question is asserted not to exist at the time.

We define a state as a complete description of every element for a fixed time; in other words, a state is a conjunction of assertions. In this conjunction, every element is assigned one and only one value of x_2 in every class of properties. A state can be represented by an $m \times n$ matrix. Each row of the matrix is a set of numbers that assert what value a given element has in each of the m classes of properties. Each column tells us the various values that the elements have of any given property. Zeros mean that the property is irrelevant (see assumption (2) above). The first column corresponds to the individuating property; none of the values of this column are the same except for the value 0. Evidently, the class of all states can be ordered, and we let S_i stand for the ith state. But since we shall want to refer to the time associated with each state, we shall introduce couples (S_i, t) to stand for the ith state which is defined for a time t.

(4) At any instant of time only one state is valid; that is, only one state can "occur." In other words if S_i is true, then every other S_j not equal to S_j but defined for the same t is false.

(5) But more generally, we say that, if S_i is true, then for every t there exists one and only one S_j that is true. This is the well-known "closed system" property of a system. Given a valid state of the system at any time, the system's whole history can be exactly defined. We express this assertion by introducing a class T of valid states. The closed system assumption then states that if the couple (S_i, t_0) is in T, then for every t there exists one and only one S_j, such as the couple (S_j, t) is in T.

Thus, associated with each (S_i, t) there is a chain of states satisfying the conditional stated in (5), each element of the chain corresponding to a specific moment of time.

Consider now a subclass of states all of which are defined for the same time; each state is exactly like the other except for one of the elements and one of the properties. The states of the subclass differ in their assertions about the value of the element in some class of properties. This amounts to saying that in the matrices a different number appears in the row corresponding to the element and the column corresponding to the specific value of x_3. We stipulate that the first property, the one that individuates, remains the same in all states. In other words, we are conceptualizing a number of descriptions of the world at a certain moment of time in which an element takes on one of a range of values in a morphological class.

Thus, for any morphological class of properties there corresponds (on a one-to-one basis) a class of states. We designate any member of this class of states by $\bar{S}_i$. Suppose there are q values the element takes on in the x_3th class. For any t_0, we have q couples $(\bar{S}_i, t_0)$. For each couple, if we assume this couple is in T, then for any t_1 there is just one couple (S_k, t_1) in T. This enables us to set up a one-one (or many-one) correspondence between the class of $\bar{S}_i$ and the class of the S_k which satisfy (S_k, t_1) in T given $(\bar{S}_i, t_0)$ in T. Suppose we designate members of this second class of states by $\bar{\bar{S}}_k$. There are at most q members of this class.[1] (We note that t_1 may be less than, equal to, or greater than t_0.)

Now, we shall examine any given characteristic of the $\bar{\bar{S}}_k$. For example, we may examine whether an element "located" by the first

[1] Some of the members may be identical.

property exhibits some other property. Or we may examine whether there is any element at all that exhibits a certain property, and so on. Let "$\bar{\bar{S}}_k$ in U" mean that in $\bar{\bar{S}}_k$ the examination yields the answer "yes." Let r be the number of "yes" answers.

Then we say that r/q is the conditional probability that "$\bar{\bar{S}}$ in U" is true at t_1, given that an element has a certain morphological property at time t_0. In other words, we can precisely define the idea of the effect of a change of an element. We say that any state of a chain of states is the cause of any state defined for a later time. Hence we say that r/q measures the probable effect of a random variation in an element of a state upon a certain aspect of a later state.

Evidently, this definition of conditional probability could be extended by considering several elements. When this is done, we can refer to the morphological property of an element, *and* the morphological property of its environment, the environment being everything else in the state except the element. If there are k elements which can exhibit properties in $q_1, q_2, q_3 \ldots q_k$ ways respectively, then the number of members of $\bar{S}_i$ is q_1 times q_2, times $q_3 \ldots$ times q_k. Further, in the "consequents," $\bar{\bar{S}}_k$, we may examine whether an element has a certain morphological property. Finally, we may extend the $\bar{S}_i$ and $\bar{S}_k$ by taking ranges of values along t. Further, we can examine the changes in the properties of the elements in the $\bar{\bar{S}}_k$ in terms of changes in the elements in the $\bar{\bar{S}}_i$—i.e., introduce correlations.

These extensions are not our chief concern here. We now want to introduce the relation of producer-product, which holds between elements of $\bar{S}_i$ and $\bar{\bar{S}}_k$ relative to exhibited properties.

Roughly, an element a of one state is a producer of an element b of another state if a is "necessary" for b. This means that if a did *not* occur, then b would not occur. More precisely, if the state in which a occurs were changed so as to delete a from its location, that is, to assign a the value of o in the first class of properties, and everything else were kept the same, then no element like b would occur in the original b's position in the later state. We now attempt to restate this characterization of a producer-product in the language we have adopted.

Consider an element a of a state S_i and assume that S_i represents some $\bar{S}_i$ with respect to the vth morphological property ($x_s = v > 1$). Consider now another state S_i' in which there is an element a' having the same location as a but not the property x_v (that is, it has a value of o for this property). (Thus, a' is in the same location as a but differs from it in some significant way with respect to the vth property). S_i and S'_i are alike in all other respects (that is, the remaining elements have the same properties).

Consider now the couples (S_i, t_0) and (S'_i, t_0), and the uniquely defined couples (S_j, t_1) and (S'_j, t_1) which satisfy

$$\{(S_i, t_0) \text{ is in } T)\} \text{ implies } \{(S_k, t_1) \text{ is in } T\}$$

and $$\{(S'_i, t_0) \text{ is in } T\} \text{ implies } \{(S'_k, t_1) \text{ is in } T\}.$$

As a takes on different values of the vth property, the members $(\bar{S}_i, t_0)$ of $\bar{S}_i$ generate a class $(\bar{\bar{S}}_k, t_1)$, and (S'_i, t_0) generates a state (S'_k, t_1). We now want to examine the difference between $(\bar{\bar{S}}_k, t_1)$, and (S'_k, t_1), since this difference is entirely attributable to the element a and its morphological property.

Suppose we examine an element b of the members of $\bar{\bar{S}}_k$. Suppose that b always has the value w for the first property, and always has a value $y > o$ for the zth property. In other words, b is always located at the same place, and always has the zth morphological property. But suppose that in S'_k there is no element at the wth location, or that if there is one, it has the value of $y = o$ for the zth property. Then, if $t_0 < t_1$ we say that a is a *producer* of b by virtue of a's vth morphological property, and b's zth property, and with respect to t_0 and t_1.

It may happen that a b located at w with the zth property may not be found for some of the states in $\bar{\bar{S}}_k$. We could then define the ratio of success to total tries, and thus define the *probability* of production.

We can also consider whether a given a of S_i satisfies a certain producer relation: for example, whether it reproduces elements with its own properties, and so on. In effect, these producer relations define a property of an a which is quite distinct from the properties we have already considered. These new properties we call *functional* properties. It is clear that one can now consider whether an a is a producer of a b by virtue of a functional property—and define probability measures relative to functional properties.

The extension of the system discussed above to "behavior" and "outcome" is fairly straightforward and need only be outlined here. We want to be able to talk about the behavior of the "same" element over a range t_0 to t_1. So far, by our notation, we have assumed that the states refer to the same set of elements. In application, this assumption would require a rule for asserting that an element defined for one time is the same as an element defined for a later time. Furthermore, we may want to group together some of the elements and make assertions about the "same" group at different times. For this purpose, we may not restrict ourselves to exactly the same elements for each moment of time; as in the case of a club, corporation, or nation, the rule may reject some elements and include new ones as time changes. The chain provides a history of the same identical individual, that is, of members of the identity class.

Each element of the chain describes the properties of the same identical individual. Consider one of the properties, for example, the yth morphological property. The identical individual takes on specific values w of this yth property over time. Thus, for every t, there is a value w. We say that the couple (w, t) represents a *behavior pattern* of the identical individual. In kinematics, the function $s = f(t)$ is thus expressible as a behavior pattern, as are any set of differential equations defined for specific boundary conditions in physics. But the property in question may be functional, and hence the behavior pattern itself may be a functional behavior pattern. In such a case, the couples (w, t) indicate what potential products of a certain kind the individual may or may not have over a period of time.

Thus, one can describe whether an identical individual is a potential producer of a given "result" by virtue of some property of its behavior over t_0 to t_1. The producer-product relationship in this instance is merely a straightforward, though tedious, extension of the producer-product relationship for elements. The product may be an element, set of elements, or a behavior pattern of such elements. In particular, the product may be what we have called the choice of the individual, or it may be the outcome of a behavior pattern of the individual.

According to this account, we would say that "an individual chooses a behavior pattern" means that if the individual had not occurred in a certain location of a series of states, no behavior pattern of the given type would have occurred in a certain location. More precisely, we say that an individual chooses a behavior pattern by virtue of one (or more) of its properties; this means that if the individual had not had a property of a certain kind (morphological or functional), no behavior pattern of a certain type would have occurred in a specified "region" of a series of states.

"Choice" of behavior is therefore definable in terms of a relationship between one (or more) properties of an identical individual and one (or more) properties of a specified behavior pattern of the individual. The fact that a person exhibits behavior is not a sufficient basis for asserting that he *chose* the behavior. Indeed "*X* chooses *A*" is ambiguous until we have specified by virtue of what property of *X* the choice was made.

Turning then to the characterization of value discussed in this chapter, we have suggested that the values of outcomes are a basis of predicting choice when the subject knows the conditional probabilities. We suggested that this "when" is better replaced by "because." In the sense of "choice" just given, this means that values are the basis of predicting choices which are made when a person's knowledge is a producer of his action.

If we say that a person chooses an action by virtue of his knowledge, we mean that had he not been cognizant of the conditional probabilities, he would not have behaved as he did. In a way, this has a strange sound, because a person might do the same thing even if he were partially ignorant of the outcomes. The point is that the test of whether knowledge produces the act must be a "crucial" test; that is, ignorance must be such that the degree of ignorance makes a difference. Hence, when we say that a person chooses an act because he knows the consequences, we mean that if he were "sufficiently" ignorant, he would choose otherwise. The criteria of sufficiency depend on how precisely we wish to predict.

One conclusion is clear from this discussion. There is no reason to suppose that any direct observation of a person's behavior could be a sound basis for asserting that a choice has been made, especially since evidence of choice is based on a comparison of behavior in different circumstances. Intuitively, however, an observer may feel that a person "clearly" makes the choice because of his knowledge or some other property.

The formal scheme given above outlines the means-end scheme. Two remarks seem appropriate. (1) This formal system, which is essentially stated in the terms of classes and real numbers, is not the only way of defining psychological concepts. Enough has been said in this book to indicate that there is no "ultimate" reference for any set of useful concepts. (2) The definition of producer-product may seem to rest on a "counter-factual" proposition if T is defined as the class of real occurrences of events in time. For then "(S, t_0) is in T" is true for one and only one state. Hence, when we construct S_i' by changing an element in S_i, it must be the case that either "(S_i, t_0) is in T" or "(S_i', t_0) is in T" is false. But if "implies" obeys the rules of ordinary sentential calculus, a false proposition implies anything. Thus "(S_i', t_0) is in T" always implies "(S_j, t_1) is in T" if "(S_i', t_0) is in T" is false. However, this system contains no assertions about which (S_i, t_i) belong to T. The assertions are all conditionals: "If (S_i, t_0) belongs to T, then (S_j, t_1) belongs to T." Nevertheless, a scientist must make assertions like "(S_i, t_0) is in T"—or must he? E. A. Singer, in *Experience and Reflection* (12), has argued convincingly that science never asserts such occurrence statements. Instead, science sets down imperatives of the form "Let S_i be taken to occur at t_0." Science does assert theoretical conditionals, but never can make unconditional assertions (which are really ideals). The purported difficulty concerning vacuously true conditionals, therefore, never arises except in the limit—which never occurs. The difficulty is indefinitely postponable. Singer's "solution" is not the only one that has been proposed concerning counter-factuals (nor, indeed, did he himself consider the problem as such). But in view of the other insights that accrue from Singer's analysis of scientific concepts, it seems to be to be the most fruitful approach to the problem.

RATIONAL BEHAVIOR

8

Summary

and

Intent.

In this chapter we consider the possibility of interpreting, "X ought to do A" in stronger terms that those suggested in the last chapter. Specifically, we consider the concept of rational behavior. If a clear definition of rationality could be found, then we might say that, "X ought to do A" means that "X would do A if his behavior were rational."

We are to consider rationality in a very specific way, and the conclusions we reach are based on this restricted consideration. "Rational behavior" is to be defined in terms of a set of "axioms"; the test of the validity of the axioms is to be based on commonly accepted intuitions about rational behavior. If the axioms are thus validated, they enable us to predict the behavior of rational

219

people in the manner indicated in the last chapter, that is, the axioms provide a basis for *measuring* the value of outcomes.

The discussion of this chapter will arrive at a negative answer to the question whether rational behavior, in the sense just mentioned, "exists." This does not mean that rational behavior is a useless concept in the behavioral sciences. The answer is negative because the proposed methodology is based on notions of intuitive adequacy, and not because the concept is fruitless. At the end of the chapter we consider an alternative concept of rationality.

We center our attention on one approach to an intuitively adequate concept of rationality, namely, that adopted within "contemporary utility theory."

It should be reemphasized that few if any workers in contemporary utility theory have consciously accepted the thesis put forward in the last chapter that the aim of value measurements is to predict behavior under conditions of perfect availability, knowledge, and equal preference for each act as such. But in actual experimental work, every effort is made to clarify the situation for the subject so that he is aware of the choices open to him, and every effort is made to eliminate a preference for the choices as such. One might say that the standard conditions defined in the last chapter are taken to be "obvious" by most researchers. The only exception to this remark is the question of the state of knowledge of the subject. This important exception will be reexamined in more detail in this chapter.

2 · *One Utility Scale.*

The program of predicting behavior by means of the concept of rationality can be accomplished in many conceptual models of contemporary utility theory by assigning a single "utility" measure to each outcome. More precisely, there is a method of assigning a single number ("utility") to each outcome, and a single probability measure to each action-outcome combination, such that a person's choice of an action can be predicted in terms of the "maximum expected utility." This seems to be true of most current attempts to measure utilities; the exceptions are those studies which do not assume that all outcomes of actions can be ranked, or assume that some are incomparable, or, as was suggested in the last chapter, assume that utility maximization is not the sole criterion.

In a way, it is astonishing to think that there is but one measure of value associated with each outcome. In the case of the primer cap we mentioned in our discussion of measurements even in the simplest conditions, at least three distinct measures are required to predict the probability of detonation (the mean-critical firing stimulus, the variance, and the "velocity effect").

It is true that before the appearance of von Neuman and Morgenstern's work, it was sometimes believed that mere maximization of an "average" or "expected" utility was not enough to predict rational behavior, but that the variance, and other properties of the distribution of utilities, are also required. But von Neuman and Morgenstern raised again the classical hope of finding one utility measure which together with the probabilities would enable one to predict rational behavior. Since that time this hope has, if anything, increased in strength.

3 · *Utilities and Gambles.*

Our story can therefore begin with von Neuman and Morgenstern's approach to the problem of measuring utility. Their approach marks an episode in the historical development of utility-theory briefly mentioned in Chapter 2. This episode seems to have been both an ending to one phase of the history, the dispute as to whether utility as such is measurable at all, and the beginning of another phase, the attempts to use "gambles" in estimating utilities. A gamble is a choice between alternative actions which are not certain to produce desired outcomes.

The use of gambles in the sense of contemporary utility theory was apparently first suggested by Ramsey, but von Neuman and Morgenstern provided the explicit framework from which most of the contemporary work has sprung.

We begin by considering a set of axioms for human behavior. These may be regarded as a (partial) theory of behavior of a rational individual. Each axiom is presumably testable; that is, the terms and relations in the axioms can be so interpreted that the axioms are susceptible to some kind of check. The crucial point will be to decide what an adequate check really is. If a person fails to behave in the manner described by the axioms, there are two rather obvious alternatives open to the researcher: he may say that the axiom is still valid for all rational persons—on intuitive grounds; or he may say that the axiom is false. There are more subtle alternatives as well, as the discussion will show.

The best plan to follow will be to set down each axiom as given by von Neuman and Morgenstern (slightly paraphrased), then illustrate its meaning in terms of an actual choice situation. Finally, we consider the significance of the whole set of axioms as an intuitively adequate concept of rational human behavior.

In order to illustrate the axioms, suppose a community educational-planning board is interested in making explicit its attitudes towards these objectives: no more than twenty-five students in each elementary class ("student"), at least $4000 per annum for all teachers ("salary"), physical examinations twice a year for all students ("health"), and recreational facilities within three blocks of every home ("recreation").

There is a technical point to be mentioned in connection with these objectives. Von Neuman and Morgenstern are actually thinking in terms of choices of commodities. The subject is faced with a set of alternative courses of action. If his choice is successful, he receives a certain commodity; if it is not, he receives nothing. The objectives we have just mentioned are not really of this kind. Failure to reach a salary level of $4000 may not be a complete loss, and attaining a level over $4000 may have an additional value for the Board. But we assume for purposes of illustration that the objectives have the same characteristics as single commodities: failure to attain them is worthless, and overreaching them adds no increment of value. In Chapter 10 we consider the problems entailed in relaxing this restraint; actually, the restraint could be relaxed with considerable additional complexity in the method we are to study in this chapter.

4 · *The Language Base of the Theory.*

We begin, as one frequently does in axiom construction, by presenting first the linguistic base of the axiom set. This base consists of terms and relations, the "meanings" of which are assumed. Any interpretation of the set tries to assign operational meanings to these terms and relations in such manner that an experimenter can follow a set of instructions and thereby test whether a subject's behavior complies with the axioms. As was pointed out in the last chapter, the base can be conceived of as a set of conceptual "links" with other concepts of science. But I suspect that most contemporary workers in utility theory think of the base as a set of concepts that can be readily translated into "simple" empirical operations—a point of view which has been criticized earlier in this book.

The language base consists of:

(1) A set of utilities, *u, v, w,* and so forth. These utilities can be understood as the "values" of outcomes (objectives)—what an outcome is "worth" to a person. The reader is not initially forced to regard these values as numbers—the numerical translation is a derived result of the axioms. However, although this brief characterization may help the reader to understand the symbolic statements that are to follow, nevertheless it does not suffice to explain how *u, v, w,* and so on, are to be interpreted in empirical research. The letter *u* is not to be taken as denoting an outcome, but a "quality" of the outcome that represents its value to a person. In terms of the last chapter, a utility *u* denotes an item of information associated with an outcome and a person which enables a researcher to predict the person's behavior under specified circumstances. Thus "utilities" do not inhere in outcomes, or in people, but are devices for studying people and their relationships to outcomes. Now the intuitive adequacy of the axioms does depend on how one interprets the symbols *u, v, w.* As we shall see, if one interprets utilities in the manner just suggested, the axioms are not intuitively obvious at all. For the present, we will postpone this problem, and act as though the "utility of an outcome" is a clear concept.

(2) A relation of prefence with respect to these utilities. The relation is symbolized by $<$. If *u* and *v* symbolize utilities, then $u < v$ always makes sense, and means that *u* is less preferred than *v* (that is, *v* is more preferred than *u*, which can be symbolized $v > u$). In the illustration we are considering, it is therefore meaningful to ask whether the utility of "health" is greater than that of "recreation."

The empirical interpretation of "$<$" is also quite difficult to give, but, as in the case of "utilities," consideration of this problem will be postponed until we have examined the axioms.

(3) Real numbers between o and 1. We let a, β, γ and so forth, stand for real numbers in the open interval, $0 < a < 1$. These numbers will stand for probabilities in the sequel.

(4) An "operation" on the utilities and the real numbers. This operation will be symbolized for the moment as (a, u, v). The empirical interpretation of the operation is the utility to the subject of a "gamble"—where the subject receives utility u with probability a or else utility v with probability $(1 - a)$. For example, $(0.5, u, v)$ might be interpreted as the value of a choice which has a 50 per cent chance of gaining the salary level of $4000 but only by having more than twenty-five students per class, or else has a 50 per cent chance of gaining minimum classes but only by sacrificing the $4000 minimum salary level. This may seem an odd choice for a planning board, but reflection will show that such boards are frequently faced with evaluating some sort of gamble rather than just the objectives as such.

We will see later on that the operational interpretation of (a, u, v) also involves some serious difficulties.

Since we do not yet know that u and v can be interpreted as numbers, we cannot express (a, u, v) as an algebraic operation. But eventually we will know this as a theorem of the axiom set, and then we can interpret (a, u, v) as the "expected" utility of the "gamble"; we can then write (a, u, v) as $au + (1 - a) v$, where au is multiplication, and $+$ and $-$ are addition and subtraction in ordinary arithmetic. Since we know we will be able to do this, for the sake of clarity, we will adopt the notation $au + (1 + a) v$ in the sequel.

(5) The symbol "$=$" between two utilities means that the utilities are identical. Hence $u = u$, and if $u = v$, then $v = u$, and if $u = v$, and $v = w$, then $u = w$. Again, an operational interpretation of "$=$" will be required in the sequel.

5 · *Meaningfulness in the Theory.*

There are two propositions which help to summarize the previous remarks about the language base:

(1) If u and v are utilities, then $u < v$ is a meaningful assertion.

(2) If u and v are utilities, and a is any real number between o and 1, then $au + (1 - a) v$ is a utility.

There two assertions simply state that it is always meaningful to compare utilities in terms of preference, and a "gamble" is a utility. In terms of the discussion of the last chapter, a "utility" is what the researcher takes to be the value of an outcome for a person. In the case of our illustration, "$u < v$" could thus be interpreted as "the value ascribed to 'health' is less than the value ascribed to 'salary'."

6 · *Ordering of Utilities.*

Consider now two axioms of the theory which read as follows:

A_{10}: Given any two utilities, either they are identical, or else one is preferred to the other but not conversely.

A_{11}: If $u < v$ and $v < w$, then $u < w$.

These two axioms provide an ordering of the utilities. A_{10} says that if the utilities are not identical, then one is preferred to the other. A_{11} (the so-called "transitivity axiom") states that if u is preferred over v and v over w, then this implies that u is preferred over w. Thus the board may decide that salary $<$ recreation $<$ student $<$ health. This (according to A_{11}) would imply that salary $<$ student, salary $<$ health, recreation $<$ health. Of course, the axioms do not preclude salary $=$ recreation; that is, the utility of "salary" may be identical with the utility of "recreation."

For those unfamiliar with these two concepts of ordering, it may be useful to note that "is the ancestor of" fails to order all the people in the history of humanity, because, though A_{11} holds (if A is the ancestor of B, and B is the ancestor of C, then A is the ancestor of C), yet A_{10} fails (if A and B are different people, it does not follow that either is an ancestor of the other). And if there are an odd number of people evenly spaced around a circular table, the relation of "being closer to in a clockwise direction" does not order the people, for though A_{10} holds (if A and B are distinct, one must lie closer to the other in a clockwise direction if the number of people is odd), yet A_{11} fails (A may be clockwise closer to B, and B to C, yet A may not lie clockwise closer to C).

We should recall that as yet, we do not know what is being ordered if A_{10} and A_{11} hold because we have still to decide how to interpret "utilities." Vaguely, we can think that the axioms are the basis of ordering preferences, that is, ordering outcomes in terms of "degree" to which a person prefers them. But this vague characterization needs clarification.

7 · "Sure-thing" Axiom.

The next axiom is:

A_{21}: Suppose u is preferred to v. Then u will also be preferred to any gamble involving a probability a of obtaining u and a probability $(1 - a)$ of obtaining v. That is, u is preferred to $au + (1 - a) v$.

For example, suppose the board prefers "health" to "student." From this, according to A_{21}, it follows that the board prefers "health" to any outcome where the health program may be risked (for example, where there is a 90 per cent chance of its success) but the minimum student requirement may be met (with a 10 per cent chance). That is, as long as "health" is preferred, the board would never risk this objective by lowering the chances of attaining it and *correspondingly* increasing the chances of attaining the less-desirable "student."

The intuitive appeal of the axiom lies in the fact that if A is preferred to B, and A can certainly be obtained without B, why should anyone adopt another action that risks A by equivalently increasing the chances of gaining B, instead of merely accepting the assurance of A without B? Axiom A_{21} is one form of what is called the "sure-thing" principle: a rational person chooses the "sure-thing" rather than any gambling choice that risks it in favor of a less-desirable outcome.

A_{21} has an analogous form when u is less preferred than v: in this case it will be less preferred than any gamble involving a probability a of obtaining u and a probability $(1 - a)$ of obtaining v. That is, if it looks as though the board will not be able to attain "health" but will attain "student," and someone comes up with a plan that will attain "health" with a 50 per cent chance, or else "student" with a 50 per cent chance, the board will adopt this gamble. The gamble gives them a chance of getting what they most want, while the plan that leads only to "student" does not.

It will be noted that these two axioms imply an indifference for risk-taking or gambling as such because, if the board likes to take chances, it might prefer the gamble even though it wanted "health." The gamble would itself have a utility, a notion that is partially ruled out by A_{21}. Or, alternatively, and perhaps more realistically, the board might dislike gambles because of the difficulty of explaining them to the community, and hence might still pursue "student" even though a gamble for "health" were available; in this case the analogue of A_{21} would fail. The problem of the utility of gambling becomes a critical one in application, but is not insurmountable, as we shall see.

8 · *Axiom of Utility Differences.*

A_{22} is the most complicated of the axioms, and is most easily understood by representing utilities along a straight line. On strictly formal grounds, we have no "right" to do this, since we do not yet know that utilities can be graphically represented. But for purposes of communication, this method of explaining the axiom is simplest.

Suppose three utilities have been ordered, so that "health" is preferred to "student" and "student" to "recreation." This means, in some vague sense, that "student" lies somewhere in between "health" and "recreation." Hence it seems natural to ask: *Where* does it lie? We would like to have some means of testing the planning board so that the location of "student" can be properly assigned. One can easily understand why this motive exists. If we only have information on the ranking of these three outcomes, then we can only decide "obvious" policy issues, not subtle ones. If the board had only three choices at its disposal, each of which leads to only one of the objectives at the sacrifice of the other two, then it would be apparent which choice should be made. With available funds for instituting only a health program, or a small-class program, or a recreation program, they "ought" to choose the health program.

But in reality such simple choices rarely exist. The board can decide to try to raise more funds, and the outcome of such a campaign may be in some doubt. By investing some of their money in such a campaign they might threaten the health program, even though they thereby increase the chances of gaining one of the other objectives. To understand their problem and to try to give it some sensible answer, we need to know how the three objectives are related to each other in some more precise sense.

Suppose the true preferences appear as follows:

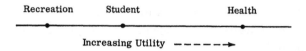

This case represents the notion that "health" is of paramount importance. What evidence could be gathered which would show that "student" lies nearer to "recreation" than to "health"?

Here the concept of a gamble becomes quite useful. Suppose the board is considering two plans. Plan I consists of investing all available resources in reducing the class size ("student"), so that neither "recreation" nor "health" would be attained. Plan II consists of investing a part of their funds in a recreation program and the rest in a campaign to raise more funds; they estimate that such a course of action has a 25 per cent chance of gaining "health" or else a 75 per cent chance of gaining "recreation." What ought they to do? The choice they ought to make seems to provide evidence concerning the location of "student." If they chose the second plan, this would mean that "student" falls closer to "recreation," that is, down nearer the bottom of the scale, because the board is willing to adopt a plan with a relatively small chance of gaining "health" at the complete sacrifice of "student." But suppose "student" and "health" were close together:

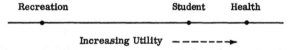

In this case, the board would adopt the first plan because there is no point in sacrificing "student" for a plan that gives some small chance for gaining a slightly more important objective or else a large chance of gaining a minor objective. In other words, in this situation "recreation" *is* minor because it plays a very small role in the board's considerations: they are not tempted by plans that weigh "recreation" heavily and "health" a little bit, if they have a sure-thing plan for gaining "student."

The purpose of axiom A_{22} is to postulate the existence of choices which will provide the necessary evidence for locating v between u

and w when $u > v > w$. Supposedly, unless such choices "actually exist," there is no way of gathering the necessary evidence. This is a consideration to which we will want to return when we examine the axioms critically, since A_{22} seems to say something about the real world of potential action-choices.

A_{22}: Let $u > v > w$. Then there exists an a, $(0 < a < 1)$, such that $au + (1 - a)$ is preferred to v. Also, there exists (another) a, $(0 < a < 1)$, such that v is preferred to $au + (1 - a) w$.

Thus there exists some gamble, made up of an a chance of gaining "health" and a $(1 - a)$ chance of gaining "recreation," which is preferred to "student." A_{22} postulates that such a gamble exists, no matter where "student" lies between "health" and "recreation." If "student" is of minor importance compared to "health," as shown in the first diagram, a may be any number above 0.1, say. But if "student" is a major objective, and lies close to "health" in the preference ordering, then the postulated a may have to be quite large, for example, greater than 0.9. No matter how close "student" is to "health," A_{22} asserts that there will always be some "health"-"recreation" gamble which will be preferred to "student." Another way of saying the same thing is that if no "health"-"recreation" gamble is preferred to "student," then "student" has a utility identical with or greater than "health."

A_{22} also asserts that there is some "health"-"recreation" gamble which is less preferred than "student." If "student" lies near "recreation," the postulated a may be quite small, for example, less than 0.1. But if "student" lies near "health," the postulated a may be any number less than 0.9, say.

The reader will now sense that a plays a critical role in assigning numbers to the utility values of the objectives.

9 · Ordering of Choices in a Gamble.

The remaining axioms are less important for our purposes here; they are concerned with some aspects of gambles. A_{31} states that the utility of a gamble is independent of the manner in which the two choices are offered. In terms of the original notation for a gamble, (a, u, v), this axiom reads:

$$A_{31}: (a, u, v) = (a, v, u).$$

Thus, A_{31} asserts that a gamble of an a chance of attaining "health" and a $(1 - a)$ chance of "student" has the same utility as a $(1 - a)$ chance of "student" and an a chance of "health."

A_{32} reduces utilities of gambles to simpler forms. Suppose, instead of offering an a chance of some specific objective, one offers an a chance of a gamble. Represent the gamble as a β chance of u ("health") and a $(1 - \beta)$ chance of v ("student"). Such a gamble must always have some utility. Hence one can combine this utility with the utility of "student" by means of another gamble: a chance a of obtaining the gamble, or a chance of $(1 - a)$ of obtaining "student." This is a very complicated choice—certainly not one ever discussed at board meetings! The axiom states that the complicated gamble reduces to a simpler gamble: an a times β chance of attaining u, or else a $(1 - a\beta)$ chance of attaining v:

$$A_{32} \cdot a[\beta u + (1 - \beta)v)] + (1 - a)v = a\beta u + (1 - a\beta)v.$$

A_{32} in effect tells us that we can multiply through a sum:

$$a[\beta u + (1 - \beta)v] + (1 - a)v = a\beta u + a(1 - \beta)v + (1 - a)v$$
$$= a\beta u + av - a\beta v + v - av = a\beta u - a\beta v + v = a\beta u + (1 - a\beta)v.$$

10 · *Formal Characteristics of the Utility Scale.*

We turn now to a critical examination of these axioms. First of all, what do they accomplish if they can be interpreted satisfactorily and are valid? Second, how can they be interpreted—or, what amounts to the same thing—what constitutes legitimate evidence for their validity?

What they accomplish can first be stated in somewhat general terms as follows. If people behave as the axioms prescribe, then it is possible to use observations of certain of their "simple" preferences between utilities to derive a measure of the utility of outcomes of actions. This measure is such that the person will always act so as to maximize his expected utility, that is, the sum of the probabilities of the outcomes times their utility—provided such an action is available and the person has a knowledge of the probabilities and an equal preference for the available actions.

The way in which utilities are measured can be understood by an example. Suppose there are a finite number of objectives, with distinct utilities u, v, w, and so on. Let the lowest utility have the value o, and the highest the value 1. The utility, v, of any outcome in between the highest u, and lowest w can be measured in terms of that a which makes the gamble $au + (1 - a)w$ have a utility equal to v. It can be proved from the axioms that such an a always exists and is unique. Thus if v is near the lowest utility, then a will be quite small since for larger values of a the person will prefer the gamble (which gives some chance for gaining u) to the certainty of v (which is not very much preferred to w). Hence v will have a value (a) nearly equal to o. If v is near the highest utility, then a will have to be near 1 before the person will swing over to the gamble.

If a can be used to measure utility in this case, then it can be shown that any linear function of a can also be used to measure utility. That is, the selection of o and 1 as the extreme values is arbitrary; but whatever extremes are used for a finite set of utilities, the remaining "in-between" utilities keep the same relative positions.

A certain point needs to be emphasized in connection with this maximization property. Suppose there is a set of outcomes, O_1, O_2, . . . O_n for which one has derived the utility measures u_1, u_2, . . . u_n. From this information one cannot infer the value of the "package" consisting of O_1 and O_2; that is, a perfect chance of gaining O_1 and O_2 does not necessarily have the value $u_1 + u_2$. But if one does want to obtain the value of the package by the method of this chapter, then it may be possible to conduct a separate test in which the package is one of the discrete items presented to the subject. The remark is relevant to the next chapter, where the value of "packages" of outcomes is assumed to be equal to the sum of the values of the outcomes alone.

In general, over the set of outcomes with utilities u_1, u_2, . . . u_n, we can infer that a person who behaves in accordance with the axioms of this chapter will choose that act which maximizes $\Sigma p_i u_i$, provided the number of possible outcomes is finite. If the outcomes are describable along a continuous scale (or a set of scales), and associated with each choice there is a function $dp_i(x)$ which gives the probability that the outcome will lie in the interval to $x + dx$, and $u(x)$ is the utility of an outcome in this interval, then the person will choose i so as to maximize

$$\int_a^b u(x)\ dp_i(x),$$

where a and b are the limits within which all outcomes fall (and it is assumed that $p_i(x)$ behaves "properly" in a mathematical sense). Thus x might be a dollar scale. An examination of the person's preferences relative to a sample set of dollar values might show that his utility curve follows the "Bernoullian hypothesis":

$$u(x) = a \log x + b,$$

that is, that the utility of money is a linear function of the logarithm of the dollar value. This has the common-sense property that a salary increment of $1000 has less utility to Mr. Curtice of G.M. (who reputedly grossed over $700,000 per annum) than it does to Teacher Jones (who grossed $3000 per annum). In this case, if dollars completely characterize all relevant aspects of the outcome, then a person will act so as to maximize

$$\int_0^\infty [a \log x + b] \, dp(x),$$

that is, so as to maximize

$$\int_0^\infty \log x \, dp(x),$$

since the act that maximizes the first will also maximize the second.

The axiom set we have been considering predicts behavior. Furthermore, the axiom set can be interpreted in such a way as to assign a specific meaning to "X ought to do A"; namely, "The choice of A maximizes X's expected utility."

11 · Are These Axioms Tautologies?

A number of questions naturally arise with respect to the previous discussion. First of all, there is the question as to whether the axioms are "valid." There is one plausible sense in which the answer to this question is obvious. One can argue that the axioms define utility (as well as "choice"), and hence the axioms are "true" in the sense in which any definition is true. This is the basis on which some take the axioms of geometry to be true. And just as there are several alternative "definitions" of lines and planes, so there are alternative axioms of utility that define the concept in another way. But then it must be admitted that the axiom set would have small value for the student of behavior, whatever might be its interest for the student of axiomatics.

I gather that most students of modern utility theory look for content, as well as formal interest, in the axiom system; they believe that there are certain criteria of rational behavior which are intuitively satisfactory, and that these criteria can be expressed axiomatically in such a way that one can predict the choices of a *rational* person. In other words, for them, "rationality" is not a concept that can be defined arbitrarily; there are specific intuitive criteria that must be met by any set of axioms purporting to define the concept. In this sense, "X ought to do A" means "If X were rational, he would do A," where "rational" means "acting in accordance with the intuitively satisfactory criteria (axioms) of rationality."

This is also the sense in which many persons use the concept when they speak of inconsistent behavior. In a narrow sense, a person is inconsistent if he makes diametrically opposed choices in the same situation. In a broader sense, he is inconsistent if his behavior does not accord with some commonly accepted standard, for example, if when he chooses A over B, and B over C, he chooses C over A. In other words, "inconsistent" behavior may be taken by some to be behavior which contradicts an accepted axiom of rationality.

In effect, according to this viewpoint, the meaning of "ought" has a more specific sense than that suggested in the last chapter, because in addition to freedom of choice and knowledge about the probabilities of the outcomes, "ought" also connotes an obligation to behave rationally. It should be noted that the concept of rationality is free of any ethical connotations. A person can behave rationally in the sense prescribed by the axioms, and yet have a high utility for goals that are ethically—or—socially—bad. Hence "X ought to do A" in the sense we are considering does not imply that X's behavior is ethically "right."

Can we assert that the axioms of rationality are to be verified solely by intuitions concerning the meaning of rationality?

Anyone who believes that a clear and precise intuition about the correct meaning of a concept can be sufficient evidence for the correct definition of the concept subscribes to the philosophy of "rationalism," best exemplified in the works of Spinoza and Leibniz. Such a person might very well expect to run into all the difficulties that plagued the traditional rationalists. The seventeenth century thoroughly explored this idea, and their struggles and failures are apt to be repeated by those who adopt their philosophy without regard to its pitfalls.

What is the lesson of rationalism? Simply that human experience always turns out to be too rich for intuition. Find an idea that is intuitively clear. Human experience will then turn up with another idea which is also clear and satisfactory but seemingly contradicts the first. The rationalist is then led to redefine his terms to "escape" the paradox.

Consider an obvious example. It is clear that nothing can be both A and not A. But this table on which I write is both green (on top) and black (underneath). I mean to say, then, "nothing can be both A and not A in the same place."—"And at the same time." But to me it is green and to you, color-blind as you are, it is gray. "Yes—and to the same person." My eyes say it is green, my hands that it is hard. "Yes—and to the same person in the same aspect of his experience." Thus our concepts will not stay still because our experience does not.

This matter can be stated somewhat differently as follows. A "principle" like "Nothing can be both A and not A" is a part of the equipment of the observer of Nature; it provides him with a convenient way of recording the results of his observations. But the activity of observation continuously forces him to reinterpret the principle, for example, to reinterpret what "be" and "A" and "not-A" mean.

This is a familiar procedure in science. We maintain certain laws of science because they provde convenient ways of observing Nature. In order to maintain the laws, the terms and relations contained in the expression of the laws have to be reinterpreted.

Consequently we cannot say that the principle is an accurate account of Nature as such; or, rather, if we do say this, we must understand that "Nature" is a construct of the observer, and that the "correct" properties of Nature depend on the procedures of the observer.

Similarly, the "laws" of rational behavior are constructs of the observer of human behavior. These laws can be maintained by reinterpreting the concept of "preference" (or "choice") and the terms that denote the objects of preference. In this sense, the axioms of rationality are not false; but we may finally reject one or more of them because we are driven to very awkward interpretations of preference and the domain of objects over which the preference relation is applicable.

We can now illustrate how this procedure of maintaining rationality might work out in the case of the axioms just considered. The point of the illustration is to reemphasize a methodological idea at least as old as Kant, who asserted that we would not observe regularity in Nature had we not first put it there: We would not observe rationality in human behavior had we not first put it there.

12 · *Empirical Interpretation of Axiomatic Systems.*

The technical problems which we face in considering the empirical validity of a set of axioms are enormous and are only vaguely suggested by the comments made above on intuitive adequacy. Present purposes will be served best by indicating the technical difficulties and suggesting why the solution of these difficulties precludes any simple intuitive check of the axiomatic assertions.

One might attempt to describe the procedure of validation superficially as follows. Consider a symbolic expression of the form "$u > v$." We try to construct an assertion which can be empirically tested and which has an "isomorphism" with the symbolic assertion. For example, "this cup of tea is preferred to this cup of coffee" is (presumably) such an empirical assertion; the subject ("this cup of tea") corresponds with the symbol "u," the connecting verb (is preferred to) to "$>$," and the object ("this cup of coffee") to "v." Assume for the moment that the empirical assertion is testable directly and is true. Then we say that under the interpretative process "$u > v$" is true. We also stipulate that any other occurrence of "u" in any expression of the axiom set must also correspond with "this cup of tea"; and similarly for the other symbols. Finally, we stipulate a rule for checking axioms as follows. If the axiom has a sign for implication, and if what precedes this sign is empirically valid, then what follows must be valid, or else the axiom is false.

The reader can readily detect difficulties with this account. One minor but troublesome problem is that u, v, w, and so forth, seem sometimes to denote objects, sometimes properties of objects (for example, "tea-ness" rather than "this cup of tea"), and sometimes numbers (as in the gambles). But the major difficulty lies in the methodological supposition that there are simply testable empirical assertions.

The implication of the earlier chapters of this book is that every system of empirical assertions must be embeddable in a broader system. Once we give up the possibility of direct test, then our only recourse is to say that the axioms of a system permit adjustment of observation. Thus, briefly, "$u > v$" may correspond to a recorded observation ("the subject did choose this cup of tea rather than this cup of coffee"). The transitivity law enables us to adjust two observations ("$u > v$" and "$v > w$") to a third observation ("$u > w$"). If the set of adjusted observations are statistically consistent then we provisionally accept the rule of adjustment (that is, the transitivity axiom). If the set is not consistent, we may do one of a number of things: reject one or more observations, reject the rule, or modify our criterion of consistency. More to the point, whether we conclude that the adjusted set of observations is consistent or not, we are always driven to enlarge the set to be adjusted, and this means that we have to find richer rules for adjustment and hence embed the axioms within a more general system.

To illustrate this point, consider again "$u > v$." The observer's report might be conditioned by whether or not in a given context the subject was observed to choose the cup of tea. This would be a rather crude observation, presumably requiring no elaborate observational setup. It would certainly not be strange if transitivity proved to be a poor rule of adjustment in this case. Very often we would find subjects who choose tea instead of coffee and coffee instead of milk, but choose milk instead of tea. We could argue in such cases that the subjects were indifferent with respect to the choices and thus assert that a set of consistent observations may include both "milk instead of coffee" and "coffee instead of milk." In other words, the criterion of consistency would not demand complete agreement of all adjusted reports. If we chose a less rigid rule of consistency, then we might find that the transitivity "holds," that is, its use leads, in most circumstances, to a consistent set of adjusted observations. But clearly there is no intuitive ground for expecting this to happen. The choices of a person who does not care, or who chooses in a random way, might not lead to a consistent set of adjusted observations even with a very loose criterion of consistency.

The reason why transitivity seems to be a correct rule intuitively is that we interpret the observational report of "$u > v$" in a different manner. We really want to say that "tea is preferred to coffee" is true if the person chooses the cup of tea because it is tea, and not for other reasons. In the language of the last chapter, a person prefers tea to coffee because his knowledge of the outcomes produces his choice. Now there is clearly no direct way of observing such a choice, but there are evidently a number of ways in which one might arrive at an observational report that such a choice had been made. Normally, we would collect other relevant information besides the observation of a simple choice, for example, choices of like tastes, or a behavior pattern that conforms with certain social styles.

Under this interpretation, it may happen that in some cases the transitivity rule should yield a consistent set of adjusted observations of preference, for if the subject's knowledge produces choice A in a given environment, where B but not C is present, and his knowledge produces choice B where C but not A is present, then under certain conditions A will be produced when C but not B is present.[1]

But we shall find that this effort to interpret "$u > v$" within a broader conceptual framework leads us to no obvious conclusion concerning the other axioms.

13 · *The Closure Axiom.*

Consider, for example, A_{10}, the closure axiom, which is interpreted to assert that the subject will always prefer one of two outcomes, or else be indifferent. But which is better, hearing Beethoven's *Ninth Symphony* or seeing El Greco's *Christ?* Or compare either of these to the Golden Gate Bridge. A subject asked to express a preference or make a selection may walk away, remain silent, or respond irritably.

One answer to this objection is to point out that if preference is given a behavioristic interpretation, then a person must choose one of the available actions. If he does not select, he is indifferent. In other words, the preference relation is given this interpretation: it means

---

[1] The technical analysis is tedious, but can be outlined here. Let X occur in a certain environment S_1, A and B in an environment S_2. X stands in a producer-product relationship to A but not to B. If S_2 is changed to contain C where A occurs, then X stands in a producer-product relationship to B, but not to C. Then the transitivity rule states that if S_2 is changed to contain C where B occurs, X will stand in a producer-product relationship to A. The rule is not tautologous, but can be made so provided S_1 and S_2 have certain characteristics.

selection when the subject must choose one of the alternatives, either because he is forced to do so by external commands, or because the logic of the classification forces the observer to assign his behavior to one of the categories.

But under the interpretation we have been considering we cannot say the subject's choices are forced by the experimenter, for then they clearly would not be the products of the subject's knowledge. Or, if the subject really cannot compare A and B, he may choose A because it is mentioned first, or because he thinks Jones likes it best. In either case, his adoption of the action is not an indication of a preference: he did not adopt the action *because* it led to A (the knowledge of its leading to A was not a producer of the action).

Specifically, we can say that "A is comparable with B for a subject" is true in a given situation if the subject's knowledge of the outcomes is a potential producer of A, or of B. In line with our earlier discussion, "is comparable with" may be transitive in certain cases, but very often does not obey closure. Hence we can argue that A_{10} is either trivially true if we adopt one specific meaning of preference, or else is very likely false if we adopt a meaning of preference more in accord with the usefulness of the concept.

All is not lost, of course. We can point out that preference comparisons of commodities and of outcomes can be made in a large number of cases, even in the sense we have adopted here. Convincing evidence for this assertion is to be found in much of consumer behavior, where a conscious sacrifice of one commodity for another is common experience. Hence we could interpret the terms "u," "v," and so on, to refer to comparable outcomes. This means that A_{10} is not an axiom describing rational behavior, but rather an axiom that may define our research intent: we intend to study outcomes which the subject can compare.

In sum, it appears that under an acceptable interpretation of "preference" we cannot argue that even a rational subject will order outcomes in terms of his preferences, but we can argue that the outcomes that can be ordered by preference constitute an important class in the study of human behavior.

There is still the problem of interpreting the identity sign in A_{10}. That is, what behavior would constitute evidence that the utilities of two outcomes are identical? One answer would be that the probability of choice of the two actions is equal; for example, where the conditions remain stable, the adjusted observations of choice made because of a knowledge that the action leads to A are as frequent as the choices made because the action leads to B. One cannot say that indifference concerning utilities occurs when the subject exhibits a fifty-fifty split, for example, by using a random device like flipping a coin, because the utilities may not be comparable so that his exhibitions of behavior are no evidence of preference.

It is very important to note that the failure of A_{10} to apply to behavior generally does not imply a failure of the general program outlined in the last chapter. This program consists of an attempt to predict behavior choices when the subject knows the consequences (and other specific standard conditions apply). If the subject is placed in a position where he cannot compare the utilities of A and B (and these are his only choices), then this means, in the language of the last chapter, that the probability of *choice* is zero; that is, he will not choose either action because it leads to A or to B. The required prediction can be made *because* it is known or estimated that the utilities are incomparable. In other words, the failure of A_{10} may lead us to a workable theory of behavior just as much as its acceptance does.

It should be noted that from the viewpoint of this book, a workable theory of values can dispense with ordering outcomes because of the behavioristic meaning we have assigned to values: measures of outcomes that permit prediction where the subject is influenced by his knowledge. In some cases the subject may not make any choice at all; in others the theory of his choice may be much simpler than a theory of ordering. Thus we may be able to give a meaning to a recommendation of the form "X ought to do A," even though we do not adopt a model in which the outcomes are ordered.

Enough has been said to indicate the way in which a methodological interpretation of "preference" and the terms, "u," "v," and so on, may conflict with an "intuitively adequate" set of axioms. Before considering the moral of this discussion, it is worthwhile mentioning some aspects of the axioms which appear to give trouble, but according to the interpretation we have adopted here, actually do not.

14 · *Doubts About the Sure-thing Axiom.*

Consider axiom A_{21}; apparently this assumes that gambling *per se* has no value. But even though u is less preferred than v, it may not be less preferred than a gamble (a, u, v) if the subject does not like to gamble. That is, the subject may choose u rather than gamble on gaining a higher utility v in order to avoid the sense of taking a risk.

However, in the last chapter we argued that the standard conditions for ascertaining preference are those in which the subject equally values all the alternative actions. Thus, the program of Chapter 7 requires that a person's behavior be adjusted to the conditions of A_{21}. Hence, if "preference" is interpreted in terms of choice in a standard environment, there is no reason why A_{21} should not hold. If the subject does want to avoid risk—or else likes to gamble— then we have to adjust observations of his behavior to predict what he would do if he were indifferent towards gambling and not gambling.

Again, A_{22} is an axiom which *apparently* raises some questions about the nature of reality. One form of it says that if $u < v < w$, then there "exists" some gamble $au + (1 - a)\ w$ which is less preferred than v. Such a gamble may fail to "exist" because no such gamble exists in reality. The implication of the von Neuman-Morgenstern theory is that gambles "exist" for any real number a lying in the interval o to 1. This assumption seems to imply an untenable theory of reality. But there is the prior question as to how a should be interpreted.

If a is interpreted as the "true" probability of the occurrence of utility u, then A_{22} would be a reasonable assumption for choices that can be made in the laboratory, or in consumer-preference tests because in such cases, by the use of random devices, one can construct almost any value of a that one wishes. But if the choices are ones that would be made in more practical situations, then no gamble may exist with a prescribed value of a. Any uneasiness the reader may have felt in the example of the community planning board is probably a result in part of this difficulty. What evidence do we have that the board would choose (say) a fifty-fifty gamble of "health" or "recreation" to a sure-thing gain of "student"? We can, of course, ask them. But this means using the evidence of introspection at a point where introspection is undoubtedly weakest. The notion of a gamble is not easy to understand, and it is virtually impossible for people to say with any degree of confidence what they would do if the gamble were really presented to them.

In the case of the planning board, it would be extremely difficult to conceive of a hypothetical illustration of 0.50 "health" or 0.50 "recreation," in order to test the board about their utility for the gamble.

But this criticism of A_{22} is not so much a criticism of a theory of reality as it is a criticism of methods of application of the axiom. The "existence" of a in A_{22} need not imply a "real" choice. It is always meaningful in science to assert that "X would occur if A occurs," even though A never occurs.

To explain this, consider again the theory of axiom interpretation which has been sketched in this chapter. Any purported observation, according to this account, is a combination of an observational report and a rule of adjustment. The observation tends to be taken as an observation of reality if any set of adjusted observations with which it is combined in a certain way is consistent. Since the observation includes implicitly the acceptance of a rule of adjustment, we can say that the rule also can be taken to describe reality. But the rule potentially adjusts observations that are not observations of reality. Thus, the transitivity rule could be used to adjust preferences when the preferences were the opposite of the observed. What shall we say about the potential reference of a rule of adjustment? Apparently, we must say that the rule is valid even when the referents are not accepted observations, or else we would be caught in an insurmountable impasse of circularity in defining observation itself. Now A_{22} asserts that there is an a having certain properties. If there is no observation of reality which asserts this about a, what are we to infer? Not that A_{22} is an inadequate rule of adjustment, for A_{22} combined with the other axioms may provide a consistent set of observations. The "existence" to which A_{22} refers is not the existence of an acceptable observation, but a number which can be used to adjust observations. Hence A_{22} does not fail if "reality" is poor in the number of different gambles it holds.

15 · *Subjective Probabilities.*

But having said this much is not to deny the existence of methodological difficulties in using A_{22}. One of these should now be
discussed, since it is critical to the analysis of rational behavior. The
a of the gamble is supposedly the true probability of the occurrence
of an outcome with utility u. A serious objection can now be raised
to the interpretation of a "gamble" which has been suggested above.
A person will act, not in accordance with the true probabilities
described by the gamble, but in accordance with his own estimates
of the probabilities, that is, his "subjective" beliefs. In the experimental work that has been done in utility theory, this statement has
been substantiated even when the probabilities in the gamble should
have been "obvious" to the subjects. For example, people often do
not believe that the occurrence of a head or a tail is equally probable in the toss of a coin; that is, they exhibit behavior which apparently denies this belief. Thus, suppose there are two gambles:

A: (head) (10¢) or (tails) (9¢)
B: (head) (9¢) or (tails) (10¢)

A subject may always choose A. Further, he will continue to
choose A even though the alternative gamble is actually "better" on
the basis of the probabilities:

A: (head) (10¢) or (tails) (9¢)
B: (head) (9¢) or (tails) (11¢)

Granted that the utility of 11¢ is greater than the utility of 10¢, the
fact that the subject continues to choose A over B is evidence that he
thinks heads is more likely to occur than tails.

It is therefore plausible to argue that people have their own
notions of probability and that these determine their choices. This
seems to land the interpreter of the von Neuman-Morgenstern axioms on one of the horns of a dilemma. *Either* (1) the a in the
gamble is the true probability, in which case the sure-thing principle expressed by A_{21} will fail because, to the subject, the a in the
gamble may be much higher (or lower) than the true value of a,
and he will see the gamble as very much better (or very much worse)
than it actually is. *Or else* (2) the a in the gamble is the subjective

probability, in which case there is no guarantee that these subjective probabilities will combine in the manner prescribed by A_{32}. Indeed, unless an axiom set is presented for subjective probabilities, there is no way of knowing whether any of the elementary "laws" of probability hold.

Despite this objection, the "gambles" of the von Neuman-Morgenstern axiom set can be given an interpretation in which a is taken to be the true probability, as we have indicated in the previous chapter. The axioms are then to be construed as predictions of behavior choices if the subject were to know the true probabilities (and were to have equal familiarity with the alternatives). But in this case the axiom set itself is not a complete theory of rational behavior, because it fails to supply a theory that will adjust observations of behavior when the subject is in partial ignorance, to predicted behavior in circumstances where he knows the true probabilities. At best, the theory contained in the axioms predicts behavior when the true probabilities are the same as the believed probabilities.

The manner in which the theory could be extended is the critical problem. One way is to make attempts to educate the subject about the true probabilities and then attempt to construct laws of behavior from observations in these circumstances. This is certainly what is done in scientific studies of organization policy decisions such as operations research, where every effort is made to convince the executive that the chances of success are those estimated by the researcher.

In sum, there does not, at present, exist a theory of rational behavior because, *if* the a in the gamble is a true probability, then no one knows how the rational person will choose between gambles. That is, no one knows in general how to predict rational behavior under conditions of complete knowledge from behavior under ignorance.

16 · *Testing a Theory: What Is Evidence?*

We turn now to some general conclusions. The entire discussion illustrates a serious methodological problem in connection with the interpretation of a formal set of axioms into an operational language suitable for empirical verification. It illustrates as well why in a book of this type it is not possible yet to express one's ideas in a formal language.

If the interpretation of a formal system is made in terms of another formal system, then the decision problems of interpretation are clear cut, even though they may be quite difficult to solve. We know that we want to translate one language into another in such a manner that the axioms of one system become the theorems of the other, and in case of failure in this effort we may be able to discern clearly why the failure occurred.

But the kind of interpretation with which we have been concerned here is very different. It is far more complicated than the kind of exercise we often impose on logic students, where we ask them to illustrate how a syllogism like "No a is b, no b is c; therefore no a is c" fails. In such a case the student is supposed to have a clear idea of how "no . . . is . . ." is to be interpreted, for example, in terms of nonoverlapping circles, and he has a fairly clear idea of what "a," "b," "c" stand for; for example, they stand for circles. Indeed, he probably uses an intuitively obvious set of axioms about overlapping circles to "prove" the failure of the logical rule.

In the problem which we have been considering, however, the interpretation must meet much more stringent requirements which have never been precisely stated. They are the requirements of empirical investigation. We have already examined at some length in Chapters 4 and 5 how the suitability of these requirements depends on ill-defined empirical criteria. This vagueness of what-is-wanted is apparent throughout this chapter. We would like to interpret the preference relationship so that it is economical to observe whether or not in a given empirical situation it actually occurs. But this economic motive conflicts with other desires. In order to keep the observation of preference simple, we have to restrict what the experimenter does; we have to insist that "u," "v," and so forth denote only certain objects or choices, and we have to make very strong assumptions about the state of mind of the subject. But as soon as we relinquish the operational simplicity of "preference" we are driven to a more-complicated process of verifying a specific case of preference. We have no clear guides that tell us how an interpretation should be constructed.

In this book we are interested in examining the problems of the empirical study of values as deeply as possible. For this reason, we have tried to question every "given" that one may accept in practical or theoretical studies. It is for this reason that a formal exposition of the subject matter seems to be impossible, given our contemporary formal science. At present, formal science proceeds by formalization and interpretation. But the requirements of interpretation (and hence of formalization) have not been worked out for empirical science; indeed, at this stage we are justified in being sceptical about whether the current methodology of formal science is adequate to the task of value measurement which we have posed. This does not deprecate current formal methodology any more than it does current empirical methodology; both are probably fruitful stages on the way to something far richer.

Thus, the reason that models of decision-making cannot be verified by criteria of intuitive adequacy is to be found in the process of obtaining the empirical information, a process that drives the concepts to a depth that cannot be reached by intuition alone. This reason, however, does not preclude the use of judgment as evidence for or against a theory since judgment is a process that is developed in accordance with observational depth.

17 · *A Moral Comment on this Chapter.*

Some serious students of values probably cannot help but feel that efforts to measure utilities by means of relatively simple choices are not only thoroughly naïve, but also a hopeless waste of research effort. In the complex situations that normally beset a decision-maker, it seems foolish and perhaps intellectually dishonest to suppose that observations of simple preferences give any evidence at all regarding one's true values. It is much as though a naïve observer of the world would expect to discover great truths by examining a few rocks on its surface.

To this comment, the serious student of utilities very often replies with that ever-satisfying phrase of the intellectual: "the first approximation." After all, science was not born in a day. We must proceed from elements to complexes.

If the concept of "first approximation" is taken seriously, then it becomes at the same time nonsense. One could only know that an approximation was first if one knew something about the end point and the other steps. Furthermore, there is no virtue *per se* in being

"elementary," and there are so many ways to be elementary, that no
one can be sure he is being elementary in the right way.

No doubt about it. Modern utility theory can be made out to be
as foolish and naïve as you want. So can any other approach to
values. Thomas Cowan argues convincingly for a "new logic" in the
study of human behavior (2a). But no one knows what this new
logic should be like. It becomes more and more apparent that the
so-called "methods" of physical sciences are not appropriate for
measuring the critical aspects of human behavior, but we are still
groping for an adequate substitute. Diversity and intensity of research effort seems to be the only reasonable possibility ahead of
us. Somehow, too, the lines of communication should be left open.
This means, I suppose, that no one deprecates the serious work of
another, while all join in critical appraisal of their own work and
that of others.

It should be quite clear, therefore, that I consider both the formal
and empirical study of utilities to be very important. Without that
work, a careful analysis of the methodological issues would be impossible.

18 · *Indebtedness.*

The task of setting down a list of references for work in modern
utility theory is practically solved by the existence of two very
complete bibliographies, one by Edwards (5), the other by Savage
(7). My review of Savage (2) contains a few additional items.

Some specific comments on the methodological remarks of a few
of the authors cited in the bibliographies above may help to make
the comments of this chapter clearer.

Davidson *et al.* (3) argue for the transitivity of preference on the
ground that otherwise there would be no "rational" rule for selecting one among a set of alternatives because no alternative would be
at least as much preferred as every other. They give no specific
defense that the notion of rationality implies a maximally preferred
choice. It seems to me that it would have been much simpler and
more forceful to say that if transitivity fails, then in a special sense
maximization cannot be used to predict behavior, and therefore it is
desirable on the grounds of convenience to structure choices and
situations so that transitivity holds. In the same manner, these

authors object to the "Archimedian" axiom (A_{21} and A_{22}) of von Neuman and Morgenstern, on the grounds that there may be some value incomparably greater than all other values (in which case, given $u > v > w$, there would exist no a such that v is preferred to $au + (1 - a)w$—(where u is the highest good, and v and w are "lower" goods). Again, the question of whether this example refutes A_{21} and A_{22} on the grounds of intuition seems irrelevant. If a person could be shown to be dominated by such a *summum bonum,* but acted in accordance with the axioms of all other utilities, then the axioms still function as adequate predictions of behavior, with the trivial exception that whenever the *summum bonum* enters into the picture, the subject makes that choice which maximizes his chances of attaining this outcome.

In other words, from the point of view of this book, the issue is not whether the axioms satisfy an intuitive notion of rationality or explicate what people ordinarily mean when they talk about rational behavior. The issue is whether the axioms provide a basis for predicting behavior of certain types of people under specified conditions.

Indeed, Davidson *et al.* point out that such philosophers as Perry and Lewis felt it to be intuitively clear that values cannot be measured in the sense of measurement of the physical sciences. They show that this "intuitively clear" idea was faulty because it was based on a fuzzy concept of measurement, which failed to recognize the manner in which behavior choices might generate measurements. Certainly neither Perry nor Lewis, nor any other philosopher who has "felt positive" that values cannot be measured, ever thought of the notion of gambles, and the manner in which choices among gambles could be the basis of a utility scale unique up to a linear transformation. Consequently, their intuitive rejection of the measurability of values is itself of questionable value. I cannot help feeling that the same remarks apply to most of the discussions of the intuitive adequacy or inadequacy of axioms for measuring utility and defining rational behavior. If an axiom is shown to be "counterintuitive" there may still be a perfectly sensible manner in which it can be used to predict behavior; and if the axiom is felt to be intuitively satisfactory, there may be a perfectly meaningful sense in which it cannot be used to predict behavior (for example, the operational vagueness of the terms).

These remarks apply to Savage's discussion of Wald (7) as well as Chernoff's discussion of Savage (1), both of which seemed to be guided by this vague desire to be intuitively adequate.

Marschak (6) takes a somewhat different position with respect to the axiom of transitivity of preferences; he seems to think that this axiom implies a rational obligation, comparable to the obligation to be rational that is apparently inherent in the "laws of reason." In other words, if a person prefers A to B and B to C, then he "ought" to prefer A to C. What is the meaning of this "ought"? As I understand him, Marschak argues that the meaning is essentially the same as that contained in the following sentence: "If a person believes that all a's are b's, and all b's are c's, he *ought* to believe that all a's are c's." If the logical inference belongs to a formal language where the rules of inference are given explicitly, then there may be a clear sense in which a person "ought" to assert "all a's are c's" or at least ought not to assert the contradictory. The rules of formal language are comparable to the rules of a game. "You ought not to play bridge with a pinochle deck" means simply, "If you do play with a pinochle deck, you are not playing bridge." In the same way, "you ought not to deny all a's are c's, having asserted that all a's are b's and all b's are c's," simply means, "If you do make such a denial, you are not making acceptable statements within *this* formal language."

But it is well known that it is impossible to set up such simple formal rules for the English language, primarily because this language functions in so many diverse and complicated ways. Every simple assertion about how English "ought" to be used has exceptions. "All the angles of a triangle are less than 180°" and "All the angles of a triangle are equal to 180°" can both be asserted without contradiction. One must add stipulations about "using a term in the same sense throughout the argument." But these stipulations become very difficult to state in such a way that they can be applied unambiguously. The meaning of a rational argument posed in the English language has yet to be made clear—if it ever can be. In short, the laws that describe rational arguments in ordinary discourse are as difficult to find as the laws that describe rational preferences.

The theory of interpretation of a formal system adopted here follows Singer's ideas (9) closely.

REFERENCES

1. Chernoff, H., "Rational Selection of Decision Functions," *Econometrica*, 22 (1955), pg. 422.
2. Churchman, C. W., Review of L. Savage's *Foundations of Statistics*, *Operations Research*, 4 (1956), pg. 254.
2a. Cowan, T. A., "Discussion," *Phil. Sci.*, 16 (1949), pg. 148.
3. Davidson, D., J. C. C. McKinsey, and P. Suppes, "Outlines of a General Theory of Value," *Philosophy of Science*, 22 (1955), pg. 140.
4. ———, and P. Suppes, "Experimental Measurement of Utility by Use of a Linear Programming Model," *Technical Report No. 3*. Stanford University, Applied Mathematics and Statistical Laboratory, April 2, 1956.
5. Edwards, W., "The Theory of Decision Making," *Psychological Bulletin*, 51 (1954), pg. 380.
6. Marschak, J., "Why 'Should' Statisticians and Businessmen Maximize Moral Expectation?," J. Neyman (editor), *Proceedings of the Second Berkeley Symposium on Mathematical Statistics and Probability*, University of California Press (1951), pg. 493.
7. Savage, L., "The Theory of Statistical Decision," *Journal of the American Statistical Association*, 46 (1951), pg. 55.
8. ———, *Foundations of Statistics*. New York: John Wiley & Sons, Inc., 1954.
9. Singer, E. A. *Experience and Reflection*. Philadelphia: University of Pennsylvania Press, 1959.

ADDITIVITY
OF VALUES

9

Summary

and

Intent.

In this chapter the problem of measuring the values of objectives is approached somewhat differently from the method discussed in Chapter 8. Here we shall assume that numbers have been assigned to the objectives by some method, and we wish to test whether or not a given number assignment is valid. In effect, the intention is to investigate ways in which additional evidence can be developed to increase one's confidence in a value scale.

We begin by discussing some existing methods for assigning value numbers to objectives. There are a great many ways in which this can be done. Very often people estimate dollar worth even for such "intangibles" as friendship, an eye, or a life.

Even when direct dollar estimates have not been made, there are a number of indirect methods of ascertaining a person's dollar estimate of the worth of an objective. Indeed, as we shall see, his past behavior may reveal that he has implicitly weighed an objective along a dollar scale, even though he is unaware of the fact.

One can also ask people to assign weights to objectives without any reference to monetary units. Most people seem willing to do this, even though they are not sure what the weights "really" mean. Or, the researcher may himself assign weights by some method, based, say, on a partial theory of the person's behavior.

How can these number assignments be tested? What does "testing" mean in this context? These questions are relevant to the discussion of theory-testing given in Chapter 5. In that chapter we argued that theories are valid to the extent to which they can make experience (observations) consistent by means of adjustments. In effect, a "good" theory explains the differences or similarities in the observations of the same items or events. In this chapter we therefore assume that a method of number assignment to objectives is confirmed to the extent to which it enables us to adjust independent observations of behavior so that a consistent set of observations results.

2 · *Antipathy to Number Assignments.*

At the outset one can adopt a thorough scepticism with regard to most number assignments to human values because so often a proposed method of evaluation seems to be obviously inadequate. For example, job-evaluation schemes assign numbers to certain factors associated with the job; obviously in many cases the numbers do not reflect the value of the factor for either the company or the worker but rather some sort of compromise designed to keep the system working as smoothly as possible.

This skepticism amounts to asserting that the onus of proof lies with the number assigner; it asserts that we should ignore number assignments unless they can be reduced to an acceptable basis. But such an attitude rejects without reflection the possibility that persons can in some sense estimate their values quantitatively, and that the estimates may roughly satisfy the conditions of value measurement which we have discussed earlier. Although we may feel that it is "very clear" that one cannot assign a dollar worth to the loss of an eye, a life, or a customer, nevertheless we are obliged to justify this feeling. In other words, we must ask ourselves how we would test a proposed method of estimating, say, the dollar worth of an "intangible" objective, rather than exclude any such proposal purely on intuitive or feeling grounds.

3 · *Assigning Dollar Values to Objectives.*

For purposes of illustration, we will confine our attention for the moment to the assignment of dollar values to objectives, recognizing at the same time that there are many other methods for making number assignments. Many companies view the future with respect to a number of goals, for example, both return on investment over a given period, and market position. Market position is (say) the per cent of the company's product that is sold relative to the total sales of all products of the given type in the market. This percentage is not a dollar figure, but executives may be willing to estimate that an increase of 5 per cent in the market position in one year is worth $10,000,000 to the company. In terms of the meaning of value measurement adopted here, this implies that if a company could increase its market position by 5 per cent in one year at a sacrifice of, say, $7,000,000 in the annual net return, management would consider such a plan favorably. The reason for this sacrifice may lie in long-range objectives, or in some prestige ambitions of management, or in a number of other factors.

In many cases the worth of an objective is taken to be its monetary value as computed by accounting figures, or the money that would be received if some item was sold by its owner. We have already mentioned in this book the problem of the marginal value of money, but this problem has certainly not discouraged the entrepreneur from interpreting dollar worth as true value.

If the objectives are defined in more personal terms, however, most people become disinclined to assign dollar values to them. No one likes to say that a friendship is worth less than $5000—meaning thereby that if some satanic character would add such an increment to one's income, one would be willing to have the friendship cease.

Suppose we see how, despite this personal feeling against assigning dollar worth to personal objectives, one's past behavior, or one's judgment, can be used to arrive at such assignments.

Consider this example. A person is engaged in certain activities over a period of time in which one or more events may occur that are undesirable. But in the system in which he works some signal always occurs which tells him that the event will take place if his activities continue to be the same. During the interval between the signal and the signaled event, he may be able to adopt preventative measures which entail certain monetary sacrifices.

Now such an entrepreneur may not want to estimate the dollar cost of the undesirable event, for example, an accident injurious to people. But he may be convinced that there exists some preventative action which is less costly than the occurrence of the event and which almost certainly does prevent the occurrence. We can now say that the cost of the cheapest action that is certain to prevent the occurrence *is* the value of the avoidance of the undesirable event.

In a way, this example may not seem appropriate since attention has been shifted from the undesirable event to the preventative action. But in terms of the value-measurement program which this book adopts, the example does provide evidence of value because it enables us to predict choices when the person knows the conditional probabilities—provided a preventative action is available. But such a subset of the general class of value-measurement environments may be quite important, for example, in planning hospital emergency actions, making recommendations for expediting customer emergency orders, recommending policies in "ditching" aircraft, and so on. In effect, the "value" in this case predicts behavior in some, but not all, environments.

Evidently the same method of dollar assignment could be used if the event were desirable, rather than undesirable. In this case the signal tells the person that if he does not adopt somewhat costly actions, the event will not occur. He may then estimate that the value of the event is greater than the sacrifice entailed in making it occur. If a sure-fire, expediting act exists, its cost is the value of the desired event: for example, a special trip by a salesman to "clinch" a customer, or adopting city-planning policies today that will remove tomorrow's slums.

There are other ways to arrive at dollar-value assignments to objectives. Very often in industrial practice it is possible to learn enough about an operation to understand how the values must be interrelated. For example, a manager may have two objectives he wants to attain over a period of time: to reduce his inventories to zero and to satisfy all customers. A dissatisfied customer is defined as one who wants to purchase the item at a specific time when the manager does not have the item in inventory and receives less satisfaction if he has to wait. Actually, in more general terms, the two objectives each constitute a set of objectives—to have zero units of inventory, one unit of inventory, two units, and so on—or to have zero dissatisfied customers, one dissatisfied customer, and so on. Now suppose it is possible to estimate that the value of the first series of objectives decreases linearly as the number of units of inventory increases. This situation can best be described by talking about costs rather than positive values. In other words, the objective of having exactly x units in inventory costs c_1x. Similarly, in order to keep the discussion simple, assume that the objective of having exactly y dissatisfied customers costs c_2y. If inventory minimization and customer satisfaction are the only two objectives, then to measure their value for the manager we need only know the values of c_1 and c_2. Actually, in many cases we can show that we need only know the relative values of c_1 and c_2. Indeed, if the manager's only decision is to select the number of items he wishes to purchase at the beginning of some time period, then one can set up an equation which will predict his behavior under standard value conditions—provided he knows something about the consumer demand. This knowledge may be in terms of a constant rate of demand, or else some probability distribution of demand.

Let s represent a decision concerning the amount to be stocked ($s = 0$, or 1, or 2, and so forth). Then, in some cases, a function of the following type can be constructed which represents the total cost to the manager of making a specific selection of s:

$$TC(s) = c_1\, f(s) + c_2\, g(s)$$

where $f(s)$ gives the average size of the inventory over the time period, and $g(s)$ gives the number of dissatisfied customers over the period. $TC(s)$ in this instance is not a continuous function since s occurs only in units. But normally $f(s)$ and $g(s)$ are such that there is one value of s (or at most two adjacent values) that minimizes $TC(s)$ and

such that this minimum depends on the ratio of c_1 to c_2. The graph
of the function $TC(s)$ is something like that shown in Figure 5.

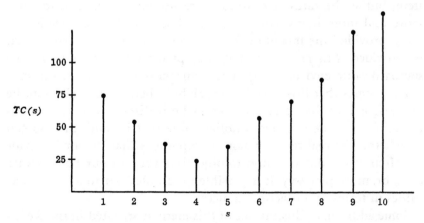

This graph predicts that the manager would select $s = 4$ if he knew
the probability of customer demand, and the consequent average
size of inventory. Thus $T(s)$ is a predictor of behavior: the manager
will choose that s for which $T(s)$ is minimum once he understands
the consequences of each choice. If the manager does not choose
$s = 4$, then he is either ignorant of the consequences of the choices
of s, or the predictive equation is wrong.

But the curve in Figure 5 cannot be drawn unless c_1 and c_2 are
known or rather the relative values of c_1 and c_2. Suppose the manager feels that he cannot assign a cost to customer ill will. Now the
problem can be transposed to another graph which is less determi-
nate than that shown in Figure 1. For any given value of c_1/c_2, there
exists an s_0 which minimizes $TC(s)$. Hence we can plot a graph
relating s_0 to c_1/c_2 similar to the one shown in Figure 6:

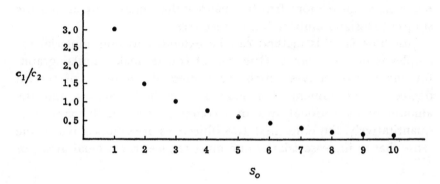

This figure means that if inventory minimization is three times as important as customer satisfaction, the manager will stock only one item, but as the ratio of c_1 to c_2 decreases, his best plan is to stock more and more items. Any selection of s_0 is, in fact, a selection of c_1/c_2, provided the model of the manager's behavior is correct (that is, provided $TC(s) = c_1\ f(s) + c_2\ g(s)$ predicts his behavior in the standard-value environment). The manager does, in fact, select an s. If he assumes that this selection is "right," then, by his selection, he has assigned a value to c_1/c_2, whether he realizes it or not. Furthermore, if c_1 can be assigned a dollar value that is valid, then so can c_2, whether he realizes it or not. The point is that by our behavior we often assign dollar values to objectives without our being aware of it; or, more precisely, it is possible for an observer to assign dollar values in terms of our action choices.

Some additional illustrations of this method are cited in the References of this chapter.

One may wonder what can be learned from this example. If the aim of research is to recommend an action to the manager, it looks as though we have admitted defeat at the outset, for we have assumed the manager's action to be correct, and thereby derived c_1/c_2. We can hardly then use c_1/c_2 to tell the manager what to do. But in this chapter we are discussing ways of obtaining number assignments of values which can then be checked independently by other evidence. In this sense, the illustration represents a powerful device. It is predicated on a partial theory of behavior represented by the equation $TC = c_1\ f(s) + c_2\ g(s)$—a theory which is certainly not self-evident, since considerable research is required to substantiate it (indeed, in most cases equations of this simple type will not suffice). Provided the partial theory is valid, one can then obtain value estimates in a much more fruitful manner than merely by asking the subject to assign numbers to the objectives.

Just how far this method can be extended to nonindustrial examples is not yet known. One can, of course, make similar graphs for any two objectives which are expressible in terms of certain degrees of attainment. For example, teacher's salaries and the amount of recreational area in a community are both expressible quantitatively. Suppose these two objectives are competitive in the sense that to increase salaries one must reduce recreational areas, or to increase recreational areas one must reduce salaries. Then Figure 7 might seem to be as appropriate as Figure 6.

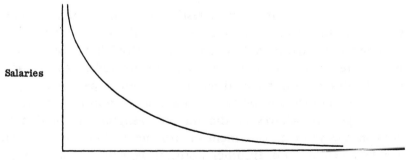

Salaries

Recreational Areas

But of course the trouble is that we do not know what line is really correct in Figure 7 unless we can develop a partial theory of behavior comparable to that described by the inventory equation.

Finally, in this discussion of number assignments to values, it is important to point out a lesson to be learned both from the example of preventative action and the selection of stock size. Our chief objective is to predict behavior under conditions of knowledge. Once this is realized, we have a much firmer basis for studying human values. For one thing, we may not even have to assign a number to the objective as such, for a partial theory of behavior may enable us to predict by means of other numbers, for example, the cost of preventative action that are more readily obtainable. In some cases it may happen that what appears to be a rather irrelevant type of information may still be the basis of prediction. For example, suppose one cannot obtain the costs of producing items, but one can estimate the total labor hours for any given production schedule. This may be a sufficient basis for predicting behavior provided one can make certain assumptions concerning the relationship between true costs and labor hours. This is a point to which we shall return later in the chapter.

In other words, there can be no doubt that, in the past, research into human values has been hampered by the researcher's desire to assign specific numbers or rankings to specific objectives, whereas the program of value measurements may progress by far more devious and subtle methods.

4 · *Testing Number Assignments.*

We turn now to the problem of testing a specific number assignment to the values of objectives. Actually, the entire program of measurement discussed in Chapter 5 is involved here. But it will simplify the discussion and more realistically reflect the present status of value measurements if we consider only a part of this program. The simplest answer to the question of testing is to assert that if a person behaves as the number assignments predict he should in the value-measurement environment, then the numbers are to be taken as valid. In other words, if we educate the manager to understand the probability of a customer demand and the average inventory that will result, we can observe whether he does adopt the policy based on a prior estimate of c_1/c_2. This type of test is of course rather naïve as far as managers of industry are concerned since managerial decisions are normally very complex, and it is very difficult to determine what action has actually been adopted. But in situations where the standard-value environment can be constructed, there can be no objection to testing behavior within it.

In general, in this discussion we will adopt the position that relatively independent confirmations of the number assignments tend to increase confidence in the numbers. If the independent evidence conflicts with the number assignments, then there is no fixed methodology for trying to discover the underlying basis of the inconsistencies. No doubt more is learned about a person if the independent evidence does conflict with prior evidence concerning values; science has always progressed via its discovered inconsistencies. To date, there is no agreed-upon set of decision rules in science that tell the researcher what to do if inconsistencies arise. He can, of course, examine each of the elements that gave rise to the inconsistency. Often, he can just as well let the inconsistency ride and continue to develop more evidence concerning a person's behavior. Or, he can argue that time and conditions change and that other variables are needed to predict behavior.

In this chapter we are primarily interested in some independent checks on number assignments to values. It really does not matter which comes first—the number assignments or these checks. But for sake of discussion we shall assume that number assignments have been made and see what other evidence either supports them or refutes them.

5 · *The Meaning of Independent Tests.*

It must be recalled that testing measurements always takes place within the context of some theory. In other words, in order to decide whether or not an independent test is relevant, one must make explicit the theory which justifies the relevance.

Consider, for example, a case where numbers have been assigned to a set of objectives $O_1, O_2, \ldots O_n$. One may adopt a theory discussed in the last chapter, namely, that personal judgment of preference is transitive over this set. That is, if a person says O_1 is preferred to O_2, O_2 to O_3, and O_3 to O_4, then one can predict he will say O_1 is preferred to O_4. Note that this theoretical statement is not necessarily dependent on the number assignments to the objectives. Indeed, a person may fail to comply with the transitive property of preference judgments and one may still assign numbers to the objectives that permit prediction of his behavior in the standard-value environment.

If one does adopt the transitivity assumption, and if one further adopts the assumption that the ordering of objectives that results is in agreement with the true ordering, then tests of "paired comparisons" of objectives may provide independent evidence for the number assignments. That is, if the number assignment gives the same ordering as the paired comparisons, there may be independent evidence for the validity of the numbers.

Is the evidence really independent?

The answer to this question depends on what we take independent evidence of a theory to mean. This is a general problem applicable to any discipline, and whatever meaning we attach here to the concept of independence is presumably pertinent to any other investigation of nature.

One way to approach the problem is to draw on statistical theory. Suppose two experimenters are observing the same phenomenon, and each makes reports at specific points of time. If we could assume that the phenomenon remained constant throughout the period of observation, then we could observe the fluctuations in the experimenters' reports. If these fluctuations went up and down together, we might argue that the reports were not independent; indeed, if we used statistical terminology we would detect a positive correlation between the errors of the experimenters' reports, and by definition such correlation would be taken as evidence of nonindependence.

Some examination of the logic of this argument seems to be required. We note that the inference about dependence could not be made if the reports had fluctuated in a corresponding fashion, *unless* the phenomenon had remained the same (or changed according to a different pattern from that described by the reports).

What is the point of insisting on stability of the phenomenon? Evidently to guarantee in some sense that one experimenter's report influences the other's. We would not have this guarantee if the changes in reports might have been produced by the changes in the phenomenon itself.

This suggests that the statistical measure of correlation reflects a more general concept of the independence of evidence. In fact, the concept of producer-product discussed in Chapter 7 seems to be the underlying relationship we require to explain dependence and independence. A report made at one time by an experimenter may be a producer of another report made by the same or another experimenter. This means that had the producing report been different in some sense, then the produced report would not have occurred; that is, some other kind of report would have been given. Therefore the basic reason for requiring (in this instance) the stable state of the phenomenon is that if the phenomenon changed, the conditions for a producer-product relationship between the reports would not obtain. More generally, one report may be a probable producer of another, in the sense that reports of its type by one experimenter are probably producers of reports of a given type by a second experimenter. The probability of production is a measure of the degree of dependence of one report on another.

Therefore, correlation of errors in reports may or may not be an indication of dependence of the reports. We note, for example, that one set of reports may depend on another but not vice versa; whereas if one set of reports is correlated with another, then the latter is correlated with the former ("is dependent on" is not a symmetric relation, while "is correlated with" is).

What if two reports each have a common producer? Would this imply a dependence? Evidently not, for both reports must have at least one common producer, namely, the phenomenon itself. Furthermore, both reports must have other common producers since a number of aspects of the environment are essential for the existence of the reports: the air, light, temperature, and so on.

Suppose we grant, then, that the degree of dependence of one type of evidence on another is the probability that the second produces the first. In the case of number assignments to objectives, the test of paired comparisons yields independent evidence of a person's values if the number assignment does not produce the ordering in the paired comparisons. The methodology of tests for independence is not our concern here; statistical correlation may provide one basis —experimental design another. We do assume that agreement of independent evidence increases confidence in the number assignments—an assumption which is actually a part of a broader philosophy of theory-testing.

This discussion illustrates in another way the thesis that what is taken to be factual evidence for a theory itself depends on a model which describes the experimenter and his environment.

6 · *Additivity of Values.*

Consider now another test of the validity of number assignments. In many cases, the values of specific objectives apparently can be added in order to predict a person's choices with respect to combined objectives. Thus if numbers V_1 and V_2 can be used to predict choices relative to objectives O_1 and O_2 respectively, then $V_1 + V_2$ can be used to predict choices with respect to the combined objective O_1-and-O_2.

In other words, we are interested here in the possible validity of the following assertion:

Additivity axiom: If V_1 is an acceptable value of O_1 and V_2 an acceptable value of O_2, then $V_1 + V_2$ is an acceptable value of O_1-and-O_2.

Even this statement needs to be further refined, but the formal problems will detract from the general purpose of this discussion, and are therefore treated in the Appendix of this chapter. But it is important in this context to make clear what is meant by the objective O_1-and-O_2, as well as the meaning of V_1 and V_2. We first consider those situations in which O_1 and O_2 can only be pursued separately.

That is, the decision-maker knows that no course of action is available which has any chance of obtaining them both. Suppose V_1 and V_2 together with the known chances of attaining each objective, are predictors of the person's behavior in this subset of circumstances. The additivity assumption states that $V_1 + V_2$ is a predictor of behavior when the package (O_1-and-O_2) is an available objective. Suppose the theory of behavior which we adopt is a maximizing theory. For example, the theory might state that the person will choose that action A_i which maximizes $P_{i1}V_1 + P_{i2}V_2$, where P_{i1} and P_{i2} are the probabilities of attaining O_1 and O_2 respectively, given that A_i has been chosen. If this theory is adequate when the package is not available, then the additivity assumption states that it will be adequate when the package is available. That is, the person will choose that action A_i which maximizes

$$P_{i1}V_1 + P_{i2}V_2 + P_{i(12)} (V_1 + V_2),$$

where:

$P_{i1} =$ probability that if A_i is adopted, O_1 will occur but not O_2.

$P_{i2} =$ probability that if A_i is adopted, O_2 will occur but not O_1.

$P_i(_{12}) =$ probability that if A_i is adopted, O_1-and-O_2 will both occur.

It is obvious, first of all, that the additivity axiom is not obvious, that is, does not define rational behavior or meet the requirements of intuitive adequacy. Enough has already been said in this book to indicate that axioms of behavior are intended to provide the observer with one way of looking at the world, and need not be validated by intuition alone. Additivity of values is therefore a framework for observation.

In effect the axiom provides a certain way of defining the objectives. The outcomes of a person's actions can be defined in a number of ways by combining the properties of future states according to various patterns. For example, consider a set of objectives which is clearly not additive: the possession of a plant, the possession of the machinery, the possession of raw material, and the hiring of machinists and other labor to run the machinery. Any one of these objectives without the other three may be relatively worthless; but the combination of all of them may be quite valuable. Alternatively, someone may like ice cream and may like oysters, but he might not like ice cream-*and*-oysters. This last example indicates the need to define the operator "and" in the expression "O_1-and-O_2." Oysters on top of ice cream may be distasteful (who knows?), but oysters and ice cream in the same meal may be very suitable.

This suggests that it is often possible to define the objectives and the operation of combining them so that the additivity axiom holds. For example, instead of "possession of a plant" in terms of its use, suppose one speaks of "possession" in terms of selling price. Then the values of the four objectives may be additive. Perhaps the entrepreneur does not want to sell, but rather to produce. Nevertheless, it may happen that he acts as though the parts of his business have values that correspond to their potential selling price. If so, then the observer can reconstruct the entrepreneur's objectives in terms of "selling" objectives, and can use the additive values to predict behavior. This reconstruction of the objectives of a firm is actually what takes place when balance-sheet data are taken to reflect the "value" of a firm's holdings.

Of course, selling is only one basis for redefining the objectives. It is quite possible that production can be segmented into parts in such a way that the production activities of each part can be assigned specific values and the values of the activities are additive. In other words, we reconstruct the objectives so that they are not defined in terms of plant, machinery, raw material, and labor, but in terms of separate activities each involving all of these, and so that the decentralization of activity brings about an additive set of objectives.

Once we grant that the observer does have a wide latitude in the definition of a person's objectives, we can sensibly ask whether a set of objectives defined so as to satisfy the additivity property has any advantages.

A detailed discussion of the advantages of one way of observing the world as compared to another would lead into too great a digression. But it is not hard to show how additivity may provide independent evidence for the validity of number assignments. Suppose there are four objectives O_1, O_2, O_3, and O_4, and that these are preferred in this order: O_1 is preferred to O_2, O_2 to O_3, O_3 to O_4. One can test whether O_1 is preferred to O_2-and-O_3-and-O_4. One can also test whether the value number assigned to O_1 is greater than the sum of the values assigned to O_2, O_3, and O_4. If these tests are independent in the sense defined above, then confidence of the validity of the number assignment may be increased. More details concerning the use of additive values are given in the References of this chapter. There seems to be some indication that in many cases additivity does provide independent evidence. There are a number of other additivity tests that can also be used; specifically, if there are a large number of objectives, the additivity property may be quite useful in simplifying the problem.

The strong additivity assumption may be modified somewhat. This can be done by conceiving the values of two objectives as made up of three components: the value of each objective alone plus the incremental value of the package over and above the values taken separately. That is,

$$V(O_1\text{-}and\text{-}O_2) = V_1 + V_2 + V_{12}$$

a formula reminiscent of the formula for conditional probabilities, except that in this case V_{12} may take on either negative or positive values. That is, there may be a negative or a positive increment of value entailed in having the objectives "occur together." If the values are additive, then V_{12} is zero; hence, the additive case may be considered within the more general framework of this formula.

If the only available evidence is personal response to questions, it may be very difficult for the subject to give any sort of reliable information concerning V_{12}. But in conjunction with other tests, this value may be estimated.

We may also note that if one is studying three objectives, then a "triple value increment" may be involved:

$$V(O_1\text{-}and\text{-}O_2\text{-}and\text{-}O_3) = V_1 + V_2 + V_3 + V_{123}$$

One may then inquire whether it is feasible to conceive of the objectives so that

$$V_{123} = V_{12} + V_{23} + V_{13}.$$

It should also be noted that formulas involving incremental values of the package are not tautological in the sense that they necessarily apply to any way of defining a person's objectives and available courses of action. Thus, for a given set of two objectives, and a satisfactory V_1 and V_2 in the sense explained on page 261, there may not exist any number V_{12} which enables one to predict a person's behavior with respect to $O_1\text{-}and\text{-}O_2$.

Finally, in this discussion of additivity it is worthwhile to recall the methods of the last chapter and ask whether the utility values determined by gambles can be used to evaluate a package. The answer is there is nothing in the method of the last chapter that precludes studying packages; that is, one may insert O_1-*and*-O_2 in one of the "boxes" of the gamble. In fact, this would provide a check on the additivity assumption.

7 · *Other Tests of Number Assignments to Values.*

Enough has already been said to show how number assignments to values can be checked by other means. The rest of this chapter consists of brief summaries of some additional methods available to the researcher. Further details are supplied in the References.

(1) *Utility differences.* In addition to ranking a set of objectives, the subject can be asked to rank the value differences between objectives. Thus if O_1 is preferred to O_2, O_2 to O_3, O_3 to O_4, one can ask whether the value difference between O_1 and O_3 is greater than the value difference between O_2 and O_4. If this question is meaningful to the subject, then his response may supply independent evidence for the validity of a number assignment; for example, if the difference between O_1 and O_3 is greater than the difference between O_2 and O_4, then presumably $V_1 - V_3 > V_2 - V_4$.

We may note that some questions about utility differences are logically redundant (for example, whether in the instance just cited the difference between V_1 and V_4 is greater than the difference between V_2 and V_3). Nevertheless, such redundant questions may supply independent evidence, since there may be no reason to suppose that the subject himself makes the logical inference.

One can pose the question whether the judgment about value differences makes any sense, that is, whether a subject can respond meaningfully to a query about value differences. Various behavioristic interpretations of the judgment are possible, however; for example, one can assume that the difference represents a difference in utilities, as defined in the last chapter.

(2) *Uncertainty situations.* If one is testing a number assignment and a theory of behavior, then it is always possible to set up a series of situations involving uncertainty of the actions relative to outcomes, and see whether the predicted behavior conforms with the actual choices. That is, if the person has initially assigned numbers to the objectives, or the experimenter has estimated these

numbers by some device, these situational tests can be used to test the number-assignment hypothesis. This method is no more than a generalization of the gamble discussed in the last chapter, although it may not be necessary to have the probabilities of the outcomes of the choices add up to 1. One could in this case use more-realistic situations than those allowable by the restricted conditions of a gamble. As in the other cases, some theory of behavior is required to use these situations to test number assignments.

(3) *Long- versus short-term objectives.* As we have pointed out earlier, and will consider in more detail later, it is possible to consider a person's actions with respect to objectives at a number of different points in time. There is no reason, therefore, why a knowledge of a person's long-term values may not be used to estimate or check his short-term values, provided one defines the standard for the value measurements of short-term objectives in terms of a knowledge of the chances of success relative to the long-term objectives. Thus, suppose a man wants, above all, to survive over a period of years, no matter what the cost. This represents a theory of behavior in which the person first maximizes his chances of long-term survival, and then, if the set of maximizing actions contains more than one member, chooses that one which maximizes the value of the other relevant objectives. If one assumed such a theory, then it might be possible to test a given number assignment to the values of short-term objectives which are relevant to long-range survival.

(4) *Latent values in questionnaires.* In recent years there has been some interest, especially in psychology, in studying personality in a somewhat indirect way. Instead of setting up a battery of questions which are directly concerned with some personality characteristic (for example, love of religion, or ability to learn), one sets up test batteries from the responses to which the experimenter can estimate a minimum number of "factor loadings" which explain the responses. Insofar as methods of this type have been applied to values, the tests have been mainly concerned with personal attitudes —usually attitudes with respect to policies or institutions.

Translated within the framework of this book, the method seems to be the following. Consider the response to a question as an indicator of an action which the subject would adopt if he were free to do so or if he were in a position of authority to do so. What set of values for what objectives would enable one to predict the responses that were actually made? This question itself is not precise enough since some restraints on the size and nature of the set of possible objectives would have to be imposed. For example, one might ask: Given a set of objectives, what is the *minimal* subset with its associated values that would enable one to predict the responses?

(5) *Surrogates.* We have already mentioned in this book the possibility of using only a subset of the outcomes to predict behavior under the standard-value conditions. A rather simple case of such "surrogate" values has already been mentioned in connection with accident prevention. Thus a signal occurs warning the decision-maker that unless he adopts an emergency action, an accident will occur. Suppose that in the general course of things he can take steps to prevent the accident by (say) adopting maintenance policies. In other words, we are considering three objectives, all of which are important for the decision-maker: (a) no occurrence of accidents, (b) no occurrence of emergency actions, and (c) no occurrence of maintenance. In general the last two are desirable objectives since emergency actions and maintenance are costly. In order to avoid accidents, the last two objectives may have to be sacrificed to some extent. The difficult problem in this context is to estimate the value of the first objective, especially if the accidents entail loss of life or limb.

If, as was suggested above, we adopt a theory of the decision-maker's behavior to the effect that there exists at least one emergency action which is less costly than the accident, and which is virtually certain to prevent the action, then consideration of the first objective, which is so hard to evaluate, is not necessary to predict behavior in the standard conditions for value measurements. The costs of maintenance plus the costs of emergency action are all that need be considered. The cost of the best emergency action is substituted for the cost of the accident, that is, it is a "surrogate." Such surrogate values can be used to check prior estimates of the cost of an accident.

Other examples of surrogate values are cited in the References.

8 · *Various Theoretical Approaches to Value Measurements.*

Although this book emphasizes the methodological problems of value measurements, one cannot help but be impressed by the multitude of possibilities open to the investigator. The number of alternative methods have by no means been exhausted. Indeed, every field of inquiry that is concerned with value measurements has developed its own methods, and these tend to differ drastically from those of other disciplines. The following list of these fields is itself impressive—and perhaps not exhaustive: genetics, psychoanalysis, clinical psychology, learning theory, attitude research, consumer research, education, industrial relations, managerial-accounting, political science, city-planning, theory of civil rights, jurisprudence, welfare economics, and ethics. Few can wonder that any discussion of value determinations is naïve with respect to the total resources of the human intellect.

We may note here several different theoretical structures which might enable one to predict choices in the standard-value environment. Some of these have already been suggested in the chapter.

Let P_{ij} be the measure of effectiveness of the ith action for the jth objective. Let V_j be a single number assigned to the jth objective.

(a) The person will choose that action which maximizes some function of P_{ij} and V_j; for example, $\Sigma P_{ij} V_j$.

(b) There is an objective, O_k, such that the person will choose that action which maximizes P_{ik}. If two or more actions maximize P_{ik}, then he will choose that one which maximizes $\Sigma P_{ij} V_j$ for $j \neq k$.

(c) [A generalization of (b)]. There are k sets of objectives, O_{11}, $O_{12}, \ldots O_{1m}, O_{21}, O_{22} \ldots O_{2p}, O_{31} \ldots O_{3q}$, and so forth. The person chooses that action which maximizes some function of the P_{ij} over the first set of objectives. If two or more actions maximize over the first set, he chooses that one which maximizes over the second set, and so forth.

(d) There exists a set of numbers V_j, and V_{jk}, V_{jkl}, and so on assigned to each objective, pair of objectives, triplet of objectives, and so on, which together with P_{ij}, $P_{i(jk)}$, $P_{i(jkl)}$—the measures of effectiveness for each objective, each pair, each triplet, and so on—enables one to predict behavior (an example of this theory is given in the Appendix of this chapter).

(e) The action choices of the subject are classified along certain scales (for example, amount of a resource that is used). The choices are constrained; that is, the subject only makes choices within certain limits along the scales. Within these limits, he maximizes the expected value, or behaves according to other criteria mentioned in (b) and (c) above. An example of this model is linear programming. This possibility might be considered as an outcome of the classification of available actions; but it may happen that the subject wants to avoid certain kinds of action "at all costs," that is, will never choose the action even though he knows it may lead to certain objectives. In the terminology of Chapter 7, his preference for certain acts is very low.

(f) Associated with each action is a probability of learning with respect to a class of objectives; the subject chooses that action which maximizes this probability (subject to constraints).

9 · *Indebtedness.*

Much of the material of this chapter comes from work with R. L. Ackoff. The additivity axiom is discussed in our joint paper (2). The treatment of preventative action was developed in conversations with him. Uses of cost functions for studying behavior is illustrated by Feeney (5). Utility differences are illustrated by Davidson, Suppes and Siegel (4). Cooper, Charnes and Mellon (3) have treated the problem of cost surrogates in some detail. Their work is an extension of the research of Modigliani and Hohn (6), whose paper also considers some aspects of the long-range versus short-range objectives.

An ingenious method of assigning value numbers to objectives is given by J. W. Smith (8) and Auman and Kruskal (1).

N. M. Smith (9) has written extensively on the use of long-range objectives for measuring the value of short-range goals. He also discusses the additivity assumption within his system, but I think fails to emphasize that his conclusions concerning the "marginal" properties of additivity hold only within his system. As nearly as I can follow his argument, he does not seem to allow a value of a "thing" in an intermediate state to be partially independent of the end-state value.

Some references to the methods of measuring values of tastes of food are to be found in (7). For a more complete bibliography on value assignments, see (2a).

REFERENCES

1. Auman, R. J., and S. B. Kruskal, "Assigning Quantitative Values by Qualitative Methods in the Naval Electronics Problem," *Naval Logistics Research Quarterly*, 6 (1959), pg. 1.
2. Churchman, C. W., and R. L. Ackoff, "An Approximate Measure of Value," *Journal of the Operations Research Society of America*, 2 (1954), pg. 172.
2a. Churchman, C. W., "Decision and Value Theory," *Progress in Operations Research*, Vol. 1 (edited by R. L. Ackoff), New York: John Wiley and Sons (to appear).
3. Cooper, W. W., A. Charnes, and R. Mellon, "A Model for Optimizing Production by Reference to Cost Surrogates," *Econometrica*, 23 (1955), pg. 307.
4. Davidson, D., S. Siegel, and P. Suppes, "Some Experiments and Related Theory on the Measurement of Utility and Subjective Probability," *Technical Report No. 1*. Applied Mathematics and Statistics Laboratory, Stanford University (1955).
5. Feeney, G. J., "A Basis for Strategic Decisions on Inventory Control Operations," *Management Science*, 2 (1955), pg. 69.
6. Modigliani, F., and F. Hohn, "Solution of Certain Problems of Production Planning over Time Illustrating the Effect of the Inventory Constraint," *Econometrica* 23 (1955), pg. 46.
7. Peryam, David R., Francis J. Pilgrim, and Martins Peterson, *Food Acceptance Testing Methodology*. Washington, D.C.: National Academy of Sciences, National Research Council Advisory Board on Quartermaster Research and Development, 1954.
8. Smith, J. W., "A Plan to Allocate and Procure Electronic Sets Using Linear Programming Techniques and Analytic Methods of Assigning Values to Qualitative Factors," *Naval Logistics Research Quarterly*, 3 (1956), pg. 151.
9. Smith N. M., Jr., "A Calculus for Ethics: A Theory of the Structure of Value," *Behavioral Science*, 1 (1956), pp. 111 and 186.

APPENDIX

The additivity axiom states that the value of a "package" is the sum of the values of the components of the package. This Appendix is an interpretation of this statement within the context of value measurement given in Chapter 7.

Let K be a set of objectives $O_1, O_2, \ldots O_n$. Assume a set of actions available to a decision-maker: $A_1, A_2 \ldots A_m$. Consider these sets of numbers:

p_{ij} = conditional effectiveness of the ith action for the jth objective, given that none of the other objectives can occur.

$p_{i(jk)}$ = conditional effectiveness of the ith action for the attainment of both the jth and k^{th} objective, given that no other objectives occur.

$p_{i(jkl)}$ = conditional effectiveness of the ith action for the attainment of the jth, k^{th}, and l^{th} objective, given that no other objectives occur, and so on. Similarly for $p_{i(jklm)}$, $p_{i(jklmn)}$, and so on.

V_j = a "value" number assigned to the jth objective by itself.

$V_{(jk)}$ = a value number assigned to the "package" consisting of both the jth and k^{th} objective. Similarly for $V_{(jkl)}$, $V_{(jklm)}$, and so on.

Let $P(A_i)$ be the probability that A_i will be chosen when the subject "knows" p_{ij}, $p_{i(jk)}$, $p_{i(jkl)}$, and so on, and has no preference for the A_i as such.

The axiom states that if there exists a function of p_{ij}, $p_{i(jk)}$, and so on, and V_j, $V_{(jk)}$, and so on, which predicts $P(A_i)$ for all i when $p_{i(jk)}$, $p_{i(jkl)}$, and so on, are O then this function will predict $P(A_i)$ for all i when $p_{i(jk)}$, $p_{i(jkl)}$, and so on, are different from O, and $V_{(jk)} = V_j + V_k$, $V_{(jkl)} = V_j + V_k + V_l$, and so on. In more precise terms, consider a set K of four members, a_1, a_2, a_3, a_4. Suppose $\sim a_1$, $\sim a_2$, $\sim a_3$, $\sim a_4$ stand for the absence of a_1, a_2, a_3, a_4 respectively, and that $a_1 u a_2$ stands for the logical sum (disjunction) of a_1 and a_2. In the first instance we have considered

(1) $a_1 U \sim a_2 U \sim a_3 U \sim a_4$
(2) $\sim a_1 U a_2 U \sim a_3 U \sim a_4$
(3) $\sim a_1 U \sim a_2 U a_3 U \sim a_4$
(4) $\sim a_1 U \sim a_2 U \sim a_3 U a_4$

and to these we associate value measures V_a, V_b, V_c, V_d, together with effectiveness numbers p_{i1}, p_{i2}, p_{i3}, and p_{i4}, relative to the ith action.

Then we considered the set:

(5) $a_1 U a_2 U \sim a_3 U \sim a_4$
(6) $a_1 U \sim a_2 U a_3 U \sim a_4$

and so on.

The effectiveness measures for this set are designated by $p_{i(12)}$, $p_{i(13)}$, and so on. We let the value measures for this set be $V_{(12)}$, $V_{(13)}$, and so on.

We similarly consider the set

(7) $a_1 \cup a_2 \cup a_3 \cup {\sim} a_4$
(8) $a_1 \cup a_2 \cup {\sim} a_3 \cup a_4$

and so on, and symbolize the effectiveness measures by $p_{i(123)}$, $p_{i(124)}$, and so on, and we let the value measures for this set be $V_{(123)}$, $V_{(124)}$, and so on. Finally we consider

(9) $a_1 \cup a_2 \cup a_3 \cup a_4$,

and let $p_{i(1234)}$ be the effectiveness measure, and $V_{(1234)}$ be the value measure.

Suppose we construct a function $f(i)$:

$$f(i) = p_{i1}V_1 + p_{i2}V_2 + \ldots + p_{i(12)}V_{(12)} + p_{i(13)}V_{(13)} + \ldots$$
$$+ p_{i(123)}V_{(123)} + \ldots + p_{i(1234)}V_{(1234)}.$$

Suppose further that $P(A_i) = 1$ if $f_{(i)}$ is max over all i, and $P(A_i) = 0$ otherwise, *provided* that $p_{i(12)} = 0$, $p_{i(13)} = 0$, . . . , $p_{i(1234)} = 0$ for all i. Then the axiom states that $P(A_i) = 1$ if $f(i)$ is max, for all $p_{i(12)}p_{i(13)}$, and so on, when we let

$$V_{(ij)} = V_i + V_j, \quad V_{(ijk)} = V_j + V_j + V_k,$$

and so on.

As was pointed out in the chapter, one methodological issue of great difficulty is the interpretation of the disjunction $a_i \cup a_j$.

SENSITIVITY AND CHOICE

10

Summary

and

Intent.

In this chapter we shall consider another approach to value measurements. This approach illustrates two aspects of the problem which have not been stressed before. First of all, we have already noted that the objectives may be classified along certain scales, and we should now consider why such a classification might be useful. Second, we have mentioned that the decision-maker does not always make the same choice even in the same circumstances; his choice may be described in terms of a "probability of choice," and the importance of this point needs to be considered.

The method to be discussed is based on a "sensitivity" model. In very general terms, a sensitivity model is an image in which a phenomenon is first

273

characterized as being in state S_1 (in our case, the subject does not choose a certain act); then one aspect of the environment is changed along some scale; the phenomenon eventually begins to exhibit a new state S_2 with an assignable probability (in our case, the subject sometimes chooses the act); finally, as the "stimulus" is increased, the phenomenon is observed to be only in state S_2 (the act is always chosen). Further generalizations of this model (for example, to several states) are possible but need not concern us here.

2 · *Sensitivity of Choice.*

We have already noted that choice changes if the conditional probabilities change. But we also may be able to relate changes in the probability of choice to certain measurable aspects of the objectives as well. For example, consider the problem of top-management policy formation in a company. We have seen how difficult it is to express the value of all company objectives in dollar units. Suppose, instead, one were to list a set of objectives as follows:

net return	total personnel
total sales	labor peace
share of market	legality
gross return	technological leadership
security	

In a sense, these are not objectives at all because it would be impossible to gauge the effectiveness of a policy relative to any one of them unless its meaning were made more precise. This might be done by trying to find a scale in terms of which each objective is defined, for example, as follows:

net return in dollars per annum
total sales in units per annum
gross return in dollars per annum
security in probability of no bankruptcy over a year
total personnel in average number of people over a year
labor peace in work days per annum per regular worker
legality in minus dollars per annum (such as fine or lawyer fees)
technological leadership in number of contributions to scientific journals per annum

Each of these scales would require a great deal of effort to make it meaningful for the purpose of policy formation. But these technical problems can be put aside for the time being in order to determine how the scaling of objectives might be used. It is clear that each qualitative objective has been translated into a set of objectives definable by some point along the associated scale. For sake of nomenclature, let us call the scale associated with one of the list of objectives the "objective scale," and in specific cases, the "net-return scale," the "market-share scale," and so on. This nomenclature may help to remind us that the selection of an appropriate scale for a given objective is not obvious and may require considerable research effort. It must be kept in mind that an objective scale defines an "objective set," that is, a subset of objectives defined by points on the scale.

The sensitivity model which we consider in this chapter assumes that in any given environment there are a set of policies (alternative decisions). For each policy there is a value on each objective scale, such that the policy is certain to attain any of the set below this value, and certain not to attain any of the set above it. We shall call this the critical value of the policy relative to an objective scale. We next assume that given two policies which have the same critical values with respect to all sets of objectives except one, the probability that a fully informed subject will choose that policy with the higher critical value on this one is at least as great as the probability that he chooses a policy with a lower critical value. This means that "all other things being equal," the higher the policy reaches on the objective scale, the more likely it is to be chosen.

Put otherwise, we consider a model of behavior in which the subject is conceived to be pursuing sets of objectives; each objective set can be characterized by a variable x_j. In any specific environment, each action determines a single value along each x_j—the critical value of the action. If we think of n objective sets as defining an n dimensional space, then each action defines one point in this space. Associated with each point in the space is a probability of choice:

$$\text{Probability of choice} = f(x_1, x_2 \ldots x_n)$$

We are to assume that f is monotonic nondecreasing. Evidently, if additional alternatives are presented, then f, the probability of choice of one action, may be altered. We can say now that the value of any objective set is the set of measures necessary to define the function f for any set of alternative actions. If all f's belong to the same family of functions, then the value of an objective set will be the set of parameters which determine a specific function of this family.

An alternative model which we shall also consider is one in which there are m specifically defined objectives and a set of alternative actions defined by morphological properties. In any given environment one can assign a "probability of success" to each alternative action relative to each objective. We are interested in a function of these probabilities of success which determines a subject's probability of choosing a specific action. We think of the environment as an aspect of nature which can be changed in such a way that the identity of each alternative choice remains fixed. We are interested in changes in behavior as a function of changes in the environment. As before, we assume that an increase in the probability of success, all other things being equal, never results in a decrease in the probability of choice.

Thus, in general, we are looking at models of behavior which relate probability of choice to certain "stimulating" aspects of the alternative choices on the environment. In the first case, we want to see how choice varies as the alternatives are changed relative to their degree of attainment along an objective-scale; in the second case, we are interested in variation of choice for fixed alternatives and varying probabilities of success. We use the term "stimulus" or "stimulus variable" to represent the changing aspects of the situation.

We have now to consider the concept of probability of choice which is central in this model of behavior.

3 · *Probability of Choice.*

We have already noticed in Chapter 7 that exhibition of behavior on the part of a person is not equivalent to the choice of the behavior. For choice to occur, the behavior must be produced by some property of the subject—in the technical sense of production given in that chapter. Specifically, we argued that for value measurements, the choice must be produced by the person's knowledge.

If we decide to define probability in terms of relative frequencies, then the reference class will be all actions that the person *chooses* in a certain type of environment. The measure of probability of choice of an action is the frequency of choices of this action relative to all choices defined by the reference class. Or, as we argued in Chapter 6, "probability" may be defined in terms of judgment and no doubt will have to be for many value studies of decision-makers.

4 · Is Probability of Choice Meaningful under Conditions of Full Knowledge?

Some question may arise concerning the meaningfulness of a probability of choice under the conditions of the standard for value measurement. If a person knows what his choices imply as far as outcomes are concerned, one would normally expect him to choose only one action. The only exception to this might seem to be the case where two or more actions are equally effective, in which case, since there is no preference for the acts as such in the standard value environment, the probability of choice would be equally divided among the actions. Or, put otherwise, an equal probability of choice would be taken to mean equal preference.

Possibly some of the confusion concerning probability of choice has come about because it seems natural to define a preference relationship over pairs of available actions. When this is done, it seems reasonable to assert that either one act is preferred to another —in which case it will certainly be chosen if the two acts are the only available ones, or else the person is indifferent—in which case the acts will be chosen with equal frequency.

But, of course, such a preference relationship need not be adopted by the researcher in order to carry out the program of value measurements. Thus the pertinent question is whether any useful purpose is served by introducing probabilities of choice other than 1, 0, or (in the case of two alternatives) 1/2. In order to answer this question, we need to reconsider the concept of an "action." In the Appendix of Chapter 7 we discussed various ways in which actions might be defined: in terms of physical properties, morphological properties, or functional properties. Whatever classification the researcher chooses, he is not forced to keep each action type distinct from the others. If an overlapping of the classes of actions seems desirable, then, of course, it may very well turn out that a person exhibits a probability of choice lying between o and 1 for each of the action types. Thus there is one rather obvious case where a probability of choice may be useful.

Second, the standard conditions for value measurement given in Chapter 7 do not completely specify all the determinants of behavior. Specifically, it was left undetermined whether the person knows the consequences of action for objectives that occur in the more-distant future. If a person does not know the consequences, then the values of short-run objectives may only predict a probability of choice which reflects this uncertainty about future goals.

Finally, there seems to be no reason at all why the researcher must think of personal choice under conditions of perfect knowledge as a "deterministic" choice. In order to attain such determinism it may be necessary to classify actions and objectives in such detail that the costs of research are enormous, or the research is not even feasible. In other words, a general approach to value measurements should not preclude economic methods of classification.

5 · *Sensitive and Insensitive Ranges.*

Suppose we assume that probability of choice may be a fruitful concept and examine some interesting aspects of the sensitivity models that might be developed. We consider, therefore, one of the two models described earlier. In some cases a change in a stimulus variable may not yield any change in the probability of choice. For sake of a name, let us call such a range of a variable for which no change in choice occurs an "insensitive" range.

For example, consider an environment in which there are two available choices A_1 and A_2, and one qualitatively defined objective, O. It may happen that the probability (P_1) that A_1 leads to O is very high compared to the probability (P_2) that A_2 does. Increases in P_2 will not lead to any change in behavior. Thus the entire range from o to P_1 is an insensitive range with respect to A_2.

As another example, consider a simple situation consisting of two actions and two outcomes, in which there is no preference for the actions as such and the person knows the conditional probabilities that the outcomes will occur. Suppose A_1 has o chance relative to both O_1 and O_2; A_2 a perfect chance relative to O_2 and a o chance relative to O_1. We keep A_2's conditional probabilities fixed, as well as A_1's chance relative to O_2. The stimulus consists of increasing A_1's chances relative to O_1. It may happen that no matter how this stimulus is increased, A_2 is always chosen. Indeed, this would occur if the subject's intention relative to O_2 had a measure of 1 in the simple intention model discussed in Chapter 7, p. 191. In such a case, the entire range from 0 to 1 is insensitive with respect to A_1.

However, if we change A_2's conditional probabilities relative to O_2, to 0.5, then the range may become sensitive, that is, the subject may eventually choose A_1 instead of A_2.

It seems reasonable to assert that if the range becomes sensitive for some conditional probability P of A_2 relative to O_2, it will also be sensitive for all probabilities less than P.

Within a sensitive range, the usual sensitivity measures apply. These measures describe the properties of a sensitivity curve. In the simplest case, the value of the stimulus at which the probability of choice becomes 0.5, and the "slope" of the sensitivity curve at this point provide a sufficient basis for predicting behavior relative to other values of the stimulus. Chapter 5 gives an example of a sensitivity analysis in the field of physical chemistry; the Appendix of this chapter provides an outline of a sensitivity model for models in which "probability of success for an outcome" is the stimulus.

6 · *Degree of Attainment as a Stimulus.*

Suppose now we consider the first sensitivity model, where an action's degree of attainment along an objective scale is conceived to be the stimulus.[1] It is interesting to note some of the commonly recognized aspects of policy-making which can be defined by this concept of sensitivity. For example, a decision-maker may refuse to consider any policy unless it attains at least a certain minimum net return. No matter how excellent policies may be along other objective scales, they will not be chosen if they fail to meet this minimum requirement. In such cases, there are large insensitive ranges for the other objective scales. Specifically, for each objective scale there may be a "need" point—a minimal "survival" measure. The set of all need points has the following characteristic: imagine one policy, A_1, which exactly attains each need point (that is, the need point is its critical value); competing with A_1 are a set of policies which have

[1] See also the Appendix to this chapter.

critical values less than the need point for at least one objective scale; then, no matter what may be critical values of the competing policies on other scales, the decision-maker always chooses A_1. In other words, all ranges on the other scales are insensitive. The application of need points in business policies is familiar enough: for example, safeguarding dividends even though excellent opportunities are available for improving market position. Of course, the frustration and disaster that occurs when no policy exists that meets all need points is a well-known phenomenon too.

Where the ranges are sensitive, one may expect radically different kinds of sensitivity functions, which reflect differences in the "values" of the objective scales. For example, once all minimal needs are met, it is possible that net return becomes the predominant motive. This, translated, means that a policy that increases net return will be chosen over policies that keep net return constant, but are much higher on the other objective scales.

In job evaluation, where objective scales are frequently used, it is assumed that the "value" increases linearly with the degree of attainment on the scale, although it is usually not clear what this assumption means. In the case of the model we are considering, the assumption states that there is some linear function of the objective scales, such that those jobs which maximize this function will receive the highest pay. In other words, each scale is weighted, each job is assigned a weighted value for each objective, and the sum of the weighted values predicts the wage. It is sometimes said that the qualitatively different scales (years of experience, years of training, amount of risk, and so on) have a "common denominator"; apparently this means no more than that wage will be determined by a linear function of the weighted scales. What excites the curiosity of the researcher is why this phenomenon should occur, that is, the underlying mechanism at work which determines wages in this manner.

7 · *Preference and Probability of Choice.*

A few notes on the relationship of this chapter to those that preceded it are in order. First of all, consider the axiom set for utility measurement given in Chapter 8. The basic concept of this model is a preference relationship which holds over a class of utilities. If the preference relation is interpreted to mean a choice of one action (or outcome) as opposed to another, then probability of choice does not occur in the model. Thus, in the sensitivity model of this chapter, it is possible for a person at some time to choose A instead of B, B instead of C, and C instead of A. This could happen if the probabilities of choice A, B, and C were each 1/3, for example. Hence, if "preference" is interpreted in terms of choice, the model of Chapter 8 and the sensitivity model of this chapter may be incompatible. But it is possible to define a preference relation within a sensitivity model which will satisfy the axioms of order, namely, by defining "A is preferred to B" to be "the probability of choice of A is greater than the probability of choice of B." Hence, the model of behavior discussed in Chapter 8 can be considered as one example of a sensitivity model. The "stimulus" is the probability coefficient of gamble. It is a relatively easy matter to define sensitive and insensitive ranges for this stimulus.

Again, consider the additivity axiom discussed in the last chapter with respect to the second model of this chapter (where the stimuli are the probabilities of success for each set of objectives). Suppose we can find a function of the probabilities of success which predicts probability of choice; suppose this function can be characterized by parameters which act as coefficients of the probabilities of success. Then it may happen that we can derive a new sensitivity function where we include packages of objectives, and that the parameters associated with the packages are additions of the parameters associated with members of the package in the first function. In such a case, a generalized form of the additivity axiom would hold.

But it should be clear that in general the additivity assumption cannot be used to study values when the subsets of objectives are defined by objective scales. For example, suppose we are examining a job-evaluation plan. One feature that makes a job more valuable is the educational requirement measured in terms of years of schooling. It presumably makes no sense to talk about the additivity of grade-school education and high-school education; at least the additivity model sketched in the Appendix of Chapter 4 is not applicable because "high-school education without grammar-school education" is a meaningless objective.

However, one could develop an additivity model for scalable properties by studying the incremental values along each of the scales. In other words, we assume that the properties are additive, and that an incremental unit gain along any of the scales has the same value independent of the position on the scale. One then uses the additivity assumption to check the relative value of incremental units (for example, the relative worth of one year of school compared to one year of training).

For example, suppose the jobs are evaluated in terms of education, training, risk, working conditions, and physical effort. Suppose each of these properties is scalable, and one can sensibly talk of incremental units of each. As was mentioned before, we might assume that an incremental unit of one year of education has the same value whether the unit occurs after grammar school, high school, college, or any point. A similar assumption is made for each of the other properties. One further assumes that the value of both one year of education and one year of training is equal to the sum of the values of the increments taken separately. One can then estimate the relative values of the increments by the methods described in Chapter 9. Finally, a different test, involving a study of the maximum education, maximum training, maximum risk, and so on, will check whether the original assumptions are valid. The meaning of such tests, as always, depends on the construction of a function for predicting behavior, and the determination of the information required to specify the function for a particular decision-maker.

8 · *Conceptual Frameworks for Value Measurement.*

In the last three chapters we have discussed three conceptual frameworks for measuring values. In each case, the framework has indicated how value could be defined in terms of certain properties of a person's choices. The framework given in Chapter 8 was complete enough to predict choices in various environments, that is, it provided a way for adjusting observations of preference choices. Economically, it may not be feasible to use except in laboratory work. The additivity axiom of Chapter 9 enables one to check a given predictive system even in fairly realistic situations, but it may be awkward or even self-defeating to define objectives so that the additivity assumption holds. The framework of this chapter recommends itself primarily as a general viewpoint in the study of value measurements, without, however, considering the practical problems of application.

It should be clear that the broad program of measurement presented in Chapter 5 has not been completely covered by any of the discussion of the last three chapters. The application of methods for measuring values is still very restricted. These chapters have not discussed any theory of the change of a person's values over time. They have omitted any reference to the relationship between personal values and group values. No reference has been made to long-range ideals, that is, ethical values. The remainder of this book is concerned with generalizing the program of value measurement by examining the problems of social value, values over time, and ethical values.

APPENDIX

It is simpler to begin with the second model discussed in this chapter, in which the stimulus is the probability of success.

Let $A_1, A_2 \ldots, A_n$ be a set of available actions; and $O_1, O_2 \ldots O_m$ a set of objectives.

$P(O_j/A_i) = P_{ij}$ is the conditional probability that O_j will occur if A_i is chosen in a given environment.

$P(A_i/I) = P_i$ is the probability that an individual I will choose A_i.

In order to simplify the discussion, suppose $n = 2$, $m = 2$.

Let P_{21} and P_{22} be fixed, as well as P_{12}. We say that a given set P_{21}, P_{22}, P_{12} represents an "insensitive environment" if P_1 remains invariant for all values of P_{11}; otherwise the given set represents a sensitive environment.

Consider, now, the properties of P_1 in a sensitive environment.

Assumption 1. If $\{P_{21}, P_{22}, P_{12}\}$ is sensitive, then P_1 will be monotonic increasing with respect to P_{11}.

That is, if the value of P_{11} does affect behavior, then an increase of P_{11} means that it is more likely that A_1 will be chosen. Assumption 1 can be regarded as a definition of a "uniform positive value" of O_1; that is, if O_1 is not valued at all, or its absence is preferred under certain circumstances, then Assumption 1 does not hold.

Assumption 2. Suppose $\{P_{21}, P_{22}, P_{12}\}$ is insensitive in the sense that $P_1 = 0$ for all values of P_{11}; suppose that P_{22} is reduced to P'_{22} and that the set $\{P_{21}, P'_{22}, P_{12}\}$ becomes sensitive. Then the set will remain sensitive for all values of P_{22} less than P'_{22}. Similarly for P_{21}. Finally, if P_{12} can be increased to P'_{12} so that $\{P_{21}, P_{22}, P'_{12}\}$ is sensitive, then every set with a higher value of P_{12} will also be sensitive.

Suppose that in every sensitive environment, the sensitivity curve relating P_1 and P_{11} can be characterized by one measure μ (for example, the value of P_{11} where P_1 becomes 0.5, the slopes of the curves remaining fixed). Then

Assumption 3. Consider the set $\{P_{21}, P_{22}, P_{12}\}$ where P_{21} and P_{12} are fixed, but P_{22} varies. Suppose there exists a value of P_{22} where the set is insensitive in the sense that P_1 is 0 for all values of P_{11}, and that there exists a value of P_{22} where the set becomes sensitive. Then μ is a monotonic increasing function of P_{22} in all sensitive environments.

This assumption asserts that the point at which a person will begin to shift A_1 will increase as P_{22} increases.

From Assumption 2, together with certain mathematical assumptions concerning the sensitivity curves, it follows that $\mu > 0$ for all P_{22} in sensitive environments.

We now have expressed μ as a function of P_{22}. Suppose this sensitivity function can be characterized by one value, v; we then attempt to express v as a function of P_{21} and to find measures which identify this function. Finally, we attempt to discover a functional relationship between these measures and P_{12}. If all this were possible, the final sensitivity function would be a complete predictor over the set $P_{11}, P_{12}, P_{21}, P_{22}$ of the probability of choice of A_1.

Consider now the first model discussed in this chapter.

Let $O_1(X)$ and $O_2(y)$ be functions defined over domains D_x, D_y. The domains are ordered—or more generally each is a continuum. Next, there exists a set of environments (states), defined by a set of alternative actions. Each alternative action A_i has the following property: for all $X \leq K_1$, A_i is certain to attain $O_1(X)$, and for all $X > K_1$, A_i is certain not to attain $O_1(X)$[2]; similarly for all $y \leq K_2$, A_i is certain to attain $O_2(y)$, and for all $y > K_2$, certain not to attain $O_2(y)$. The couple (K_1, K_2) thus defines the action A_i. The set of environments is such that all possible couples are represented and compete with all possible numbers of alternatives defined in all

---

[2] Thus $O_1(X)$ is to be interpreted as the objective of attaining at least X.

possible ways. Or the set may be constrained in ways that are useful to the researcher.

We assume the following about the action-choices of any environment:

(a) Only one action is chosen; that is, the probability of choice is 1 or 0.

(b) Given only two couples (K_1, K_2) and (K'_1, K_2), and $K_1 < K'_1$, then (K'_1, K_2) will be chosen. Similarly for two couples (K_1, K_2) and (K_1, K_2'), if $K_2 < K_2'$, (K_1, K_2') will be chosen.

In the discussion of the chapter we assume that there exist functions $V_1(X)$ and $V_2(y)$ such that for any environment the two functions are sufficient to predict the action-choices of a decision-maker. More precisely, given a set of action-couples (K_i, K_j), the values of $V_1(K_i)$ and $V_2(K_j)$ are sufficient to predict which action will be chosen. For example, $V_1(K_i)$ may be simply aK_i and $V_2(K_j)$ may be βK_j. That action (K_i, K_j) will be chosen for which $aK_i + \beta K_j$ is maximum. This example is the "linear weights" model discussed in the chapter. (It is assumed that the set of action-couples is finite.)

The model could be generalized by relinquishing condition (a) above, that is, by introducing probability of choice. We would then conceive of an ordered set of environments having all action-choices identical except for one, represented by the couple (X, K_2). The values of X would order the set of environments. As X increases we would record the probability of choice of this action. We might find that the set of environments is "insensitive," as above; that is, the probability of choice of (X, K_2) is 0 (say) no matter what X is. This would mean that other actions are available which have higher values than K_2, and this precludes the choice of (X, K_2) no matter what X is. Alternatively, we might discover a sensitivity curve as we increase X, that is, the probability of choice may go from 0 to 1.

Evidently, the model could also be generalized by introducing other objective scales.

JUDGMENT

11

Summary

and

Intent.

Up to this point we have been chiefly concerned with the concept of optimal behavior of a single individual, who may be a person or any identifiable purposeful entity. The remainder of this book is devoted to a sketch of the problem of the optimal behavior of a social group.

If we were to carry over the analysis of optimal behavior which has been suggested in the earlier pages, we would say that the best action for a group to adopt is the action it would choose if it knew the conditional probabilities and had freedom of choice. But in the case of a group there are a number of ways in which this stipulation can be interpreted. Furthermore, there does not seem to be any clear indication of the best interpretation since any of these ways may prove quite fruitful in the study of purposive groups. Our endeavor, therefore, is primarily a taxonomy. The consequence of this endeavor is a classification of the many senses in which one may speak of social approval, social morality, ethical criteria, and the like.

The following is a brief account of the taxonomy that will be considered in connection with group knowledge and group values.

(1) When we say that a group "knows" something, there are a number of possible meanings we may have in mind. We may consider the group as a single individual, and try to adopt behavioristic criteria of the type already discussed in this book. The practical methodology of doing this may be very difficult to work out, but conceptually there appears to be nothing wrong.

Alternatively, one could interpret group knowledge in terms of the knowledge of the members. One rather direct way of doing this would be to say that a group knows something if and only if every member knows it. It should be noted that a group may know something, in the collective sense given above, without any member's knowing it. For example, a community may vote very effectively relative to its goals even though the members are all uncertain about the proper measures to be adopted.

In this chapter we consider a third meaning of group knowledge based on the concept of judgment which was discussed earlier in the book. This much-more elaborate meaning illustrates the breadth of opportunity open to the student of social values in terms of the ways in which these values may be defined.

(2) Next, we consider the meaning of the phrase "what a group ought to do." Again, we can adopt the viewpoint that the group is an entity, and attempt to set up rules of identification that enable us to determine what kind of behavior the group as a whole adopts when it knows the consequences of its acts. Alternatively, we can argue that a group ought to adopt an action if and only if every member wants to adopt it. In this latter sense, a group can be said to value an outcome, and an action can be said to be preferred by a group, if and only if every member has the same set of values. This interpretation of group values is certainly very limited in its scope, although from time to time there may be considerable advantage in studying ideally harmonious groups.

In the next chapter our interest will center on alternatives to the two interpretations just mentioned. These alternatives all develop from the concept that the researcher of group behavior can study the manner in which the members of a group agree to resolve group conflicts when the members are free and have knowledge. What a group wants is defined to be the resultant of this method of resolution. A great many methods of resolution are possible, and some of these will be illustrated. It will be noted that the way we have chosen to consider group values does not entail any problem of the so-called "comparison" of personal values, except in so far as a specific idea of fair comparisons may lead us to judge that one resolution rule is to be preferred to another. But our concern is not with evaluating the rules on some "rational" basis.

(3) Finally, we consider the study of a social group from the point of view of an indefinitely long time span. The possibility of doing this for individual persons is always open, but most researchers feel that the opportunity for studying decisions of a single subject closes at some moment of time, and few researchers have much interest in predicting what a subject would do if he were still alive. But many social groups have indefinitely long life spans, and to the methodologist this fact poses some difficult problems of conceptualization. Here the discussion has been restricted to two examples: organizations controlled by some type of accounting procedure, and the institution of science. The last chapters of the book introduce some long-term predictions concerning the future of the study of "immortal" groups, and tries to relate these considerations to the problems of ethics. Specifically, the last chapter considers in as general a way as possible the theme of conflict which is central to all the discussions of this book.

2 · *Belief.*

We begin by considering in more detail the meaning of "belief," because we assume that a judgment is some specific kind of belief.

It may be wise to point out why the analysis of the concept of belief is not as obvious as one might at first assume. When does a person believe that something is so? That is, what constitutes evidence for the assertion that "X believes that Y exists"? We can take it for granted that an expression of personal conviction that one believes something, is not sufficient evidence that the belief actually occurs. A person may not know he holds a belief; a person may think he holds a belief but not actually hold it.

Behavioristic evidence of belief, however, seems simple to define. Why not say that "X believes that Y exists" is true if X acts *as though* Y exists? The difficulty, of course, lies in trying to say what "as though" means in this context. We would like to say that whenever Y is present, X exhibits a certain type of behavior. Hence, if he exhibits this type of behavior now, we want to argue that this is evidence of belief in Y. However, in order that the behavior be relevant at all, it is necessary that X does not exhibit the behavior when Y is not present. Otherwise the behavior would not be any indication of belief about Y. But now the behavior criterion is useless: X adopts the behavior when Y is present, and does not adopt it when Y is absent. Hence X never behaves as though Y were present unless Y is actually present. Mistaken belief, under this theory of evidence, would be impossible.

The way out of this conundrum seems clear enough. We could say that normally X adopts a certain type of "criterion" behavior when Y is present, and does not adopt it when Y is absent, and on this occasion there is no conceivable reason why he should fail to adopt the criterion behavior. By this we apparently mean that the criterion behavior serves X's needs whenever Y is present, and does not serve his needs when Y is absent.

By these steps of reasoning, we are led to the conclusion that belief is like knowledge in that neither concept is meaningful independent of the concept of value. Belief, knowledge, and value are really aspects of the same total concept of human behavior. As our earlier discussion indicated, the choice of assigning measures to belief and values is essentially an economic choice of the researcher.

Thus, it may appear that we cannot decide whether a person believes an act is effective relative to one of his goals, or whether he simply is not interested in the goal. For example, Jones believes that it will not rain today because he does not take his raincoat along. This kind of statement makes sense as long as we can safely assume that Jones wants to stay dry. It looks as though the observer must use economic criteria to decide whether Jones is exhibiting belief or a change of interest. People often accuse their fellow men of stupidity when actually they fail to recognize what the other fellow really wants to do.

In some circumstances, the economical way to proceed may be to assume that a person's preference increases the more he receives of a given commodity (for example, he always wants more comfort or money or free time or prestige). Rewards along such a scale can then be used to test belief. The technical details of such tests may be quite difficult to work out, but at the present time it seems feasible to construct empirical tests both of belief and of value on this basis.

In effect, then, the standard conditions for measuring belief are as follows. Suppose there are a set of alternative choices the individual can make. Each of these alternatives is relevant to one objective (for example, maximal reward along some reward scale). The individual has no preference for the alternatives as such and is equally aware of the availability of each. If the individual chooses one of the alternatives in this standard environment, he believes this alternative is the most effective (or at least as effective as any other). If the choice is estimated to occur with a relative frequency less than one, then the probability of choice may be taken as a measure of the degree of belief.

The standard conditions for measuring belief need not specify one objective only. But if there are more objectives, then the experimenter must assume the relative values of each; more generally, the experimenter must assume the subject's effectiveness scores for the alternative actions.

Belief in the existence of an object can now be defined as follows. Suppose that when Y is present, X responds in a certain way (that is, Y produces a certain aspect of X's behavior). Now consider X to be in an environment where Y is absent. Suppose that, relative to X's objectives, it is not effective to exhibit the type of response that he normally exhibits when Y is present (that is, in this environment, some other available action is more effective). In contrast, suppose that if Y were present, the normal response behavior would be most effective and X would know this to be the case. Then, under these conditions, if X chooses the normal response behavior he believes that Y is present.

It is somewhat surprising that the meaning of belief in the existence of objects is so difficult to define. But the reasons for the difficulty are not hard to find. The conceptual scheme we are considering here is based on the concepts of choice and the effectiveness of choice for desired outcomes. Belief in the occurrence of events is not an unanalyzable "primitive" concept within this framework; it is actually quite a complicated idea. The complications become even greater when we attempt to define what is meant by believed-in (subjective) probabilities of the sort discussed in Chapter 6. Details of these complications would cause too great a diversion from the main theme of this chapter. See, for example, the empirical studies of Davidson, Suppes and Siegel (3), and the theoretical analysis of Savage (4).

So far we have been discussing one dimension of belief based on a person's choices. But it is reasonable to say that, although a person chooses one alternative and makes this choice regularly, he is quite uncertain about the effectiveness of the choice. What does this "uncertainty" mean? Apparently the idea of "doubt" rests on the uncomfortable feeling a person has about what is actually taking place. In other words, the individual would like to know more if he could. Thus, doubt is a measure of a person's value for increased knowledge.

One consequence of the analysis of doubt is that a person who really knows cannot doubt that he knows (which is actually a dictum of Spinoza's). If this consequence seems awkward, the analysis can be changed to remove the difficulty, but the details of this procedure do not seem to be important for the present discussion.

Doubt may be expressed along a value scale—and the consequent measure we shall refer to as the intensity of belief; the intensity of doubt will be taken as the negative of the intensity of belief.

3 · *Agreement.*

We are now in a position to define "agreement in belief," a concept that will be central to the discussion of this chapter and the others that follow. As a first step, we can say that two individuals agree about the effectiveness of an action for an objective if they have the same degree and intensity of belief about the action. A similar definition can be given for belief in the existence of objects, and belief in the effectiveness measure of an action relative to a set of objectives.

Here again there are conceptual problems in defining "sameness" which would have to be considered in a more complex treatment of the subject. Degree and intensity of belief are properties of a person's

behavior, and it is possible for an observer to compare these properties as they are expressed by two or more persons. A rigid meaning
of sameness would require that the two persons make exactly the
same kind of choices with respect to the action in question, in standard conditions. But, because a rigid concept of agreement may prove
to be useless in actual studies, it may be desirable to define "virtual"
agreement in terms of a range along the scales of degree and intensity
of belief.

It should be noted that the concept of agreement (to which we
referred in earlier discussions of empiricism and hedonism, especially in Chapter 2) is not simple to define and certainly not simple
to ascertain. Yet, surprisingly enough, agreement has sometimes been
used as an ultimate "primitive" concept, in terms of which meaningfulness and verification in science are to be defined. More detailed
discussion of this point will occur in Chapter 14.

Also, as we shall see in the next chapter, there has been considerable concern in recent years about the feasibility of comparing the
values of two or more individuals. If interpersonal comparison of
values is not possible, it is extremely difficult to ascertain whether
the "will" of the group is in accordance with the will of the members. But if the foregoing analysis of belief and agreement is correct,
then agreement among two or more people about the effectiveness
of actions is an interpersonal comparison of values since intensity
of belief is a value measurement. Those who believe that it is impossible to compare values also must accept that it is impossible to
measure agreement of belief. This is certainly an awkward consequence, especially if, as we shall argue in Chapter 14, belief agreement is a basic concept of any method of science. But in these remarks we are running a bit ahead of the argument since we have yet
to decide when an interpersonal comparison of value does make
sense within the conceptual framework of values given in Chapter 7.

4 · *Judgment.*

In Chapter 6 it was suggested that the concept of judgment is somehow richer than agreement. In other words, the fact that two individuals agree is not evidence that their beliefs constitute a judgment.
We require a concept that means more than simple agreement if we
are to use this concept as a basis of valid inference, which the dis-

cussion of probability suggests. I have used "judgment" as the name of the concept intended to accomplish this purpose.

Essentially, judgment is a group opinion. The "group" may consist of the same individual at different points in his reflective life, but for all practical purposes we can talk as though the group in question had several different members. We shall want to argue that judgment is a group belief which occurs when there are differences of opinion among the group members because, in the spirit of the earlier discussion, we want to say that sound judgment occurs when the judgment is subject to strong opposition.

Thus, the essence of the concept of judgment is the establishment of "agreement" in the context of disagreements. Judgment is a type of negotiation. We can begin with one attempt to say what this "agreement" is and then see what troubles we encounter as a result. Judgment is a group belief arrived at by a set of rules operating on the (partially conflicting) beliefs of the individual members. These rules define one, and only one, group belief. The rules are believed to be correct by the members of the group.

In order to explain this definition, we need to know what "operate on" means, and we need to know what "believed to be correct" means. The first can be explained as follows. If the beliefs of the members can be expressed in terms of degree and intensity of belief, then we simply mean that the group judgment is arrived at by means of a function of these measures. For any set of member beliefs, the function defines a unique group belief. Evidently every member's belief need not have the same weight—some may count for nothing or one may count for all.

The definition of correctness, in contrast, is more difficult. Indeed, there seem to be various meanings of "correct" in this context. For our purposes, it will suffice to mention one such meaning here. A member of a group may believe that the rule for unifying disagreements is correct because he believes that adherence to the rule will result in a "long-run" optimal policy for the group. In other words, this definition of "correctness" is based on a dynamic model of individual and group beliefs. Each individual member believes some specific X_i is correct, and the X_i differ depending on the member. The "correct" rule defines a specific group belief which certainly differs from the belief of some members—and possibly all members. Yet each member feels that eventually all members will come to believe that with respect to the set of choices of various times and places, the collective choice defined by the rule is better than any other alternative collective choice.

A simple example may suffice to explain this meaning of "correct" rule. Suppose there are three members of a group, A, B, C, and that on five occasions they are faced with two distinct alternative actions, A_1 and A_2. In each instance, each member is fully convinced that one of these actions is correct (the degree of belief and the intensity of belief are both maximum). A rule that will select a unique action in this case is the rule that selects the majority decision. For example:

	First	*Second*	*Third*	*Fourth*	*Fifth*	*Sixth*
A's choice	A_1	A_2	A_1	A_1	A_2	A_2
B's choice	A_1	A_1	A_2	A_2	A_1	A_2
C's choice	A_2	A_2	A_2	A_1	A_1	A_2
Majority rule's choice	A_1	A_2	A_2	A_1	A_1	A_2
Group's decision differs from that of	C	B	A	B	A	C

In this example, the group belief differs from that of every member on two occasions. However, if the problem was to decide what collective pattern would be best over the six instances, each member might decide that the group's selection (by majority rule) was best. This would mean that though in each instance a member is convinced that one alternative is best, he is not convinced that his collective convictions are correct.

The reason for this apparent paradoxical situation may reside in the fact that the individual member does not want to conflict overtly with other members. Specifically, in addition to other goals he himself wants and he believes the group can attain, he also wants to maintain the respect of his fellow members. Alternatively, a member may be convinced that an action is best when he makes his decision by himself, but not when he receives information about other members' opinions. In either case, that is, either interest in other members' interests or influence based on other members' beliefs, the collective belief need not coincide with the individual belief.

In the next chapter we shall examine in more detail various ways in which a group's values can be defined in terms of individual values.

The example just given is used to illustrate how a single group belief (judgment) can be generated out of disagreements among the group members. The phrase "single belief" means that there is one action that the group believes is best—or at least is as good as any other. In a stronger sense, "single belief" may mean that the degree and intensity of group belief is defined for each alternative action.

It is clear that judgment, defined in the above manner, is a matter of degree. For example, the first condition for judgment states that the members disagree. Evidently, the magnitude of disagreement is important. More important still is the origin of the disagreement. Indeed, we might have made "difference in viewpoint" a criterion instead of "difference in belief," because it seems natural to say that a "more complete" judgment takes place when the group belief takes cognizance of many different points of view. In Chapter 4 we have already mentioned this point in connection with the adequate testing of a theory. If this were a treatise on judgment we might well devote some time to considering degrees of difference in viewpoint of the members as a basis of defining the degree of completeness of a judgment. Evidently the number of members, the approximation to a single group belief, and the group's intensity of doubt would also be considered in attempts to scale completeness of judgment.

5 • Illustrations of Judgment.

As an illustration of the concept of judgment, consider the case where a series of observations are made on the same object, each observation being a report of a reading along some continuous scale. If the usual stipulations for readings are followed, the observations will disagree at least in the last decimal place. Thus the members of the group differ in their beliefs concerning the object's property—provided, of course, that the members agree that the object remains stable with respect to this property over a period of time. In this instance, every member has doubt about his belief. For example, he doubts the accuracy of the final digit.

The arithmetical average of the readings may define a single group belief concerning the best number that can be used. Furthermore, the standard deviation of the readings provides a basis for computing the group's degree of doubt concerning the average. In some cases it may happen that the group has no doubt about the accuracy of the group's belief in a digit that was doubtful to every member. Thus, each member may report to the second decimal place, the last place varying among the readings. But the average may be taken as correct to the second decimal place by agreement among the group.

Finally, since the error of the average is always greater than o, the group's degree of doubt is always greater than o.

The point of this illustration is to show that averages of a set of readings are judgments, and have the same structure of social agreement that other judgments have. Despite the precision of formalism embodied in statistical methods, basically these methods are ways of reaching a satisfactory negotiated "peace" among disputants.

We have already illustrated a type of judgment in Chapter 6 in the discussion of probability. There we did not emphasize the role of disagreement in the formation of judgment, but merely hinted at its existence in the idea of tenacity of belief in the face of counterarguments. The present discussion has attempted to characterize this somewhat elusive phrase in more general terms.

6 · *Valid Judgments.*

A judgment is not necessarily valid, even if it exhibits a high degree of completeness in the sense defined above. For example, an increase in the number of readings need not imply that the average is more accurate; a systematic bias in the readings may result in an average that tends to be sure to deviate from the "true" value.

But it may happen that a group's judgment obeys the conditions we have already characterized for knowledge. Assume for the moment that we know what the group wants; it makes a judgment about the effectiveness of various courses of action relative to its goals. These judgments may (to an observer) remain correct even though the environment changes so as to alter the effectiveness of the alternatives. In this case, as before, we would say that the group, via its judgments, *knows* the conditional probabilities of each alternative. We could also determine whether the group is free to choose each alternative, that is, is not restrained by external forces or by a preference for the acts themselves.

We have thus arrived at one method for characterizing the standard of group values. We can say that the values of objectives for a group are the measures the observer uses to predict the group's choices when the group, via judgment, knows the conditional probabilities and is free to make any of a set of choices. As before, we recognize the circularity of concepts entailed in this definition of a standard.

We remarked at the outset that this is not the only way in which knowledge of a group could be defined. Nor have we explained what kind of measures the value measures would turn out to be: whether, for example, they are measures associated with each member, or with the collective, or both. It is to this question that we turn our attention in the next chapter.

7 · *Indebtedness.*

Discussions of belief and judgment similar to that found in this chapter occur in (1) and (2).

Some of the extremely difficult technical problems of formalizing "subjective probabilities" are discussed in (3) and (4).

REFERENCES

1. Churchman, C. W., and R. L. Ackoff, "Beliefs, Opinions and Attitudes," *Int. J. of Soc. and Psych. Res.*
2. Churchman, C. W., and R. L. Ackoff, *Psychologistics* (mimeographed). Philadelphia: University of Pennsylvania Press, 1946.
3. Davidson, D., *et al.*, *Decision Making*. Stanford, Calif.: Stanford University Press, 1957.
4. Savage, L., *Foundations of Statistics*. New York: John Wiley & Sons, Inc., 1955.

VALUES
OF SOCIAL
GROUPS

12

Summary

and

Intent.

An assertion that each of us might deny but all would accept is that the values of social groups are much more important than those of any individual in the group. Collectively we demonstrate our acceptance of this assertion by our common concern for the welfare of the people, the nation, the firm, the church, the university. Of course, we do study the values of persons; consumer preferences, psychoanalysis and personality studies attest to an interest on the part of the researcher in individual values. But our chief concerns are with those values which we recognize to be the values of the many groups to which we belong. Most of us who are interested in value research cannot help but feel that the significant "payoff" lies in a better understanding of these social values. For example, although it is fascinating to determine how to maximize the profits of a firm, or the take-home pay of the members of a union, these problems seem to be of minor importance compared to the problem of developing atomic energy in a way that best serves the interests of our nation or our world.

But what is the distinction between individual and group values? Specifically, what is a "group"? And what is meant by saying that the group prefers one action, or outcome, over another?

2 · Groups.

Although the term "group" has been given a number of meanings in sociological literature, at the risk of confusion, we will adopt a very general definition of the term. A group is any manifold of persons, identifiable over a period of time, and sufficiently integrated so that its actions and objectives are identifiable. This "definition" is not intended to differentiate manifolds by some inherent property. Evidently almost any manifold of persons could be "sufficiently integrated" in the sense required by the definition; what differentiates a group from a nongroup is the researcher's intent. If he wants to take the time and effort to make the integration, he conceives of the manifold as a group. Thus if a manifold of persons is conceived of as an identical individual in the sense defined in Chapter 7, then such a manifold is a group. In Chapter 7, we required explicit rules for the identity of the individual over a period of time; it was pointed out there that a manifold might change its membership and yet retain its identity. In the case of manifolds of persons, the rules of identity may be very difficult to define satisfactorily. Chapter 7 further required that we be able to identify the individual's potential actions and the outcomes of these actions. Finally, in order to talk meaningfully about the properties of a purposeful individual, we must be able to apply Chapter 6 and 11, that is, estimate conditional probabilities and believed-in probabilities.

In other words, any manifold of individuals may be conceived of as a group; it *is* a group if the teleological conditions of Chapter 7 become the framework within which the group is studied.

The concept of group values may have a number of meanings some of which will be discussed in this chapter.

First, we may consider the group as a "collective," that is, independent of the properties of its members. In this case there are no additional conceptual difficulties over and above those already discussed in Chapter 7.

Second, we may consider the group in terms of its members and attempt to define group properties as a function of member-properties. Chapter 11 has discussed one example of this type of definition in considering the concept of judgment.

Third, we may combine the two conceptual methods just mentioned, and define the group *both* in terms of the member properties and the group properties.

These three methods of studying a group can be characterized by the following two assertions.

(1) The properties of the members are sufficient to define the properties of the group. That is, any property of the group, such as its value or knowledge or belief, can be defined as a function of the properties of one or more of the members.

(2) The properties of the members are necessary to define the properties of the group. That is, the function that defines a group property must include member properties.

The first method of studying a group denies (2) while making no comment on (1). Thus, when we study a group as a collective we do not define its properties in terms of member properties—although it may be possible to do so. The second method affirms both (1) and (2). In such studies one develops group properties as a function of member properties. The third method affirms (2) but denies (1); the group is defined partially in terms of member properties, but not entirely in these terms.

Examples of the first method are contained in such expressions as "The union then decided to strike," or "The nations ratified the treaty"—where the activities of specific persons are irrelevant in the description of the group's decisions.

The best known examples of the second method occur in voting behavior, or in the concept of welfare economics, where one can fully describe what a group does or wants in terms of membership behavior or values.

The third method is used to describe competition, and more generally, organized behavior. In this case the researcher is not interested in deriving group action and values solely in terms of membership action and values; he uses the collective properties as well, and speaks of the "over-all objectives of the company, or the union." These objectives need not be derivable from the objectives of the members, but membership action and values are nevertheless essential in giving a complete description.

In addition to various methods of studying group behavior, one may also wish to consider the properties of members of the group which arise because of their group membership. Specifically, what values does a person hold because he is a member of a group? This question is theoretically answerable by ascertaining a person's values when he is not a member of the group, and when he is a member of the group. That is, the question is answerable by studying differences in free behavior under these two circumstances.

Finally, we may sensibly ask what the group wants its members to do, that is, ask questions about the social mores of the group. In view of the fact that there are at least three distinct ways of understanding group wants, there will be at least three distinct ways of understanding group morality.

We turn now to a more detailed discussion of the various aspects of group and member values which have been briefly outlined above.

3 · *The Group as an Individual.*

When the group is taken as an individual, the conceptual problem of giving meaning to group values is simplest, but the significance of the resulting concept may be very difficult to understand. Group values in this case consist of the information needed to predict the group's behavior when the group "knows" the conditional probabilities associated with the alternative actions. Knowledge in this context can be defined in terms of the concept of judgment discussed in the last chapter, or it can be defined in terms of the collective behavior of the group. In effect, judgment was defined in the last chapter by the second method mentioned above: the beliefs of the members are necessary to define judgment, and, in addition, if one is given a set of member beliefs of a certain kind, including a belief in a way of settling differences, the group judgment can be derived. But one could ignore the manner in which the members generate judgments and pay attention only to the decisions of the whole group. The two approaches to group knowledge provide different ways of studying group values; that is, *what* a group values depends on how we define what a group knows.

Despite repeated skepticism concerning the "existence" of a "collective mind," there is nothing very startling about the concept, and in many instances this manner of studying a group is by far the most effective. For example, an executive committee of a firm may make various decisions; it is irrelevant for some purposes to determine *who* makes the decisions, and why he makes them. Instead, we can take the collective actions of the group and study them as though they were the actions of one individual. These actions often give clear indication of what the committee wants—and these wants need not be derived at all from the wants of the members. Of course, if there is some doubt about the group's values, one may be driven to investigate how the values are generated, and hence to investigate membership attitudes. In this case, the mechanism of the generation of group values becomes supporting evidence for an hypothesis about the group's collective values.

Thus social groups do have "minds of their own" in the rather obvious sense that the group's purposive behavior can be studied independently of the properties of its members. The interesting questions about collective social groups are not concerned with the existence of such groups or the utility of the collective concept. Rather, we want to know how the group's values are related to the member's values in various contexts. We know that in cases of national emergency, the lives and freedom of citizens are sacrificed for the sake of the survival of the people. In more peaceful times, the individualists at least preach the necessity of ultimately serving the citizen's goals—not the state's. Indeed, extreme individualism always takes the membership goals to be ultimately important—consideration of group goals being only a means to the ultimate end. The group mind is thus supposed to be subservient to the individual mind.

In the case of business firms there seems to be little question that individualism does not apply; the goals of the firm predominate, and they cannot be identified with the goals of any individuals—including the stockholders. On the national level, however, individualism is being fought out, at least verbally.

4 • *The Group as a Set of Individuals.*

It is common practice to consider the group as a collective with collective goals; it is just as common to view it as a collection of individuals with a collection of individual goals. In the latter case, we try to see how we can define the values of the group solely in terms of properties of the members.

In this attempt there are evidently a number of possibilities. If the group can adopt one of a finite set of actions, then we could simply say that the group "prefers" that action which the majority of members prefer. Or, we could weight the membership vote in terms of some property of the members such as money, intelligence, or status. Any such method of defining an optimal group action constitutes a decision rule for the group which is explicit as long as it can be decided what is optimal for each (relevant) member. In other words, once we are equipped to measure a member's values, and once we have a rule for combining these measurements, we can determine what is optimal for the group.

The preceding paragraph, which at first sight may seem obvious enough, poses a number of problems that are not easy to answer. Mention of some of these will help us to understand the kind of research which the "individualistic" concept of a group entails.

(1) When we speak of the group's "preference for actions," are we referring to the group's beliefs or to the group's values for objectives served by the actions?

(2) Should the membership vote depend on the real values (or knowledge) of the members, or on their opinions concerning their true values or their beliefs in the effectiveness of the actions?

(3) What is meant by "optimal for a group" in this context? That is, can we adapt the notion of values defined in Chapter 7 to this concept of group values?

(4) It is unrealistic to think that each member has his own set of selfish values which he wants to pursue; actually, a member may want to do that which a certain number of his fellow members want. That is, in addition to his other values, he values serving other people's interests. Alternatively, he may want to thwart the interests of others. Can this value of the

group member be defined within the framework of "individualistic" groups?

(5) Finally, no mention has been made of the influence of members on each other; the final "voting" is often far less significant than the prior process which produces the votes. This process should certainly be included in any account of the decision rules which define the optimal group choice since the results of the voting are, in reality, an outcome of this process.

Adequate consideration of these questions would require far too much space relative to the purposes of this book. Our present aims will best be served by grouping the first two and then the last three questions together.

Questions (1) and (2). When the membership of a group expresses preferences for various alternatives, they may be expressing their beliefs in the effectiveness of actions for common goals, or they may be expressing their values for the goals served by the actions. There is nothing in the usual voting situation that indicates which of these two activities is taking place.

Since our interest in this book is concentrated on the measurement of the values of objectives, we want to consider that aspect of voting which entails an expression of the membership's values for objectives. Furthermore, we are concerned with the actual measure of membership values, not the member's estimates of their values. In other words, we narrow the total problem of voting to a consideration of how to generate a measure of group values of a set of objectives from the measures of the membership values.

It is readily recognized that in many social voting processes there is no effective way of either splitting the belief problem from the value problem, or of determining the members' true values. In particular, we have learned the risks of having any subsection of a social group decide what each member really wants. In the case of elections, then, we do not know of an effective method of generating group values from true membership values. In a sense, national elections do not represent what the citizens really want. The results of an election constitute a set of beliefs in the effectiveness of actions and beliefs in one's own value and this may very well be what we want the national election to represent.

But such election procedures constitute only a small part of group activity. When we try to study plans for urban development, or a hospital, or a church, or a union, or a consumer population, we may very well want to determine what actions best serve the interests of the group when such interests are defined in terms of the true interests of the members. Even in these cases we run the risk of one man's enforcing his notion of what another man wants. As we shall see in Chapter 14, an important aim of science has been to develop methods of agreement so that this risk is minimized.

Questions (3), (4) and (5). Even if we grant that the problem before us is restricted to one of generating group values from individual values, what does the "generated" group value really mean?

In recent years there has been some concern on the part of welfare economists in the adequate methods of generating group preferences from individual preferences. The so-called "paradoxes" of welfare economics are relevant to the question posed above and to the whole problem of defining group properties in terms of individual properties.

Essentially the paradox amounts to this. The decision rule which transforms the members' values into the group's values should at least rank the objectives in terms of their importance for the group or the actions in terms of their preference for the group. This derived ranking should satisfy some fairly obvious criteria. For example, suppose by some chance one of the actions is made unavailable; this event should not disturb the ranking provided the actions are independent and exclusive. Furthermore, some economists believe that it is not reasonable to use anything more than a member's *ranking* of the objectives in determining the group's preference. To go so far as to use numbers to weight a member's values seems to imply that we can compare the values of two or more people. This notion of mapping everyone's values onto a common scale has seemed impractical, possibly because it apparently is derived from the notion of directly comparing the feelings or sensations of two distinct individuals—an absurd comparison since we cannot "get into" anyone's head to do the comparing.

Whatever may be the reasons for discarding interpersonal comparisons of value (above the simple comparisons of ranking), if the reasons are cogent, then it can be shown that there is no common-sense "democratic" decision rule for combining the members' interests to form a group interest. Details of the argument, as well as a precise definition of "democratic" in this context, are to be found in Arrow's analysis in *Social Choice and Individual Values.*

It should be noted that the comparison of values (or utilities) is not excluded on any a priori grounds, if we do not insist on equating values with so-called "directly apprehended" feelings. Indeed, there seems to be an obvious sense in which we could say that two persons have exactly the same set of values. This would occur if the same model of their behavior could be used to predict choices in the standard conditions. Further, even when two persons differ in their values, it is at least conceivable that we can measure how much they differ. These measured differences would be the information required to predict one person's behavior, given information about the other's behavior in the standard conditions. In some models of behavior, the differences in values would be linear functions of the parameters of the models.

The problem, therefore, of the comparison of values is really the methodological problem of theories of behavior. But the problem we are concerned with here is not only a problem of comparison. We also need to provide a fruitful definition of group values in terms of individual values; that is, we need to know how to use the comparisons when they occur.

Thus, quite apart from the so-called "paradox" of welfare economics, it is very difficult to understand what we mean by a "satisfactory" method of ascertaining group preferences from individual preferences. We may argue that there are intuitively obvious criteria for such satisfactory rules, but in this book we have tended to avoid the pitfalls of intuition as a sole guide for reaching conclusions. Indeed, it is not difficult to make a convincing case for the invalidity of each of Arrow's axioms in *Social Choice,* just as we did for the axioms of utility theory in Chapter 8.

We could argue that a "satisfactory" method of going from individual values to group values depends on ethical standards, but, as we shall see in Chapter 16, the definition of ethical standards does seem to depend on some way of comparing individual values. Instead, in the study of this problem, we shall follow the theme already developed in Chapter 7. There we argued that the researcher was not to be restrained by concepts of rationality in his understanding of an individual's values. He is to use whatever model of behavior seems most suitable to provide a consistent image of a person's choices.

Therefore, we are to look for a model within which the member choices and the group choices can be made consistent. The simplest approach seems to be one of considering how the members themselves feel about the way their values should be weighted.

Suppose for each member, in isolation, we can assign values to a set of objectives. Suppose, too, that for any member we can assign values to alternative methods of arriving at the group preferences in terms of membership "isolation" values. These values would predict how the member would act if he were free to choose the method and knew the consequences of any method. If all members would choose the same method, there would seem to be no problem. Of course, all members might agree on a voting method, only to find out that one consequence of the method might be that a person could veto the decisions of everyone else. If this left some members dissatisfied, then they could not have known the consequences of the method, that is, the observer did not really measure the value of the method for the group members.

Thus, one definition of group values is the following: suppose all members are free to choose how their own values will be used to determine group action; suppose all agree on the method; then the group values are the measures that predict choice when the group "knows" the consequences of its choices. "Freedom" in this context is used in the same sense as in Chapter 7: freedom from ignorance as well as other restraints.

More generally, we can use the concept of judgment developed in the last chapter and arrive at the following definition: group values are those weights attached to objectives by the researcher which predict group choices when (a) the members are free, and (b) the group correctly judges one method of "voting" to be best. This definition implies that there will be differences of opinion on the best voting procedure, but that the members agree on the way of resolving these differences. For example, prior to the adoption of women's suffrage, the citizens of the United States did not agree on one voting procedure. They did, however, agree on a method of deciding this disagreement—a method of campaigning and finally voting. Even after the final vote many husbands may have disagreed with the new method of voting—while agreeing with the method by which the issue had been decided. This example implies that the values of the group members need not remain fixed over the period of the decision-making. The members may agree that the group can debate the issue, and that members may try to change the values of other members prior to the actual voting procedure.

In sum, if we study group values as functions of individual values, and we want to speak of a function that satisfactorily represents the wishes of the group, one way of doing this is to include in the model of the group and its members a consideration of the member's evaluation of various decision rules.

Of course, we may impose, instead, a criterion of "satisfactory" from without—and indeed we do not hesitate to condemn the entire voting procedure of a nation even if its citizens agree to it wholeheartedly. We do this on so-called "ethical" grounds of the type discussed in Chapter 16.

5 · *Methodological Requirements of a Voting Procedure.*

We will say that a method of generating group values from individual values that satisfies the criterion of agreement or judgment given above is a "voting procedure." That is, a voting procedure is a way of defining group goals when the members use judgment to determine how their individual values are to be weighted.

It is reasonable enough to ask how detailed the agreement needs to be. For example, would it suffice to derive a rule that selects the most preferred action for the social group? At first glance it seems that the answer must be affirmative; that is, the complete ranking of the courses of action by the social group seems to be irrelevant for all practical purposes since all we want to know is what choice the group will make.

But this first glance is not very perceptive. We are not concerned with actions as such, but rather with the objectives served by the actions. A voting procedure must determine choices in a wide variety of circumstances. Hence agreement on the best action (for example, agreement on how to select candidates for an elective office) does not necessarily constitute a voting procedure in the sense used here because it may not be applicable in (say) cases of war emergency.

The procedure must be general enough to be applicable in a wide variety of circumstances; in other words, an ideal voting procedure would measure the values of the group in the sense of measurement adopted in this book (see Chapter 5).

6 · *The Group as an Individual Composed of Members.*

We turn now to the study of groups where information about the properties of the members is necessary but not sufficient to determine the properties of the group. Specifically, we consider those situations in which the group exhibits certain values because its members have certain values, but the values of the group are not defined solely in terms of the membership values.

It is important to keep in mind that we are discussing alternative schemes for studying group values. A group may be studied in terms of several alternative schemes, and the researcher usually tries to find that scheme that best serves his purposes. Hence, when we say that the group values are not defined in terms of membership values, we do not intend to say that such a way of conceptualizing the group is impossible. We merely say that in the conceptual scheme adopted for a particular study such a derivation cannot be made.

The conceptual scheme we are now considering is in a sense "organic." The group is made up of elements with differing characteristics, and out of these differences arises a coherent type of group behavior that is not identified with the properties of any one of the members.

7 · *Conflict.*

Central to the idea of such an "organic" group is the concept of conflict. Our aim now is to try to characterize this concept in detail sufficient to arrive at a better understanding of the organized group.

Suppose there are two individuals, A and B, living in the same environment. Suppose this environment is such that if A attains some goal O_A (for example, A's possession of an item) then B cannot possibly attain a goal O_B (for example, B's possession of the same item). Suppose, finally, that the value of O_A for A is very high, as well as the value of O_B for B. Then clearly A and B are in conflict in the environment. On the other hand, if the environment is such that when A attains O_A, B cannot help but attain O_B, then A and B are not in conflict at all; we would normally say that they were cooperating.

We note that this description of conflict and cooperation suggests one rather obvious definition of the "degree of conflict." The degree that A's attaining O_A reduces the chances that B attains O_B seems to be the crucial aspect of conflict. This degree could be represented by $P(O_B/\sim O_A,N) - P(O_B/O_A,N)$—the probability that O_B will occur given that O_A does not occur in the environment (N) minus the probability that O_B will occur given that O_A does occur in the environment. Similarly, $P(O_A/\sim O_B,N) - P(O_A/O_B,N)$ is also relevant; this is the degree to which the occurrence of O_B reduces the chances of the occurrence of O_A. However, the symbolism is faulty since the probabilities are meaningless unless we specify the actions adopted by A and B. Futhermore, the differences in the probabilities is not enough because the degree of conflict between A and B also depends on the values of O_A and O_B for A and B respectively. We may also note that "conflicts with" is not necessarily a symmetrical relationship: A can conflict with B while B cooperates with A. This nonsymmetry of conflict becomes quite important in studying social groups.

We therefore want to consider the three following problems: (1) the definition of the degree of conflict in terms of action choices, (2) the weighting of conflict by the values of the objectives, and (3) the nonsymmetry of the conflict relationship. These considerations will enable us to characterize the concept of an organic group.

(1) The meaning of $P(O_B/O_A,N)$ and $P(O_B/\sim O_A,N)$ can be made more precise as follows. Consider an environment defined over a time span, t_0 to t_1. This environment is such that one can state the probability that O_B will occur, given a course of action defined over t_0 to t_1. Consider two such environments which are alike at t_0 and at t_1, except that, at t_1, O_A is present in some region of one environment and absent in the other. Then $P(O_B/O_A,N)$ is the probability that O_B will occur in the first environment (where O_A occurs at t_1) if the optimal action is adopted (that is, the action that maximizes the chances that O_B occurs). An analogous definition can be given for $P(O_B/\sim O_A,N)$.

In the limiting case, the degree of conflict of B with A is based on the following components: let P_{AB} be A's chances of success with respect to one of his objectives when B's objective is certain to occur, and P_{AB}' be A's chances of success when B's objective is certain not to occur. If $P_{AB}' - P_{AB}$ is positive, then there is conflict; if it is o, there is independence; and if it is negative, there is cooperation.

This characterization can be generalized to several persons, to several objectives, and to a relaxation on the certainty of occurrence of O_B.

The technical difficulties of this definition are not completely specified here since the two environments defined above need not be unique (there may be several ways of passing from a state at t_0 to a state where O_A occurs at t_1). But further consideration of these difficulties would carry us too far from the main purpose of this discussion.

(2) If conflict depends in part on the values of the conflicting parties, what do these values mean? We have said that value measurements predict A's behavior under conditions of knowledge. Since B and his actions are part of A's environment, this means that the value of O_A predicts (in part) A's behavior when he knows what B is going to do. Similarly, the value of O_B predicts (in part) B's behavior when he knows what A is going to do. Can we simultaneously consider the values of O_A and O_B for A and B respectively? There seems to be no reason why we cannot, given the definitions of value in these terms.

There is, however, the important question of the correct recommendation for A when he does not have any knowledge about B's actions—a problem that has received a great deal of attention in game theory. The game-theory approach attempts to analyze values in situations where one knows that one's opponent will do his best; in this case the seeming circularity in determining correct recommendations may be quite difficult to overcome. In a sense, we have avoided such problems by the definition of the value standard. In many analyses of game theory, the values ("payoffs") of all players are "given," but there is no prior knowledge of the play they will adopt. This analysis, therefore, seems to assume that in practical situations one could know enough about a person's behavior to ascertain his values, but not enough to ascertain his choices. Within the framework of value theory adopted in this book, this position is almost an absurdity because value determination is, in general, only possible in terms of a comprehensive theory of action-choices.

Nevertheless, there is an interpretation of game-theory analysis which does reveal its importance. This consists of saying that the researcher has an hypothesis about the subjects' beliefs and/or values; he wants to determine in a conflict situation whether this hypothesis holds. Usually, the hypothesis is stated in terms of the player's subjective probabilities of the other players' choices. The strategy adopted in a game by a player may supply evidence for or against such an hypothesis.

(3) There is, finally, the question of how the measures just discussed should be combined to develop a measure of conflict. To recapitulate, these are the measures of the degree to which the occurrence of O_A reduces the chances of O_B, and vice-versa, and the respective values of O_A and O_B for A and B.

The natural inclination is to say that the degree to which A conflicts with B is V_B (the value of O_B for B) times $[P(O_B/\sim O_A,N) - P(O_B/O_A,N)]$. That is, we simply "weight" the interference measure by the value of O_B for B. This multiplication function seems natural since we will want to say that the conflict increases as either of these components increases, and is o if either component is o. More precisely, if O_A does not affect the occurrence of O_B at all, either favorably or unfavorably, then the degree of conflict should remain invariant with changes in V_B. Similarly, if B is indifferent regarding O_B, that is, O_B is irrelevant in predicting B's behavior in the standard-value environment, then the degree of conflict should remain invariant with changes in the degree of interference. This is all the justification that can be given for the simple multiplication of values and probabilities at present; whether this measure of conflict is really correct depends on how conflict measures are to be used. Furthermore, it may happen that there is no way of associating one and only one real number with each objective (as Chapter 7 points out) so that the proposed definition of conflict may not apply. But enough has been said to enable us to proceed to use the concept in the study of organic groups.

8 · *Organic and Organized Groups.*

The degree of conflict between A and B may be positive both ways: A conflicts with B and B with A. Further, A and B may both be aware of the conflict, and as a result adopt certain actions. Consider, now, a severe case of this kind, say, a gladiatorial contest. Here the social group made up of A and B displays certain activities and greatly amuses C who looks forward to a neatly performed decapitation. It may be perfectly sensible to say that the group, *A-and-B*, "wants" to amuse C—in the collective sense of group want discussed above. But *A* and *B* individually may be indifferent to amusing *C*. More precisely, *A*'s and *B*'s individual interest in *C* is irrelevant in the study of the group. Hence without the conflict of interests, the group collectively would not have the amusement of *C* as its purpose; but the interests of the conflicting parties are independent of this purpose. In other words, the interests of the members are necessary but not sufficient to define the group purpose. There is, of course, the question whether in gladiatorial combat the conflicting group really has values in the sense adopted in this book. But, whatever may be the virtues of this example, it seems clear that we may expect to find the implied model a very fruitful way of studying groups. To recapitulate, this model asserts that the group is composed of conflicting members, and some conflict pattern is better than any cooperative pattern relative to the group objective. We call a group so conceived an organic group.

But not all organic groups are organized. Organizations are usually thought to be groups whose members are self-conscious of the group goals and adopt controls to make sure the goals are properly pursued. We therefore suggest the following definition of an organization: it is an organic group in which the values of some, but not all, members are the same as that of the collective group, and where these members attempt to control the membership conflict to serve the group aims. In this sense, we could have a "badly" organized group: one in which the control is not optimal. This characterization suggests various "degrees" of organization, and the need for more technical clarity. But our present interests will best be served by an illustration: an industrial firm.

9 · *Organized Groups.*

Anyone who has observed the operations of an industrial enterprise cannot help but notice the predominance of conflict that takes place. This conflict is well recognized to occur in the case of management and labor; indeed, there can be no question that management values the objective of increasing net worth much more highly than labor does. None of the usual managerial propaganda about the need of labor's cooperation in the "common" goal of the firm is relevant to the issue. The objective which labor values most is increased real income for each worker, and it only regards management's objective as one possible means to this objective. Management, in contrast, regards the welfare of the labor force as less important than the increase of net worth. The conflict is real enough and is not to be resolved by any pleas on either side for greater cooperation. A union that forgets its primary objective in order to avoid industrial crises ceases to serve its membership.

But even this patent example of the conflict theme in industry does not portray the complete picture. Practically every industrial firm is so structured that its divisions must be in conflict with one another. In other words, the functions assigned to the divisions are such that increase in success of one division must eventually imply decrease in success of another. The function of the sales department is to maximize sales either in terms of total dollars, total units, share of the market, or percentage of a prior year. This function represents a set of objectives which the sales department as a group values quite highly. Often, in order to accomplish these objectives, customers have to be satisfied on an emergency basis. From the point of view of the sales department these "red-tag" orders are essential; without them the company's market position would suffer seriously.

But a "red-tag" order for the production departments means an interruption in a smoothly operating schedule. The setup costs and morale costs may be quite serious. The production department wants to maximize quantity and/or quality of output at minimum cost. This certainly cannot be done effectively if emergency orders occur frequently. Furthermore, it is *not* the sales department which suffers from the effects of these orders; the increased costs are scores against the effectiveness of production management.

This example is only one of many similar cases of industrial conflict within management itself. Personnel policy conflicts with the policies of all other departments; and again a department must bear the brunt of adverse scores of performance because of personnel policies not under its control. The finance department may want to cut inventories because they represent the most risky part of the firm's working capital. Cutting inventories may very well mean a poorer showing for both production and sales.

But these conflicts may not be mere accident or stupid inefficiency on the part of top management. It may indeed be a rather clever scheme for getting the most out of people.

The unjust scoring system, in effect, produces a conflict group.

As sales improve, then (after a point) production does not improve but, on the contrary, shows up poorly, and vice versa. But the conflict group, as a group, does accomplish the objectives of the total firm. It seems perfectly justifiable to say that if a scoring system could be devised within which there was no divisional conflict, the firm would not operate as well (relative to its collective goals) as it does under some scoring system that entails conflict. This is not to say that any conflict scoring system is better than any cooperative one; in defining an organic group, we did not specify that all conflict patterns are preferable to any cooperative ones, but rather that some conflict pattern is preferable to all cooperative ones.

In other words, which works better—a firm whose members cooperate, or a firm whose members conflict? The answer is not obvious, but there can be no doubt that in many cases it is the latter which best accomplishes the firm's objectives. This is also the verbal argument of proponents of free competition: let firms conflict even to the extent of destroying one another, because thereby we as a nation profit most.

But firms are also organized in that the managerial conflict is designed and controlled; otherwise the conflict might have the unfortunate ending in which one of the divisions is victorious. No division ever "wins" in the sense that it annihilates or controls the opponent. If this happens the objective of the firm would not be served optimally. The firm is so designed as to keep the conflict in control—not letting it sink into the calm of peaceful cooperation nor rise to the level of mortal combat.

I have chosen to call such a designed conflicting group an "organization." Much time might be spent in justifying this language, especially since "organization" means so many things to so many people. At least it is clear that any social group which is designed to promote and control conflict in order to accomplish an over-all objective is "organized." Whether all organizations can be so conceived is a question not to be debated here.

It is of interest to note that in the case of industrial organizations, the internal conflict between (say) production and sales could be resolved by a compromise. That is, if we can discuss the objective of the company as a whole, it may be possible to indicate the optimum balance between the aim of reducing production costs and the aim of increasing sales. But this so-called "optimal" policy may *not* be the best course of action for a company to adopt. By letting the individual departments conflict, the firm may be able to motivate greater departmental effort than by imposing an "optimal" plan. This is quite a different point from the much-discussed theme of "suboptimization." Suboptimization is generally thought to be the attempt to optimize the functions of one division (or member) of a group. As indicated above, the scoring system may be such that optimization of a division's score is disastrous. Hence, suboptimization may be very bad policy. But alternatively, the attempt to find an "over-all" solution may be equally disastrous if this means an attempt to resolve the conflicts between divisions.

10 · *Institutions.*

In concluding the discussion of organic groups, I would like to broaden the illustrative material somewhat and try to characterize social institutions.

Conflict appears to be an essential ingredient in the activities of almost all social groups; in other words, the most fruitful conceptual schemes for the study of groups are those that include the concept of conflict. One fascinating aspect of the understanding of groups is the manner in which conflict occurs. In the case of social institutions the role of conflict seems to be very subtle indeed.

I think that social institutions such as religion, science, and law have at least the following characteristics:

- (a) they have a history which has produced a classical body of judgments; the judgment may be about issues of *method,* that is, how to accomplish certain tasks, or about issues of *content,* for example, what state of affairs actually occurs at a certain time;
- (b) they have as one of their objectives the indefinitely prolonged survival of the institution, that is, the "immortality" of the social group;
- (c) membership in the institution depends on whether a person does or does not serve the institutional objectives; and
- (d) within the institution there is a conflict between "conservative" and "radical" elements—the one aiming to preserve the classical body of beliefs, the other aiming to change it.

Thus, institutions are social groups which show an intense interest in survival. The evidence of this interest is the development of a "classical" framework. But, dialectically, institutions do generate their own changes via conflicting aims and methods of their members. Otherwise, an institution's concentration on its classical role may very well lead to its destruction.

Chapter 14 uses "science" as an illustration of this concept of an institution. But it is noteworthy that many industrial companies now show pronounced tendencies to become institutions, that is, to try to set up a classical doctrine of their methods and objectives; they try to emphasize survival of the company; and they try to institutionalize the radical-conservative fight within the activities of the company.

11 · *Social Morality.*

Enough has been said in this chapter to indicate the problems associated with defining the values of a group and the behavior choices of a group. A successful solution of these problems would enable us to say (in one of the many senses) what a group wants and what it does not want. An ability to say this enables us to say something about social morality, that is, to say what a social group wants its members to do.

Evidently, social morality is of tremendous importance to all of us who live our lives in one group or another, because we must try to find out what is expected of us by the various social groups to which we belong. Even if we decide to oppose the will of the group or to leave the group, there seems to be an obligation to understand the group's desires with regard to its members. Further, we discover that the morality of various groups to which we belong differs. We find that the will of the family conflicts with the will of the club or the company. Modern man lives within the scope of many disturbing conflicts of social morality.

The aim of this book (which is the aim of a reflective observer) is to try to understand what social morality means and to try to understand how social morality enters into the determination of human values.

At first sight, the meaning of social morality seems to be easy enough to define. The group wants certain objectives. Why not say that one of these objectives is a specific action of one of its members? What the member "ought" to do in this context is what the group wants him to do.

If we pose this definition within the conceptual framework of Chapter 7, we arrive at the following: the value of a member's action for the group is a predictor of what the group would do if it had knowledge of the consequences of its choices. As was indicated in Chapter 1, this means that if the social group knows the consequences of action choices of its members and were free to enforce these choices, what it chooses is what its members "ought to do" on grounds of social morality. But the discussion of this and the last chapter has revealed the inherent ambiguity of this earlier characterization, for we have cited several meanings of group knowledge and several ways of defining group choice. It appears, therefore, that social morality can have several meanings, depending on the choice the experimenter makes in defining these underlying concepts. Nor does any choice seem forced on us by rational or intuitive considerations.

Thus, consider the choices of a member of a firm, union, or nation. In one sense, the social morality of the member depends on the group's collective goals; he ought to choose to die for his country if need be, or forsake family for the good of the firm. But he just as reasonably ought to do what (say) the majority want him to do.

The meaning of a social "ought" depends on which way we conceptualize the group. This is not a very startling conclusion except that it does reveal the futility of many discussions about *the* will of the people, *the* good of the firm, *the* un-American activity, *the* scientific method, and so on.

12 · *Personal Values in a Group.*

It should be noted that the discussion of Chapter 7 does not logically precede the discussion of this chapter. That is, we do not *first* determine personal values and *then* determine group values. The "environment" which Chapter 7 uses to define knowledge and value may be (and almost always is) a social environment. Hence, although this chapter classified group values in terms of membership values, there is no intended implication of methodological priority.

13 · *Bargaining.*

In conclusion, we can reflect that the problem of group values is essentially the same as the bargaining problem between individuals with partially conflicting interests. The egoistic model of bargaining is developed by starting with the values of the bargainers in isolation. That is, the effectiveness of each alternative open to the bargainer is determined relative to a situation in which no other bargainers occur. The result is an egoistic "payoff" matrix. We may then try to do one of two things: describe how each bargainer modifies his choices when other bargainers can change the probabilities of the outcomes, or determine a "fair" or "rational" bargaining procedure. In either case, the model attempts to provide a valid description or a defensible rationale based on a function of the egoistic payoffs. The alternative approach is a model of bargaining which defines the values of various settlement procedures for the bargainers; this is the model discussed in the chapter. In the case of the egoistic model, it seems to be very difficult to find "fair" bargaining methods even in relatively simple situations. In the alternative, the study of choices made by the bargainers when they are aware of the outcomes of their choices is the basis for estimating the value to them of a particular settlement procedure.

Consider, for example, the so-called "prisoner's dilemma" problem of two players. Let the outcomes be defined in terms of monetary payments as shown in the accompanying figure.

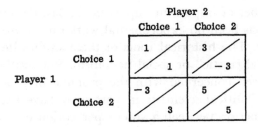

(The first entry in each block is the payment made to Player 1, the second is the payment made to Player 2.) If the players do not communicate, what is the fair or rational method of play? One answer is that both "ought" to select choice 2, although in experiments this group behavior pattern occurs far less often than does both selecting choice 1. The experimental result is not unexpected, of course, because both players may believe that the other will shift to choice 1, which belief may in fact be correct. The actual choice made, therefore, gives some evidence of the value of safe settlement for the two bargainers. In any event, a nonegoistic model would not assert that the payoff matrix given above measures the values of the choice outcomes for the players, and would require the values of the outcomes in the bargaining context before the optimal solution could be obtained.

In the more general and important instances of labor-management disputes and international disagreements, there may be a way of studying the shifting patterns of choice in order to develop a theory of the value of settlement methods for the disputants. But such a study would require some estimate of the perspectives of the bargainers and the degree of validity of each perspective. The point is that we do not need to know the (egoistic) values of the participants before we can decide what is a fair settlement. The behavior of enlightened bargainers defines the meaning of fairness. In this connection, we should repeat an earlier warning: what is fair for one group of bargainers need not be ethically valid.

14 · *Indebtedness.*

The rationalist literature on the derivation of group values from individual values is quite large. Arrow's book, *Social Choice and Individual Values* (New York: John Wiley & Sons, Inc., 1951) inspired a number of important papers in the last decade. As far as I know, there has been no experimental work on the utility of group decision rules. The historical roots of these studies lie in the great tradition of "altruistic" or social hedonism. Practically every social science has been concerned with the problem of group mind and group value. Political scientists in particular have been concerned with the distinction between a voter's perception of a situation and his values for the outcomes. It is well recognized that the citizen of a democratic state is asked to make judgments about the true state of affairs when he has only the most meager evidence and is at the same time subject to all kinds of conflicting persuasions. His vote therefore cannot be construed as an expression of what he wants.

ASSETS AND TRANSACTIONS

13

Summary

and

Intent.

We turn now to a detailed consideration of organizational decision-making. In order to make the discussion specific, we return to the problem considered in Chapter 3 and ask ourselves whether it is possible to generate data which help the management of an enterprise to select an optimal choice.

We can begin by recapitulating the allied defects of "traditional" accounting procedures with respect to providing measurements for decision-making keeping in mind that some of these defects are overcome by various techniques in some firms.

(1) Accounting does not reveal the profits which would have occurred had alternative decisions been made. Even though a return or investment may appear excellent to management or stockholders, or constitute a decided improvement over previous years or other competitors, there is no indication in the data themselves that vastly greater improvements might not have been made. Indeed, as business games seem to show, a firm which is pleased with its profit score may shun worthwhile changes in its policies.

(2) Accounting often penalizes some decisions illogically by making them share in overhead or other charges which do not measure the value of the decision.

(3) Accounting ignores goals other than profit and related aims.

(4) Most important, it is very doubtful whether the profit goal of accounting truly reflects the monetary goal of the organization. Specifically, accounting assumes that each transaction of the firm can be costed by itself, independent of other transactions, that the "profit" is a gross return minus the sum of the transaction costs, and that management wishes to maximize *this* "profit."

We shall want to examine this fourth accounting defect in this chapter in greater detail. But instead of making an economic analysis of the firm, we shall attempt to translate the basic idea of profit and loss into a behavioral language. In other words, the aim of the chapter is to define a "net-profit" theory of optimal behavior, and to criticize this theory. To this end, accounting concepts are generalized in such a way that monetary standards are special cases. We want to define a theory of optimal behavior in which each action can be regarded as entailing a cost and/or a return, and the optimal set of actions is one that maximizes the returns minus the costs.

We shall say that when an action is construed as increasing or decreasing specific costs and returns, the action is to be called a *transaction;* and we shall hereafter refer to the theory of behavior as a transaction theory.

2 · *Transaction Theory and Organizations.*

Perhaps the most important application of this theory is the large organization. Once an enterprise becomes larger than one or two men, a way has to be found to discover optimal decisions for the whole firm. It does no good to decide what ought to be done unless there is a method to implement the decision. But also, even in fairly small firms no one man can make all the decisions. Thus a firm has to develop a "nervous system" of its own; parts of its body must be able to make decisions without having to check with the central brain. The obvious answer to this problem is to supply each part with a scoring method, so that when a decision is made and carried out, the person in charge of the part can determine the cost and hence evaluate how well he acted. If the costs become excessively high, then, as with a sudden pain in an organic body, the central control becomes aware of the trouble and takes steps to remedy it.

As is the case with all analogies, this one breaks down, of course. The division decision-makers are humans and, in this sense at least, there are some differences between the more-or-less automatic "decisions" of a heart to beat and the decisions to invest in more labor or capital. But the analogy is valuable heuristically, because it emphasizes the need to find some way in which a group as a whole can act in a properly goal-directed manner by means of setting subgroup goals.

3 · *The Accounting Axiom: Assets.*

We turn to an explicit formulation of the transaction theory. We shall do this by formulating an "accounting axiom," with the comment that the axiom is rarely a conscious one, that we are, as always, speaking of accounting for decision-making purposes, and that we are conceptualizing in very broad terms.

First of all, we consider the general goal of increasing power in order to define the term "asset" which is basic in the formulation of the axiom.

We have not previously considered in detail the concept of power in decision-making, although it obviously appears frequently in the decisions of our culture. The concept can be defined in several ways within the means-end scheme. For example, we could say that the power of an individual X is simply the measure of his ability to attain any one of a set of his desired goals. Thus, X's power could be measured by the effectiveness of the actions he chooses relative to his specific goals. A man may be rich but weak because he lacks knowledge or poor but weak because he lacks the available choices.

This definition of power implies that the power of an individual depends on the choices he can make, on his state of knowledge, and on the goals he wants. Hence, one man may be more powerful than another because he wants less, or because he wants a different kind of thing. We would have to say, for example, that one way to "increase" your power is to simplify your life.

Our interest here, however, is in a concept of power that is independent of the individual's specific goals. This abstraction can be accomplished by defining an individual's power in terms of his potential choices. In this sense, X is more powerful than Y if X can exhibit all the behavior that Y can, and more besides. Thus, X, a surgeon, may have the ability to use certain instruments in a certain way which Y, a layman, does not; in this context, X is more powerful than Y. Similarly, a rich man is, in general, more powerful than a poor man, provided the former is aware of (can choose) the opportunities his riches provide.

There are obviously a number of technical problems which this definition introduces: for example, the meaning of potentiality of choice (which could be defined in terms of probability of choice greater than o in some environment), the classification of choices, the ranking when X cannot choose all that Y can and vice versa, and the construction of a scale. But consideration of some of these formal problems can be more properly placed in the Appendix.

Although it may be possible to measure power in terms of potentiality of choice, we often find ourselves concentrating more on an individual's resources than on the actual choices themselves. This suggests a third definition of power. We shall call the resources assets, and define an asset as any aspect of an individual's environment which produces a potentiality of choice for a set of actions. For example, a saw is sometimes an asset, because without it one cannot cut a piece of wood in a prescribed time period, and with it one can. The saw therefore is a coproducer of the cutting. More precisely, the presence of the saw coproduces a potentiality for action on the part of the individual. The individual, of course, must be able to use the saw, and hence he too is a coproducer of the potentiality; a saw may be an asset for one man and not for another.

We now want to define an individual's power in terms of the size of his assets. The *size* (or amount) of an asset is determined by the number of choices in a set of alternatives which the asset potentially produces at one time. In this regard, we note that some assets (for example, money or labor force) can be used for a wide variety of purposes, even though their size may be small. A small asset can produce only a small set of actions at one time, although it may produce any one of a number of actions. Assets that can be used for a wide variety of purposes are called *general*, those that can be used for few purposes are called *specific*. Thus, within the context of carpentry, a saw may be a general asset because it can be used for many different purposes, whereas a certain size bit may be a very specific asset, because it can only be used for drilling a specific hole. But both saw and bit are "small" assets because neither produces potentiality for many simultaneous actions in the manner that a well-equipped tool box of a group of carpenters does.

The concept of a general asset is important because it suggests that the possession of a specific asset can be treated as though it were the possession of a certain amount of a general asset. In other words, we may be able to standardize the measurement of the size of specific assets by translating each size into a size of a very general asset (for example, by translating the assets of a person or firm into monetary terms).

Evidently the proposed definition of an asset makes the denotation of the concept very broad. The assets of an urban dweller include streets, lights, stores, movies, and museums because each of these produces a potentiality for action of some kind. Many of these are assets independent of any choice of the person himself, and hence will not concern us in the development of a transaction theory of decision-making.

This suggests two kinds of theory of asset maximization, namely, maximizing socially shared assets or maximizing possessed assets. In order to make this distinction clear, we need to explain what a "possessed" asset is.

We say that an asset is *possessed* by an individual X if it produces potentiality of choice for X alone, that is, not for any other decision-maker in the environment. Possession may be a matter of degree; that is, we may want to say that an asset is possessed by X if the probability that it produces potentiality in Y is very low. Possession and ownership are not the same, of course. Furthermore, possession may be accidental in the sense that others could possess the asset but the circumstances are such that their possession does not occur. In other words, we could narrow the theory to the position that an individual wishes only to maximize absolutely possessed assets (in the sense that no other individual could possess them at the time) or owned assets (in the sense that society does not wish the assets possessed by another). In contrast, some individuals and societies want to maximize shared assets. It will be irrelevant to the discussion that follows which form of the theory applies. In other words, the theory could be used to describe the values of either a capitalist or socialist state.

The power of an individual is defined hereafter as the size of his assets. More specifically, if a general asset exists in terms of which all other assets can be measured, then an individual's power is the size of his assets when measured by means of the standard. We are therefore considering a theory of value which asserts that the decision-maker tries to maximize his power. The nature of the theory can best be explained if we introduce a behavioristic interpretation of the concept of a *transaction*.

4 • Transactions.

Consider an individual in an environment at t_1, and the set of his assets. Let each asset be computed in terms of a standard. The individual can exhibit any one of a set of alternative actions A_i. If he chooses an action A_1, then we can predict the probability distribution of the standardized size of his assets at some later time t_2. Restricting ourselves to certainties for the moment, we can associate with each A_i one standardized size of the assets at t_2; also we can associate with each A_i the difference between the final size at t_2 and the initial size at t_1. In other words, each action can be mapped on a line, the point on the line defining the difference between the size of the assets at t_1 and the size at t_2. We say that a *transaction* is the description of an action in terms of the differences. A theory of value in which an individual is depicted as maximizing the size of his assets is therefore a theory which reduces all actions to transactions; the only relevant consideration in the description of alternative choices is the difference over time in (standardized) assets. We can therefore call the theory the "transaction theory of values." The transaction theory says in effect that if all action sets are translated into transactions, the set of transactions is a sufficient basis for predicting behavior under conditions of knowledge. More specifically, the transaction theory asserts that the informed decision-maker chooses that A_i which maximizes the difference between the size of the assets at t_2 and the size at t_1.

The theory can be made to include uncertainty stipulations, but these details are of less concern here than the axiom of the theory which permits a breakdown of the decision-making process.

5 · *Breakdown of Decisions into Elements.*

This axiom asserts that the effort to maximize assets over a period of time can also be viewed as a set of separable subactions, that each subaction can be described as a transaction, and the over-all effort is equivalent to maximizing assets within each subaction. In simpler terms, an individual's struggle for power can be broken down into self-contained episodes within which he tries to maximize power without reference to what happens in the future or in other places.

For example, consider the life of an individual person. The theory not only states (1) that were the person informed, he would choose those actions that maximize the assets at the end of his life, but also (2) that his life span can be subdivided into shorter periods in such a manner that if he maximizes the growth of his assets in these periods, he will at the same time maximize his life's assets. In other words, the successful search for the long-range plan is accomplished by finding short-range plans which maximize the returns for shorter periods.

In the same manner, the theory also provides a way of searching for the over-all plan of a social group. In this application, the theory states that the group can be divided into smaller subgroups in such a manner that the set of maximizing actions of each subgroup constitutes the optimal action for the group as a whole.

The theory, of course, does not say that any method of segmenting time or the group will accomplish the desired end of predicting choice. In this respect, it is not a complete theory of value even for the individuals for which it may be valid. Discovering the correct method of segmentation may be extremely difficult and time-consuming. But the theory does direct the research effort towards elements of a total plan which presumably can be studied more readily than the entire plan by itself.

There are some obvious illustrations, even if we question whether the theory always encompasses all the real subtleties. A man's life may be describable in terms of an attempt to maximize his fortune, and his yearly income maximization may be a sufficient basis for accomplishing his objective. In such a simple form, the theory would assert that actions maximizing yearly income pose no threat to a lifetime's search for power. More realistically, the time segments might be broken down into relatively independent periods of unequal length. Similarly, a business firm may divide its organization in such a way that within "cost centers" or "profit centers," cost minimization or return maximization is taken to be the optimal choice. And even urban communities, socialist republics, and labor unions find the need to segment their activities and account for the performances within each segment.

The Appendix of this chapter provides a sketch of a formulation of the theory. We now turn to some obvious and some subtle criticism. For the purposes of the present discussion, we can note that the two important axioms of the theory are the following:

Axiom 1 (*"Asset Maximization"*). Over a time span t_0 to t_1, the decision-maker, who is free to choose among a set of alternatives and knows the consequences of each, will select that alternative which maximizes the standardized size of his assets.

Axiom 2 (*"Closed System"*). The optimal activity for the period t_0 to t_1 can be subdivided in such a way that it consists of asset maximization within each subdivision.

6 · Is Axiom 1 a Tautology?

Axiom 1 proposes a specific framework of values, which of course may not seem adequate for predicting informed behavior. It says that the decision-maker tries to change his environment in such a way that at the end of some time period the set of alternative actions he can choose will be maximum. But such an objective must seem pointless to some, just as any other formulation of a "power" objective would. The natural thought is to ask what good a large potential could possibly be if one did not have any ultimate objective which would justify the effort. The answer, of course, is that by maximizing potential one does not have to concentrate on specific goals, because any goal can be pursued if the potential is great enough.

In other words, the asset-maximization axiom seems to be supported strongly by a common-sense principle: whatever else anyone may want, he also wants to increase his power, that is, his ability to gain his goals. The theory looks as though it were a description of the necessary; whoever values must value power.

To paraphrase an early theme of this book: whatever proposition has the clear support of intuition needs to be doubted and subjected to analysis. The proposition which we are asked to accept says that any value-seeker values power. The first question that comes to mind is whether the assertion is a tautology. Now if, as this book claims, values are determinants of informed choice, then it is true that every individual who values also seeks the best way of attaining his goals. This truth follows from the definition of value we have adopted, and, therefore, once the definition is accepted, the principle must be accepted. As in all tautologies, the truth depends on the truth of a definition.

But the tautology only occurs if we define power in the sense of ability to select the most effective action for a specific goal. This definition of power was discussed earlier in the chapter, and we decided that it is not equivalent to the meaning of power in terms of the size of assets. It is therefore not a tautology to assert that a man wants to maximize his power. For example, a man may want only certain specific things in this life: a comfortable home, a college education, a good wife and two successful children. The wealth he might accumulate beyond these objectives may be irrelevant. His life's goals, then, are not equivalent to maximizing his assets.

We can take it, then, that Axiom 1 is nontautological. Furthermore, it may be intuitively defensible in the case of certain persons. For example, a man who does not have a clear idea of what he wants or will want in his lifetime, might feel that he ought to choose those actions that will maximize the chances of attaining any desired end. This position is based on the horizon thesis we described earlier; it views the decision-maker as an individual with clear foresight for short periods, and blindness for the future thereafter—at least a blindness for the goals he will value. He therefore maximizes his assets for the short run. Whether this intuitive argument for the axiom is satisfactory or not is perhaps less important than the fact that many persons and social groups do appear to value their objectives in the manner which the axiom predicts. Thus, the axiom seems to provide a sound basis for an empirically valid description of the values of many important decision-makers: persons, groups, nations, and cultures.

We should note that the axiom does not explicitly mention the knowledge of the actions which the assets can coproduce. In other words, an individual may be rich in choices but not know which to select. This is true, but if the decisions in any period of time are the basis for action in the next period, then Axiom 2 does seem to imply that knowledge must exist. The next period will be one of the subsegments of time, and this axiom states that maximization within each subsegment provides over-all maximization; presumably a necessary condition for this to occur would be that the decision-maker knows how to maximize for the coming period with the assets at his disposal. In effect, Axiom 2 depicts an indefinite sequence of decision-makers; each maximizes the potentials of the next; each can do anything he wants as long as it is consistent with the power-maximization aim.

7 · Some Criticisms of Axiom 1.

Before considering criticisms of Axiom 2, we can briefly mention some of the obvious objections to Axiom 1 which have been discussed often in the literature.

First, there is the difficulty of standardizing to one general asset. This is a problem that we have discussed in many ways, and further consideration is not necessary here. The facile suggestion is to use money as the general asset, and the difficulties and possibilities of doing this have been mentioned earlier. We should note that the form of Axiom 2 that segments the plan into time periods requires a discounting method to standardize all assets over time which is a problem that has received a great deal of attention in economic literature.

There is another sense in which Axiom 1 will appear unsatisfactory to the student of business firms. We have talked about total-asset maximization, but there is a question whether a firm maximizes total assets, or net worth, or some other accounting figure. But within the behavioristic form we are discussing, these issues are not relevant. It may be that maximization of total "balance-sheet assets" is equivalent to maximization of behavioral assets because the liabilities do not threaten a reduction in real assets in the next period. If so, then the theory is equivalent to balance-sheet asset maximization. Thus the theory is a possible basis for deciding which accounting measures (if any) the firm ought to maximize or minimize. If a firm's objective is to maximize its potential for action, then risk considerations may be sufficient to determine what aspects of the balance sheet or operating statement are most important.

8 · *Criticism of Axiom 2: the Closed System.*

Applied to business firms, Axiom 2 asserts that it is possible to organize the firm into divisions and to hold each division accountable for its performance. In Chapter 3 we raised questions about the feasibility of divisional accounting in organizations for decision-making purposes. For example, there is the problem of those divisions which serve a number of other divisions. What is their objective? The problem of internal-pricing is essentially a problem of defining the "shadow" assets of each division so that at the end of the period one can determine whether "return minus costs" has been maximized. In some instances, this method may prove quite useful; in others, such as administrative departments, it may prove quite useless and costly. These problems arise because of a basic conflict between organizational structure and accounting. It may be possible to subdivide an organization's personnel and their working time in such a way that when each segment maximizes its assets the whole organization does so. But in such a case the administrative lines of authority and responsibility would not be applicable, especially if all of a person's time must be supervised by one superior.

In any event, the issue of the applicability of Axiom 2 to business firms is not settled. It should be noted that the verification of the theory depends as much on the cost of trying to apply it as it does on other empirical evidence; our earlier discussion has emphasized that verification is based in part on economic-decision criteria no matter what is being verified. But managers of firms are perhaps more aware of this fact than purer scientists.

The more serious defect of the axiom is its concept of the closed system. In effect, each time segment or each organizational division is regarded as a system unaffected by the operations of the other segments or divisions with respect to optimal performance. A useful analogy is to be found in laboratory practice. The measurements of some phenomena can occur without having to take into account the perturbations of much of the surrounding environment because the laboratory can be successfully designed to remove the significant influences of the outside world. In the same way, the costs incurred by a department may be measured, we hope, without taking into account the behavior of other departments.

But the analogy is untenable simply because, in so many cases, the cost of doing something cannot be measured simply in terms of actual outlays of cash. Consider a typical allocation problem: how to manufacture various amounts of n different products by m available methods. To set up the model for this problem, we need the cost of manufacturing x items of product i by the jth method. If we have segmented the organization properly, then according to the axiom the optimal solution of the manufacturing process will be one in which the costs of manufacturing the stipulated amounts of the n products by the m methods is minimum. But realistically the cost of manufacturing x items of product i by method j is not an historical cost, because historically the application of the method may have been faulty. We must say instead that the required cost is to be determined for the optimal application of the method.

In other words, for the theory to be valid, the imputed costs are based on a determination of an optimal subprogram. But here is the difficulty. In the case being considered, the optimal application of the method entails solving the problem of the proper job description of the foreman and the time-motion plan of the machine operator. Perhaps more seriously, it also entails solving the problem of the optimal available equipment on the market or the optimal research and development for as yet unavailable equipment. If this problem is considered properly, one must study competing uses of available capital. Thus the solution of the allocation problem depends on the solution of an over-all financial problem. The cost of manufacturing a certain product in a certain way must be defined in terms of the optimal method of allocating capital to equipment design and purchase. One may come to feel that Leibniz's metaphysics is an accurate if quaint description of today's manufacturing firms. He depicted all reality in terms of monads which "reflect" all the rest of the world. Paraphrased, to determine what any element of reality is like, one must know what the world is like. Or, to optimize any segment of an organization, one must optimize the whole.

9 · *Learning from Experience.*

Such a conclusion of course would lead the critical observer to doubt the validity of Axiom 2. His doubt would be strengthened by any of the analytical studies of a firm's operations. In each case, cost determination leads one to the study of other segments of the firm: what is best for this department depends on what is best for another.

But now we should return to the analogy of the laboratory which at first lent some conviction to the transaction theory. When we examine laboratory operations realistically, we see that these too entail an implicit or explicit interdependence. We can assume that aspects of the environment other than those that are consciously controlled do not influence our readings in the laboratory. But how do we know this? Indeed, our assumption is often quite wrong. Time after time it has been shown that the most carefully conducted laboratory measurements are subject to unknown influences that create unpredictable deviations from day to day, from observer to observer, from laboratory to laboratory. Rarely, if ever, does physical measurement satisfy the conditions of optimal performance. To know that a sequence of measurements is being conducted optimally, one must know how the environment influences the readings; that is, one must know about something more than the closed system to know that it is closed. The conduct of a laboratory is no more an instance of the axiom than is the conduct of a firm.

However, there is something in this brief account of laboratory closed systems that does suggest the great value of the segmentation of activities. We may not know that a specific method of obtaining readings in the laboratory is best, but we can conduct tests to validate or refute the hypothesis. In other words, the transaction theory may not adequately account for reality, but its acceptance in a certain form may be the best method of learning from experience. We act as though the system were closed, and let designed experience tell us whether we should continue to act in this manner.

How does experience tell us when to give up the hypothesis that the system is closed? The answer is that we must design certain tests to accomplish this purpose. For example, if we suspect that something may influence the readings, we ask ourselves whether the influence may vary with time, or the observer, or the laboratory. A designed test will help us to answer the question thus posed. But the test can only do so if we estimate the variance of our readings, that is, only if we can estimate error as well.

In other words, no scientist seeks to obtain absolute agreement of observational reports, because such agreement contains no information about the nature of the system. Whenever agreement occurs, the scientist will push his readings to the next decimal place or refine his classification so that there is disagreement among observer reports. When disagreement occurs, it is possible to learn from experience.

Within scientific practice, then, one might argue that some form of Axiom 2 is equivalent to the theory of closed systems, and that the theory is valid because the scientist is trying to optimize the method of learning from experience. He does this by attempting to learn the most in a segment of experience. He is successful because he has a criterion of failure.

If the transaction theory could be used to depict the efforts of learning of the scientist, we might be encouraged to apply it in the same way to the behavioral theory of a business firm. To this end, we would argue that firms are not trying to maximize assets directly, but are trying to learn how to maximize assets. Within each division of a firm, we would say, there is an effort to learn from experience how to maximize assets just as each laboratory learns how to become more precise.

But the analogy is seriously defective, simply because cost data do not include statistical variances. Even if a test of the closure of the system were economically feasible, we have no way of conducting it. Hence, acceptance of the theory leads the manager to accept certain divisions of his operations as closed systems, and the data which the firm generates never tell him directly that the closure is incorrect. Of course, he does learn about gross miscalculations; he learns that too stringent a financial policy (which minimizes the cost of borrowing capital, say) is drastically hampering the efficiency of the manufacturing operation. This type of learning is something like the experience of an engineer who finds that the laboratory tests certifying the properties of a steel bar were clearly defective because the bridge falls down.

The most important problem of managerial accounting based on the transaction theory is to develop data that will reveal when a system is not properly closed. One way to go about solving this problem is to try to supply measures of statistical variations in costs, and hence, hopefully, to apply the resources contained in the literature of experimental design and statistical control. Those who have taken this step discover deep and mystifying complications; if current statistical theory is applicable to the control of segments of a firm, it is no simple matter to discover the application.

For one thing, many managers are unfamiliar with the concept of error as a useful informational device. A scientist does not take it as a confession of failure to assert that there is positive, probable error in his measurements. Rather, he realizes that without some estimate of error the measure itself is meaningless. But accountants and managers want their cost data "exact." They think of "cash on hand" as the most precise measurement because there can be relatively little error in this figure. What they do not seem to realize is that a precise figure in this sense of precision also contains very little information about the state of the system. Or, rather, if a firm's goal is to learn, it learns least from precise figures.

The effort to be precise discourages the manager from living with discrepancies. Thus, he tries to resolve different estimates of depreciation because he feels that there should be one figure, not a range. He might be persuaded to accept a range if he could see how he could learn thereby.

However, one does not receive much encouragement from modern statistical theory because this theory is so strongly oriented towards statistical deviations of observations in controlled experiments. The elements of the theory are discrete observational reports. Hence to apply statistical theory to costs, one has to try to conceive of a cost estimate as a function of discrete pieces of information. But this manner of interpreting cost estimates is at variance with practice. True, the costs are often weighted sums of discrete numbers, but the elements themselves are not considered to be results of a set of observations.

One might try to conceive of independent judgments of costs as the "elementary observations" that statistical theory requires. But, at the present time, there is no evidence that this approach will work.

Possibly, then, the fault lies also with the elementalism of statistics; we may need a theory of testing closed systems that does not rely on any set of elementary informational inputs.

10 · *Conclusion.*

The transaction theory may be the basis of developing a theory of learning for the firm, which at the present time seems to be the most critical problem of the theory of the firm. But just how this basis will be accomplished, that is, just how the firm's data-processing must be modified or statistical theory changed, is not clear. We seem to require a way of subdividing the organization so that each subdivision can be taken as a closed system. Within each closed system, the managerial effort is to maximize return (or minimize cost). This effort continues until there is a signal that the system is not closed, either to the effect that its efforts disturb the efforts of some other system or are disturbed by some other system. Such a signal might be a shift of a cost figure outside the range predicted by the theory of the subsystem. This is what standard-cost variances are sometimes supposed to accomplish in a crude way. The whole system would learn optimally if the signals were optimally sensitive. I doubt whether current statistical measures of error are useful for this purpose. Nor do I as yet see any feasible alternative.

Perhaps the need can be put most forcibly as follows: find a cost system for the divisions of a firm so that the firm would know at each period (1) that it had or had not performed optimally, and (2) what is the most fruitful next attempt if nonoptimal performance occurred.

APPENDIX

Let A_i stand for an alternative in the set A.

Let B_i stand for an object in the environment N.

Let X_i be an individual in the environment.

Let $A_i(X)$ stand for a behavior pattern A_i exhibited by X.

B_i produces $A_i(X)$ in N if B is a necessary condition in N that $A_i(X)$ occur.

Let N be a set of environments (for example, a set of environments the properties of which agree within certain limits).

B_i potentially produces $A_i(X)$ in any instance of N if the probability of production is greater than 0.

B_i is an asset for X_i relative to A_i in N, if B_i potentially produces $A_i(X)$.

B_i is a possessed asset for X_i relative to A_i if for all $X_j \neq X_i$, B_i is not an asset.

The generality of B_i for X is the number of $A_i(X)$ in A relative to which B_i is an asset for X for all instances of N.

The size of B_i for X is the number of $A_i(X)$ relative to which B_i is an asset for X in any one instance of N.

Let b_i be the size of the asset B_i.

Two assets B_i and B_j are the same type if they potentially co-produce the same actions in a specific environment N.

Axiom 0. There exists a set of entities M such that, given any asset B_i, with size b_i, a subset of M could replace B_i in environment N and have exactly the same size and type as B_i. We call the size of M corresponding to any B_i the standard size of B_i.

A transaction set is a classification of actions in which each element describes the initial and final size of each asset of X over a time interval t_0 to t_1. According to Axiom 0, all transactions can be standardized. If the difference between the initial and final standardized size is negative, it is called a return; if the difference is positive, it is called a cost.

Axiom 1. There exists a transaction classification such that the free individual attempts to maximize the sum of the standardized size of all returns minus the sum of the standard size of all costs.

Axiom 2. Let $A_i(X)$ be an optimal alternative of a decision-maker X relative to the time period t_0 to t_1, according to the criterion of Axiom 1. X may be a group composed of subsets. A_i can be expressed as a set of actions a_{ij}, in such a manner that:

(1) each a_{ij} occurs in a time segment t_i to t_j falling within the interval t_0 to t_i;

(2) each a_{ij} is a member of the set of all alternative actions of some subset of X in the interval t_i to t_j;

(3) each a_{ij} maximizes the standardized size of the assets relative to the time segment t_i to t_j relative to the set of alternatives of the subset of X,

(4) A_i consists of at least two distinct a_{ij}'s.

DECISION
METHODS
OF SCIENCE

14

Summary

and

I n t e n t .

In this chapter we consider an illustration of institutional decision-making. Specifically, we have in mind a taxonomy of scientific methods, meaning thereby the description of the manner in which choices are adopted by the institution of science. This discussion will have an unfamiliar tone even for students of scientific method, and therefore some brief account of the method of approach is desirable.

Two things seem to me impressive about the activities of the institution of science. One is that its goals are rarely if ever defined in such a way that they clearly differentiate between good and bad choices, and certainly almost never become a dominant consideration of the individual scien-

339

tist. The other is that science has developed fantastically complicated and fruitful ways of reaching judgments, that is, agreements generated out of disagreements. In this chapter I want to recapitulate my impressions of this judgment process and try to view the scientist and his community as subjects of decision-making research. Hence, I am not concerned with defining "the" scientific method but rather with trying to understand some of the ways in which scientists come to reach conclusions.

When we speak of science as a decision-making activity, certain semantic confusions are almost bound to arise. Science in our day has attained an aura of purity, and to think of a scientist as we would a business executive is apt to be poor taste. The accepted picture of a scientist is a man driven by intellectual curiosity which can only be satisfied by the objective examination of the facts which Nature presents to him. His basic apparatus is intelligence, integrity, curiosity, observation, thinking, and creativity. None of this suggests that he makes his decisions for any other reason than the attainment of pure knowledge. Indeed, the scientist may announce discoveries which have unpleasant repercussions for his entire community. A social scientist may discover that the vast majority of people want to suppress certain minority groups. The announcement of this discovery may result in severe hardship for many persons. The scientist's decision, however, is presumably based on his own objective findings, and not on a desire to maximize pleasure, or profit, or any other like quantity. Similarly, some persons feel that atomic physicists only discover and are not politicians interested in their discoveries' applications.

Hence, if we propose to consider scientific method from the point of view of decision-making, we may straightway run into semantic confusions. Do we mean to deny the objectivity of the scientist? Are we trying to assert that the decisions of the scientist can be forced into some scheme whereby the right decisions are defended in terms of maximizing some utility?

So far, the answers to these two questions can be kept in abeyance. Our only need at the present time is to recognize that scientists do make decisions. These decisions may be statements in books or journals; they may be modifications of beliefs; they may be the planning and carrying through of experiments and other research projects; they may be, for applied science, actions leading to bridges, products, therapy, and bombs. In all cases, decisions are made. We want to ask ourselves what kind of decision theory science uses to select one decision from a group of alternative decisions. The question, so posed, does seem to require that we look at science in an unusual manner. But whenever one scientist criticizes another, he evidently attacks the other's decision-making, though most scientific criticisms fail to expose at the same time a general and "correct" theory of decisions for science.

One final comment is required. Why should one study how scientists make decisions? And granted that such a study is possible, is it of any benefit to scientists? Furthermore, granted that it is of some benefit to scientists, who but the active scientist at the reflective end of his life is best qualified to report on what scientists do?

These are all typical questions the scientist raises concerning the activities of the philosopher of science. E. B. Wilson's review of Braithwaite's *Nature of Scientific Explanation* is an example (see pg. 28). Wilson makes out that Braithwaite is talking only to philosophers, and is not talking about what scientists do. He points out that scientists do very complicated things. They often hold on to two mutually contradictory hypotheses, their pattern of "explaining" does not follow any rigid, logical sequence, and so on.

Some philosophers of science have felt the impact of these remarks to the extent that they have divorced philosophical activity from scientific as completely as possible. They have done this by devising a one-way road called reconstructionism. They assume that the task of the philosopher is to analyze and clarify certain procedures of scientific inference in such a manner that the procedures meet carefully defined criteria of justification. Thus in formal science, they have taken seriously the concepts of simplicity, consistency, and proof, which are the hallmarks of mathematics. They have analyzed these concepts and refined them to a point that meets rigid standards of analysis. The result has been of doubtful value to mathematicians, whose papers continue to use only a rudimentary framework of deduction. In empirical science, philosophers have tried to refine such concepts as explanation and degree of confirmation which are part and parcel of scientific discourse. Yet these analyses have had virtually no influence on physical scientists, who continue to work "successfully" without bothering about the logical difficulties inherent in the concepts they employ.

As Wilson points out, Bridgman's work in operationalism had far more influence on scientists than all the efforts of reconstructionists despite the fact that Bridgman's philosophy lacks rigor and ignores certain issues that are important to the philosopher. Bridgman was talking about a matter that does directly concern the scientist: his everyday use and application of his concepts. He provides a general frame of reference, based on physical operations, in terms of which the scientist can better understand what he is doing and better report his results and conclusions to other scientists. Bridgman's efforts have been much like those of the practicing mathematical statistician who has gradually succeeded in convincing scientists that a proper analysis of data depends on a proper design of the research. The statistician has done this without a precise analysis of "statistical inference" or of "research design." It cannot be said that either Bridgman or the statistician have contributed greatly to the aims of the philosophical reconstructionist.

Yet Wilson is wrong, in a sense, in his attack on professional philosophers. How can he prove that their reflections are useless? It is true that some sciences, such as physics, have attained social acceptance, and have perfected the procedures of acceptance of results in a way that meets with widespread social approval and support. There seems to be no short-range need to devote a considerable part of their energies to an examination of their methods. The point is a simple and perhaps very obvious one that concerns the whole of decision theory. There is no advantage *per se* in examining and reflecting upon a decision process. Such examination may be disadvantageous in that it is costly of time and effort and may stop the decision-maker from taking certain actions because he has become reflective and therefore cautious. One may decide not to examine the justification of one's decisions, just as well as one may make any other kind of decision. But whether in the case of physical science a study of the decision processes is desirable is not obvious. The success of physical science may be largely attributable to the amount of time and resources put into the effort and not to the methods used; an analysis of the methods might vastly reduce the need for such large expenditures.

Efforts by such philosophers as Hempel (5) and Ackoff (1), do show the advantage of philosophical thinking for the social sciences where general acceptance is far from being attained. Social scientists need much more careful scrutiny of their activities than a clarification of concepts or better experimental designs. This chapter, if it serves the social scientist at all, serves him by outlining the many methods at his disposal. The far from definitive results reached here may become, along with other contemporary efforts of the same kind, a vehicle for opening up possibilities for social research which may be closed to the present-day social scientist, either because he is unaware of them, or believes them to lie outside the province of "accepted" scientific methods.

This does not say that all philosophy of science must be a service to the scientist whose decision processes are made in a state of doubt. The one-way reconstructionism of the physical sciences is merely one-way for today's thinkers, and like much of research-for-its-own-sake, may eventually become in time the basis for a general reconstruction of physics, that is, may become research-for-another's-sake. The ultimate justification of pure research, after all, is that by ignoring the eventual usefulness of the results one may best accomplish this usefulness.

With this apology we can turn to a discussion of types of decision-making available to the scientist.

2 · Some Concepts.

The classification which follows depends on some concepts which will now be defined. We have already discussed one of these: "judgment." In this context a scientific judgment is a conclusion accepted by a group of scientists. It should be recognized that this group may be smaller than the entire body of scientists. Or, more generally, the accepted method of resolving disagreements proceeds first by a consideration of an issue by a subgroup (a "discipline," or selected group in the discipline). This subgroup is characterized as "experts." Once the subgroup comes to a conclusion, that is, makes a judgment, then the entire body of scientists also accepts the conclusion. In the subsequent discussion we will be chiefly concerned with the judgment process of subgroups.

We say that a person "agrees" with an assertion (or action) if he is a member of the subgroup, and the subgroup has made a judgment. It will be recalled that a member may in some sense "disagree," but yet agree with the method of resolving disagreements. We are therefore adopting the term "agreement" in a special sense.

We consider now two kinds of judgment. One we call "primal" and the other "inferential." A primal judgment is the agreement on an assertion (or action) which is not based on any other judgments. For example, the "fact" that something occurred at a certain time and place may be a primal judgment for a group. An inferential judgment is a judgment which asserts a rule for "inferring" other assertions (or actions) given that certain judgments have been made. "Inferring" has the following property: If A has been judged true (or optimal), and an inferential rule R infers B from A, then on the basis of the rule alone, B is agreed to be true (or optimal). Inferential judgments may be primal. Primal and inferential judgments need not be consciously accepted by the group.

In effect then, the group judges certain things to be so, and also judges what follows from these primal agreements. We shall call what follows "commitments."

We now want to distinguish between conventional and nonconventional judgments, having in mind the difference between an arbitrarily accepted assertion or rule, and one that is supposed to be "universally" valid. The difference seems to depend on whether or not the agreement occurs because a person is a member of the group. More specifically, we say that a judgment is conventional if the rules of group membership produce the agreement (in the sense of production given on p. 214). Thus, if one plays chess, he becomes a member of a group, and he agrees that the bishop moves only on the diagonals because he is a chessplayer. In contrast, nonconventional agreements are not produced by the conditions of membership in the group. The agreement that Mercury is nearer the Sun than Venus is not produced by the rules (say) that define the group called "astronomers."

Next we say that an inferential judgment is formal if the rule is recognized by the group, that is, the group is aware of the rule. Otherwise, an inferential judgment is nonformal. ("Awareness" requires defining in this connection, but for our purposes here we can simply point out that "X is aware of A" means "X is sensitive to the way in which he responds to A.")

Finally, we say that a set of group judgments and commitments is "deductive" if the group seeks to find the commitments inferred from its primal judgments, and is "inductive" if the group seeks to find what agreements would infer their primal judgments. In other words, deductive processes seek to find what follows from agreements; inductive processes seek to find what agreements would lead to the agreements already made. (It should be noted that in this sense "induction" is not restricted to the so-called "empirical" sciences.)

We now briefly describe the eight types of judgment processes that arise from combining conventional-nonconventional, formal-nonformal, and deductive-inductive judgments in all possible ways.

3 · *Conventional, Formal, Deductive Judgments.*

These judgment methods are to be found in symbolic logic and mathematics. In strict axiomatic methods the degree of formalism may be quite high; that is, an intense study is made of the inferential rules. This has necessitated the construction of artificial languages which permit this scrutiny and ease the burden of discovery. In mathematics proper, there is less interest in the inferential rules and more in the commitments (theorems). To a careful logician, many of the judgments of mathematicians seem based on inadequate evidence since the inferential rules are so loosely expressed.

The primal judgments are often called axioms or axiom sets. These together with the rules of inference are "arbitrary." That is, it is "meaningless" to ask whether they are true or false. Interest centers on the commitments that follow from the primal judgments and inferential rules.

It is important to note what is not conventional in these group activities. First of all, there are nonarbitrary goals which are being pursued, although these may not be stated explicitly. These goals provide criteria of significance and elegance of the type we discussed in Chapter 4. For example, it is usually considered essential that an axiomatic system be rich enough to generate "unexpected" and "important" theorems. Often, the axiom system should be rich enough to prove a set of theorems of a certain kind. These goals are not "conventions"; that is, most members of the group believe them to be absolutely valuable (their value does not depend on whether the evaluator is a mathematician).

Second, the fact that a commitment is inferred from the primal judgments is not conventional; that is, any qualified observer can check whether the rules have been applied correctly.

The value of a group member lies in his ability to discover important commitments which cannot easily be discovered. That is, the value of a member is based on his ability to forecast accurately the unexpected but significant theorems and to discover the method of proof.

This group therefore values precision and originality. It often regards the less precise sciences fundamentally as attempts to become more precise about subject matters that seem intractable in this regard. In contrast, in its adoption of conventionalism with respect to primal judgments, the group feels itself free from the plaguing issues of nonconventional primal judgments.

4 · *Nonconventional, Nonformal, Deductive Judgments.*

This method is deductive, but the interest of the members of the group is in "true" axioms and true conclusions. Furthermore, no stress is laid on precise methods of deduction and the construction of artificial languages. Instead, the group borrows terms from common languages, and the meanings of the terms are supposedly clear to the group members. The group may also coin some terms or construct symbols which are defined within the original, supposedly clear language. The supposition of clarity can at least theoretically be tested by determining whether the terms of the language denote the same objects or images, or connote the same ideas and concepts. But this scientific group usually does not try to perform such tests unless confusion in communication becomes obvious.

Examples of nonconventional, nonformal deductive methods are to be found in economics, philosophy, political science, and, in general, in fields where the presentation of material is in an "essay" form and is not an inductive generalization on a report of empirical data. In each case there is some language in common use, and the readers supposedly ascribe the same meanings to terms as do the writers. It is not easy to discern what "same meaning" connotes here, but it is usually believed that ultimate agreement on an assertion implies that all members accept the same meanings of the terms. This amounts to a "relativistic" Platonism: in each person's mind there is a set of ideas and relations, and appropriate choice of language will call forth the ideas the writer intends to evoke. But attainment of this state of mind is not inborn; it is, in fact, a consequence of training programs in the schools. Furthermore, the language of one group may have the same physical signs and symbols as the language of another group, with totally different meanings. There is no attempt to create a universal language in this type of scientific method.

Thus we are considering a group whose members can speak meaningfully to each other, though they are only sporadically interested in testing for the existence of a common understanding. The next step is to agree on certain "principles"—sometimes euphemistically called "basic truths," "principles," "self-evident assertions." What these agreements are, that is, what kind of decision is being made, is not always easy to say. In fact, scientists who adopt this method speak in vague terms with respect to these principles: "it is clear that . . . ," or "evidently, . . . ," or "few can deny . . ." are common expressions. The reader will find examples spread throughout this book, which relies rather heavily on this method for its exposition. Someone proposes an assertion and defends it. His defense is based in part on other judgments (commonly accepted findings) of the group, and in part on the force of his language. The assertion is scrutinized by his colleagues (for example, by reviewers of articles and books). Perhaps it is agreed to at once, perhaps only after long debate and restatement. Furthermore, a judgment once made may be changed in time when some other group member rises to challenge it. Often the defense of a judgment is based on "facts," but the factual support is only one basis of accepting the principle or postulate, and hence the method is primarily deductive.

Since the rules of inference are not precise, there may be disagreements on the commitments. In this case, unlike the conventional, formal, deductive commitments, the commitments themselves may be judgments.

This scientific group also recognizes a distinction between "significant" or "fruitful" principles, and "trivial" or "irrelevant" ones. Again, the members are not self-conscious about these terms, and there is virtually no intention to investigate them for their meaning. But books and articles may be unimportant, significant, or very important depending on whether the author has "stated the obvious" or "brought to light a significant truth that few have previously recognized." Successful papers are ones which carefully scrutinize the obvious and reveal in the commitments the need to agree on the nonobvious, or else to change an obvious judgment accepted by all.

This group therefore values originality, depth of penetration, and generality. It does not regard precision as a desirable attribute of its decision-making because it feels that attempts to formalize always leave out the really deep nuances or else (as I feel in the case of the present book) make premature methodological commitments.

One may be struck by the crudity of this description of a scientific method. I have intentionally concentrated on the mode of reaching decisions and not on the intellectual values that supposedly accrue, because these values are not, in the case of this method, conscious determinants of the judgments and hence not part of the explicit method of the group. Also, the general description shows that many other activities also fall into this type of decision-making. In the case of science, the group agreement must be almost universal. Every "rational" and trained scientist is free to think about the matter and should, on the basis of his own thoughts, come to agree with the rest.

It is always possible to point out the weaknesses of any such decision plan, and these weaknesses have repeatedly been evident in areas like economics and philosophy where this method is most frequently used. The vagueness of language is one point. Failure to admit confusion is not a sign of understanding, as many a teacher knows. It may take years before two disputants realize they have employed different meanings for the same terms, and the lack of disagreement about the meanings of terms is thus no sign of mutual understanding. Again, the failure to provide "objective" criteria for principles and consequences has been the source of the greatest irritation for opponents of this method.

Despite these weaknesses, one cannot deny the great strength of the method. Because it does not have to rely on a language understood by the very few, and can include so many people, its judgments have the flavor of validity. Its very vagueness permits openness on many issues; that is, it does not need to make final judgments on every aspect of a problem. Because it uses a common language, it can touch people's feelings and intuitions and hence find more-than-rational support in the agreements of its members.

5 · *Nonconventional, Formal, Deductive Judgments.*

This group is interested in introducing precision into the deductive methods of disciplines like economics, law, and philosophy. Its aim is to validate first principles but not at the expense of precision. Mathematical economics and philosophical analysis are examples. It differs from the conventional, formal, deductive group in that the primal judgments are supposed to be nonconventional, and from the nonconventional, nonformal, deductive group in its insistence that the inferential rules be made explicit. This has led to the mathematical or logical language of its discourse.

In addition to precision, this group often values parsimony. One of its chief objections to the second group is the easy manner with which the latter proposes basic principles. To this group, a basic aim is to discover the minimal set of judgments that must be made in order to arrive at a certain set of commitments (and in this regard the group may more naturally fall into the "inductive" class).

The method is like that of traditional geometry, except that this geometry, to our modern eyes, suffered under a defective rule of inference. Traditional geometry believed in the immutability of its axioms; all persons at all times were to judge them to be true. But the "geometric method," tightened in its inferences, loosened in its insistence on timeless acceptance, is as useful today as it ever was. In Chapter 8 I argued against this method, as applied to modern utility theory, because I felt that there was too much concentration on one aspect of the process of agreement, namely, whether a member of the scientific group can or cannot think of a counterexample. This, it seems to me, has led us away from an interest in other kinds of evidence, such as empirical studies and experiments, and has often resulted in needless disputes. It should be noted, in this regard, that although precise language may force intuition to the ultimate test, it does so at the cost of making the issues less open than the less-precise methods permit.

6 · *Conventional, Nonformal, Deductive Judgments.*

This group does not seem to require elaboration; it is essentially one of speculation. The group wishes to speculate on the consequences of certain assumptions without agreeing with the assumptions themselves. It does this by means of loosely defined rules of inference. Presumably these rules are nonconventional.

7 · *Nonconventional, Nonformal, Inductive Judgments.*

This group comprises one part of the empirical sciences. Here the emphasis is on agreement of fact. But the real interest lies in what can be generalized from the facts. The facts are the primal judgments. The generalizations are assertions which, if true, would "explain" the facts. Explanation usually means that if the generalizations were accepted, then the inferential rules would lead to the facts.

Since facts in this case are agreements, and since there is a strong tendency of Western man to agree on what has occurred or is occurring if one has the opportunity of observing and a strong tendency not to agree on what cannot be observed, this group is disinclined to make judgments about the future. In contrast, it does not feel the necessity of formalizing the "reverse" influential rules that lead to acceptance of generalizations. This means that the group is usually content with a version of a common language, and that its facts are often expressed qualitatively, that is, in terms of class membership.

Examples of this method are to be found in sociology, anthropology, political science, much of business administration, clinical psychology, psychoanalytic research, and many other fields.

In this group, the value of a member lies in his ability to observe significantly and with refinement; or in his ability to generalize cautiously and meaningfully. Precision is not necessarily desirable for it may wipe out the refinements of meaning which common expression can give, and may represent a costly and insignificant effort to quantify for quantification's sake. This group does value very broad theories, but only if they are presented with real insight, that is, are apt to be accepted. Otherwise, the group encourages special research with a limited aim. Its primary aim is data collection; contemplation and speculation are always subservient to this aim.

It will be recognized that although many of the members of this group have a keen interest in human values, they feel caught on the horns of a dilemma because it seems to be virtually impossible to agree on even the most rudimentary assertions about values. Any possibility of ethical "facts" is ruled out by the group because such agreements would be so drastically different from the usual agreements about what has been observed.

This book, of course, has been directed mainly against using the nonformal inductive method in the study of human values. In particular, it has attacked the notion that facts are agreements based solely on observation. Once one analyzes the manner in which factual judgments are made in the scientific community, and tries to evaluate the process, the possibility of a "science" of values become a reality. "Facts" are themselves agreements conditioned by the values of the scientific group.

8 · *Nonconventional, Formal, Inductive Judgments.*

Here a great deal of emphasis is placed on discerning the rules of generalization. As before, formal methods entail the construction of precise, artificial languages. Two aspects of the process of generalization are important. First of all, there is an explicit formalization of the theory so that it is possible to decide precisely what alleged facts are deducible and what are not. This formalization often suggests the title "inductive-deductive" for the method since as much time and effort may be put on theory construction as on the observations. Second, there is an explicit decision rule for selecting one from a set of alternative generalizations (here often called hypotheses). In some cases only one aspect may be emphasized. Thus physics has studied theory construction intensively, but has paid only little regard in this century to the concept of hypothesis-testing. In contrast, experimental psychology has emphasized hypothesis-testing but has, until recent years, shown considerable hesitation in developing mathematical theories. Of course, in a deeper analysis of what each has been doing, one finds that both have been implicitly concerned with theories, as Chapter 4 argues.

This group values precision and an interest in controlled observation. It is not concerned (in the short range) with extensive fact-finding, although it often expresses the optimistic hope that its discipline will gradually move into more-and-more significant areas. The group therefore considers experimentation to be the most important fact-finding method. Facts of minor importance (in terms of their usefulness outside the group), which are elegantly obtained, may be highly esteemed by the group.

Much of the argument of this book has been in terms of the mores of this group; on the one hand, we cannot help but appreciate the need to define what factual acceptance means in the area of value research, but, on the other hand, we have to take a dim view of the possibility that the judgments of this group alone will gradually develop into significant theories of value. It seems better to say that in the area of human values we should not restrict ourselves to experiments which meet this group's demands for precision but should also conduct research on live organizations and hope that somehow it may be possible to compare the results and use one as support for the other.

9 · *Conventional, Formal and Nonformal, Inductive Judgments.*

I find no very obvious representation of this group. The activity is a "counterfactual" argument in which the facts are arbitrarily assumed, and one tries to see what would be implied in the assumptions. This sort of thinking is often the prelude to empirical investigation, but aside from science fiction writers, does not seem to be peculiar to any group.

10 · *Methodological Camps.*

The tenor of description in the account made above implies real disagreements on methodology among scientific disciplines, and this implication comes as no news to the academician. In the face of it, he may adopt one of several attitudes. He may say that his group's method is scientific, and its members are scientists; he may even allow this for some of the other groups; but the rest he may regard as "investigators" or "researchers." If he says this, he no doubt does so on the basis of the judgment of nonscientists: physicists are scientists because the public agrees they are, while sociologists are not scientists because the public is not "agreed." However, he may say that each group represents a style and that each person should choose the style that best fits his personality. If he says this, he ignores the problems of promotion in rank or support of research since decisions about these are often made by persons who belong in different groups from that of the applicant. Or, he may say that the groups should give up their autonomy and recognize that the appropriate method "depends" on the type of problem and the available evidence. If he says this, he takes upon himself the burden of proving, to the satisfaction of *all* groups, that a certain method is optimal relative to a specific problem area.

He may, in contrast, feel that the differences are healthy, and that the institution of science thrives on methodological disputes.

This treatment has not suggested any criterion of "good" and "bad" in connection with the disputes except in terms of human-value research. It seems to me that although the institution of science may be organic (that is, its disputes serve a common set of goals) it is in no sense organized (no one is conscious of the goals nor controls the scientific activity relative to them). But there are certainly strong indications on the part of some members of our society that they would like to see science become organized.

11 · *Disagreement as an End.*

There is one thing worthy of note about attempts to classify human beings: most of us would just as soon not be a member of any of the classes. It will be interesting, therefore, to mention a theory of scientific activity in which the scientist is not taken to belong to any of the classes given above. This may seem startling because the classification was clearly exhaustive. But a little reflection shows that the classification assumed that every member of each group wanted to reach agreement, and that the differences arose because of the nature of the agreements they thought important. In other words, we were classifying those who believe that truth is a kind of agreement.

What if scientists really want to reach disagreement and only use agreement as a means of doing this? Suppose we see how such a viewpoint might be justified. We begin by saying that if the group reaches perfect agreement on a question of fact, its intent is to refine the question so that disagreement occurs. This refinement might take place by stating the facts in quantitative terms out to one more decimal place or by refining the classes if class assignments are being made. These disagreements pose the problem of resolution by use of a theory of observer differences, for example, or environmental differences or random "inputs." Once the disagreement is resolved, that is, a judgment is reached, the scientist seeks to destroy the principle of resolution, perhaps, by making observations under different conditions or by further refinement of the factual reports. Such a scientist might accept the value of precision, or generality, or insight, as a means for establishing a new basis for disagreement. In any case, his primary aim is not to solve a problem but to dissolve a proposed solution.

Would such a scientist be considered perverse? Possibly, if there were no methodological controls. But his establishment of new disagreements is based on a philosophy of agreement. He does not merely obtain an arbitrary dissent of his colleagues. He must obtain this dissent in the face of the established rules of agreement of his group, and this may be a very delicate task requiring a high degree of ingenuity and creativity. To some he may appear to be a gadfly that keeps his group from becoming too self-confident or from resting on its laurels. To others he may appear to be the essence of the scientific: science, in the activity of research, is the discovery of new problems.

One may seek to find a compromise between agreement- and disagreement-seekers by proposing that the scientist is an ideal-seeker and not just a problem-solver (as the next two chapters will suggest).

Whatever may be one's attitude on this matter, we begin to sense a counter theme to the one adopted in this book, namely, that man is a problem-creator, not a problem-solver. In the extreme, it may be that some scientists always seek certain kinds of disagreement, and have no interest in the resolution or solution of problems. These themes, which will be considered in more detail in the next chapters, can conveniently provide a concluding note on this one.

12 · The Radical.

Chapter 12 suggests that institutions always display a radical and conservative tendency. It is not difficult to suggest how radicalism may be characterized within the framework of the discussion of judgment made in Chapter 6. The aim of radicalism is to create disagreements; the aim of conservatism is to create and maintain agreements. In each of the groups discussed above, the radical element will attack the strongest core of agreement: the structure of an axiomatic system, the first principles of a discipline, the facts, the method of experimentation or hypothesis-testing, all the unconscious or unquestioned presuppositions. For the radical mind there are no agreements which cannot be attacked; for him every agreement is based on some other implicit or explicit agreement. In other words, he recognizes no legitimate primal judgments, although he must admit that his group often makes such judgments. But he is also loyal to his group, and he must generate doubt within the rules of judgment-making his group permits. The philosophical radical, in contrast, tries to generate doubt without loyalty to any one group.

The conservative tries to strengthen the agreements of his group. He sometimes does this by relinquishing the least-acceptable judgments in order to hold onto the stronger ones; this may be the reason that some judgments tend to become tautologies.

The intent of this book is philosophical radicalism. Its primary attack is against the judgment that there is a distinction between what is (or was) and what ought to be (or will be). This attack has necessarily entailed other doubts of established beliefs as well. Yet, any student of radicalism recognizes the strong conservative tendencies that underlie its operation. In this case, we have committed ourselves to an analytic approach—to the means-end schema, to the principle of controlled observation, to the value of precise analysis. The next chapters will attempt to bring these commitments into clearer light so that they can more adequately be attacked. Specifically, we must ask ourselves whether radicalism in some sense is not always a means to an end, or whether it stands as an ideal in its own right.

As for the immortality aim of institutions which Chapter 12 proposes as essential, this needs to be defined, and its definition depends on understanding the role of the concept of "time" in the analysis of values.

REFERENCES

1. Ackoff, R. L., *Design of Social Research*. Chicago: University of Chicago Press, 1953.
2. Churchman, C. W., *Theory of Experimental Inference*. New York: Macmillan Co., 1948.
3. ———, "Critique of Scientific Critiques," *The Review of Metaphysics*, VII (1953), pg. 89.

4. Carnap, R., *Logical Foundations of Probability*. Chicago: The University of Chicago Press, 1950.

5. Hempel, C. G., "Foundations of Concept Formation in Empirical Science," *Int. Encyl. Unified Science*, II, No. 7 (1952).

VALUES
AND TIME

15

Summary

and

Intent.

The discussion of the last four chapters gives clear indication that the problem of values can be considered from many viewpoints. Especially important in this regard is the social context. We say that the size and diversity of the social group which is being studied determines the *scope* of the value research. Persons, families, clubs, associations, firms, communities, institutions, nations, cultures, and ages seem to represent a ranked set of groups according to the relation of broader scope. The "diversity" which characterizes this scope is based on differences of values, that is, differences in the values of objectives. As the social group is increased in scope, the problems of defining what it wants become quite different, and require a different methodology.

There is another, related sense of scope which is based on time. Time enters into the model of goal-directed behavior of a single individual in two ways. First of all, it seems obvious enough that a person does not maintain the same values even in comparatively short periods of time. The measurement of values, however, must be based on a theory of a person's behavior that describes the development of his value structure. Second, as was mentioned on p. 198, the model of Chapter 7 is ambiguous concerning a person's knowledge of goals which lie beyond those that are pertinent to a study.

This chapter tries to suggest some ways in which the first problem could be treated, by outlining some theories of a person's value structure over time. The attempt should also provide some insight on the second problem because the importance of long-range objectives in the study of a person's behavior depends on the way in which his goals evolve in time. Perhaps long-range goals never play a part in determining his free choices, or perhaps they are all-important. In either case, the researcher can decide how to remove the ambiguity of the standard for value measurements.

The same remarks apply to social groups, and especially to those with life spans extending over several generations. It seems, perhaps, more reasonable to say that what the group really wants can only be ascertained from a theory of its developing value structure over a long period and not in terms of the values during a shorter time span. This would seem to be especially true of the history of nations. The meaning of our Constitution is not contained in the values of the national objectives for its framers, nor in those of Jacksonians, or Northerners, or New Dealers, but rather in the pattern of the development and changes of the values of these groups and many others.

2 · Classification of Value Theories.

It is not my intention to construct detailed theories of values but rather to try to classify the various forms which such theories might take and to suggest in each case how within the theory one might frame a general concept of value. This classification is based on the manner in which a person's (or group's) values depend on time. We therefore start with a theory which is atemporal in this sense: the values of the individual depend solely on environmental properties. That is, choice can be predicted solely in terms of the environment in which the choice is made. We then consider four temporal theories of value, based on two concepts: consistency and termination. We say that a set of objectives is consistent if there is some future objective which fully explains the individual's values for the components of the set. For example, a long-run profit picture may explain a company's short-run preference for some objectives over others. Nonconsistent sets of objectives are ones for which no more "ultimate" value exists. A set of objectives is "terminal" if a person's behavior can be predicted in terms of them; that is, the effectiveness of his choices for more-distant objectives does not provide any better estimate of the probability of his present choice.

We therefore have the following five theory types:

(1) Values are predictable from the environment ("situational" theories).

(2) Values are predictable from a series of ultimate goals spread out over the life span (theories of temporal, terminal and consistent goals).

(3) Values are predictable from a series of sets of incompatible goals spread out over the life span (theories of temporal, terminal and inconsistent goals).

(4) Values are predictable from an unattainable "goal" (theories of temporal, nonterminal and consistent "goals").

(5) Values are predictable from a set of incompatible, unattainable "goals" (theories of temporal, nonterminal and inconsistent "goals").

In the total life of a person or a group, more than one type of theory may be most appropriate for a period of time in explaining the person's value structure.

3 · *Situational Value Theories.*

It has frequently been noted that an individual's values are determined by his environment—either family upbringing, social milieu, or the organizations to which he belongs. If this observation were carried to its fullest extent, we would be led to assert that the values of a person's goals are all predictable from environmental measures. Indeed, if we did assert this, we might come to doubt the advantages of a means-end schema, for the values of a person are predictors of his choices. If these predictors are functions of environmental measures, then we might more economically ignore the goal values and simply describe a person's behavior as a function of his environment only. We would, in effect, give up a teleological framework; thus teleological theories of behavior are those in which the measurement of the values of goals is essential (or most economic) in predicting choice among two or more alternatives.

As an example of an ateleological theory, consider the proposition that in certain task-oriented groups some of the group's members are not interested in the problem to be solved but rather in the way the group gets along. An internally conflicting group may automatically produce a strong drive on a member's part to bring about peace at all costs. The means-end model would characterize this behavior as follows: when X is in a conflict environment he values cooperation very highly. Thus, if he were given two choices, the one bringing the group closer to a solution but with considerable conflict between members, and the other leaving the group internally at peace but not any nearer the solution, he would choose the second. But then it might be simpler to say that such a person does not have goals; he is driven to choose certain acts by his environment. In other words, given a specific type of conflict between certain kinds of personalities in his social environment, one can predict the choices he will make. In the next chapter we shall see another example of a theory of behavior which raises questions about the optimality of the means-end schema. Of course, even in the example cited, goal-seeking may be an appropriate way of understanding behavior if the person's drive is not as pure as that described; for example, if the solution of the problem does have some real value for him. In such a case we would have a mixed model in which the prediction of choice depends partly on environmental measures and partly on future goals.

4 · *Temporal, Terminal, Consistent Goals.*

It should be understood that throughout this book we are not implying conscious choice on the part of the decision-maker. Hence a theory of his behavior is not necessarily equivalent to his conscious plans. This remark seems especially pertinent in connection with the theory of terminal goals. This theory views a person's or group's life as a set of segments, in each of which one or more goals predominate. The observer, in other words, views the decision-maker as essentially a set of problem-solvers, though it is not essential in this theory that any problem actually be solved, nor that the decision-maker be aware of the segmentation.

In order to understand this theory we require a more precise definition of consistency. First, this definition can be phrased loosely as follows. A set of goals, no matter how much they appear to conflict, are consistent if there is some ultimate future objective which fully explains their relative importance. More precisely, consider a means-end schema in which an individual X pursues a set of objectives $O_1, O_2 \ldots , O_m$ defined for a future time t_1. Suppose we can assign values $V_1, V_2, \ldots , V_m$ to these. But suppose we can define an objective O' at a later time t_2 with the following property: there is a set of probability measures which describes the probability that O' will occur at t_2, given a certain state at t_1 (or, if O' is measured along a scale, the degree to which O' is attained in t_2, given a certain state at t_1). Specifically, suppose there is a probability measure which describes how likely O' is to occur if only O_1 occurs in t_1 or only O_2, and so on, or only O_1 and O_2, or O_1 and O_3, and so on.[1] Thus for every combination of objectives occurring at t_1 there is a probability that O' will occur at t_2. Now suppose that the decision-maker's values for the objectives and combinations of objectives at t_1 are functions of these probabilities alone. Then we say that the objectives at t_1 are consistent.

It may happen that a set of objectives is not consistent relative to an ultimate objective because the decision-maker is ignorant of the probabilities described above. We mean by the stipulation, therefore, that the set is consistent if the decision-maker did have the knowledge, that is, that adjustment for ignorance would fully explain the deviation between his values and those predicted by the probabilities.

For example, a company may place certain weights on annual

---

[1] It will be noted that in this theory it may be more convenient to use the concept of "state" rather than "objective," where a state is a sufficiently broad description of a segment of the world at t_1 to measure the probability of O' at t_2. In effect the decision-maker places values on whole states, and not specific objectives. But this technical consideration need not deter us from talking about objectives, as is commonly done in all planning, because we can insist that the objectives be so defined that a phrase such as "O_1 alone" denotes a state with the desired property.

profit, dividends paid, labor-wage level, technological developments, market position, and total sales. An astute observer might be able to discern that all these implicit weights can be explained by recognizing that the company is "actually" pursuing one five-year goal: maximization of the discounted, average net profit.

Similarly, a man may sacrifice his pleasures or his creative hours in the expectation that such a sacrifice will serve a long-run goal of pleasure or creativity.

This model is adequate to describe both the dilettante and the devoted man. The former may pursue one objective for a while, but eventually drop it. Nonetheless, during the pursuit, the one ultimate goal predominates. The devoted man pursues his ultimate goals for longer periods.

It is important, for our later discussion, to understand how the consistency stipulation might fail. Logically, its contradictory says that at no time t_2 later than t_1 is there a conceivable goal which has the properties ascribed to O' above. This is certainly a very strong statement, especially if, as we intend, t_2 may "tend to infinity." But we should remember that all along we are discussing alternative conceptual schemes. It may be possible to find the goal that makes a man's life pursuits consistent, but it may be much simpler to use a theory of inconsistent pursuits instead. Before turning to this possibility, we consider the nonterminal "goals" that may make a set of objectives consistent.

5 · *Temporal, Nonterminal, Consistent "Goals": Ideals.*

We have already introduced the idea of unattainable "goals" in Chapter 14, and will discuss them in more detail in the next chapter. Here, we can briefly note that a man's life, or the life of a social institution, might best be understood by interpreting every value of a short-run objective to result from a degree of approximation to an unattainable "goal." In other words, we search for a scale of approximation in terms of which the attainment of any one or more objectives can be defined. Then we find that the value of any state at t_1 for the decision-maker depends on its approximation to the unattainable ideal. Such ideals seems to occur in science (perfect knowledge, or perfect precision), in legal institutions (perfect cooperation), or in industry (perfect production and distribution).

6 · *Temporal, Inconsistent, Terminal Goals.*

This theory finds no single goal that explains a segment of a person's life pattern. Instead, it may be possible to find a set of goals, and to determine a person's values for short-run goals in terms of the probabilities and a set of relative weights. The weights may remain fixed or vary as functions of time. But, presumably, no more ultimate goal explains the weights so that the decision-maker is "basically" split on the goals he seeks. There is no moral compunction to be consistent, of course, nor is even such a consideration appropriate because, in saying that a man's life is divided on the ultimate goals he pursues, we mean that there seems to be no point in seeking a goal that would explain his "inconsistency." For example, throughout his life a man wants security and prestige, and it may seem fruitless to look for some long-run "pleasure" principle which "resolves" the conflict.

The theory we are now considering is very general; it pictures a life in terms of basic "goal sets" which then explain all the "ups and downs" of the values of other objectives. It allows for moods of depression and elation, of chivalry and cowardice, of chastity and adultery, by permitting relative values of the goal sets to change as functions of time or the environmental variables.

7 · *Temporal, Inconsistent, Nonterminal: the Inexplicable.*

The account above assumes that there is a set of goals whose relative weights provide predictors of the values of intermediate goals. But there is nothing in the concept of inconsistent goals which implies the existence of such a set of ultimate goals. Perhaps no such goal set exists. Even so, we might find the explanation of a man's values in a set of weighted ideals (unattainable "goals"), an explanation often sought to solve the mystery of the devious ways of man. Indeed, we have no evidence that the ideals we seek, for example, of knowledge, of production, or of cooperation, are consistent, that is, are all incorporated in some master ideal which can be approximated without limit. It may be, then, that mankind is a species pursuing unattainable and ultimately conflicting ideals.

But it may be that not even the introduction of ideals explains a person's or group's behavior. Perhaps to any observer such decision-makers are afflicted with a perverse chaos which never permits any dominating "long-term" objective or ideal, or any environment, to account for the pattern of their changing values. This seems to be the present fate of many observers of decision-makers today, but we hold open the faith that our present inability is a result of ignorance. However, it may be that it is not so much ignorance as a commitment to a means-end schema that accounts for our failures in some cases. In the next chapter we shall discuss one such example of the chaotically goal-oriented person, namely, the person dedicated to conflict. But we should note that the "chaos" is of our own making; the pattern of values is chaotic because it has nothing to do with goal attainment.

8 · *"The" Values of a Decision-maker.*

Postponing for the moment the consideration of this troublesome personality, we can bring these reflections to a close by returning to the remarks made at the beginning of the chapter.

A theory of temporal, consistent, and terminating goals would permit us to talk sensibly about "the" value of a person, company, or institution, for the value would be the value of the long-range goal which explains the short-range values. Furthermore, this theory provides a clear answer to the methodological question of ignorance or knowledge of future goals in the definition of a standard in values, namely, knowledge of the consequences of choices relative to the ultimate goals, but not beyond. Similar remarks apply to the theory of consistent ideals, where knowledge of the degree of approximation of a state to an ideal is to be assumed in determining the value of the state.

Similarly, the value of a decision-maker in a theory of inconsistent goals may be the relative weights of the ultimate goals. Again, the question of knowledge in the definition of the standard is solved by the nature of the theory.

It should be noted that the measurement methods discussed in Chapters 8 and 9 would, from the viewpoint of this chapter, provide evidence for or against a given theory, but would not by any means provide the sole type of evidence since these measurement methods themselves are not yet complete. As Chapter 4 argues, we are able to measure a decision-maker's values to the extent that we are able to construct a predictive theory of his behavior.

ETHICS—
THE PROBLEM
OF SCOPE

16

Summary

and

Intent.

This final chapter considers the broadest of all decision problems, the decisions about right and wrong. We begin by trying to differentiate ethics from other aspects of decision theory primarily for the purpose of defining a problem and not to suggest that such differentiation occurs in actual decisions. Once the problem of ethics is defined, we examine some answers. This examination leads us again to the theme suggested in all three of the last chapters—the possibility that conflict is an ultimate goal of the human race. We then re-examine the means-end hypothesis to see whether its underlying presupposition can be made explicit and try to formulate an alternative hypothesis. Both hypotheses are methodological, and the

365

crucial test is a test of economy and fruitfulness. But the crucial test seems also to be a matter of feeling. This conclusion leads us back to the question of the science of ethics. Here we recall the various decision methods outlined in Chapter 14 and ask ourselves whether any of these is applicable to the testing of ethical theories. The conclusion seems to be this: a science of ethics is possible if and only if a science of science is possible, where a science of science is the study of the adequacy of scientific method as a goal-directed decision process. Hence, in some sense, a science of ethics requires that we go beyond any of the methods described in Chapter 14.

2 · What Is Ethics?

Is there a definition of ethics that can be framed within the means-end schema of human behavior? Specifically, the problem is this: Is there any meaning of an ethical judgment which can be framed within a behaviorist theory of decisions and which at the same time corresponds to Kant's concept of a categorical imperative? The categorical imperative, it will be recalled from Chapter 2, is a recommendation for action which is not hypothetical. Kant distinguished between two kinds of optative sentence: (1) "If p is true, then X ought to do A," and (2) "X ought to do A." In the first the proposition p was considered empirically testable, as was the entire conditional sentence. Kant, of course, held that the second sentence was not empirically testable.

To translate this distinction into the conceptual framework of this book, we start with the meanings of "X ought to do A" which we have been considering so far. If X is a person, we defined the expression to be a prediction of choice of behavior when X is "free" to choose. If X is an individual in a social group, we defined the expression to be a prediction of what the group would choose X to do, given the standards of free choice. If X is a social group, we defined the expression to be a prediction of a free group choice in one of the several possible meanings of this term. If the decisions of X are considered with respect to time, then if X's behavior accords with a certain theory, there may be a set of ultimate values which are the basis of defining what X ought to do. The "conditionals" of these interpretations of "ought" are the specific individual or group being studied. In other words, "X ought to do A" means "*if* prediction of some *Y*'s behavior is the relevant consideration, then *X* ought to do *A*." If there is an analogy to Kant's categorical imperative, therefore, it is a meaningful assertion of the form "*X* ought to do *A*" which does not depend for its meaning on some particular individual or social group.

What such an assertion would be seems almost obvious at this point in our story. If "*X* ought to do *A*" is not to depend for its meaning on some particular group or individual, it can only depend for its meaning on the most general group or individual possible. Suppose we call this "mankind," recognizing that by adopting such nomenclature we run the risk of excluding ourselves from all the presently available scientific groups described in Chapter 14. For now we assert that the problem of ethics is to predict the choice of mankind: "*X* ought to do *A*" means "*A* is what mankind would choose *X* to do, given an opportunity of free choice." There seems to be little hope of reaching any agreements on (a) what mankind is, (b) what mankind's free choices mean, and (c) verification that a certain kind of choice would be made by mankind.

Yet despite this discouraging note, it is important to follow through in reflection the various possible interpretations of the ethical problem that this discussion implies. Only then will we be in a position to assess properly the possibility of a science of ethics.

We can note at the outset two aspects of this interpretation which have been suggested in earlier chapters. First of all, we said that there are several equally plausible interpretations of group choice. One would expect this observation to hold for mankind as well, so that if it is at all possible to study the choices of so general a group, there will be several ways of doing so, and these may be expected to result in different kinds of ethical research, just as we have different kinds of research into social morality.

Second, we have already introduced the concept of "scope" into the framework of value research, and one might reasonably expect to use this concept in an attempt to approach a meaning of mankind. The two dimensions of scope that were singled out in the last chapter are time and the size of the social group; from the point of view of this chapter, these two dimensions coalesce since enlargement of the social group evidently entails inclusion of groups defined for various times. The concept of "relevant" scope may permit us to bring the ethical problem within feasible limits, as we shall see below.

We can thus rephrase the proposed definition of the problem of ethics: How can one give meaning to the prediction of choices of a Y with maximum relevant scope taking cognizance of the various possible interpretations of choice? We note that the problem so stated permits a negative answer: no such meaning is possible. But the research entailed in arriving at such an answer is nonetheless ethical research.

The general position we take in this chapter can be put in other terms. We have said that a man's values are the basis for describing the influence of the future on his present choices. Social values are a description of how a social group wants a man's future to influence his choices. Ethical values are a description of how all interested men want a man's future to influence his choices. Each man himself is an important ingredient in the determination of the ethics of his conduct, for the man that he will be is often the person most concerned about his present values. A man who listens to the voice of his future self is to this extent listening to the voice of his moral conscience; his present despair would lead him to suicide were it not that he-who-will-be wishes otherwise. This may be the hand that deters him from debauchery and murder. The "long-range plan" of a firm is the estimate of what will best satisfy the requests of the firm's management twenty years from now: what would the future management ask of the present if it could do so? If the citizens of three generations from now could vote in our present elections, what would their campaign be like?

In this book we can only outline the various ways in which mankind's values can be described, providing the detailed considerations of any one way would clearly entail a treatise of considerable length. But before we turn to this matter, we should discuss the various denotations of the X which "mankind" wishes to behave in certain ways.

3 · *Individual and Social Ethics.*

Traditional ethics has tended at times to concentrate attention on the problems of right and wrong conduct of individuals. It is clear that most reflective men turn eventually to a deliberation on the conduct of their lives, and ask themselves what it all means and whether a richer life could have been led. Such deliberation may lead to a change in the pattern of living, or a basic change in attitude. In our own age there is a strong interest in the value of individual behavior. Some seek the aid of psychoanalytic therapy, some go through a religious revival, some become members of cultural or political associations, some "find art."

It is doubtful, however, whether these deliberations are based on ethical considerations; very often the need is one of finding a way to live with oneself, and the desirability of this end is taken for granted.

Although there may be a sense in which one could study the ethicality of individual conduct, I hazard the guess that in our Western culture today we are far more interested in the ethics of social groups, and especially the ethics of institutions: nations, industry, labor, education, communities, and churches. We live in a world of social conflict, and the reflective mind is driven to seek intellectual support for his social loyalties. Is it a "good thing" to be American or un-American? Are the goals of our large industrial firms ethically justifiable? Does "Big Labor" have the welfare of the people in mind? And so on.

Whichever interest we may have, individual ethics or social ethics, we can sense that the ethical researcher may reasonably be expected to restrict the scope of mankind to whatever group is relevant. The great artistry of science lies in its ability to recognize simultaneously that every event depends on virtually everything else and yet to be able to estimate what occurred in a specific instance. In some sense mankind has an interest in the actions of every person and group, but it may be possible to narrow the scope to those members of mankind who had, have, or will have a "virtual" interest. In other words, the ethics of conduct depends on all who could have some significant concern with the conduct. Each person in his life's pattern, therefore, is surrounded by his particular ethical group. This is the group of persons (including himself) with a true interest in his conduct. In the case of the nations today, however, we suspect that this ethical group may be quite large: large enough to include a good portion of the generations of centuries to come.

4 · *A Classification of Answers to the Problem of Ethics.*

In classifying possible answers to the question of the values of a group with maximum scope, we keep in mind the formal scheme of Chapter 7. The answers to the question state some hypotheses about the wishes of a "maximal group" with respect to the behavior of some person or group. They also suggest how this wish might be ascertained. In Chapter 7 we distinguished between a person's preference for actions and his preference for goals. This suggests one division in the classification, between answers phrased in terms of right actions and answers phrased in terms of good goals. The latter type of answer is separable in terms of the relevant scope of the group involved. The classification then appears as follows:

  (a) Ethical conduct can only be defined in terms of the structure of conduct; man prefers certain acts and abhors others.
  (b) Ethical conduct can only be defined in terms of the goals of restricted social groups.
  (c) Ethical conduct can only be defined in terms of unattainable goals.

After examining this classification, we shall ask ourselves in what sense it is incomplete, and the answer will suggest a fourth possibility.

  (d) Ethical conduct cannot be defined in terms of the attainment of either patterns of behavior or goals, but must be defined in terms of conflict.

5 · *The Right Act: Morality.*

Students of ethics are familiar enough with the answer to the ethical problem which asserts that any man who is free to think about the matter will inevitably arrive at the conclusion that certain acts are right in themselves, and others are not. Candidates for right actions have been many: honesty, loyalty, equal regard for all; and for wrong actions: murder, adultery, stealing. Much of this thinking has been formalized into our legal systems and our manners.

The way in which the right action is to be discerned has been described variously by philosophers: sometimes in terms of moral education, sometimes by clear insight (conscience), sometimes by anthropological studies which purport to find those properties of conduct that all societies have esteemed or deprecated.

The ethical theory of right actions is similar to the situational theory of behavior described in the last chapter. This theory predicted a person's choices in terms of the environment; the ethical theory of right conduct predicts mankind's preferences for individual choices in terms of the structure of the act, which, in general, would be defined in terms of environmental variables.

It must be understood that this ethical theory is by no means naïve even in the light of available anthropological evidence. For we are considering the interest of an enlightened mankind, not the opinions of each person, tribe, nation, or culture. The answer asserts that every man who understands the nature of conduct and its consequences, will prefer the same type of act. He will, in fact, ignore the consequences even though he knows what the outcomes may be. The answer obviously imposes a severe burden on the researcher to define this enlightenment since one might too readily fall into the tautology which defines enlightenment in terms of the choices a person makes. Nevertheless, it may be that if the cultures of the world were to come to a common understanding of enlightenment, their members would at the same time agree on the criteria of right conduct. Put in the more general terms of Chapter 11, it may be that the cultures of the world will come to a judgment about what is right and wrong. We certainly have no strong evidence to the contrary.

However, it seems altogether too strong to say that this model of ethical conduct is the only one at our disposal. Men do select actions in terms of goals, and this way of conceptualizing a man's behavior is obviously quite fruitful. Further, men often explain their judgments about the ethicality of conduct in terms of the goals which this conduct serves. It is not very easy to see how a model of ethics in terms of conduct alone would explain these goal-seeking interests of mankind. An argument of methodological economy, therefore, would cast some doubt on the usefulness of the proposed answer.

6 · *Independent Goals.*

This answer to our question is based essentially on a segmentation of mankind in terms of its interests. It visualizes groups of men pursuing their separate goals in such a manner that the goals of one group are of no concern to another group. More precisely, two groups (or individuals) X and Y are distinct in their evaluations if X does not wish Y to act in any specified way, and vice versa. This, in turn, means that if X were free to choose he would not influence Y's behavior. One answer to the ethical problem, therefore, is based on the theory that one can fruitfully examine mankind as a set of distinct goal-directed groups. The answer is similar to the segmentation theory of individual behavior discussed in the last chapter. There the segments were defined in terms of time, and here they are defined in terms of social groups. This chapter and the last follow similar patterns, but have a different objective, the one seeking to understand one man's (or group's) life, the other seeking to understand all man's life. This latter aim must include the possibility of group segmentation as well as time segmentation.

One extreme of the ethical position we are considering would propose that in an enlightened society each man leads his own life and social morality disappears as a motivating force. One might even drive the model to a further extreme and say that, ethically speaking, a single man's lifetime ought to be a series of terminating episodes. At the other extreme would be a theory of ethics defined in terms of long-range plans. This would view the group as engaged in a long struggle to solve certain problems: to provide adequate housing, to provide better schools, to secure a certain market position, to secure a free world. What lies beyond the problem once it is solved is not an ethical concern of the group, but will, of course, be a concern of some later group.

This answer to the ethical question is probably the most commonly adopted because it is the most attractive in terms of feasibility: it is at least conceivable that a group of scientists could agree on the relative values of a particular group. It is also the kind of answer which appeals to those who seek peace of mind, religious salvation, and liberal reform. Each sees the job to be done in terms of a specific goal and is not concerned with other goals because these concerns are taken to be irrelevant.

It should be noted that the proposed answer is a positive answer to the question asked. It attempts to show how one could ascertain the wishes of mankind with respect to conduct by proposing the hypothesis that only a segment of this enormous social group is ever relevant. The answer would therefore be conceptually different from a negative answer which would deny that any feasible method is available to discern ethical criteria.

And yet the answer is disturbing because it is predicated on a segregation of man's interests in an age where such segregation seems to be impossible. Further, it ignores those thinkers who talk either in terms of progress or nihilism, because it refuses to look for patterns that would substantiate any indefinitely prolonged struggle of men. What should we say if such a pattern could be revealed? Possibly the issue can be posed in this manner, using the theme of the last chapter: social groups may appear to be distinct in their evaluations if we study their values by defining short-term standards but may not be distinct if we lengthen the time-span. In any case, we should examine the alternative viewpoint of nondistinct social groups.

7 · *Nonindependent Goals.*

There are at least two ways in which one can view human progress. One is to take man as the great accumulator, engaged in the endless effort to add more units to the growing stockpile of power, of information, of natural resources. The other is to view him in the endless effort of gradually approaching certain ideals: cooperation, perfect knowledge, complete distribution. The two ways are in some cases easily translated into one another, because a boundless scale can often be expressed as a bounded scale. Yet there is undoubtedly some difference in feeling attached to the two descriptions.

Because we have already discussed the concept of power in Chapter 13, it seems preferable to dwell here on the second, idealistic scheme.

There certainly is evidence that the activities of some of our major institutions can best be described in terms of ideals. Thus the "aim" of science is precise answers to important questions; the "aim" of industry is maximum production and distribution at minimum cost; the "aim" of our legal system is maximum cooperation with minimum restraint. Each of these "aims" could be defined along some scale. For example, science's "goal" is to increase the degree of knowledge of all men, industry's "goal" is to increase the effectiveness of each man's optimal choice, and our legal system's "goal" is to create a social environment with the maximum degree of cooperation. Each one of these "degrees" has been discussed earlier in this book.

I have put quotation marks around "aim" and "goal" in discussing ideals because the supposed aims are not attainable, and hence are not goals in the sense which we have used the term throughout the book. At least in the light of our present understanding it seems safe to say that perfect knowledge, productivity, and cooperation are impossible to attain. But it does not require any elaborate extension of the means-end schema to incorporate ideal seeking into it, provided the ideals are definable in terms of scales and provided points short of the ideal are attainable. We then have a model of behavior in which each goal nearer to the ideal is preferred over a goal more remote, and we may be able to weight the preferences. Eventually if each point, no matter how near the ideal, is attainable with some positive probability, and if the social group always prefers attainable goals nearer to the ideal, then the group is an ideal-seeker. This is a brief account of material described in more detail elsewhere. (See (1), (2), and (3) in the References of this chapter.)

The validity of the theory depends on whether the social group with maximum scope actually displays idealistic behavior. One difficulty is apparent at the outset. According to the account just given, we need to show that such a social group has certain preferences, for example, that it prefers goals that approximate more closely the ideals. This is rather an imposing task when we consider the whole of mankind, past, present, and future in terms of the science of our century. We could be complacent and expect that an expanding social science should one day find the method of attaining judgments about mankind's wishes. We could even suggest that such a method would be based, not on a total agreement of all men, but on some sort of evolutionary trend of the type mentioned in Chapter 1. Such a trend is actually an extension of the concept of judgment presented in Chapter 11. We pointed out there that judgments are the results of disagreements arrived at by agreements on methods of settling differences; but judgments, once reached, are broken into conflict of belief when new evidence or new group members are added, and they later may be resolved again. If there is a pattern of these breakdowns and resolutions of judgments about the values of human ideals that is adequate to explain relevant aspects of human history, then such a pattern could at the same time be a basis for forecasting, and possibly a basis for estimating what ideals man really wants to pursue.

Some may feel happier with a more-modest approach to ideals. This involves combining the notion of ideal-seeking and distinct social groups. The problem of ethics would then be answered by differentiating between ideal-seeking institutions, such as science, law, or a large corporation, and seeking to find a pattern for each institution. Thus each institution would be the basis for an "institutional ethics." But such an answer should be regarded as a step towards the more general answer, because it is hard to conceive how ideal-seeking could forever remain differentiated. Indeed, many citizens feel that science has gone "too far" in its growth because we apparently know how to destroy the world but we are far from attaining a world cooperation which would prevent the holocaust. One could question, therefore, whether knowledge or precision is *the* ideal of science, for a world in which culture is destroyed may not permit any further scientific effort. Science's ideals must also include social cooperation. It thus seems better to say that the ideals are separable conceptually for purposes of study but are integrated in the sense that the effectiveness in approximating one eventually has an influence on the approximations to the others.

8 · Conflict.

But now we must turn to a serious charge of lack of realism, based not on the feasibility of a method of inquiry, but on a failure to discern the crucial aspect of man's activities. More to the point, the classification of ethical answers depends on a supposition, and the supposition needs examining. More generally, the entire taxonomy of the book makes this supposition in some form, and possibly the whole structure is misconceived.

The supposition can be stated in a number of ways. It is a supposition that man primarily seeks goals; that man is a problem solver; that man wants to maximize some benefit—knowledge, power, cooperation, peace of mind, or whatnot; that men, ethically speaking, are brothers; that, as Singer says (5), man seeks to cooperate with man in the conquest of Nature.

We should at least try to say the opposite to see if it makes sense.

If it does not, then what is asserted above is also nonsensical, or at best tautological. Man does not seek goals; he seeks instead for the process of goal-seeking. Man is not a problem-solver but a problem-creator. Man does not want the benefits of the good earth; he wants instead conflict and differentiation. He wants to conflict with other men in the search for his own individuality.

Now there is a sense in which one could object to the "nots" in the discussion above because if man seeks anything, he seeks a goal. Thus, if he "seeks" to create problems, then problem creation is his goal. But, in this sense, the goal-seeking hypothesis says very little; it could only fail if there were no way to use information about future states in predicting man's free choices.

The point of difference between the means-end philosophy and the conflict philosophy is a matter of emphasis. The means-end schema emphasizes the goal attainment; it considers the decision-maker to be engaged in selecting courses of action that lead him to goals. The goals are where he wants to be. But the conflict scheme emphasizes the problem; the problem is where the decision-maker wants to be. This difference can therefore be described best in terms of the mechanism of goal generation: the first does not and the second does assert that generation of goals depends on the particular nature of the problem. One might point out that this mechanism can be absorbed in a means-end schema since use of this schema apparently makes no commitment about the way in which the values of goals are generated. But, as Chapter 4 argues, the choice of a plan of measurement is based on decisions of economy, and it may be that if the nature of the problem is the determinant of behavior, then the means-end schema is not the most fruitful. Instead, a preferable schema might be one which considers two basic elements, the decision-maker and the alternative set of problems, and predicts choice in terms of the "value" of the problem, not the value of the goal that is sought. This schema would require a taxonomy of problems, just as the means-end schema requires a taxonomy of means and ends.

9 · *The Conflict Hypothesis.*

Whatever may be the formal properties of the schema appropriate for a conflict philosophy, it is relatively easy to give a free characterization of one form of this philosophy. This is the philosophy of individualism; each person seeks to be distinctly different from everyone else. A man believes that his true self contains this essential distinction so that this seeking is a "natural" development. Seeking individuality leads inevitably to conflict because conflict is the expression of difference. Instead of ending a discussion with "I think we all agree that . . . ," the adherent of this conflict philosophy would vastly prefer "I think we have finally found a solid basis for disagreement." He sees the welfare of human societies to depend on differences, not agreements.

Within himself, he also looks for conflict, and this is what drives him to be a problem-creator. He looks for problems which, if solved, only generate new and more difficult problems. The problems themselves have to have a certain quality that appeals to him personally, and his individualism is expressed by the problems he tackles. His concern is not with "efficiency," or with "team cooperation." Concentration on efficiency seems to be concentration on problem solution, and the team is the obliteration of individuality.

10 · *A Possible Resolution.*

It must be admitted that the conflict personality presents a problem to the intellectual student of ethics. Conflict as an end seems to be opposed to the aims of intellectual activity itself. But we could propose one solution which apparently resolves the differences if they are real ones. This has already been suggested in the first chapter. We could recognize within an ethical scheme of ideal-seeking the need for conflict or at least the need for dissatisfaction with goals once achieved. Indeed, this seems implicit in the notion that each point nearer the ideal has a higher value than points more remote, because then the ideal-seeker tends to pursue the more-difficult problem (assuming, as we do, that closer approximations are more difficult). Thus conflict in some sense is essential in the pursuit of nonconflict ideals: science, productivity, and cooperation.

We could even agree to turn the tables and make conflict *the* ideal, by arguing that man clearly does not pursue any kind of conflict, for this would very well lead to his destruction. Instead, he seeks a particular kind of conflict which is inspiring and creative. The definition of these vague terms is to be found in the other ideals.

The "suitable" conflicts are conflicts over ways of discovering new knowledge or creating better products or establishing a fuller cooperation. More generally, we also seek to find a suitable environment for conflict where "suitable" is defined in terms of the "peaceful" ideals.

11 · *But.*

Whether this proposed resolution would satisfy the proponent of the conflict theory is not easy to say. In one very significant sense it does not, because he is bound to point out that individuality is lost if we all favor the same type of problem. At this point he may be inclined to resort to feeling, and defend his position in terms that are not even understandable to the intellectual.

12 · *Feeling.*

This comment recalls the general policy of the book, which has been to try to rephrase the issues of feeling in a form amenable to the tests of analysis and experience. We all know that our values are a result of the way in which we feel about things, and that social values are agreements of feelings. Furthermore, ethical problems often seem to be solvable in terms of the refined feelings of enlightened men.

But the reflective mind has to turn to other sources of evidence because feelings are "subjective" states of mind, are "intangible," "inexplicable," and so on. These phrases are the defense mechanism of the feeling type, a defense against the invasion of analysis and observation into matters that are not analyzable or observable.

Yet what feelings describe are terribly important matters for reflection. Further, reflection must recognize, as Chapters 4 and 5 argue, that the methodology of analysis and observation is defensible only if one assumes the answers to certain questions of value. One may do this arbitrarily on the basis of group agreement of the sort described in Chapter 14, or else one may decide to invade the untouchable area of feelings.

We seem almost driven to assert that the opposition of reflection and feeling is a fundamental opposition of psychological types, as Jung seems to suggest (4).

But perhaps the opposition is not as fundamental as a first glance would suggest. We might take a lesson from the history of biology in this regard. Half a century ago the intellectual world was split into mechanists and vitalists. The mechanists would only admit into the "living" those whose behavior was predictable by mechanical (or physical) laws; the vitalist insisted on a basically unpredictable force. The argument, it seems to me, was a true conflict because if the vitalist was right, then *all* mechanism was threatened. All mechanical theories would have to include the proviso "as long as no vital forces intervene." The whole ideal of precision would become an absurdity if even a simple law of kinematics had to be expressed as "$\frac{d^2s}{dt^2} = k$, if there is no élan vital around."

The historical lesson seems to be that both sides were wrong: mechanism for insisting on one type of natural law; vitalism for insisting on the impregnability of the vital force to any analysis.

So here, reflection has to face the problem of revising its methodology in order to analyze and observe values. But by doing so, it may, after a laborious process, come to understand what feeling grasps directly. Gradually, we begin to see what life may mean in terms of fantastically complicated models of organic structure and behavior; so we may gradually understand what values mean in terms of even more fantastically complicated models of decision-making. The reflective mind allows its "lameness" of feeling to be a virtue. In effect, the reflective mind tediously "transcends" its psychological type.

But this is not enough to have said, because in ethics we assert what ought to be—and the transcendence catches us up. The reflective observer is always going from the world inwards; or rather his greatest problem of evidence is the report of the subjective mind. Hence, for him, an ethical system must be a system that proceeds from a world of selves to the role of the self. He can see what each self ought to do once he can see what the world of selves ought to do. The other side of this picture depicts each self as working out its own meaning and inferring what kind of a world there must be so that each can realize himself. To the reflective mind, again, there may not seem to be any difference in the two viewpoints. But to a feeling mind the difference is all important. This mind feels that reflection may be willing to see many selves sacrificed for the sake of a rational world view, whereas the sacrifice of any self, for the feeling type, is as major a calamity as could possibly occur. For a Butler, for example, the failure of conscience is an evil not measurable in terms of degrees, whereas, for a Bentham, the social program merely lags a bit whenever social legislation fails to maximize happiness.

We cannot say, then, that the reflective observer transcends this problem of types; he cannot throw into the picture the elements of self-realization as though they were value elements of one or more individuals because this misses the entire point for the "other side."

The conclusion seems to be that analysis and observation, as the reflective mind now conceives them, are inappropriate to the understanding of values as the feeling type conceives them. Our reflective lameness may be of our own making.

And this brings us to a challenge with which a book such as this can most appropriately end.

13 · *The Challenge.*

It seems to me that, at the present time, we cannot find scientific support for any one of the ethical theories discussed in this chapter if science is to be defined in terms of one of the methods discussed in Chapter 14. I think, besides, that it is doubtful we ever will. The moral, however, is not the futility of the study of ethics, but the appropriateness of redefining our science. Indeed, the justification of any method of science seems to rest on ethical grounds unless we are to adopt the position that a certain type of agreement is good in itself. Science cannot justify its existence in terms of the satisfaction of intellectual curiosity because this so-called "satisfaction" is based on a certain method of agreement or judgment. The method itself has to be justified. The justification depends on adoption of one of the ethical theories discussed in this chapter. Therefore it seems that we can conclude that a science of ethics is a necessary condition for a science of science.

But if we do conclude this, then we must face the challenge of conflict and feeling. What seems to be the distinctive contribution of the twentieth century to the theory of human progress is the recognition that there can be no progress without conflict. The challenge is to develop a science which can understand what this means.

REFERENCES

1. Ackoff, R. L., "On a Science of Ethics," *Philosophy and Phenomenological Research,* IX (1949), pg. 663.
2. Churchman, C. W., and R. L. Ackoff, *Methods of Inquiry.* St. Louis: Educational Publishers, 1950.
3. ———, *Psychologistics* (mimeographed). Philadelphia: University of Pennsylvania Press, 1946.
4. Jung, C. G., *Psychological Types.* New York: Pantheon Books, 1959.
5. Singer, E. A., Jr., *Modern Thinkers and Present Day Problems.* New York: Henry Holt and Co., Inc., 1923.

INDEX

INDEX

Lightning Source UK Ltd.
Milton Keynes UK
UKHW02n0843270218
318539UK00009B/289/P